CONSCIOUSNESS AND THE BRAIN

A Scientific and Philosophical Inquiry

Contributors

E. M. DEWAN
Lexington, Massachusetts

SIR JOHN C. ECCLES
University of Buffalo

GORDON G. GLOBUS
University of California, Irvine

KEITH GUNDERSON
University of Minnesota

PETER H. KNAPP
Boston University

GROVER MAXWELL
University of Minnesota

KARL H. PRIBRAM
Stanford University

C. WADE SAVAGE
University of Minnesota

IRWIN SAVODNIK
University of Pittsburgh

MICHAEL SCRIVEN
University of California, Berkeley

R. W. SPERRY
California Institute of Technology

WALTER B. WEIMER
Pennsylvania State University

WILLIAM C. WIMSATT
University of Chicago

CONSCIOUSNESS AND THE BRAIN

A Scientific and Philosophical Inquiry

Edited by
Gordon G. Globus
University of California, Irvine

Grover Maxwell
University of Minnesota

and
Irwin Savodnik
University of Pittsburgh

Plenum Press · New York and London

Library of Congress Cataloging in Publication Data

Main entry under title:

Consciousness and the brain.

Includes bibliographies and index.
1. Mind and body. 2. Consciousness. 3. Brain. I. Globus, Gordon
G., 1934-   II. Maxwell, Grover. III. Savodnik, Irwin. IV. Title.
[DNLM: 1. Consciousness. 2. Neurophysiology. 3. Psychophysiology.
4. Philosophy. WL102 C755]
BF161.C69   128′.2   75-44478
ISBN 0-306-30878-9

First Printing − June 1976
Second Printing − November 1977

© 1976 Plenum Press, New York
A Division of Plenum Publishing Corporation
227 West 17th Street, New York, N.Y. 10011

Printed in the United States of America

Preface

The relationship of consciousness to brain, which Schopenhauer grandly referred to as the "world knot," remains an unsolved problem within both philosophy and science. The central focus in what follows is the relevance of science—from psychoanalysis to neurophysiology and quantum physics—to the mind–brain puzzle.

Many would argue that we have advanced little since the age of the Greek philosophers, and that the extraordinary accumulation of neuroscientific knowledge in this century has helped not at all. Increasingly, philosophers and scientists have tended to go their separate ways in considering the issues, since they tend to differ in the questions that they ask, the data and ideas which are provided for consideration, their methods for answering these questions, and criteria for judging the acceptability of an answer.

But it is our conviction that philosophers and scientists can usefully interchange, at least to the extent that they provide constraints upon each other's preferred strategies, and it may prove possible for more substantive progress to be made. Philosophers have said some rather naive things by ignoring the extraordinary advances in the neurosciences in the twentieth century. The skull is not filled with green cheese! On the other hand, the arrogance of many scientists toward philosophy and their *faith* in the scientific method is equally naive. Scientists clearly have much to learn from philosophy as an intellectual discipline.

A specific case of the importance of communication between philosophers and scientists may prove illuminating. This example concerns a well known objection to Feigl's psychoneural identity thesis. According to Feigl (1967), "The raw feels of direct experience as we 'have' them . . . are empirically identifiable with the referents of some neurophysiological concepts." However, Sellars (1963) has raised what appears to be a troublesome objection to Feigl's identity thesis, an objection which has been variously discussed in the philosophical literature (Meehl, 1966; Capek, 1969; Weimer, this volume; Globus, this volume; Maxwell, this volume). Meehl states the "grain objection" as follows: "a small phenomenal red patch is typically experienced as a continuous homogeneous expanse of red hue," whereas the brain comprises a "'gappy,' heterogeneous, discontinuous conglomerate of spatially discrete events." If mental and neural terms refer to the *same* entity, how could it be that experience is without grain whereas the brain, comprising discrete neurons which fire digitally, is "grainy" both in space and over time?

It should be noted first that the classic "mind–body" question has been rephrased as a "mind–brain" question, indeed a "mind–neuron" question. Thus, science has already entered into the formulation of the issue, although "the neuron" is so familiar to us that it hardly seems to be part of a scientific language.

But why should the assumption be made that the digital events of neuronal firing correspond in some way to mind? Why should sharply localized neurons in space–time be contrasted with the differentiated continuum which is consciousness? Pribram (1971) has proposed, for example, that slowly varying "graded" electrical changes at the synaptic junctions between neurons are coordinate with awareness, rather than the digital event of nerve impulse firing. Pribram's "junctional microstructure" provides a persisting pattern in space and over time by effecting a spatiotemporal integration of the myriad influences impinging on any neuron. (Pribram even ties this model to rather recent scientific discoveries in holography for which Gabor won a Nobel Prize [Gabor, Kock, & Stroke, 1971].) Since Pribram's junctional microstructure has no spatiotemporal grain in the manner of the discrete firing of discrete neurons, the "grain objection" to Feigl's identity thesis may be totally undermined. At the least, it becomes an issue decidable on *empirical* grounds.

On the other hand, suppose it were decisively determined empirically that Pribram's junctional microstructure is indeed the neural "correlate" of mind. Would scientists then have resolved the problem which has perplexed philosophers for so long? The answer is clearly negative, for the nature of the correlation is an inherently philosophic issue. Is the presumptive "correlation" between mind and the junctional microstructure actually an identity as Feigl (1967) would have it? Are they separate realities which somehow interact in some liaison cortex, following Eccles (1970)? Does mind "emerge" from the neural events, as Sperry (1969) argues? Is the apparent correlation a spurious issue stemming from our failure to appreciate the nature of language (Ryle, 1949)? And so forth. Even given the fact of a clearly demonstrated and specified correlation, the ontological and epistemological issues remain quite as mysterious as ever.

The present volume juxtaposes philosophical and scientific strategies of approach to the world knot in an attempt to clarify issues and effect rapprochement. It is somewhat distantly related to an informal conference on consciousness and brain which was held in Newport Beach, California, in the spring of 1973. The conference, sponsored by the Department of Psychiatry and Human Behavior, College of Medicine, University of California, Irvine, and by the Minnesota Center for Philosophy of Science, University of Minnesota brought together scientists and philosophers in a pleasant ambience for presentation of ideas and discussion. The cost of the conference was underwritten by the Department of Psychiatry and Human Behavior. We express our appreciation to Professor Louis A. Gottschalk, Chairman, for this funding.

Following the conference, we asked the participants to write a paper, or in some cases write up a presentation or discussion of another presentation. Thus, the papers reflect a result of the conference, and stand as independent contributions to the scientific and philosophical literature on the relationship of consciousness to brain. We have provided an introduction to each contribution in order to emphasize the main strategies and provide a bridge to related papers in the volume. Since there is considerable cross-referencing to other authors, we have provided a name index for contributors, as well as a subject index. Although many readers whose primary training is in science may find the articles by philosophers quite difficult, and those whose training is in philosophy may find the scientists' articles equally arduous to comprehend, the effort to understand both strategies would seem rewarding.

It is our conviction that intrinsically human and spiritual issues are integral to the mind–brain relationship, so that its importance far transcends the mere intellectual excitement of struggling with such a magnificent mystery. Since, as Eccles observes, "The hardest problem a man can ever have is the relationship of his own brain processes to his mental states!" academic chauvinism, like other forms of narcissism, is maladaptive, and the contribution of both philosophers and scientists would seem most welcome. We offer this volume with the hope that it may help unravel the world knot.

REFERENCES

Capek, M. (1969): The main difficulties of the identity theory. *Scientia* **CIV,** 1–17.

Eccles, J. (1970): *Facing Reality.* New York: Springer-Verlag.

Feigl, H. (1967): *The "Mental" and the "Physical,"* Minneapolis: University of Minnesota Press.

Gabor, D., Kock, W., Stroke, G. (1971): Holography. *Science* **173,** 11–23.

Meehl, P. (1966): The compleat autocerebroscopist: a thought experiment on Professor Feigl's mind/body identity thesis. In: *Mind, Matter and Method.* Ed. by P. K. Feyerabend and G. Maxwell, Minneapolis: University of Minnesota Press.

Pribram, K. (1971): *Languages of the Brain.* New Jersey: Prentice Hall, Inc.

Ryle, G. (1949): *The Concept of Mind.* London: Hutchinson.

Sellars, W. (1963): *Science, Perception and Reality.* London: Routledge & Kegan Paul.

Sperry, R. (1969): A modified concept of consciousness. *Psychol. Rev.* **77,** 532–536.

Contents

8

9

10

1   Introduction

Although we tend to talk glibly of *the* "mind–body problem," Weimer makes clear in the following article that there is in fact a cluster of mind–body problems—indeed, a cluster which has changed and grown over the history of philosophy—and, in so doing, he provides a broad perspective on the area. Certainly the "world knot" is a complicated one, and many strands dangle teasingly from it. *Contra* those who believe that the data of science will allow us ultimately to unravel it, he argues that scientific knowledge is part of that epistemological problem which is itself integral to the world knot. It may not sit comfortably with scientists that they are part of the problem rather than providers of the solution!

For Weimer, "sentience," "sapience," and "selfhood" are all "a result of the central nervous system's ability to structure and restructure its own activity." When it comes to what we know, there is an inescapable distinction between phenomenal experience (known "by acquaintance") and the discursive knowledge of the nonmental domain (known "by description") which transcends that experience. Since we can only know a nonmental entity by description, it is impossible to say whether "the physical is or is not intrinsically identical to the mental," and ontological skepticism results.

Each of the mind–body problems is basically a problem relating to meaning in the sense of Frege; i.e., "the concepts pertaining to the mental realm do not mean the same thing as those pertaining to the nonmental realm, and that *is* the problem." It follows in a straightforward manner for Weimer that "the only way to solve the mind–body problem is to resolve what meaning is, and explicate how it is manifested in the natural order."

In the final sections of his paper, Weimer proposes what

1

appears to be a novel strategy that is closely related to radical Chomskian notions (Chomsky, 1968) and the often overlooked work of Hayek (1952). [As Weimer (1973) has discussed elsewhere, the philosophical basis for this position is inherently Platonic in outlook.] Since meaning, within the tranformational approach, which Chomsky largely initiated, is generated by deep structures intrinsic to the brain, then, in principle, the mind–body problem can be solved by an appropriate conceptualization of deep structures. A model is provided by ambiguous figures, such as the Necker cube, or ambiguous sentences, wherein two alternative surface structures are transformationally related in terms of their relationship to an underlying deep structure which is ambiguous. Thus, "persons," which as Strawson (1959) has argued are conceptually prior to "minds" and "bodies," entail distinct surface manifestations *because* the deep structure which generates those surface manifestations can be viewed both ways with equal legitimacy. In effect, Weimer speculates that the mind–body problems require "an account of the grammar of deep structural reality that explicates how it is written into mental and physical surface structures."

What, then, is the relationship between these two surface structures, since there is no causal connection between them? First of all, the mental and nonmental realms are "different phases, or modes of instantiation, of existence," just as the matter of classical physics differs from the plasma of quantum physics. Causal laws do not obtain across phases, but within phases; however, *invariance laws* do obtain across phases.

Although Weimer's argument is compelling, it leans upon linguistic and psychological views of meaning which remain at present problematic, and those who are realists at heart may find it difficult to accept that the distinction between "the mental" and "the physical" is simply a function of different meaning created by the brain. (In linguistic terms, the distinction would be between ways of speaking and ways of being.) Further, even if it were admitted that the difference between the mental and physical realms is ambiguous, there is no obvious connection between that kind of ambiguity and the ambiguous sentence, "Praising professors can be platitudinous." The two phases have *incompatible* properties, e.g., the mental is private and unextended whereas the physical is public and extended; but there is nothing incompatible (except in the sense that both cannot be had at once) about "to praise professors can be platitudinous" and "professors who praise can be platitudinous." In any case, Weimer's proposal would seem to be a considerable advance over those views on mind–body which simply reduce the problem to one of disparate mental and physical languages, since he suggests an underlying unitary but ambiguous deep structure which generates those languages.

REFERENCES

Chomsky, N. (1968): *Language and Mind.* New York: Harcourt, Brace & World.
Hayek, F. A. (1963): *The Sensory Order.* London: Routledge, 1952. Reprinted by University of Chicago Press.
Strawson, P. F. (1959): *Individuals: An Essay in Descriptive Metaphysics.* London: Northern & Co. Ltd.
Weimer, W. B. (1973): Psycholinguistics and Plato's paradoxes of the Meno. *American Psychologist* **28,** 15–33.

1 Manifestations of Mind: Some Conceptual and Empirical Issues

Walter B. Weimer

The conference that generated this volume focused upon brain and consciousness. Consciousness is the major mental phenomenon discussed, and recent data from brain science, neuropsychology, and technology are assayed in an attempt to understand how consciousness is related to brain, and what problems that relationship poses. Since these are focal issues on many pages, I wish to point out that consciousness is just one exposed tip of the mental iceberg, and that fundamental mind–body issues remain no matter what is said of consciousness. My primary task is to overview a major cluster of mind–body problems from which consciousness may become a focal problem. This is not to demean consciousness as a problem, but to put it in perspective as one of many pressing issues. Having located the major issues, I wish to turn to the second focus of the conference: the role of data in conceptual problems. This book contains empirical data relevant to the mind–body problems, but none of them are decisive, and some remarks why this is to be expected are in order. Finally, the manner in which mind and body are manifested in the natural order has always been puzzling, and I believe that recent conceptual advances in linguistics and cognitive

WALTER B. WEIMER·Pennsylvania State University

psychology help clarify the issue. Integral to this issue is an explication of the relationship that obtains between mind and the physical and biological orders, and the focal problem of the causal efficacy of consciousness. Thus this essay concludes by examining how mind and matter could be derived, and how the mental realm could be causally efficacious in the natural order.

THE NATURE OF THE ISSUES

Although the semblance of organization that it provides may be misleading, it is worth compartmentalizing various aspects of the mind–body problems. By listing problems and exhibiting their interrelationships we can achieve a synoptic perspective from which to locate the issues discussed in the literature. Contrasting the major problem areas with the domains of inquiry from which they are addressed yields Figure 1 as a first approximation to the "world knot." By filling in this matrix, and noting how the contents of various cells interact, we can

Problem	Area of inquiry		
	Epistemology	Ontology	Technology
Sentience	Knowledge by acquaintance (tacit knowledge) ?	Intrinsic properties of onta (manifest image)	Mystical experience Biofeedback ↓
Sapience	Knowledge by description (conscious and tacit)	Structural properties of onta (scientific image)	Esoteric ↑ psychology Learning and the control of behavior
Selfhood	Personal knowledge	Persons as objects in the natural order	Consciousness and the location of self

Figure 1. Some major objects of investigation in the mind–body complex, grouped by problem area and area of inquiry. The listing is neither definitive nor invariant: for example, whether tacit knowledge is a problem for sentience is not clear; certain aspects of esoteric psychology involve both sentience and sapience.

sketch *what* the major mind–body problems are, and *why* they are problematic.

The major problems are familiar from Feigl (1967). *Sentience* refers to our phenomenal experience, to what Tolman (1935) felicitously called the "raw feels" that we live through. The problem of sentience is that we cannot tell how it exists within and relates to the remainder of the nonmental universe. *Sapience* refers to knowledge or intelligence, which likewise is an attribute of the mental realm not obviously reducible to the properties of the nonmental realm, and which could not likely have been generated except by minds. *Selfhood* refers to the individual that "is" a person, which is that compound mental and physical entity who is the subject of conceptual thought. Selfhood is problematic because persons are logically singular entities which are simultaneously mental and physical.

The prototypic statement of the mind–body problem since the time of Descartes is, "What are mind and body, and how do they relate to one another?" The classic answers are the more popular of the 17 "moves" or "positions" that C. D. Broad (1925) so beautifully summarized in the last chapter of *The Mind and Its Place in Nature*. Thus one can hold that both mind and body exist or that one does not (dualism, or mentalistic or physicalistic monism), that neither exists except as an appearance (neutral monism), etc. The relation can be interactionistic (Cartesian or other), parallelistic, epiphenomenalistic, or nonexistent (reductive monism), etc. On top of all this can be superimposed the question of emergence, which asks whether mind (or matter) is emergent in the universe with respect to the other. Unfortunately, these standard moves presuppose that we are clear on what we *know* about mind and matter, and that is decidedly not the case. Epistemology places severe constraints upon ontology, and thus simultaneously sharpens what the mind–body problems consist in and rules out the standard positions.

Epistemology and the Inescapability of Dualism

Neuropsychology has progressed to the point that it can assert that everything human beings can perceive, conceive, or do is a result of the CNS's ability to structure and restructure its own activity. Everything mental arises from the functioning of the active nervous system: The CNS is the place of mind in nature. This truism from neuropsychology has enormous implications for epistemology. All our knowledge is a matter of the activity of our nervous systems: in this sense the Kantian admonition that human knowledge is a construction in the mind of man must be true. But what is human knowledge, and how does it come about? Granted that neurophysiology (which, like all empirical discipline, is contingent and fallible) is on the right track, what can we know, and how does this constrain what we can say about mind and body?

How we know can be answered, at one level, by explicating how knowledge results from the structuring and restructuring of neural activity. This question can be answered, at least in principle, by advances in cognitive and neuropsychology. But *what* do we know? Here we are forced to admit a dualism: on the one hand we have knowledge by acquaintance, phenomenal experience; on the other hand, we have knowledge by description, discursive knowledge, of the nonmental realm. These types of epistemic activity reflect a qualitative difference: acquaintance is not and *cannot* be description, and vice versa (despite the fact that we can know by acquaintance the referential basis of a description, and can describe experience with which we are acquainted). Although knowledge by acquaintance and description may have the same *reference* (when both refer to our experience), they do not have the same *sense*. As Russell (1948) and Maxwell (1968, 1970) have argued, our only knowledge of the nonmental realm, including our bodies, is purely by description of its structural properties. The only intrinsic properties of objects which we know (if indeed we know any), are those of the events in our brains comprising our phenomenal experience. All knowledge is ultimately related to our experience, but knowledge by description transcends experience. At this level of analysis, the mind–body problem of sentience arises: we do not know the intrinsic properties of any nonmental entity, and therefore cannot say that the physical is or is not intrinsically identical to the mental.

Our epistemic dualism thus has a disturbing ontological consequence. That consequence is that the only tenable ontological position is one of agnosticism: we can never *know* whether "the mental" is or is not ontologically "the same" as "the physical." Any claim in this regard must rest upon arguments that are purely conceptual in nature, for no contigent knowledge claim can ever address this issue. A Utopian physical science that exhaustively specifies all the structural properties of every object in the universe cannot tell us whether the intrinsic properties (of which those structural properties are higher order properties) are the same as those with which we are acquainted. In this sense, sentience is not a contingent (i.e., scientific) problem at all. The problem is posed by the mere existence of raw feels and knowledge by acquaintance, because we cannot get from our epistemic situation to an ontological specification. That acquaintance exists is beyond reasonable doubt; what it is remains totally un-known. Since this is so, the standard mind–body moves, especially physicalistic monism, must be rejected.

Pursuing this point, the presently popular "neural identity hypothesis" must likewise be rejected as a contingent claim, since it cannot be *known* to be true (or false). If it is to be endorsed, it must be on conceptual grounds instead of empirical ones. But there is one thing wrong with the claim in any case: it begs the ontological question at issue. "Appreciation of the psychoneural identity hypothesis from a biological perspective leads to the idea that *physical reality can be directly known and it is precisely consciousness* (consciousness *per se* and phenomenal content) *that is this noninferred physical reality*" (Globus, 1972, p. 298). Ignoring the fact that we cannot *know* anything *directly* (see below), there is no basis for the claim that the reality with which we are acquainted is *physical*. That is, we can never know that it is or is not physical. All we can do is ascertain a correlation of *reference* of acquaintance (consciousness) with events known by description (patterns of neural activity). But reference is not the issue: to make the strong claim above, we must identify the *sense* of "consciousness" or "acquaintance" with "physical" or "neural." But this cannot be done, precisely because acquaintance is not description: we can never know the ontological point at issue. Epistemic dualism is compatible with correlation of reference for mental and physical phenomena, but it requires ontological agnosticism and thus rules out the identification of sense.[1]

Even granting some headway on the "How" and "What" problems of knowledge will be of little help unless we simultaneously address a third mind–body problem: *who* has knowledge? This is the problem of selfhood, of the epistemic "I" who is the singular subject of conceptual thought. What sort of entity could be both a singular subject of thought and also a mass of cells and neural impulses? How can we reconcile personal knowledge (by acquaintance) of the self with the advancing knowledge by description provided by the physiological and psychological sciences? Where and how, to put it another way, are *persons* in the "physical" world? Here we arrive at another paradox: what we know of the self by acquaintance is radically different from what we know about our bodies and nervous systems by description. Consider what we know by acquaintance in entertaining some proposi-

[1] Arguing that current physics discloses onta (basic entities or "existents") having properties "congruent" or "symmetrical" with consciousness *per se* does not mitigate against this. The epistemology of physics is no different from that of psychology and philosophy, and is confronted with the same ultimate dualism (see Wigner, 1967). The "ontological" claim in physics is thus a reflection of its (conceptually prior) epistemic status.

tion (say, that life is all too short). In understanding that proposition, whether in a flash of insight or by drawing out its implications over time, you are, both logically and phenomenally, a singular subject of conceptual activity. *You* have knowledge, and you are a single entity in all instances of conceptualization. But our scientific image, with its postulational knowledge by description of the nervous system as a functioning pattern of neural impulses (Hayek, 1952; Eccles, 1973; Pribram, 1971) does not disclose a unitary self, or indeed any self at all. As Sellars (1963) has argued, there is a difference in "grain" between experience and the self with which we are acquainted, on the one hand, and what we know of neural functioning, on the other. It is the *difference* in grain that is the problem for our understanding of self, not merely that there is grain. Everything that we can know, most especially our experience, results from the structuring and restructuring of the nervous system's activity. But what we know by acquaintance has a different grain than anything yet found in neural activity.[2]

Continuing in this manner we can build a detailed matrix of mind–body problems and explore the particular shape each one assumes depending upon which domain(s) of inquiry we relate it to. We cannot answer any one problem (say, sentience) without simultaneously addressing many different domains of inquiry: to epistemology, ontology, and technology could be added ethics and value theory, the discrepant pictures proposed by what Sellars (1963) has called the manifest and scientific images, etc. However, regardless of what columns we add to the three in Figure 1, there is an order of constraint applying to the ones listed: what we know about epistemology con-

---

[2] What Sellars means by the difference in grain between experience and the nervous system comes out in this passage about the relationship of occurrent color to microparticulate reality:

"It does not seem plausible to say that for a system of particles to be a pink ice cube is for them to have such and such imperceptible qualities, and to be so related to one another as to make up an approximate cube. Pink does not seem to be made up of imperceptible qualities in the way in which being a ladder is made up of being cylindrical (the rungs), rectangular (the frame), wooden, etc. The manifest ice cube presents itself to us as something which is pink through and through, as a pink continuum, all the regions of which, however small, are pink. It presents itself to us as ultimately homogeneous; and an ice cube variegated in colour is, though not homogeneous in its specific colour, 'ultimately homogeneous' in the sense to which I am calling attention, with respect to the generic trait of being coloured" (Sellars, 1963, p. 26).

When applied to the problem of selfhood,

"If the human body is a system of particles, the body cannot be the subject of thinking and feeling, *unless thinking and feeling are capable of interpretation as complex interactions of physical particles;* unless, that is to say, the manifest framework of man as one being, a person capable of doing radically different kinds of things, can be replaced without loss of descriptive and explanatory power by a postulational image in which he is a complex of physical particles, and all his activities a matter of the particles changing in state and relationship" (*Ibid.*, 27).

The problem is that such a replacement of the manifest conception of persons as singular subjects cannot occur without the loss of precisely those characteristics which are definitive of persons. This is the mind–body problem of selfhood.

strains what may be said in ontology, and the problems of technology only make sense against the backdrop of epistemic and ontological specification. Thus one aspect of the world knot is that what can be said about one domain constrains theorizing in another, yet the pictures developed across domains are often discrepant, i.e., violate those constraints.

Equally important, and more often addressed in the literature, are the conflicts that occur within a single cell in the matrix. Consider the ontological problem of selfhood. The problem is that persons are basic entities in the manifest image, yet they have both mental and physical aspects simultaneously. How can a "basic" entity be this sort of compound? Or look at sapience as an ontological problem: What are we to make of the "third world" of the products of human knowledge that Popper (1972) and Eccles (1973) make so much of? How can we reconcile Plato's three worlds of material existence, consciousness, and recorded knowledge? How can we, as inquiring creatures of the second world, have both a material existence and produce knowledge in the third world?

Most of the issues discussed at this conference concerned new data from one or another science or technology. Thus a technological problem of sentience concerns mystical experience and altered states of consciousness; esoteric psychology and learning provide technical problems in sapience; and Sperry's research on consciousness and selfhood is a technological breakthrough in selfhood. Thus the empirical issues depend for their character upon prior conceptual and "philosophical" issues, and these latter positions change as a result of the influx of new data. In this way the mind–body complex grows and changes, adding new dimensions, increasing both our knowledge and our ignorance at the same time.

Consciousness as Sapience: The Act–Object Distinction

Consider the pure experience of a raw feel. So long as the mere undergoing of experience is at issue, there is no need to split the process of sensation into an object sensed and a sensing subject. James (1904) and Russell (1945) were correct in abolishing the act–object distinction in sensation. The having of a raw feel is truly nonconceptual, and "pure experience" involves neither subject nor object. But pure experience is *un*conscious: being aware of experience *as* experience transcends sentience for sapience. Knowing an experience *as such*

is a conceptual activity; consciousness, as awareness, is *always* awareness of something as an instance of some abstract classification. Thus
we must distinguish sensation, on the one hand, from perception and
conception (i.e., cognition, which includes consciousness), on the
other. We cannot follow James and Russell in the cognitive realm. We
can abolish the act–object distinction in sensation, but not cognition.
Intrinsic to all cognition is a subject of conceptual activity (the "I" in
esoteric traditions) who has awareness (both of and as an object in
consciousness). Pure consciousness must of necessity be "consciousness of consciousness" rather than consciousness of nothing: the latter
is unconsciousness. What we are conscious of is thus not identical with
our acquaintance, but is rather a restricted part of it. That which is left
over is part of our tacit knowledge (as Polanyi [1958, 1966] uses the
term). But consciousness, like thinking, is knowledge by description
(quite often, of entities which are ingredients in sensory acquaintance).
We can *have* acquaintance, to be sure, but that is all: the moment we do
anything with acquaintance, such as label it or acknowledge it, we do
so in thought. Thought, in words, images or whatever, is knowledge by
description, and is vastly richer than our acquaintance can encompass
(we can know by description all the abstract propositions and concepts
of science, but we can never experience them: we know the meaning of
"the largest integer" or "Light is the limiting velocity in the universe," but *not* by acquaintance).

Thus the point I am attempting to make is that consciousness,
as a mind–body problem, is in the same cell as thought and discursive
knowledge, and that (depending upon the domain of inquiry) that cell
is in the row labeled "sapience" in Figure 1 and *not* "sentience."
Consciousness is thus a focal issue, but not the only one, in this aspect
of the world knot. There is far more to the mental realm than just
consciousness. Let us now consider another problem of sapience: the
problem of tacit knowledge.

Tacit Knowledge and the Problem of Meaning

Tacit knowledge, as Polanyi (1958, 1966) has defined it, is
knowledge of which we are focally unaware and can almost never
formalize. The vast majority of human knowledge is tacit in this sense.
Consider our ability to recognize faces *as such*, i.e., as instances of
human faces. Each of us can exhaustively separate everything in the

universe into the categories of "face" or "nonface," despite the fact that we have never been taught how to do this, and have never experienced the majority of faces that exist. The domain of perception has as its main problem that of thing–kind identification, the problem of how we perceive particulars of X as instantiating the class X. Every time we succeed in recognition, we have instanced tacit knowledge. How do we know Δ is a triangle? Psychology hasn't the faintest idea (Weimer, 1973). We do know certain aspects of what is involved: the mind must be operating with a set of abstract categories that transcend experience, and the rules of determination which are the mind must assimilate surface-structure particulars to these deep structural categories.The mind can never know particulars *as such* (see Hayek, 1969). Our explicit knowledge can't cope with the recognition of even the simplest phenomena, and it is totally powerless to formalize how, for instance, we can recognize a significant problem in science as being either significant, or a problem, or scientific.

But tacit knowledge is not limited to perception. As both Polanyi's writing and cognitive psychology point out, it is characteristic of all conception, and hence of all human knowledge. Concept formation is an instance of it (see Cassirer, 1923, 1957), as is our knowledge of language (the transformational revolution has as its basic insight Chomsky's [1965, 1968] emphasis that we know more of our language than we have learned or can tell). All the higher mental processes that are characteristic of man reflect the same picture: the knowledge and ability which makes us human is tacit. It is as if we have two heads, one explicit and formal, the other tacit and intuitive (Ornstein, 1972), and the latter is almost infinitely smarter than the former. How this can be so is equally much a problem in the mind–body complex as is consciousness.

In its most essential form the problem of tacit knowledge is nothing more, nothing less, than the problem of meaning. In this sense there is only one problem in psychology, and everything in the field is a manifestation of it in a particular area. We have been grappling with this same problem since the dawn of reflective thought, grasping at it without ever reaching it at all.

This problem has many names. In the language of behaviorism, it is a matter of stimulus generalization or of stimulus equivalence. In the terminology of Gestalt psychology, it is the problem of contact between perceptual process and memory trace: the so-called "Höffding Step." Among philosophers, the question is usually formulated in terms of "universals" and of "abstraction from particulars." For Bruner and his associates, it is the problem of categorization. In computer technology, it is called "character recognition" when only letters and numbers are to be identified, or more generally "pattern recognition" (Neisser, 1967, p. 47).

The problem of when stimuli are equivalent *is* the problem of stimulus recognition which *is* the problem of concept formation, *ad infinitum*, all of which together constitute the problems of meaning. Stimuli are equivalent, in the last analysis, only because they *mean* the same thing to the organism. No matter where one turns in psychology there comes a point at which we run straight into an insurmountable wall. All we can do is look up and see that written on that wall are all the problems of the manifestations of meaning. Should anyone think that any current approach resolves the mind–body problems, let him explicate the meaning of meaning and its manifestations.

Manifestations of Meaning in the Mind–Body Problems

I contend that each problem of mind and body that Figure 1 represents is at heart a problem of meaning. In each case the concepts pertaining to the mental realm do not mean the same thing as those pertaining to the nonmental realm, and that *is* the problem. Indeed, one manifestation of the problem may be seen in answering the question, where is meaning in the physical universe? Here one of the "paradoxes" that Pribram (1971) finds so stimulating arises: the answer is simultaneously everywhere and nowhere. The resolution of this paradox would answer, at least in essentials, the classic problems of mind and body.

This essential tension between the presence or absence of meaning, and the differences in its modes of manifestation, comes out clearly in the favorite metaphors used to render intelligible the relationship of mind to body. Sellars uses the idea of a difference in grain to point out that a phenomenal colored expanse does not mean the same thing as packets of light quanta emitted from a colorless source. Globus, following Bohr and the Taoist tradition, talks of the complementarity of mind and body. The double-aspect or double-knowledge metaphor has served the same purpose for Spinoza, Leibniz, Wundt (the founder of psychology), and many contemporary theorists. By emphasizing the difference in perspective, or point or view, from which the mental and physical are seen, these metaphors bring out the inescapable epistemic dualism of acquaintance and description, and locate the ultimate nature of that dualism in meaning. The only way to solve the mind–body problem is to resolve what meaning is, and explicate how it is manifested in the natural order.

THE ROLE OF DATA IN PHILOSOPHY AND SCIENCE

Like all enduring issues in philosophy, the problems of mind and body are both conceptual and empirical. Advances in mind–body understanding typically consist in clarifying conceptual points and assimilating new data to emerging conceptual frameworks. Scientific (or empirical) data are relevant to the issues, but can never resolve them. The conceptual issues can be changed (sometimes clarified, sometimes confused) by data, and data can be changed by conceptual frameworks, but problems can only be solved at the expense of creating others. The role of data in the assessment of scientific theories and conceptual frameworks is both a methodological and an epistemological problem, and in the second sense is part of the mind–body problem that it is to help solve. Thus a second issue I wish to discuss is that of the role and relevance of data in the mind–body problems. How can it be that data are relevant (indeed indispensable) but not decisive? Now we must address the issues compartmentalized in the third column of Figure 1, under the heading of "technology." It has been the success of modern technology that has provided all the data that transcends phenomenological observation and introspective report. Had it not been for the development of neurophysiology and psychology beyond purely observational and correlational disciplines, the mind–body complex would be largely an historical curiosity (in technology-minded Western cultures).

Data in Conceptual Issues: Two Case Studies in the Mind–Body Problem

Data are relevant to the conceptual issues of the mind–body complex, but their role is neither in confirmation (as the inductivist would have it) nor in refutation (whether decisive or conventional, as Popperians contend). No methodology of scientific research is adequate to the task of explicating the role of data in scientific growth (although I believe a combination of Kuhn and Popper's views is the most adequate framework presently available; see Weimer, 1974). Indeed, one of the most informative tasks the historian and psychologist of science can perform is to expose the discrepancy between even the most sophisticated scientist's philosophical preachment and his actual research practice. The scientist's tacit knowledge enables him to learn significant things about the natural order, but philosophical reconstruction lags far behind in its attempt to explicate that tacit ability. Sometimes data seem relevant to inquiry, sometimes not. Let us examine two cases in which data are admitted to be relevant, to see their effect upon mind–body conceptual issues.

Consider first the newly christened "science" of psychophysiology, and its research on operant conditioning of autonomic bodily functioning, and the technique of biofeedback. This field was given scientific legitimacy in the late 1960s, largely due to the sophisticated research of Neal Miller and his associates. By painstakingly controlled research, these investigators showed that subjects (both animal and human) can exert control over bodily functioning that had previously been regarded as not modifiable by "voluntary control." By making cues explicit and instituting reinforcement contingencies, it is possible for a subject to learn to control blood pressure, the temperature of various parts of the body, threshold of stimulus input and pain, etc. Indeed, we can even control our brain waves: biofeedback, as an operant conditioning technique (Kamiya, 1968; Brown, 1974), lets us produce alpha and other EEG patterns virtually at will or "on command." Thus we have "hard" scientific data for the "causal" effect of mind on body that even the behaviorist must acknowledge. So long as we can establish appropriate cues and reinforcements, our volition can exert control over bodily and neural functioning, control that was undreamed of in scientific circles even a decade ago.

What effect has this "new" data had upon the mind–body positions? None whatsoever. No theorist was ever persuaded to or dissuaded from a theoretical formulation on the basis of data *alone*, and the mind–body "theories" are no exception to this rule. If a theorist believed in interaction before, he will cite such data as support, and if he didn't, it won't matter anyway. For example, no one need abandon the identity theory because there is evidence for mental control of bodily processes, and it is hard to imagine how *any* data could make a materialist (such as the Australian group of Smart, Medlin, etc. [see Presley, 1967; Armstrong, 1965]) decide to have a mind that he could change.

Indeed psychophysiology fits nicely into Kuhn's conception of paradigmatic normal science research, and testing a theory is the last thing these studies do. If science were corrigible by data then the "evidence" that has been available for fully 3000 years from oriental and esoteric psychology would have affected our thinking, but it has only appeared in "hard" science with the rise of laboratory psychophysiology. Prior to that we simply dismissed reports of yoga masters who could lower their pulse, walk on coals, sleep on nails, meditate on command, etc., despite an enormous literature of documented cases and the teachings of enduring esoteric traditions. Yet this esoteric data is exactly what psychophysiology is corroborating: we have taken the yoga and zen doctrines into the laboratory and corroborated their accounts quite uniformly, whereas before Miller, Kamiya, *et al.*, published, we dismissed this "data" as nonexistent and on a par with that of astrology.

It is thus slightly ironic that subsequent investigations have not replicated some of Miller's "classic" results. Here the informativeness of failure is quite in accordance with Kuhn's (1970) account of it in normal science research: failure reflects on individual competence, *not* the theory. It is amusing that Miller, who legitimated the field and established the paradigm, may now be adjudged an incompetent experimenter by the paradigm's standards. But Miller legitimated another area of research in his classic study on fear as an acquired motive (1948), that has since proven to be quite "solid." This has occurred despite the fact that Miller's study was virtually inconclusive: He reported that "a majority" of the subjects learned the correct response, but inspection of the data indicated that the "majority" was 13 out of 25 rats!

Other data may have a more dramatic effect. An example is the work of Sperry (1969) and his associates on commissurotomized patients. His arguments for the causal efficacy of consciousness and its localization in the dominant hemisphere are cited throughout this volume, so there is no need to repeat them here. But now the tantalizing question arises: Why is Sperry's research having such a dramatic effect, while the psychophysiology and biofeedback research is not?

One reason is that brain localization-of-function research is compatible with virtually all conceptual positions in the mind–body problem. The localization of consciousness does not threaten any theory, and can be accommodated as an empirical refinement by all. Further, Sperry's results are dramatic in the sense that no theoretical position anticipated hemispheric localization: this was an unanticipated discovery, and therefore newsworthy. Sperry's claim that consciousness has causal potency is another matter: despite its novelty in the hands of a contemporary neuropsychologist, it is historically an old position. Emergent, or physical$_1$–physical$_2$,[3] interactionism has a "pre-history" very much like that of the esoteric traditions that preceded psychophysiology.[4] But the evidence that Sperry sees as forcing him to endorse emergent interactionism can be accommodated with no trouble by the identity theory, Berkeleyean idealism, or any other position. Everyone can admit that the data are relevant to the mind–body problems, but since all theories can stretch to accommodate it, no decisive result obtains. Once again the point: data are relevant, but never decisive. One cannot hope for consensus in even conventional falsification: Popper's (1963) model of science, despite the appeal of its slogans, is not correct (Lakatos, 1970; Kuhn, 1970).

Methodology as an Epistemological Problem

A major problem of the methodology of scientific research is to explicate the nature and role of data in theoretical systems. The growth of science depends, in ways no one yet understands, upon the generation of theoretically motivated data. Recent advances in our understanding of science as an ongoing enterprise can both clarify and reinforce the contention that data can never resolve the mind–body issues. We can see this by examining the role of factual propositions in the assessment of scientific theories. The two problems most discussed in methodology are *inference* and *acceptance*. These are the problems of what do we (and can we legitimately) infer from data, and when do we (and ought we to) accept a theory on the basis of evidence.

With regard to the problem of inference, it has become clear that science infers *to* facts rather than *from* them. From data we can infer nothing at all. This is because facts are theoretical entities: all factual attribution is relative to a thoretical (or conceptual) framework. One can only attribute factual status to an observation if a theory is available to determine that it is indeed significant, i.e., a fact. Facts are theoretically significant observations, not neutral or "hard" data. The data relevant to the mind–body problem is like all other scientific obervation in this

---

[3] The physical$_1$–physical$_2$ terminological distinction was introduced by Meehl and Sellars (1956). An entity or event is physical$_1$ if it is in the space–time manifold. An entity or event is physical$_2$ if it is explainable by (Utopian) physico-chemical theory. Thus emergent phenomena are physical in the broad sense of physical$_1$, although they are not physical$_2$. The emergence theorist denies only that physico-chemical theory can encompass emergent phenomena; he is not claiming that they are insubstantial or "ghostly."

[4] Interestingly, the history of psychophysiology extends back to the ancient Greeks even in the West. But when, as a historian of psychology, I pointed this out to current investigators, they were dumbfounded: they thought they were daring pioneers, working in a field that had not existed 15 years ago. Sperry (1969) is likewise unaware that his position has been endorsed before, and thus makes claim that are quite amusing to an historian.

regard: without a theory (either explicit or tacit) of what constitutes observing and what there is to be observed, nothing will be seen at all. This thesis of factual relativity is well known from Popper's (1959) discussion of the "empirical basis" of science, from Hanson's (1958) discussion of observation, from Kuhn's (1970) account of the role of data in paradigm clashes, and indeed was familiar to Goethe, whose famous dictum that "were the eye not attuned to see it, the sun could not be seen by it" is the essence of the doctrine.

All this is commonplace today in philosophy of science, but the theoretical "contamination" inherent in data has an obvious implication for methodology that is overlooked by inductivists and empiricists: it destroys induction as the "method" of science (as Popper and his disciples constantly remind us; see Agassi, 1966; Feyerabend, 1970; Lakatos, 1968; Popper, 1959, 1963, 1972). If facts follow from theories rather than lead to them, then the assessment of rival theories cannot be based upon factual support. No theorist has ever accepted or rejected a theory on the basis of data alone. The factors governing theory choice are neither factual (as the inductivist claimed) nor logical (as Popper would have it), but psychological (see Weimer, 1976). Explication of the nature and role of data in the assessment of scientific theories is the role of a Utopian psychology of inference and expectation. When all is said and done, it will be a psychological account of the scientist's tacit knowledge, and his inferential processes, that provides the key to methodology. But we need not have the final account to see that data are not decisive in the acceptance or rejection of a theory: the case studies that the Popperians have provided (see Agassi, 1963; Feyerabend, 1970; Lakatos, 1970) make the point beautifully, and show very clearly how data may be relevant to conceptual issues even though it cannot be decisive.

But if this is so, then methodology merges imperceptibily into epistemology. How scientists infer, what they learn from the data their theories generate, is an epistemic problem that is part of the world knot that it was to help resolve. That is, what human knowledge is, how it is acquired, and who has it are all aspects of the mind–body problem. Everywhere we turn in methodology, psychology, and epistemology we encounter another facet of the problem.

THE MANIFESTATIONS OF MIND AND BODY

Thus far there has been little constructive commentary. I have concentrated upon presenting mind–body problems as genuine, unresolved issues centering around the problem of meaning. The discussion of the role of data was negative in that there are cogent reasons why the world knot is not just an empirical issue, and why data cannot be decisive even in scientific problems. Now it is time to balance this dreary picture with some positive, if highly speculative, conjectures as to how mind and body manifest themselves in the natural order, and how they can be said to be related.

Beyond Neutral Monism

If the outline thus far sketched, of an epistemic dualism and an ontological agnosticism, is accepted, flirtation with neutral monism seems immanent. But if we accept the physical$_1$–physical$_2$ interactionism of mental phenomena causally influencing bodily actions and processes, then a dualism seems equally immanent. Can we reconcile these disparate tendencies?

Acceptance of emergent interactionism requires us to admit both mental and physical phenomena on equal ontological footing. That is, since epistemology cannot adjudicate the issue, we are equally in the dark about the ontological status of either. No reductive position is tenable, whether it reduce ultimately to either mental or physical. Thus no *monism*, as it is typically conceived, is acceptable.

But a true *neutralism*, which allows the mental and the physical to be manifestations of some other, third mode of being, is still tenable. Such a position would *not* be that initiated by William James and refined by Bertrand Russell. As elaborated in *The Analysis of Mind* (1921) and subsequent publications, Russell's position was similar to a double knowledge view: Physics and psychology look at different "appearances," but appearances are deceiving, for underlying disparate appearances is something which does not possess the characteristics of either matter or mind. Russell's position is clearly monistic: that which exists ultimately or fundamentally is neither mental nor physical, at least as we *typically* conceive those concepts. But is it really a neutralism? Russell's proffered "neutral third" realm of existents turned out to be sense data. Even after he had explicitly rejected phenomenalism and endorsed realism, Russell did not escape from mentalism. In Russellian neutral monism it is the physical which winds up being a deceiving appearance of something else, and that something else is sense data, which are paradigm exemplars of mental phenomena.

Feigl (1967) is thus correct in rejecting Russell's neutral monism as merely a variant of phenomenalism.

Two major problems face any genuine neutralism which does not reduce one mode of being to the other. First, the "neutral" substratum out of which the mental and the physical are somehow manifested must be given ontological specification such that it is not an unknown and unknowable fiction postulated solely to save otherwise discrepant appearances. Sooner or later we must have theoretical specification of its intrinsic and structural properties. Second, one must render intelligible (provide a model for) the *manifestation* of two disparate modes of being out of a further, third mode of being. That is, it is necessary to provide a model of *how* the mental and the physical could be "manifestations" of something else.

The *a priori* implausibility of neutralist doctrines in the past has been a combination of these two problems. To the first I have nothing to contribute. I find it unfruitful to speculate upon the nature of the substratum when we have, as yet, no plausible characterization of either the mental or the physical. This is an immense problem, but one for *all* theories of mind equally, not just neutralist theories. But admitting this first problem, there are some things we can say about the second one, thanks to the recent revolution in linguistics and cognitive psychology. Recent applications of concepts stemming from the theory of Post languages[5] make clear what we intuitively mean by "manifestation of mind and body."

The theory of Post languages and the technical concept of a transformational rule provide a rigorous account of how mind and body can be said to be related. Transformational grammars specify how different surface structure strings can be related to (or derived from) a common underlying, or deep, structure. At least in principle, the problem of the manifestation of mind and matter is solved. What

---

[5] The theory of Post languages (stemming from the work of E. L. Post, 1943) has as its domain all "languages" composed of symbols that can be concatenated. Any conceivable language can be understood by specifying this ordered four-tuple: $(V_T, V_N, \sum, F)$. V_T refers to the terminal vocabulary items; in the case of a natural language, these are surface lexical items, i.e., words. V_N refers to the nonterminal or abstract, underlying entities such as *NP, VP, det., aux.,* etc., which determine what traditional grammar referred to as "part of speech." $\sum$ refers to the axiom set of the language. Contemporary linguists consider only one: *S*, intuitively understood as sentence, although in principle an indefinite number are allowed. The key for our purposes is *F*, the "Post productions" or formation rules. These rules of the grammar specify how terminal strings result from the application of rewriting rules to the axiom set and nonterminal vocabulary elements. Intuitive rewrite rules for natural languages are $S \rightarrow NP + VP$; $NP \rightarrow ADJ + N$, $N \rightarrow Boy$; etc. The transformational revolution in linguistics may be understood as the realization that natural languages can only be generated by grammars utilizing very powerful rules called transformations. Transformational rules rewrite strings of symbols (rather than single symbols) into strings of symbols. Other, less powerful rules can rewrite only a single symbol at a time.

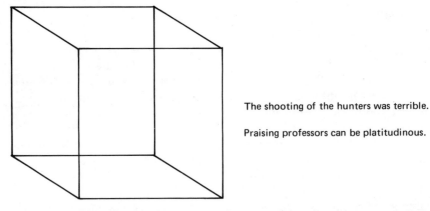

The shooting of the hunters was terrible.

Praising professors can be platitudinous.

Figure 2. Examples of deep structural ambiguity. Both the ambiguous sentences and the Necker cube are cases in which one surface object has two deep meanings or representations. Persons as simultaneously minds and bodies are ambiguous in this manner.

we now require is an account of the grammar of deep structural reality that explicates how it is written into mental and physical surface structures. What we must explain is the deep structure ambiguity of those aspects of reality (persons) which are alternately known to be mental and physical. But the point remains: I propose that the transformational model of perception and language, now being developed for the entire realm of "higher mental processes," is (more properly, will be) an adequate model for the problem of the model of manifestation of mind and matter.

The mental and the physical may be transformationally related in the manner in which the two "interpretations" of a Necker cube are related, or the two surface structure representations of deep structurally ambiguous sentences (see Figure 2). In essence, deep structure ambiguity is the basis from which a transformational model *could* derive the alternative manifestations of "the mental" and "the physical" realms. Deep structure ambiguity occurs when two disparate entities, in terms of their sense or intension, are manifested in the same referential basis. This is precisely the problem with persons as the referential basis for both mind and body. The surface-deep structure distinction and the transformational model of their relation is sufficient to explain how the mental and the physical could be alternative manifestations of a third, common, underlying (deep) substratum or "structure."

Such a view rules out any strict monism because transformationally related phenomena (generically or neutrally construed) are not merely "translations" (and hence disguised identities) of one another.

Physicalistic doctrines fail because they attempt to *translate* the mental into the physical, rather than admit both phases as distinct. The converse holds for the failure of mentalistic doctrines that deny matter as an appearance. But transformationally related surface phenomena *are* distinct: the Necker cube is two objects manifested in one set of lines, not just one object seen from different perspectives. "Persons," in this view, are deep structurally ambiguous objects like the Necker cube: they are simultaneously and indivisibly minds and bodies, as Strawson (1959) and Sellars (1963) have argued. The mental and the physical are thus related and "interact" in the manner in which the alternative "readings" of a common ambiguous structure are related and interact.

Mind, Matter, and the Nature of Interphasic Relationships

Now a problem arises: on the one hand, arguments such as Sperry's for the causal efficacy of consciousness in human action are compelling; on the other hand, the relation between the mental and the physical modeled by transformational analysis is not causal in any usual sense of the term. Sperry, Eccles, and Pribram all argue in one or another manner for attribution of causal potency to consciousness in their contributions to this volume, and I am in agreement with their contention. But it should be clear that surface structures do not cause alternate surface structures in the transformational model: one perspective of the Necker cube does not cause the other, any more that one interpretation of an ambiguous sentence causes the other. The traditional interactionist position which holds that mental phenomena causally interact with physical phenomena must be rejected if the transformational model is accepted. Thus we face a new question: How are we to understand the relationship obtaining between the mental and the physical if they are alternative surface structures derived from a common deep structure?

We can gain some insight into the problem by considering the similarities and differences in *inter-* and *intra*-phasic relationships. There are different phases, or modes of instantiation, of existence. Classical physics, for instance, deals with matter (neutrally construed) in what we can call the *ordinary* phase. Laws of nature for ordinary matter are the paradigm exemplars of causal relationships: the concept of causality had its first application in scientific analysis in explicating the relationships obtaining between entities within the ordinary phase of matter. But the 20th century has seen the rise of a new physics, that deals with the instantiation of "matter" in a new mode of existence: *plasma* physics. The laws of nature for plasma (ionized gases at high temperature and pressure) are not those of ordinary physics: quantum laws are not classical laws. Once again, within the phase boundaries of plasma, the relationships that natural laws explicate can, by stretching the traditional analysis,[6] be called causal (but *not* microdeterministic). But no causal relations obtain *across* phase boundaries from ordinary to plasma physics. The laws relating ordinary and plasma physics are *invariance* laws rather than causal laws. Invariance laws specify constancy of formal structure of entities with respect to permitted changes in the entities, and can apply both within and across phase boundaries. Within phase domains, causality may be one type of invariance (see Lazlo & Margenau, 1972), but across phase boundaries that type of invariance does not apply.

The different phases of plasma and ordinary matter are no longer questioned. More controversial is the contention that there is a *biotonic* phase of existence, which is the phase of living things. Many eminent authors have argued for admitting the biotonic phase as irreducible to any inanimate phase, among them Elsasser (1958), Schrödinger (1945), Von Neumann (1966), Wigner (1967). There is no space to argue the case here, and I simply assume the existence of this phase of existence, at the price of abandoning the reductionists' tidy, if simple-minded, view of the universe. For our purposes, there are two important things about biotonic laws: first, they are emergent, in terms of complexity and organizational properties, with respect to inanimate laws of nature; second, they are likewise not causally related to other phases. Once again, within the phase boundary causal specification appears to be applicable (although the "billiard ball" model of ordinary matter causality is clearly inapplicable); but across the phase boundaries, causal specification does not hold. It does not make sense to say that physical systems "cause" life, despite the fact that it is both sensible and illuminating to speak of a physical substratum underlying a living system.

---

[6] Causality, on the usual analysis, is a succession of events sufficient to permit microdeterministic state determination of the system involved. That is, a system is causal if a linear sequence can be traced from event to event leaving no "unfilled" gaps in the chain of events. Linear or causal interactions among contiguous events are microdeterministic and involve a direct transference of energy from one event to the next in the chain. "Billiard ball" interaction is paradigmatic of causal interaction in both respects. Only laws of nature which are formulated in terms of the interactions of events could conceivably by linear and/or microdeterministic, and hence causal. But the interphasic invariance laws, which relate events in terms of the laws of nature, deal with entities that are not only separated in space–time but also in different phases of existence. Thus they are nonlinear and nonmicrodeterministic: they have neither of the properties which may be considered definitive of causal analyses. Such invariance laws are at best macrodeterministic and nonlinear.

But the mental realm is not coextensive with the biotonic phase: not everything that is living is also mental. It is perfectly acceptable to be a panpsychist and hold that *life* is *not* an emergent property of the universe, but rather coextensive with the inanimate realm. But the mental is not just the living: attributes such as sentience, sapience, and selfhood are emergent with respect to living systems (and *ipso facto* to inanimate systems). Thus if a biotonic phase of existance be admitted, it is implausible to deny a *psychic* phase for the mental realm, despite its restricted localization in the central nervous systems of the highest primate(s). Again the same picture emerges: within the phase boundary, causal specification is possible, but none is permissible across phase boundaries. As before, the type of causality that occurs within the psychic phase is neither the classical mechanical concept of ordinary matter physics, nor the quantum mechanical concept. Russell aptly called the causality that occurs in the mental realm *mnemic causality*, in virtue of the central role of memory in all psychological processes. Mind may be defined as a group of events in space–time (a physical$_1$ system) connected by mnemic causal laws. Wherever mnemic relations are found, attributes of the mental will be in evidence.

Consciousness, in its causal potency, is a mnemic relation. The mind responds *directly* to its experience, as Sperry has emphasized:

> Perceived colors and sounds, etc., exist within the brain not as epiphenomena, but as real properties of the brain process. When the brain adjusts to these perceived colors and sounds, the adjustment is made not merely to an array of neural excitations correlated with the colors and sounds but rather to the colors and sounds themselves (Sperry, 1969, pp. 535–6).

But equally, mind is a system of neural impulses that exist within the biotonic phase (to say nothing of the electrochemical system that instantiates it within the physical phase). How can these systems be related? Can we understand their interaction in causal terms? Asking the question suffices. The relationships between the phases are lawful and necessary, to be sure, but they are not causal as the term has heretofore been used in science. We may be able to state lawful relations obtaining between the various phases of existence which coreferentially constitute a person, but it is clear that such laws will be invariance principles rather than causal relations. Mind cannot cause matter, nor vice versa. Classic emergent interactionism, which postulates that the interaction is causal, cannot be correct.

Thus if mind has causal efficacy, it is only with regard to the entities of the *psychological* phase of "matter." And indeed, this fact is implicitly recognized in extant theorizing. Consciousness is said to cause *behavior* or *action*. Behavior and action are *psychic* concepts: they cannot be reductively defined in terms of any of the other phases of being. For instance, psychological behaviors are functionally rather than physically (or physiologically) specified: to attribute to a psychological subject the ability to "leap a barrier" or "write a signature" or perform any behavior whatever is to attribute to that subject the ability to execute an infinitude of physically specified movements. The mental realm in which consciousness is causal is simply not the same as, nor specifiable solely in terms of, anything except the psychological phase of existence.

From this perspective, it becomes clearer what Russell meant when he said, "An event is not rendered either mental or material by any intrinsic quality, but only by its causal relations" (1951, p. 164). What we require at this point is a theory specifying the coimplication relations holding between events that exist simultaneously in more than one phase of existence. Mind and matter are corelated in a context of constraint that utopian invariance laws may specify. Perhaps we shall never know why the relations that obtain do so, but at least we may aspire to a specification of what those relations are. At present, it seems that these relations exemplify what Leibniz had in mind in talking about compatibility and existence. The framework in terms of which the phases of existence are related seems to be one of Leibnizian *composibility* rather than causality[7] (see Weimer, 1976; Shaw & McIntyre, 1974).

To return to the neutralism modeled upon deep structure ambiguity, notice that the relationships it postulates are "compatible" with the analysis of relationships obtaining between phases of existence. The rules of a grammar that specify the derivation of terminal

---

[7] Compossibility defines possible worlds that are internally consistent. Because the actualization of some possible events is incompatible with that of others, the possibilities split into mutually exclusive systems of "compossibles." The phases of existence, which instantiate onta as physical, plasmic, biotonic, or psychic, constitute a compossible system (which is the *actual* world, one of indefinitely many *possible* worlds). The relationship between the phases is one of compatibility rather than causality.

The problem of science is to explicate that compatibility, literally the corelations, obtaining between onta within the various phases of existence. Following Leibniz, and more recently Mach (1902), Einstein (see Clark, 1971), Weyl (1950, 1952), and Wigner (1967), I believe that symmetry theory considerations govern the relationships between phases. The invariance laws relating phases are invariably symmetry laws. If this is so, then the task of psychological science involves uncovering the coimplication relations obtaining among phases. The formal structure of causal laws within one phase will be mirrored, according to symmetry group theory principles, in the other phases. Thus there is a context of constraint supplied by the formal or structural properties within each phase, because those same formal characteristics must have their symmetry theoretic counterparts in the other phases. If the compatibility of phases is correctly captured by this symmetry theoretic analysis, then mind and matter are coimplications of the compossible system which is the actual universe.

strings in a surface structure instantiation have the conceptual necessity (or nomological necessity) associated with laws of nature, but,
although they are in this sense compelling, they are not causal.
Rewrite rules do not cause S to turn into $NP + VP$, any more than
nonterminal elements are caused to become terminal elements: derivation is not causation. In this respect the rules of a grammar resemble
invariance laws relating phases of matter. Figure 3 shows the relationships involved in mind and matter (ignoring the biotonic phase).
Causal specification occurs only within a phase, and the relations
between mind and matter (and life) is compossibility rather than
causality.

Dewan (this volume) proposes that *mutual entrainment* is a
model for how consciousness as a superadditive control system could
be causally efficacious. Although this may be true, it is a data claim
rather than an explanatory hypothesis. Entrainment is a fact rather than
an explanation. Furthermore, there are no cases of entrainment relations *across* phase boundaries. Thus entrainment cannot explain how
consciousness is related to physical (or even physiological) movement
of the body. As Eccles rather gleefully notes, the problem of voluntary
control, of why my fingers move my pen when I will to write this
sentence, is completely mysterious granted a purely physical account of
the universe. If we grant the account sketched above, it is no longer so
mysterious, but it definitely remains completely unexplained. We
presently have no idea how to characterize the relationships that must
hold across phase boundaries such that the mental realm can coexist
with certain complex physical and biotonic systems.

The account I am proposing has more in common with parallelism than traditional interactionism, although it admits the causal

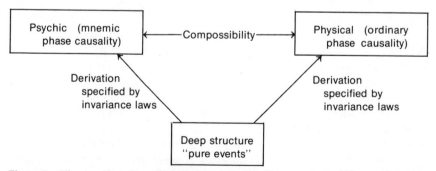

Figure 3.   The manifestation of mind and matter in a framework of Leibnizian Compossibility. Because of the epistemic limitations on knowledge by description, we will never
know whether the deep structure of reality (neutrally construed, pure events) is or is not
intrinsically the same as our acquaintance.

efficacy of mental phenomena (but restricts it to the psychic phase). Leibnizian parallelism, interpreted as a descriptive account of the cooccurrence relations obtaining between mind and body, is not at all incompatible with emergent interactionism. Mind and body, as disparate surface structure manifestations of existence, are related by invariance laws which denote compatibility within a framework of compossibility. These latter relations are, descriptively at least, a form of parallelism. Despite the mere parallelism of our descriptive understanding of their relation, mind as the psychic phase of existence is still empirically emergent in the universe, and mental phenomena are causally efficacious in the affairs of "persons." But as to how this can be, I can only say that we need more data to tell.

CONCLUDING CAVEAT

In concluding, it is worth restating the three major points I have attempted to make, and the consequences they entail for future research on the world knot. First, the constraints upon epistemology (emphasizing the dualism of acquaintance and description, and leading to the thesis of structural realism as an account of scientific knowledge) prevent us from making definitive progress in ontology. Our epistemic predicament forces us to remain ontologically agnostic. We are forced to acknowledge that ontological prescriptions for the nonmental realm must be based upon contingent theories of the structural properties of such onta. This in turn forces upon us the primacy of structural analysis, and helps to direct research away from hopeless ontological tangles. This is certainly not a solution to any aspect of the mind–body complex, but it does at least locate the problems in which progress can conceivably be made in the domains in which they occur. Second, the core of the resultant epistemic problem is the problem of meaning and its manifestations. All our endeavors are an effort after meaning—in this quest science, philosophy, and common sense are on a par. Again, this is not a solution to the myriad problems we face, but it does characterize their intrinsic nature. Third, the conceptual advances of transformational linguistics and the theory of Post languages do suffice to solve the structural problem of the manifestation of mind and body. Granting the reasoning leading to it, the conception of mind and body as alternative surface manifestations of an underlying deep structure obviates this minor but heretofore irritating problem. And, if correct, the symmetry theoretic analysis of interphasic relationships holds a definite hope for the future. It suggests that if we ever succeed in solving one of the problems of meaning within one phase of existence, we will have a key to its counterparts in other domains in the symmetry of invariance laws. Success in a first step would automatically unlock many other doors.

Whether this picture of our current status will be seen as enlightening and optimistic, or sterile and depressing, will depend upon the expectations of the reader. If definitive progress in ontology is desired, then it is depressing, for neither the mental realm known by acquaintance nor the nonmental realm known by description can yield such information. On the other hand, the contingent arguments for realism are warrantedly assertible: there is a world external to our senses, and *if we can know anything at all*, we can know its structural properties by description. And since structural properties of onta are, in the last analysis, properties of intrinsic properties of onta, we need not be reluctant to identify the system we know by acquaintance with the system our contingent theories know by description. But such identification is the beginning of the world knot, not its resolution.

REFERENCES

Agassi, J. (1963): *Towards an Historiography of Science, Beiheft 2, History and Theory*. Wesleyan University Press.

Agassi, J. (1966): Sensationalism. *Mind*. N.S. Vol. **75**, 1–24

Armstrong, P. M. (1965): *A Materialist Theory of Mind*. London: Routledge & Kegan Paul.

Broad, C. D. (1925): *The Mind and Its Place in Nature*. London: Routledge & Kegan Paul.

Brown, B. B., (1974): *New Mind, New Body*. New York: Harper & Row.

Cassirer, E. (1953): *Substance and Function & Einstein's Theory of Relativity*. Orig. Chicago: Open Court Press, 1923. Reprinted by Dover Press.

Cassirer, E. (1957): *The Phenomenology of Knowledge*. New Haven: Yale University Press.

Chomsky, N. (1965): *Aspects of the Theory of Syntax*. Cambridge: M.I.T. Press.

Chomsky, N. (1968): *Language and Mind*. New York: Harcourt, Brace & World.

Clark, R. W. (1971): *Einstein: The Life and Times*. New York: World Publishing.

Eccles, J. C. (1973): *The Understanding of the Brain*. New York: McGraw-Hill.

Elsasser, W. (1958): *The Physical Foundations of Biology*. New York: Pergamon Press.

Feigl, H. (1967): *The Mental and the Physical*. Minneapolis: University of Minnesota Press.

Feyerabend, P. K. (1970): Against method: Outline of an anarchistic theory of knowledge. In: *Analyses of Theories and Methods of Physics and Psychology*. Ed. by M. Radner & S. Winokur, Minnesota Studies in the Philosophy of Science Vol. IV, Minneapolis: University of Minnesota Press, 17–130.

Globus, G. G. (1972): Biological foundations of the psychoneural identity hypothesis. *Philos. Sci.* **39**, 291–301.

Hanson, N. R. (1958): *Patterns of Discovery*. Cambridge: Cambridge University Press.

Hayek, F. A. (1963): *The Sensory Order*. London: Routledge, 1952. Reprinted by University of Chicago Press.

Hayek, F. A. (1969): The primacy of the abstract. In: *Beyond Reductionism*. Ed. by A. Koestler & J. R. Smythies. New York: Macmillan, pp. 309–333.

James. W. (1904): Does "consciousness" exist? *Journal of Philosophy, Psychology and Scientific Method* **1**, 477–491

Kamiya, J. (1968): Conscious control of brain waves. *Psychology Today* **1**, 57–60.

Kuhn, T. S. (1970): *The Structure of Scientific Revolutions*. Chicago: University of Chicago Press, 2nd edition.

Lakatos, I. (1968): Changes in the problem of inductive logic. In: *The Problem of Inductive Logic*. Ed. by I. Lakatos, Amsterdam: North-Holland Publishing Co., 315–417.

Lakatos, I. (1970): Falsification and the methodology of scientific research programmes. In: *Criticism & the Growth of Knowledge*. Ed. by I. Lakatos and A. Musgrave, Cambridge: Cambridge University Press, pp. 91–196.

Lazlo, E. & Magrenau, H. (1972): The emergence of integrative concepts in contemporary science. *Philos. Sci.* **39**, 252–259.

Mach, E. (1902): Science of Mechanics: *A Critical and Historical Account of Its Development*. Chicago: Open Court.

Maxwell, G. (1968): Scientific methodology and the causal theory of perception. In: *Problems in the Philosophy of Science*. Ed. by I. Lakatos and A. Musgrave, Amsterdam: North-Holland Publishing Co., pp. 148–160.

Maxwell, G. (1970): Theories, perception, and structural realism. In: *The Nature and Function of Scientific Theories*. Ed. by R. Colodny, Pittsburgh: University of Pittsburgh Press, 3–34.

Meehl, P. E. & Sellars, W. (1956): The concept of emergence. In *Minnesota Studies in the Philosophy of Science* Vol. 1. Ed. by H. Feigl & M. Scriven, Minneapolis: University of Minnesota Press, 239–52.

Miller, N. E. (1948): Studies of fear as an acquirable drive: I-Fear as Motivation and fear-reduction as reinforcement in the learning of new responses. *J. Exp. Psychol.* **38**, 89–101.

Neisser, U. (1967): *Cognitive Psychology*. New York: Appleton-Century-Crofts.

Ornstein, R. E. (1972): *The Psychology of Consciousness*. San Francisco: W. H. Freeman & Co.

Polanyi, M. (1958): *Personal Knowledge*. New York: Harper.

Polanyi, M. (1966): *The Tacit Dimension*. Garden City, New York: Doubleday.

Popper, K. R. (1959): *The Logic of Scientific Discovery*. New York: Harper.

Popper, K. R. (1963): *Conjectures and Refutations*. New York: Harper.

Popper, K. R. (1972): *Objective Knowledge: An Evolutionary Approach*. Oxford: Oxford University Press.

Post, E. L. (1943): Formal reductions of the general combinational decision problem. *American Journal of Mathematics* **65**, 197–215.

Presley, C. F. (Ed.) (1967): *The Identity Theory of Mind*. St. Lucia, Queensland: University of Queensland Press.

Pribram, K. (1971): *Languages of the Brain*. Englewood-Cliffs: Prentice-Hall.

Russell, B. (1921): *The Analysis of Mind*. London: Allen & Unwin.

Russell, B. (1945): *A History of Western Philosophy*. New York: Simon & Schuster.

Russell, B. (1948): *Human Knowledge: Its Scope and Limits*. New York: Simon & Schuster.

Russell, B. (1951): *Portraits from Memory*. New York: Simon & Schuster.

Schrödinger, E. (1945): *What Is Life?* Cambridge: Cambridge University Press.

Sellars, W. (1963): *Science, Perception and Reality*. New York: Routledge & Kegan Paul.

Shaw, R. & McIntyre, M. (1974): Algoristic foundations to cognitive psychology. In:

Cognition and the Symbolic Processes. Ed. by W. B. Weimer & D. S. Palermo, New York: Erlbaum Associates.

Sperry, R. (1969): A modified concept of consciousness. *Psychol. Rev.* **77**, 532–36.

Strawson, P. F. (1959): *Individuals: An Essay in Descriptive Metaphysics.* London: Northern & Co. Ltd.

Tolman, E. C. (1935): Psychology versus immediate experience. *Philos. Sci.* **2**, 356–380.

Von Neumann, J. (1966): *Theory of Self-reproducing Automata.* Ed. by A. Burks, Urbana, Illinois: University of Illinois Press.

Weimer, W. B. (1973): Psycholinguistics and Plato's paradoxes of the *Meno. Am. Psychol.* **28**, 15–33

Weimer, W. B. (1974): The history of psychology and its retrieval from historiography: Part I—The problematic nature of history; Part II—Some lessons for the methodology of scientific research. *Sci. Stud.* **4**, 235–258 & 367–396.

Weimer, W. B. (1976): *Structural Analysis and the Future of Psychology.* New York: Erlbaum Associates.

Weyl, H. (1950): *The Theory of Groups and Quantum Mechanics.* New York: Dover Press.

Weyl, H. (1952): *Symmetry.* Princeton: Princeton University Press.

Wigner, E. P. (1967): *Symmetries & Reflections.* Bloomington: Indiana University Press.

2 Introduction

Alfred North Whitehead once divided all philosophers into two groups—simple-minded ones and muddle-headed ones. With respect to the problem of consciousness, the former group may prefer to focus on the perception of that roundish red color patch referred to by the term "tomato," while the latter may abjure this simplicity and attempt an appreciation of the full complexity of the problem through an entrance into its numerous interstices. Even though both "hard-nosed" scientists and "tough-minded" philosophers may consider clinical psychological data to be irrelevant as well as muddle-headed, the sensitive clinician engaged in the psychotherapeutic encounter may well be more attuned to the true nature of the mind–brain problem than either neuroscientists or philosophers, since taking the "other mind" very seriously and with full attention is integral to his daily work.

In the following article, Knapp illustrates the extraordinary richness and poignancy of human consciousness by presenting a psychoanalytic "hour" that utilizes the method of free association for exploring consciousness, and reveals striking alternations in the state of consciousness, thinking, and boundaries of self; i.e., alternations in sentience, sapience, and selfhood. Knapp also presents findings from psychosomatic investigations and human developmental studies. He emphasizes that the more we examine developmentally earlier layers of thought and feeling, the more we find mind and brain to be "inseparably intertwined."

As a psychoanalyst, Knapp also shows us that "the unconscious" is part of the problem as well, if we are to provide a complete account of human consciousness. Of special importance, we must appreciate that the consciousness we have as highly sophisticated adults is vastly different from the primordial consciousness of earlier stages of

33

development, prior to the attainment of a "firm sense of reality." The psychoanalytic method provides data about this archaic period early in the ontogenesis of consciousness, when perceptions, cognitive "plans," and bodily arousal are not easily differentiable. (This method is said to induce "regression" to earlier modes of psychic organization.) From his ontogenetic frame, Knapp finds common ground with Cassirer and Piaget, who commonly are neglected in discussions of consciousness and brain.

The manifest dualism of brain (or body) and consciousness (or mind) originated from "a common simpler matrix" which includes motivational processes, according to Knapp. To understand a highly complicated hierarchically organized system, it is crucial to understand the genesis of that system. But Knapp also speculates that it is crucial to understand our own personal history as well, since it may be that "motivational pressures serve to give our intuitive conviction about the separate existence of outer and inner reality the characteristics of a stubborn illusion." Could it be that the bifurcation of reality reflects a way of maintaining "emotional security," that is, the bifurcation is a result of a psychological defense? Perhaps it is not reality which is split, "but merely the vision of the beholder." Although Knapp's argument is literally *ad hominem*, it is indeed curious how much emotion can be generated by an intellectual discussion of the mind–body problem! Although Knapp may be accused of psychologizing away what is inherently a philosophical problem, and although he is ambiguous about the word "split" (in that he uses it in the psychoanalytic as well as metaphorical and philosophical senses) yet some rewarding insights may obtain.

Given the context of psychoanalytic, psychosomatic, and developmental considerations, Knapp's construction of "dichotomous schemata in human experience" richly reflects the bipolarities which appear to be inherent in human mentation. But this does not necessarily imply any corresponding bifurcation of reality; the manifest bifurcation is a function of how human consciousness develops. It is through the study of the mind's ontogenesis, especially as revealed through the unique free-association method of psychoanalysis, that the mind–brain problem may be resolved. It should be noted that Knapp's ideas are quite consistent with Weimer's thesis. For Weimer, the bifurcation of reality is generated by ambiguity in the "deep structure" which generates the disparate meanings of consciousness and brain. Knapp's developmental view points to the primitive anlagen for and the genesis of that ambiguity. At the core is found the distinction between "self" and "nonself." This distinction arises from different sorts of experience, which are difficult to disentangle during development. With the emergence of a self-system, this process of splitting continues into the distinction between mind and body.

It might be said that Knapp presents a somewhat "romantic" view of the world knot; i.e., in the innocent wisdom of early childhood, the problem does not exist, and it is only through repetitive and emotionally charged splitting during ontogeny that a pseudoproblem is created. Surely some (adult!) philosophers would contend that of course there is no problem, so long as the question is not asked; but when development attains the critical juncture when conceptual thought occurs, then the problem which has been present all along becomes manifest. That one can become aware of one's own awareness, as Weimer emphasizes, is a *conceptual* activity, and it is not until this level of conceptualization is attained that the world knot can even be considered. Hence, that the mind–brain problems arise only during the course of development need not imply that they are pseudoproblems.

2 The Mysterious "Split": A Clinical Inquiry into Problems of Consciousness and Brain

PETER H. KNAPP

Felix Deutsch, a pioneer in psychoanalysis and psychosomatic medicine, took for his title of another symposium a phrase of Freud's: "The Mysterious Leap from the Mind to the Body." My modification focuses, as did the conference as a whole, on the notion of bifurcation or splitting. It is further intended to suggest that many conceptual problems concerning consciousness and brain are sophisticated present-day heirs to the problems of mind and body.

The paper will address two of these problems. Primarily it will deal with the relationship of conscious experience to the physically observable organism. Secondarily it will discuss the task of reconciling subjective feelings of volition and choice with apparent observed lawful determinism. These questions are familiar, often intertwined, but fundamentally separate; they form, if you like, orthogonal dualities.

The discussion will have its own inner bifurcation. First, using case material as a text, it will review empirical data from three

PETER H. KNAPP·Boston University School of Medicine

sources—free association in the psychoanalytic situation, investigations in the area of psychosomatic medicine, and studies in developmental psychology. It will discuss implications of these observations for the two psychophysical questions as they have been traditionally posed.

Secondly, from the standpoint of a psychoanalytic clinician, it will speculate on some motivational factors that may be relevant to the very persistence of these questions.

My aim is eminently clinical, to heal such splitting. This is not to deny that problems exist. Mind and body, brain and consciousness, as well as freedom and necessity, are phenomenological contrasts that have always puzzled thoughtful men. My aim is rather to recommend that we pay meticulous attention to observational, descriptive and conceptual approaches, and especially that we trace the origins of these contrasting phenomena. So doing, we may avoid taking subjective conviction of duality for proof of unbridgeable gaps in the universe outside us. The wiser conclusion may be that it is not reality as a whole which is split but merely the vision of the beholder.

CLINICAL VIGNETTE: A SPLITTING HEADACHE

These clinical data come from one session in the prolonged psychoanalytic treatment of a patient who has been described elsewhere, (Knapp, 1969). Busy and successful in his professional life, he had difficulties in the personal sphere which had prohibited a stable and lasting relationship to a woman. Any approach to such involvement stirred up the ambivalently colored image of his mother, a domineering lady who had been extraordinarily controlling and intrusive throughout his childhood. During that time his father had been largely absent, remaining a powerful but distant figure. Ordinarily the patient found it difficult to experience warmth or closeness to either a woman or a man, including his therapist, who at times seemed to represent one, at times the other.

Before this session quoted here (from the tape-recorded record) he was beginning to speak of terminating his treatment, although he still had significant unresolved problems. This session came only a few days before he was to make a trip overseas. He had rationalized this on grounds of his business, though there was no real need to make it at this time. His main purpose was to go skiing with an older man. He was debating how many days to take off, and, just under the surface, was preoccupied with an effort to rebel against and escape from the demands of his therapy. Hidden defiant impulses were accompanied by fears of being off by himself, weak and vulnerable.

For most of this early morning session he talked about this projected trip and his conflicts in relations to the analyst. He also referred eight times to what was for him only an occasional symptom, an episodic throbbing headache.

His first reference to the headache came almost as he entered the door. He remarked: "It's going to be a tough session for me. I don't have any dreams. I come with an empty bag of tricks, and—*come in with a headache.* I don't think it's psychosomatic, though. The apartment was very dry last night and I woke up with a *splitting headache* on the right side." He followed this by telling of a fantasy he had on the way to his appointment, namely that he would be locked out by the doctor, and be filled with righteous anger, or perhaps feel "left out in the cold," an interpretive possibility raised by the analyst, greeted with some skepticism by the patient.

In fact, after about three minutes, he switched to talking about an ambitious business venture. His *second reference* to headache ensued: "We're committing let's say a million dollars, you know, big deal; and I should have—uh—*my head should be splitting now.* I should be scared." Then he reported another fantasy. His mother was currently in another city and had sent him an unusually supportive letter about his business acumen; he imagined replying to her with a "warm, tender letter, a real love letter." He said that this was "revealing," making him feel "naked . . . unguarded." The analyst commented that his reaction was like that of a little boy talking openly, trusting a parent who cares, a notion that made the patient uneasy.

His *third reference* to headache followed: He toyed with the idea of building himself up again, boasting of his achievements, saying, "Well I've accomplished this and that. That would just be sweeping under the rug again. *This headache is*—uh— . . . I suspect it's part dry room but in part something else. Uh—I suspect it's—it's an attempt of a little boy to get love and attention . . . by coming in and *holding my head and moaning* . . . I've come here and *held my head and I moaned.*" At that point he returned to the subject of his impending trip. Focus on this led to ambivalent debate about whether or not he should stay away one or two exta days. A fleeting image emerged, "the rear end of a dark, an aborigine, naked." This was followed by more debate about his conscious desire to escape the "discipline" of analysis.

Then—about 20 minutes after the start of the hour—came his *fourth reference* to headache. "The extra day . . . is freedom, uninvolvement, back-stepping from this analysis and this commitment. *I got a headache right now again*—Ach! Ach—that's it. I can talk about it from now till doomsday and I won't come up with anything else I don't think." Focus on the headache elicited memories of a previous time away in a strange city, where the patient was managing a plant for his father. During that period he had had several severe episodes of "migraine." "I never had a headache like that in my life before. Murder. Here I was left alone. I had business down there—see? And I really had a lot of doubts about whether I could do anything. And I failed." In earlier sessions he had reported that his failures there had been not only at work but also in his sexual life.

The patient then returned to the immediate future and his indecision about when to return from his trip. His *fifth reference* to headache followed. He imagined the analyst saying, " 'Take your time; take two weeks off.' I think it would upset me. Uh—I think I would get unnerved and it would prove you didn't love me, that you weren't interested, you didn't care . . . What can I say? I just know we'll talk about this for the next three days, about when I'm coming back. Uh—*the thing comes and goes, the headache.* It's expressing something . . . a pulling and pushing. It's a *split.*" He went on to say he wished things were "hunky dory," that he could please everyone. He expressed worries about what medicines to take on his journey, at the same time feeling that he was weak and unmanly as he tried "to fill my father's shoes."

The last 13 minutes of the session were characterized by vivid fantasy, strong feeling and lively interchange. Just before the *sixth reference* to headache he said, "You're right. I'll be here. I don't know, I don't know why I'm doing this. Let's make it Monday morning." The analyst remarked, *"You held your head."* He followed, "Hmm I—I *scratched my head.* Why am I . . . going, going back and forth from Tuesday to Monday night to Monday morning; I *held by head 'cause I've got a headache.* That's why I held it. The *headache* part. You know what I feel like right now? I feel like I'm floating, floating in air, in a cocoon, in a, I don't know, an egg." He followed by saying that he had the image of looking at a vagina and seeing a clitoris. It upset him; he was confused, scared of women. Then he recalled bumping into an unfriendly male acquaintance a day or so earlier, and he expressed shame over the idea of his employees seeing him "lying here being analyzed; wouldn't that be something?"

His *seventh reference* to headache ensued after the analyst again remarked, *"You hold your head."* "Yuh," he said, "I don't know why . . . it's not planned. I don't know. *I don't know why I hold by head.* It's warm. If I take my hand away it's cold. And my eyes—you know—*my head hurts a bit here,* right through here. You know, *holding my head it doesn't feel like by head.* It hasn't—it feels like it's smaller and *like it's not my head.* My hands feel much bigger than my head. My *head's shrinking.* If I were to run my hand over my head right now I would say this *does not feel like by skull.* It feels like somebody else's. It's a *baby's head I guess* . . . no hair."

At this point the analyst asked: "If you were to blurt something out . . . instead of a headache . . . what would it be—" He replied "Shit . . . I wanna punch, you know. I wanna punch a bag . . . do something physical . . . I would stand up against the wall and pound my fist into it. I just feel like I want to—I want to be physical and violent and I don't know what the hell to do with it." The analyst suggested that he felt rage at him for his demands, yet couldn't experience the rage because he had at the same time such a need—ultimately the need for "a mother who loves you." The patient struggled with ambivalent feelings. He spoke of his long-standing fear of being a quitter, and said, "I feel like crying." . . . "I just cry. I'd sit and bawl . . . the crying is a little boy's cry. I've got tear ducts. They're running a bit now and I don't know why. I'm crying now." Again the analyst asked: "What would you say if you blurted out something instead of crying?" He replied: "I love you—something like that. I don't know—uh—be kind. I don't know, I don't know what I'd say. Shit. I don't know what I'd say . . . I don't know. I'm *split* down the middle and boy I'm fighting myself."

He remarked on hearing another patient enter the waiting room: "That little girl coughs for attention out there." Then he wondered whether he was simply trying to impress the doctor with his astuteness. This led into his *eighth reference* to headache. "I'm smart, I'm dumb. I'm mature. I'm not. I'm a child. I don't know what the hell I am . . . I never follow through. My mother always threw it up to me. I never follow through, like my father, you know. 'You don't follow through'; he used to say it—that of me, too. 'You're a quitter.' And I used to quit. Fencing; I quit on that. School I didn't quit. I was never a good student. (pause) I see cobwebs—cobwebs on the ceiling. Uh—jesus—*I don't know what the key is to this headache.*" The analyst remarked: "It came as you talked about cobwebs." The patient went on: "Spiders frighten me. I'm scared to death of *spiders*. They petrify me. Not slimy but they've got legs and stuff and I see *a big one jumping on my head and just biting me*. To show you how afraid of spiders I am, take a snake; snakes I'm afraid of, but spiders, they're worse. Now what does a spider mean? I'm doing this (holding his *forehead* with both hands); and that's what a spider's like."

This culmination of fantasy plus simultaneous expression of emotion in both verbal and gestural language marked the end of the session.

It is difficult to capture on a typed page the sense of authenticity conveyed by a session like this. Reading or, better still, listening to the entire exchange might be more persuasive. As it is the reader will have to make up his mind whether or not it was largely verbal play, a kind of compliant performance. The analyst, familiar with such performances from work with this and other patients, felt otherwise—that the session represented one of those episodes, rare but rewarding in successful psychoanalytic treatment, of intense interpersonal encounter.

The data show progressive "deepening" and elaboration of several themes. Purely within the psychological sphere, the patient started with nothing to say, "an empty bag of tricks," and ended up expressing a graphic fantasy, which might be taken to represent an archaic and threatening portrayal of the relationship to a woman; simultaneously he expressed intense emotion, tears, and the even more foreign and frightening idea of "loving" the analyst. Yet the vividness and intensity were temporary. After the interview he got up and went about his business; he was neither hallucinated nor overwhelmed.

The session also showed progression in his references to headache. At first they seemed to replace all awareness of conflict. He attributed the disturbance to an event in his physical surroundings, the dry apartment, although he followed at once with the theme of conflict over closeness in the analytic situation. As the session went on references to the pain and to his head became accompanied by and increasingly interwoven with his fantasies and feelings.

Furthermore, references to other humans, initially being confined almost entirely to the therapist, expanded to involve memories of his parents. Distinction between the analyst and these figures from the past became blurred; so also did the line between the patient himself and persons outside him—as he held his head and said it felt like a baby's, or as he saw a spider "jumping on my head and biting me."

From this single session a number of hypotheses may be derived in roughly sequential fashion. These are listed in Table 1 along with the evidence as it emerged as part of successive references to head sensation. Two broad contrasting formulations emerge almost at once:

A The headache is etiologically related to changes in the physical environment. These seem best left unspecified, though the patient speculates about "dryness."

B The headache is etiologically related to disturbing changes in the interpersonal environment. Here we postulate in addition that the symptom becomes a focus of attention obscuring these changes, yet allowing them partial, disguised expression. This second broad view would thus place the headache in the general category of conversion symptoms[1] though without yet specifying exact mechanisms. Evidence emerging from this patient at this time seems to favor this hypothesis. As the session proceeds—and the disguise becomes less complete—further subhypotheses emerge:

B_1 The headache is related to conflicting urges to move toward and away from the therapist;

B_2 The headache is in part related to self-punitive trends, counteracting assertive, defiant urges for autonomy;

---

[1] "Conversion symptom" in the technical psychiatric sense postulates a process of symbolic transformation by which an underlying hidden nonconscious conflict becomes expressed in overt behavior, usually as illness, e.g., the forbidden wish to strike becomes "converted" to a paralysis.

TABLE 1.   Hypotheses—Sequentially Derived

Evidence (patient's speech or other behavior in immediate context of references to head)	Reference	Etiologic hypotheses about headache
A "Apartment was dry" "I suspect it's partly the dry room"	 Fourth	Hypothesis A Related to changes in the physical environment (unspecified "dryness"?)
B "I come with an empty bag of tricks" "That would be sweeping under the rug again. *This headache . . .* " "I can talk about it till doomsday and I won't come up with anything else I don't think"	First Third Fourth	Hypothesis B Related to disturbing changes in the interpersonal environment. It becomes a focus of attention, obscuring and disguising these
B_1 "It's expressing something, a pulling and pushing. It's a split . . . going back and forth from Tuesday to Monday" "I'm split down the middle and, boy, I'm fighting myself"	 Fifth Seventh	Further subhypotheses, as postulated disguise becomes less complete B_1 Related to conflicting urges to move toward and away from the therapist
B_2 "A million dollars . . . big deal I should have, uh, *my head should be splitting,* I should be scared . . . " "I can point to accomplishments . . . *This headache*" "The extra day . . . is freedom, univolvement, backstepping from this analysis and this commitment. *I got this headache right now again* "I wanna punch . . . be violent"	 Second Third Fourth Seventh	B_2 In part related to self-punitive trends, counteracting assertive, defiant urges toward autonomy
B_3 "It's an attempt . . . to get . . . love and attention by holding my head and moaning . . . I've held my head and moaned" "If you said go, it would mean you didn't love me . . . *comes and goes this headache*" "I love you . . . I dunno what I'd say"	 Third Fifth Seventh	B_3 In part related to seeking love through weakness and suffering
		B_4 (Combining $B_{1,2,3}$ above) An expression serving to countract defiant urges toward the therapist by a demonstration of self-punishment and suffering
		Further subhypotheses
B_{4a} "I feel like I'm floating . . . in a cocoon . . . an egg" "This does not feel like my skull. It feels like a baby's"	 Sixth Seventh	B_{4a} The constellation around the headache involves the fantasy of being a helpless infant
B_{4b} "Spiders frighten me. I'm scared to death. They petrify me . . . I'm doing this (holding forehead) and that's what a spider is like"	 Eighth	B_{4b} The constellation involves the fearful reactions of an infant attacked by a dangerous, overwhelming mother figure

B_3 The headache is in part related to seeking love through weakness and suffering; or

B_4 (combining $B_{1,2,3}$ above) The headache is an expression serving to counteract defiant urges towards the therapist by a demonstration of self-punishment and suffering.

As the session comes to an end, the references are less to head pain and more to diffuse fantasies; in these the head is part of a total constellation, including a picture of the self and key other persons (cf. Knapp, 1969). The material both supports the combined hypotheses as just stated (B_4) and suggests still more detailed refinements:

B_{4a} The constellation around the headache involves fantasies of being a helpless infant;

B_{4b} The constellation around the headache involves the fearful reactions of an infant attacked by a dangerous, overwhelming mother figure.

Naturally there are many problems with such an approach. Hypotheses, as any perusal of psychoanalytic writings can testify, tend to proliferate. They depend heavily upon the assumptions of the observer. A Jungian, for example, might be impressed by the reference to Jesus, as the patient groped for the "key to these headaches," and be tempted to see him living out archetypical fantasies of religious suffering. Other more physiologically oriented observers might argue that the pain, triggered by events in the physical environment, was leading the patient to a profusion of pseudoexplanatory material in the hopes of gaining some relief. Even within the framework of our own hypotheses one might wonder whether the enormous effort this man was making to "think out" his conflicts was in some way contributing to the localization of his distress in the head.

Whatever hypothesis one espouses, there are problems in searching for mechanism and problems concerned with inferences as one tries to establish a general explanation within and across cases.

The vignette represents a deliberate choice of a common symptom and an active therapeutic interchange. It does not constitute "proof" of the validity of free association and its clinical assumptions of underlying meaning. It is not "proof" of the etiological relationship of hidden conflicts to the symptoms presented by this patient. Nor is it "proof" of the historical antecedents of present conflicts in his childhood.

The material does, however, *illustrate* alterations in an individual's state of consciousness, which included bizarre, primitive imagery, temporary confusion about boundaries of the self, and, simultaneously, a display of unusually powerful emotion. It thus bears on some formal aspects of consciousness as thrown into relief by free association—the method of psychoanalysis.

It illustrates, too, concomitant waxing and waning of painful bodily awareness, which at times may be presented by a patient as something alien, and at other times presented as a phenomenon increasingly involved with his fantasies and feelings. It bears on many problems of "mind" and "body" encountered by those who report conscious experiences, and who attempt to interpret such interrelationships in disease states—the subject matter of psychosomatic medicine.

It illustrates, finally, parallel waxing and waning of intense preoccupation with the process of therapy and the person of the therapist, linked to images of past figures, namely, his parents. And so it bears on the relationship of present conscious experience to prior history—the area clarified by developmental studies.

EMPIRICAL FINDINGS

Psychoanalysis and Free Association

Free association may be pragmatically defined as the language uttered when an individual is instructed to report uncritically everything that comes to his mind. At the outset we must recognize that the instruction is an impossible one and the term an abstraction. Association is never "free" in an absolute sense but rather to some extent "guided"[2] by more or less explicit expectations and reinforcements. As the listening audience becomes vaguer, the speaker supplies his own context. Close study of what he projects onto the partially "blank screen"—for example, the primordial spider in this patient's final fantasy—gives the method its power.

Thus the psychoanalytic situation involves two individuals bound together in an intricate communicative network, however much, at times, it may be convenient to describe associational chains as issuing from one speaker. Nevertheless, free association has a characteristic phenomenology. One can verify this by paying volunteers to associate (Knapp, 1973), by carrying out the procedure oneself with no manifest audience, or by studying literary attempts to reproduce the

---

[2] I am grateful to Dr. Louis Sander who attributed the adjective to Felix Deutsch.

"stream of consciousness." Clear focused perceptions yield somewhat to expanded inclusion of ordinarily suppressed details; logical manifest order is replaced to a greater or lesser extent by a flow of images, feelings, perceptions, and memories, connected by obscure leaps (cf. James, 1890). Their structure, in turn, has important implications for study of mind and consciousness and their relationship to body and brain.

Actually these data have not been fully exploited. The method has been tied to a system of treatment, and, with a few exceptions such as the work of Colby (1960, 1961), there has been little study of free association by itself. Because of its predominantly therapeutic orientation, and, more important, because of difficulties in reconciling its approach to the increasingly experimental temper of the times, psychoanalysis has had a limited relationship to the rest of science. Its theories, dominated by its founder, proliferated into a gothic structure which contained many obscurities, not the least of which concern these very problems of body and "mind."

Some involve predominantly "mind." When one attempts to study free association, or even undertakes the original task, one rapidly discovers that the mental sphere does not present a homogeneous uniform surface. This is hardly a new discovery. Introspective philosophers from St. Augustine to Husserl have pointed to the complex ramifications of thought and feeling around a central area flickeringly illuminated by conscious awareness. Freud, crystallizing awareness that had grown through the century before him (Ellenberg, 1970), developed a method for examining systematically this ramifying structure and delineating its underlying organization. These steps represented revolutionary advance. However, they posed the danger of reifying "mind" and then positing an isomorphic agency, equally reified, below it, namely "unconscious mind" (Holt, 1972).

Spatial analogies and personification, though at one time providing heuristically useful models, can lead to perplexity. This pertains both to the nature of mind and to volition. Where is an idea or feeling, what are its dimensions, when it is in the Unconscious? Who controls the gateway to motor action, the Ego or the Id?

Avoidance of the traps set by metaphors entails formulating mental processes with more philosophic acuteness. One starting point may be to examine free associative communication along the dimensions proposed for linguistic signs in general by Morris (1938). He divided language functions into three broad—though not entirely discrete—areas: semantics, syntactics, and pragmatics. Put in terms of this discussion, an emerging stream of associations conveys not only ordinary dictionary significations, cast in conventional grammatical arrangement, realizing a manifest set of intentions; it also expresses disguised meanings, in a variety of ancillary, obscure modes, and reflects hidden motives.

The semantic dimension is the most familiar. Since "The Interpretation of Dreams," not to mention "The Meaning of Meaning" (Ogden, 1923), when a speaker names a snake or a spider we seldom believe (however much he may) that he is referring only to the members of a given animal class. We look beyond to his unconscious referents. Our problem is that these may be multiple and may stem from different levels. We have not developed rules for sorting them out.

More is involved than mere translation from the language of conscious to that of unconscious processes. To pick two extreme instances, an unconscious element may be betrayed only by its total exclusion from awareness (as when our patient came in initially speaking of having only "an empty bag of tricks"); or it may be revealed through obvious, even dramatic allusions, but highly disguised (as in the patient's final fantasy of a voracious spider).

Nor is the matter settled by a simple topographical scheme, which assumes that elements are removed from consciousness by varying degrees of "depth." We recall that the patient, after imagining a "warm tender love letter" to his mother, said he felt "*naked*." A little later, as he debated delaying his return to analysis, he had a sudden image of "an aborigine, *naked*." One may suspect that the word "naked" in both cases referred to a quasiphysical sense of vulnerability in the immediate therapeutic situation, but that in both cases this was only partially conscious. In the former instance the word was used conventionally in relation to natural embarrassment over an effusive outpouring to his mother; in the other case it was used as part of a fleeting dissociated image.

I suggest that we are dealing with underlying schemata which achieve different *syntactical* forms or modes of expression. The result is statements which are similar to one another, though fitting into different organizations of a psychological field. At times different expressive modes occur sequentially (as in the "naked" imagery just given); at times they may overlap with one another (as in the patient's closing passage when he described head sensations, verbalized a fantasy, and at the same time illustrated it by holding his forehead). We may see such schemata as analogous to the "deep structures" which, Chomsky infers, underlie ordinary verbal language (1957). The analogy can be only approximate. The surface syntactical modes of expression which I am postulating for larger segments of communication are not so neatly interchangeable as those in Chomsky's typical sentences; obviously more complexity is involved and greater difficulty in removing ambiguity.

Further examination of inner experience as revealed by free association discloses a series of schemata or fantasy constellations refer-·ring to the self and key other persons. These are arranged hierarchically (Knapp, 1969). Our patient repeatedly introduced the theme of localized illness. "Under" that could be seen more generalized, alternating fantasies, on the one hand of himself as a rich, assertive, powerful man, rebelling against a controlling parent, on the other hand that of himself as a damaged child needing help from a caring parent. Still "deeper," more amorphous and pervasive, was the fantasy, also dual in nature, of himself as fused with a benign protective person or with a controlling destructive one, epitomized in his closing image of being bitten by the poisonous predator.

We see traces here of the prehistory of language. Casisirer (1953) offers evidence that the formation of subjective consciousness, the concept of self as a unified entity, observing, experiencing, acting, and acted upon, emerges slowly in primitive language,taking many different routes. Some languages have a possessive case; in some possession is indicated by prepositions; in some indicated by a personal verb form. As Cassirer puts it, "In language the personal sphere only gradually grows out of the possessive (p. 263) . . . Language represents a process of differentiation; it may be presumed to have grown out of a relatively undifferentiated state (p. 269)" (Cassirer, 1953).

Hierarchically organized constellations of self–other fantasy do not exist in an isolated individual, but in an ongoing two-person relationship. We are thus also involved in *pragmatics*, defined as "the relation of signs to their interpreters" (Morris, 1938). Language is a form of action, responding to the acts of others and aimed at achieving its own ends.

As the individual thus reacts and becomes mobilized to act himself, we can discern not only pervasive fantasies but powerful wishes, urges, strivings, and fears. In short, we enter the sphere of emotion and "drive." Here conventional dualistic ways of speaking about mind and body become embarrassed. It is as if emotional processes are sometimes assigned to one, sometimes to the other side of the Cartesian pineal gland.

Freud's early, brilliant attempt at psychophysical integration by his neuropsychological "Project" might have given his thought a different shape if he had persevered with it. Instead he turned away from the complexities of the brain to develop his successive models of a "mental apparatus" in what he hoped would be exlusively psychological terms. This step had heuristic value but did not dispose of the dualistic dilemma."Instinct" remained at the heart of Freudian conceptualization, though always assigned to a separate realm as "the demand placed upon the mental apparatus by virtue of its connection with the body" (Freud, 1915). Free association was a psychological method and could not *per se* penetrate the walls erected by its own language. The motivational forces interplaying with meaning were formulated in 19th-century metaphors—affect charge, cathexis, instinctual energy. They were not effectively linked to burgeoning 20th-century knowledge of neurophysiology, neuroendocrinology, and neurochemistry. Yet they were never abandoned. In Ricoeur's words (1970), psychoanalytic explanatory efforts refused to opt for a facile "disjunction—either an understanding in terms of energy, or an understanding in terms of phenomenology." But its crucial task remains unfulfilled—the task, as he put it, of integrating "force and language" (p. 66).

Curiously enough, its own data suggest directions in which to search for such an integration. When devices to ward off intense experience weaken in the therapeutic situation and it becomes an intensified primitive encounter, separation of subjective image and fantasy from simultaneous expressive and neuroendocrine activation becomes virtually impossible. Our patient's statement, "I've got tear ducts and they're running now and I don't know why I'm crying," or "A pulling and pushing, it's a split . . . I'm split down the middle and boy I'm fighting myself,"—may not be mere analogies; rather he may be trying to articulate the kind of core disruption which led to those analogies in primeval language, may be sensing processes which originate centrally and which spread to pervade spheres that only secondarily come to be called psychological and physiological.

The same conceptual paradigm may be found in other types of common experience. A sudden threat while driving an automobile may elicit simultaneously a sharp perception of danger, immediate action, and a racing pulse. Orgasm results from a mixture of vivid sensory perception, voluntary movement, and autonomic nervous activity. In these situations one or another aspect may be consciously perceived, first or throughout. But it is an error to fragment experience on the basis of such partial perceptions, still more of an error to assign to one or another preeminent causal status, and fruitless then to argue in the manner of James and Lange, as to how it brings about its effects across our man-made conceptual barrier.

Argument by selected illustrations does not constitute logical proof. Nor does it leave us with the necessary working model of a motivational core. That task is beyond the scope of this paper. Such a model would have to include positive and negative hedonic systems, and their obligatory stereotyped connection through feedback circuits to expressive and neuroendocrine systems; it would have to trace the progressive structures of checks and balances that these systems acquire, and, particularly, spell out their relationship to symbolic elaboration as conscious representations, which in turn reflect the social structure around the developing child.

Many details about mental functioning and its primitive strata remain to be discovered. This paper is stressing only two points. First, we must not look for the relationship of body or brain to a simple homogeneous "consciousness"; but, rather, we must observe states of organization. Second, as we examine affect and motivation, we find perceptions, plans, and bodily mobilization inseparably intertwined. In developmentally early layers of thought and feeling, it becomes progressively more difficult to apply either "psychic" or "somatic" labels, and more necessary to apply both. Diffuse mood disturbance, sweeping inhibition, pervasive anxiety, and disturbances of the sense of reality, all involve some alteration in consciousness along with concomitant alteration of physiologic function. Thus we enter the domain of psychosomatic medicine.

Psychosomatic Observations

"Psychosomatic" is a hybrid term. The word reflects and in part perpetuates the difficulties with which we are dealing even while proposing approaches to solving them. Originally it was applied to a "classical" set of disorders involving the autonomic nervous or endocrine systems or their end organs. Anecdotal evidence had accumulated, in some instances for centuries, suggesting that social and psychological factors played a role in these disorders. Though much information has been gathered about them, proof remains elusive and is complicated by our conceptual confusion.

The two broad hypotheses about headache, suggested by the earlier case material, illustrate the point. Such hypotheses have tended to be presented in dichotomous fashion. Evidence has to a considerable extent been determined by the questions asked. Voluminous information has been accumulated about many physiologic mechanisms, but, insofar as we lack conceptual bridges between symbol and symptom, gaps have persisted in attempts at comprehensive explanations uniting psychological and physiological data. The studies of Wolff (1948), for instance, have elucidated inflammatory and nervous mechanisms responsible for vascular dilation in the type of headache experienced by our patient, as well as clarifying the variety of head pains from which it must be differentiated. Wolff's studies have concentrated on "life stress" as provocation for such headaches. The question of exactly what kind of events and what kind of responses to them, in this and other patients—the question, in other words, of generalized conditions, sufficient and necessary for headache—is unanswered. We lack not only appropriate physiologic measures but refinement in formulating rules of psychological evidence and inference.

Studies of bronchial asthma have encountered similar problems (Knapp & Nemetz, 1960). Recent years have seen a profusion of information about mechanisms controlling bronchiolar obstruction, related to factors on the surface of the pulmonary epithelium, to substances bathing the bronchiolar tissues, to endocrine and nervous influences on the bronchial tree, and to brain mechanisms, which appear to play a regulatory role. The psychosomatic task is to find relevant patterns of organization in these multiple factors and to relate such patterns to symbolic and social organization. In studying asthmatics psychoanalytically, we have encountered global fantasies and primitive emotions which appear to be inseparable, interrelated aspects of a primitive core. Our hypothesis is that activation of these core processes leads to disturbance flowing from central to peripheral pathways to cause the final disease paroxysm (Knapp et al., 1976).

Such formulations are complex. The main thrust of psychosomatic investigation has been away from the clinically ill adult human to simpler models. For example, Henry (1969) in ingenious experiments has shown that social pressure, as from overcrowding, can lead to sustained elevation of blood pressure in mice. Further consequences have been histologic change in brain and heart and kidney, as well as altered biochemistry, e.g., catecholamines; thus he has provided a model that duplicates many features of human essential hypertension.

Similar approaches have studied gastric ulceration in animals. The most dramatic instance of ulcer production was that used by Brady (1958) and his colleagues in their celebrated "executive monkey" experiment. This involved four pairs of monkeys yoked together in a stress-avoidance situation. Electric shock could be avoided by bar-pressing on the part of only one of the pair. In all four pairs this monkey developed fatal ulceration, which bore a remarkable resemblance to human duodenal ulcer. This crucial experiment has had an interesting epilogue. Attempts to replicate it have not been successful. Recently Weiss (1971 a,b,c) actually found the opposite effects, using rats. They also were paired; one of them could avoid or escape the shock by appropriate bar-pressing; but in these experiments this member of the pair to a significant extent *escaped* ulceration. In an astute analysis of the two experiments, Weiss pointed out that Brady and his group had used the Sidman avoidance procedure, which calls for constant vigilance and virtually continuous bar-pressing activity. The alternative, more common, avoidance procedure used by Weiss, provides relevant feedback, giving the animal an indication of success and—to put it anthropomorphically—permitting relaxation until the next signal. Weiss was able to manipulate the amount and nature of feedback in several ways, and showed that such maneuvers had further decisive influence on the severity of gastric involvement. The relevance of this work to human peptic ulcer is still unclear. It shows, however, the sophistication of behavioral investigation that can be attained. "Stress" is not a vague general phenomenon, but can be broken down into operationally induced meanings for an animal, defined by precise experimental conditions.

Thus in a relatively simple organism, a relatively simple change in external social situation can lead to physiologic change. It could only take place with the aid of the brain and its functions. Perceptions, memories, anticipatory organization, a combination of these factors into learning—all imply rudimentary consciousness. The results would not occur in decerebrate or totally anesthetized animals. Yet we, as observers external to them, do not puzzle over such matters as the basis of animal consciousness, the relationship of his mind to his body, or the nature of his will. Rather we are concerned with the exact parameters of the situation, such as the degree to which he is the passive recipient of stimuli, or is involved in augmenting them through processes originating in his own nervous system.

The psychosomatic concept has also broadened to include almost all that has been discovered about the biochemical foundations of brain function in states of disease. A vast array of knowledge, neurophysiological, neurochemical and especially neuropharmacological, has accumulated in recent years. Some authors, like Kety (1969) defend a naive dualistic position on heuristic grounds similar to those of Freud. Avoidance of abstruse argument has permitted an unencumbered flow of data; yet it may lead us to similar conceptual barriers. The history of psychiatry up to and including the present shows that it has been dominated by one or another hidden set of assumptions, usually falling along the axis between reductionist–monist views on the one hand and idealist–vitalist trends on the other. Workers tend to concentrate on findings that seem appropriate to their implicit world view and to neglect those which appear to lie outside it.

The psychotic state of depression may serve as illustration.

Though its nosological borders are hazy, the syndrome is relatively clearcut; it is a major disturbance marked by striking psychological and physiological concomitants. For the moment we may ignore the question of whether or not it represents a lifelong, possibly inherited disturbance. As overt illness it is episodic and reversible. Let us examine two hypotheses, by no means mutually exclusive, about depression. One states that in certain instances a major blow to the systems maintaining an individual's self-esteem, particularly the loss of a key person, may be a critical antecedent of a depressive episode. The other is that a biological disturbance characterizes depression; in recent years this view has specifically implicated a biochemical alteration in monoamine metabolism and a consequent impairment in neural transmission (Schildkraut & Kety, 1967).

Although there is no dearth of dogmatists in this area, who would dismiss or ignore one or the other of these hypotheses, many informed observers would suspect that both have a good deal of validity, though each will undoubtedly be sharpened by the passage of time and accumulation of further evidence. Our question here is how can they be reconciled? Does loss, for instance, lead to an altered "mental" state, which then in some way lowers monoamine levels? Yet is not the monoamine metabolism postulated to be an intrinsic part of the mental state?

It would seem simpler and ultimately more useful to develop a model in which images, positive hedonic processes and neurophysiologic functioning are all considered to be aspects of adaptive equilibrium. Such equilibrium may be upset for one or another reason—and loss of a crucial person may be such a reason; then the organism, like the mice observed by Henry, is in a different balance, characterized by different images, hedonic stimulation, and neurophysiologic output. Logically the emphasis shifts away from linear chains of events in different realms, which pose not only epistemologic but methodologic obstacles, particularly as they become hardened into ideologies. It moves toward the study of systematic interrelationships, using a comprehensive model; this is possible only if we pay careful attention to the languages, and the levels, used in describing them.

Developmental Data

Tracing events not retrospectively, nor phylogenetically, but ontogenetically in human development, leads to a closely related state of affairs. An infant starts life with little that is recognizable as "mind" or "consciousness." Yet he is not inanimate or insensate. Reactions that appear to involve pain and pleasure, states that we readily characterize as hunger, satiation, alertness, and withdrawal, characterize his earliest behavior. He appears to be under the influence of immediate, largely hedonic elements. Significant anlagen of more elaborate conscious activities manifest themselves early in life. Spitz (1957) showed awareness in the first six months of a variety of social cues, e.g., a drawing of the human face, and the phenomenon has been observed in even younger infants by Stechler, Bradford, and Levy (1966) and Sander (1964). Diffuse strivings become progressively more focused. Awareness of nearby objects is followed by uncoordinated reaching, which achieves some success and repeats itself, leading to improved coordination. Elementary, highly stereotyped motor elements become hierarchically organized, and incorporated into wider adaptive schemata, as Bruner shows in his analysis of the integration between breathing, sucking, and swallowing (1969). The repertoire of inborn responses includes social patterns, such as smiling, which become caught up in circular reinforcement. Mastery provides some kind of early competence which gives pleasure. Pleasurable experience is rewarding *per se* and tends to perpetuate itself. Mastery and pleasure elicit rewards from the human environment which serve as further reinforcement.

Mind develops from this matrix of reflexlike responses. Piagetian investigation, supplemented by Freudian developmental psychology and by both experimentalist and ethological formulations trace the stepwise growth of such functions as imitation, symbolic representation, naming, including designation of self and others, the gradual construction of predictive and causal models, progressively more accurate anticipation, memory and learning, prelogical, and, finally, logical thought. This entire sequence depends upon progressive maturation of the body, particularly the brain; it is equally dependent upon a social system outside the developing child. This finally comes to be represented in his language and thought and integrated with an overall unity, that which makes him recognizable to himself and to others, and which gives him a "self" or personality.

Consciousness, then, like brain, undergoes progressive epigenetic differentiation. Conscious processes start from an elemental stage in which it is impossible to distinguish them from the perceptual and reflex properties of brain itself, and in which only the roots of adult structure and function can be discerned. The individual, as social–psychological organism, differentiates himself from a psychosomatic state of partial fusion with the environment. This means more than mere dependence upon the first nurturant figures. From birth on the infant's responses are locked into environmental rhythms to a far greater extent than we readily grasp. Condon and Sander (1973), for example, have studied films of newborns; apparently random movements of the infant become synchronized, in the first weeks of life, with the speech of an adult, regardless of whether this comes from a live interlocutor or a tape recording, and whether it is English or Chinese. In spite of the partial autonomy each person attains, a vast degree of interlocking interdependence persists into adult life, revealed in the filmed sequences of psychotherapy and other forms of communication by Scheflen (1966) and Birdwhistell (1971).

The point here is not merely to emphasize these facts of entrainment, nor man's residual involvement with his cultural milieu, but rather the bearing of these facts on what we call mind. As Piaget has hammered home, human mentation starts out as quasi-reflex behavior, every bit as anchored to external contingencies as the rats described by Weiss. Gradually, given appropriate stimulation and development of relevant cerebral structures, the infant assimilates patterns from the environment, accommodates to it, develops increasing capacity for self-initiated action and internalized symbolic schemes.

Von Bertalanffy remarks, almost as if echoing Cassirer:

> The distinction of 'object' and 'subject', 'body' and 'mind', 'matter' and 'soul', is not an ultimate given. Rather, it is a product of conceptual differentiation, occurring in individual and sociocultural development . . . Cartesian dualism is not a given disjunction; rather, a primary adualism (Piaget) is progressively differentiated, both in the development of the child and in cultural history. (1969, p. 253)

We have come full circle.

SOME IMPLICATIONS: KNOWLEDGE AND REALITY

Our common sense, molded by Western European tradition, tends to divide the experienced world into two contrasting spheres—brain (or body) and consciousness (or mind). My argument up to now has suggested that closer examination of experience, by free association as well as by phylogenetic and ontogenetic study, reveals that these two spheres originate from a common simpler matrix. This matrix includes motivational processes, that is, urges toward action, which contain both mobilized bodily processes and imagery in obligatory linkage. For example, the startle reflex represents the rudimentary, beginning act of escape, and simultaneously it is inflexibly linked to the perception of danger.

The ostensibly simple example of headache, as it became elaborated in a clinical encounter, suggested a number of hypothetical formulations. These included a presumed history of contradictory messages from parental figures, their internalization as conflicting images and impulses, propelling the patient toward and away from fantasied closeness, along with maladaptive influences on vascular and muscular organization, characterized, among other things, by a report of pain; the pain emerged as a result of disordered equilibrium, which had, at a different level, its own adaptive value, thus tending to reinforce and perpetuate itself. All of this is a ponderous attempt to avoid some of the pitfalls in our usual ways of speaking. It does not answer the question of why headache in this patient, as against stomach ache in another— or, actually, in him at a different time. But it permits orderly inquiry to *begin*. If it does not solve all of our philosophic dilemmas, at least it may avoid perpetuating them.

Naturally such a view does not deny that distinct component systems can be described within the human organism: on the one hand neural and motor equipment; and on the other hand perceptions, memories, images, and plans. But in simpler organisms they appear as just that—concomitant, coordinated systems fitting together into larger systems. Only in man, where complexity, specialization, delay, and apparent separation of functions abound, do we find it difficult to see them in this light, particularly since we are studying an organism with our own complexity, namely ourself.

The difficulty leads to at least two sorts of philosophic dilemma. The first concerns the nature of knowledge. The second concerns the nature of reality.

The nature of knowledge actually poses several problems: (a) how can one know one's self, since subject and object, knower and known, are the same; (b) granted at least some awareness of the contents of one's consciousness, how can one know another's consciousness; and (c) how can one know that the contents of consciousness correspond to anything beyond them?

Analogy with some man-made machines may be helpful. Take television. This apparatus can "look" at many aspects of the world, and it can also be arranged so that in some ways it "looks" at itself. Figure 1-A shows a camera (C_1) looking at a monitor. What is then "seen" on its own monitor screen—Figure 1-B—is an image of itself growing blurred

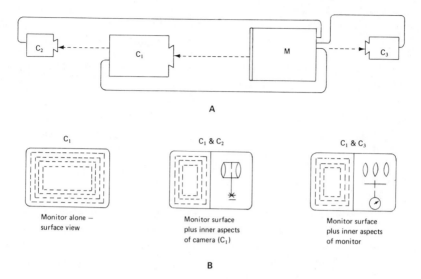

Figure 1.   (A) Camera arrangement. (B) Views on monitor.

and small as it shades off into infinity. Not a bad analogue of human introspection. Using auxiliary cameras (C_2 or C_3 in Figure 1-A) and a split screen, one can have the system "look" at parts of the monitor or parts of the original camera itself, perhaps using a dial to reflect some element of its functioning, shown schematically in Figure 1-B. Whether we use one camera or many is irrelevant, for they are essentially interchangeable. They all give reliable and predictively useful data about the world we inhabit. Thus it is possible to reproduce in a simplified model some aspects of the scanning, shifting, multiple awareness, and self-awareness that characterize human consciousness.

This analogy, like most, contains some flaws. The television machine, a critic might say, can never directly see itself and can never see, in itself or in another, the whole *act* of seeing, which is different conceptually from any particular reading on a dial. Moreover, no two cameras can ever see an object from exactly the same angle at the same moment; and all cameras schematize and distort whatever they see. In other words it is possible to force familiar epistemological uncertainties upon this model. But from our human vantage point, external to television systems, these dilemmas do not disturb us. Machines can see enough of their own or another's workings, they are enough alike, and they give information which agrees with what we take to be reality.

What more can we say, however, about that reality? To sharpen the inquiry for present purposes—what statements, in the light of these uncertainties about knowledge, can be made about the general nature of the knowing organism and about the specific "real" relationship between its neural machinery and its conscious processes, between brain and mind? Again let us use the television analogy, referring to its "machinery" of tubes and wires and its "imagery" of configurational displays. A familiar range of philosophic assertions suggest themselves.

(a) The machinery is real and the imagery is some incidental *epiphenomenon*. This strikes us as absurd, since both are "real" to us, though in different ways, congruent with their differing origins.

(b) The machinery and imagery are both real; they are each separate from the other; yet they *interact* with one another causally. This immediately embroils us in a host of problems concerned with causality; but the extreme case, which alleges that a given image by itself influences subsequent behavior of the machine, is also absurd.

(c) Machine events and image events constitute two series, which in some inexplicable way happen to *parallel* one another exactly. Here the implied duality of two separate spheres inexplicably linked in time and space seems gratuitous, since we can trace the machinery to an electronic shop, the imagery to a studio, and account for how the two come together in a performance.

(d) Machinery and imagery are both *aspects* of some underlying reality—a statement closely related to the previous one. For the mystery of the parallel procession through time is substituted the puzzle of a shift in stance, which will somehow reveal one or another aspect. The further implication of an underlying essence or substance, prior to and more fundamental than both, also seems gratuitous.

(e) Machine events and image events are *identical*. This statement is indisputable if properly circumscribed. Activation of circuitry and of image display occur simultaneously in time and space and show invariant mutually dependent regularities. (The image of a fixed chair seen by a fixed camera will always involve the same paths of circuitry and identical flow of energy.) We must of course add that circuitry and visual display belong to two different conceptual realms of discourse; and we must note that the concepts themselves have developed differently in order to describe two different components of the world. We may view them as two systems, each necessary, neither sufficient, for functional actualization of the wider system we call television.

The analogy faces further difficulties of incompleteness. It does not provide for memory or decision-making. To model them we would do better with the digital computer. That was devised by human minds to extend their power and it necessarily mirrors many essential aspects of human mentation. To design a brain, as Ashby points out (1960), is still a task of enormous complexity, but computer systems can not only save and retrieve memories and extrapolate to the future, within limits they can generate their own programs, and modify their function according to feedback, internal and external. We have gone far beyond the earliest servomechanisms, or the ingenious mechanical organism, *M. Speculatrix,* which Grey Walter created (1953), to a host of homing, planning, and thought-simulating systems for peaceful and warlike use spawned in the aftermath of the cybernetic revolution.

All of these analogies can be dangerous. They can lead to a latter-day and cybernetically adorned mechanistic view, reductionism refurbished. Artificial simplification may smuggle in one or another of the familiar philosophic assertions already mentioned; or at the least it may exclude from study many aspects of the human receiving, sending, and decoding apparatus that await clarification. A sample area is extrasensory perception. By now there is an enormous volume of experimental evidence pointing to the existence of psi phenomena. Within the psychoanalytic situation a number of observers, including myself and James Skinner, have encountered phenomena which seem only explicated by some hypothesis of nonordinary modes of communication. Our models will have to grow to encompass those and other as yet undiscovered phenomena.

The point of this philosophic analysis of television and other machines is that, taking a stand detached from the subsystems of television and computer, we have no difficulty in conceptualizing circuitry and programs as different components in a larger functioning system. The implicit assertion is that the universe is best described in terms of hierarchical organization of such systems. This paper cannot spell out a complete philosophic position. It contends that to understand such systems it is wise to examine, as Cassirer did, the historical antecedents of their organization, and also wise to beware, in describing them, of linguistic pitfalls. My view remains skeptical about the ultimate nature of reality, though I believe that it is sounder to postulate one universe rather than many. With Whitehead (1926), it suggests that bifurcation of that universe along subject–object or mind–brain lines is an unwarranted generalization, particulary marked in our Western European culture, from a split view of ourselves to the conclusion that reality beyond us is also split.

MOTIVES BEHIND THE QUESTIONS: SOME SPECULATIONS

A final mystery remains. What has been said so far is hardly being stated for the first time. Several generations of thinkers have inveighed against the fallacy of misplaced concreteness, reification, hypostatization, the "ghost in the machine," and naive Cartesian dualism—e.g., Whitehead (1926), Ryle (1949), and in the psychosomatic and psychiatric field, Scheflen (1966) and Von Bertalanffy (1950, 1965). Why should the mind–body problem persist?

Yet it does. It persists in the very term "psychosomatic." In too many ways to enumerate, our language is shot through with dualistic metaphor. Old modes of thought give a paradoxical coloring to all discussions of brain and consciousness. Writers and readers often waver back and forth. When they use analogies such as those in the previous section they say: of course, there is a program distinct from the circuitry, and of course both are aspects of the "behavior" of the total system. Yet a doubt intrudes: behind both program and circuitry was a human "consciousness" responsible for designing it (as Neisser points out [1963]). Surely *I* exist; *Cogito ergo sum*, Descartes was right after all. One begins to suspect a vested interest.

Cobb (1957) remarked that it had taken him years to overcome a personal conviction about a simplified view of a world divided dualistically into mental and physical spheres. The phenomenon is reminiscent of the resistance one encounters when trying to lay an ancient fantasy to rest—in a patient or oneself. The suspicion grows that motivational pressures serve to give our intuitive conviction about the separate existence of outer and inner reality the characteristics of a stubborn illusion.

I believe that the phenomenon can be traced to a series of bipolar distinctions which crystallize during the first 5 years of life, especially in the preoperational period of Piaget. These are: the distinction of nonself from self; awareness of bodily as against mental processes; experience of the activity of skeletal muscular systems in which autonomous, goal-directed regulation is maximal, as against visceral activity, where it is minimal; the use of discursive thought, characterized by "digital" modes of cognition, leading to discrete contrasts, versus nondiscursive thought, using "analog" modes characterized by continua; awareness of deterministic sequences of events as against the experience of inner freedom and "will."

Paramount in all of these distinctions is the tendency in the development of human mentation to think by way of dichotomous

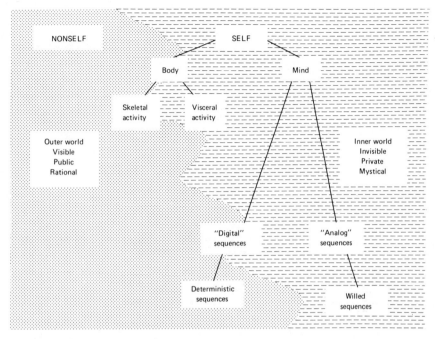

Figure 2. Dichotomous schemata in human experience.

contrasts. All these bipolarities, which are not exactly parallel to one another, tend to coalesce into a global conviction of contrasting outer and inner worlds. Figure 2 depicts graphically both the individual distinctions and the broader dualistic view of everyday phenomenological experience. An intentionally irregular boundary line is meant to suggest variation, between and within individuals, as to which components may be felt as outer, and which inner. The design is also that of a decision tree, to imply that these schemata are constructed more or less sequentially (though their exact time course must remain uncertain); they help to settle certain issues and establish positions in an individual's achievement of a dual view of himself and his environment.

These schemata are seldom precisely articulated, but rather remain vague images or maps, largely preconscious. As indicated in the earlier discussion of free association, even vaguer, unconscious components are hidden behind them. The positive "self-image" is asserted and maintained, in part to ward off feared negative elements (Knapp, 1969). A volume could be written on the typological, psychopathological, as well as philosophical, implications of this diagram. It is offered here as a preliminary sketch to guide the ensuing discussion.

In the early phases of thought, as Piaget has described them, reification is the original order of business. Split views, becoming established, seem "real." My point here is that important motivational reasons sustain the conviction of their reality. Dichotomous thinking is not only a primary mode of cognition but also a fundamental way of maintaining emotional security.

Nonself versus Self

This distinction is probably our most fundamental one, starting very early in life, being progressively refined throughout all of childhood and most of adult life. We can presume that it originated from discrimination between different sorts of experiences, those that are visible, tangible, relatively clear, originating at some specifiable distance away, in contrast to those sensed as emanating from within, often hard to localize but permeated by poignant, at times intense hedonic qualities. Soon is added awareness of outer objects, discontinuous and frequently difficult to influence, as against a personal sphere which is continuous and which gradually comes under a degree of autonomous regulation. Difficulties in sorting out the two classes are mastered only slowly and seldom perfectly. But a growing self-system emerges. It has obvious adaptive value in freeing the individual from bondage to his environment. Its extent, however, is not limited by immediate self-preservative needs. The sense of self comes to include identity markers of all kinds, possessions, group affiliations, and social qualities. The self tends to accumulate and claim all that seems desirable and to repudiate all that is felt as undesirable. Images and aspects of other persons become part of a continuing exchange, taking in and projecting outward. The body participates, serving as a vehicle to symbolize persons or parts of them (Dutsch, 1959; Mushatt, 1973). These efforts lead to the forms of splitting so important, as Pinderhughes has remarked (1969), in social partisanship and racial discrimination.

Body versus Mind

This distinction extends the process of splitting. In great part the body is visible, tangible, a quasimachine, a manifest mechanical manikin. "Mind" becomes the indefinable locus of private thoughts, wishes, longings and fantasies. Further elaboration of these apparently separate aspects of the self varies considerably. For some individuals major investment is in the mind. It becomes a refuge from demands of the body.[3] When these cannot be met, such a position may be adaptive, for example, in conditions of physical hardship, incarceration, or even prolonged illness. Absorption in things of the mind may be induced or sustained by less outwardly compelling considerations—socially sanctioned, or idiosyncratic asceticism. Under such circumstances the body may be experienced as a disciplined machine, functioning automatically out of awareness most of the time. Needless to say its claims have ways of reasserting themselves. At times demands may be veiled, as in masochistic overtones of the ascetic who "humiliates the flesh"; at times sensuality may erupt and extreme distortions of mental life may be necessary to contain it.

For other individuals the major investment may be in the body. This may be relatively free of conflict as in the bodily narcissism of the ballerina or of the athlete. It may be an exaggerated narcissistic effort to resolve neurotic conflict. Attention to bodily sensations or functions may serve to ward off conflict or disguise it, using the capacity already mentioned for symbolizing human relationships in bodily terms.

The location of the "body" thus has a curious ambiguity. Figure 2 places it at the irregular borderline between "outer" and "inner." In part it may be assigned to the external world, though seldom completely. Almost always the individual retains some impression of a tenuous zone of anchorage between this external bodily "machine" and his "self" and somehow his "mind." In extreme instances the body may be experienced as completely "out there," that is, in depersonalization, when the individual may look at his hands, or limbs, or even his whole physical self, as if these elements were detached, not belonging to "him." These are alien and frightening experiences. It is more usual for the body to be split in a subtle and varied fashion into external and internal spheres.

Skeletal versus Visceral Activity

Actually many splitting processes are discernible in the construction of different body images. Felix Deutsch (1959) spoke of the

[3] I am grateful to Dr. Howard Levine for stimulating this thought.

importance of front versus rear, right versus left, related to individual fantasies about active and passive, masculine and feminine components of the self. Pinderhughes (1969) has called attention to the upper–lower distinction, often made as a cultural one and equated with good and bad. Perhaps more general and more germane to our argument is the distinction, based on clear sensations, between, on the one hand, activity of the skeletal musculature and the outer casing of the body and, on the other hand, inner visceral elements. The outer integument and movable parts can be seen, touched, manipulated. They are quintessentially the manifest mechanical manikin. The inner elements, lungs, guts, blood, must be "sensed" through vague cues. They are difficult to influence. By various cultures these have been considered the seat of the soul. "Where the intuition of the self, the soul, the person, first appears in language, it clings to body" (Cassirer, 1953, p. 252).

One might even argue that the inner–outer split comes first, antedating in childhood the split between mind and body This would fit with Freud's frequently quoted statement that the ego was originally a body ego. I prefer the view reflected in Figure 2, that the original self (or nucleus of ego functions) begins essentially undifferentiated and that further differentiation takes place roughly as diagramed. One must allow for much interplay back and forth; various schemata serve to organize experience and provide evidence for further refinement of other schemata at different levels. Thus elaboration of all of them proceeds unevenly over long stretches of time. Further empirical study would be needed to fill out Figure 2 and establish its timetables.

The boundary between the manifest mechanical manikin and its inner fluid core also varies, both between and within individuals. Fisher and Cleveland (1958) have shown characterological differences in the extent to which individuals construct a relatively impermeable carapace around themselves as part of their preconscious bodily imagery, and also fluctuations in the degree to which different inner parts become included in this. Partly the difference may depend upon experience. First-hand acquaintance with viscera from a physiology course or from encounter with illness, even one's own, may allow them to be incorporated into the total manikin. Differences may also depend upon the way in which bodily awareness comes to be used in the individual's defensive security operations. Inclusion of customarily automatic or unnoticed functions in awareness may be a particular way of removing conflictual attention from other concerns, as well as expressing these in symbolic disguise; to wit, our patient's headache. We see the possibility of extending the conversion process to include visceral and autonomic phenomena. Mushatt (1973) has recently called attention to the wide variety of bodily functions which may express loss and separation. The recent developments in biofeedback give us hints—as have yogi teachings for years—about the extent to which visceral activity can be brought under psychic regulation.

Ordinarily the manifest mechanical manikin behaves like a responsive machine, following orders. Ideally these are clear digital instructions: yes, no, up, down, go, no-go. Behind the scenes, giving the orders, is the "I," the "mind"—with all its ambiguous relationship, as we have noted, to hidden inner visceral sources. Everyday experience reinforces; we learn to have reliable control over our limbs; accuracy is great, responsiveness to feedback is prompt. The "I" feels in control. At times this smooth arrangement becomes disrupted. The manikin's function may be impaired for any of a variety of reasons; it seems to rebel or may be experienced as under the influence of hostile, alien forces. In fact the malfunctioning bodily system, whether skeletal or visceral, often comes to feel like an enemy, or persecutor. "I want to but my body won't let me"—the individual cries in exasperation, even though the state of affairs may be a defensive solution he himself has achieved.

Discursive versus Nondiscursive Mental Activity

As language and logical thought develop, splitting becomes refined in different ways. Secondary process, discursive or, as Spence has called it (1972) "digital," thought develops. This is accurate, leads to precise and ultimately mathematical manipulations of clear "bits" of information. Along with it persists a different mode of mental experience, nondiscursive, presentational in Langer's terms (1942), or "analog" as Spence would have it. This is made up of qualities that blend with one another, a substrate of continuing imagery and feeling tone. It is here that we must look for most aspect of the self (Knapp, 1969). In this stratum is the "I" behind the words I speak. As we have seen, this nondiscursive core is integrally linked to emotional processes. It speaks, if not with clarity, with its own authority. The mind itself is split—as Pascal knew: the heart has its reasons which reason does not know.

Generally, in subjective experience the perceived world of

objects becomes figure; the personal substrate becomes ground. To paraphrase Weisman (1958) the former becomes the *content* of reality while the latter provides the *sense* of reality. At times, under conditions of altered consciousness, whether through intense personal experience, through induced "regression" in various modes of psychotherapeutic influence, or through drug use, the substrate itself becomes object. Figure and ground are reversed. Often there is then apparent expanded grasp of reality, a feeling of contact with a universe beyond our ordinary categorized and subdivided world, a heightened sense of self, an unassailable conviction of the existence of mind or even soul. First-hand, concrete experience becomes evidence which our discursive and logical modes of thought ordinarily relegate to the background. Using this evidence, for which it was not designed, reason can then feel that it has gained proof about new reaches of the world, fitting them into the old design. Castenada's (1969) drug-induced discoveries of Yaqui ways of knowledge is a case in point. It becomes a case of hallucinating is believing.

As before, we find variation in the value placed on head and heart. The very individual who has relegated his body to the status of a controlled machine, largely extrinsic to his "self," may persevere with his need to externalize. His "mind," too, may come to seem identical with perceptual and technical nervous machinery.He may insist with Skinner (1971) that only observable behavior is real. He may deny the role or even the existence of private fantasy and feelings; they are somehow an illusion, "the ghost in the *machine*" (in Ryle's words [1949] with my italics). Others may remain aware of and absorbed by the nondiscursive characteristics of experience, captivated by the ebb and flow of privately experienced processes. These individuals, too, may carry their views to an extreme, seeing the "psychic" components of life as having exclusive claims to be considered "real." For them both inner and apparent outer worlds are in fact manifestations of generalized panpsychic activity.

Still other observers may, of course, argue thoughtfully that in fact two sorts of reality exist, each apprehended by different methods—as Eccles appears to do in this volume. My own difference with this view, as stated in the earlier section, centers around questioning the validity of going from dual modes of experience to the conclusion that this reflects an outer duality. My intent at this point is not to argue further about these ontological views, but to indicate that all of them may arise from different characterologic sets and have important motivational roots. Their origins need to be considered as one formulates or criticizes world views.

Determinism versus Free Will

What has just been said applied in every sense to this final distinction, which in ways reflects a polarity between helplessness and omnipotence. This, too, can be traced to early roots in fantasy.

A starting point is the struggle, originating in infancy, between tendencies we may call "active" and "passive." The infant begins life dependent, not in the least autonomous, with a partial sense of his helplessness, which is both gratifying and frustrating. As we try to reconstruct empathetically his situation, it contains a mixture of notions of magical, omnipotent control and opposite notions of submissive fusion. The two oscillate, as we can see in the tales of childhood: the younger son, Jack, climbs the magic stalk and robs the giant; the Sleeping Beauty is passively preserved in her castle until her magical awakening. Gradually the developing human gains some realistic sense of relative autonomy. Operating within many constraints, memory systems and anticipatory schemata serve as guides toward rewards, and away from punishments. In short, cognitive activities join with and help us to attain chosen ends—granted that the choice of these has its own constraints, both biological and social.

The constraints are all too tangible and ubiquitous. At certain times or for certain persons they stand out; attention becomes focused upon the causal chains influencing behavior. Schools of thought seek resignation, even peace, possibly masochistic satisfaction, by proclaiming a belief in total determinism. More often rebellion and protest surge to the fore, attempting to magnify the role of those autonomous inner determinants of behavior, which do afford some optional routes toward goals; followers of other schools then insist upon continued reification of the inner, familiar and unique core of memories and fantasies. Thus man can proclaim his unfettered mind and the freedom of his will.

Lurking in the background of all experience, of course, is the ultimate, bleak anticipation of death. That serves as a perpetual stimulus to reify not only mind but a soul which will transcend death. The threats of helplessness, augmented by this existential anxiety, lead to inevitable defensive reactions. These are no simpler than other human reactions. We wish for a soul and fear the wish will be frustrated; so then we may adopt an exaggerated allegiance to "hard" science and end up even denying the nature of our mental functioning. Or there may be a final spiritual counterattack: the universe may be conceived as a giant machine yet somehow at the same time the creation of a personalized deity. These motivational complexities must be considered in any discussion of either "will" or "mind." They collaborate with in-grained, overlearned common-sense attitudes. Both remain perpetually ready to distort and subvert sober argumentation about brain and consciousness.

ACKNOWLEDGMENTS

Supported in part by Grant PHS-5 RO1 NH11299-0.9.

REFERENCES

Ashby, W. R. (1960): *Design for a Brain: The Origin of Adaptive Behavior.* 2nd Ed. Revised, London: Chapman Hall.

Bertalanffy, L. Von (1950): An outline of general systems theory. *Br. J. Philos. Sci.* **1,** 134.

Bertalanffy, L. Von (1964): The mind body problem: A new view. *Psychosom. Med.* **26,** 29–45.

Bertalanffy, L. Von (1969): Law or chance. In: *Beyond Reductionalism: New Perspectives in the Life Sciences.* Ed. by A. Koestler & J. R. Smythies, London: Hutchinson.

Birdwhistell, R. (1971): *Kinesics and Context.* Philadelphia: University of Pennsylvania Press.

Brady, J. V. (1958): Ulcers in executive monkeys. *Sci. Am.* **199,** 95–100.

Bruner, J. S. (1969): On voluntary action and its hierarchical structure. In: *Beyond Reductionism: New Perspectives in the Life Sciences.* Ed. by A. Koestler & J. R. Smythies, London: Hutchinson.

Cassirer, E. (1953): *The Philosophy of Symbolic Forms* I, Language. (R. Manheim Transl.) New Haven: Yale University Press.

Casteneda, C. (1969): *The Teachings of Don Juan.* New York: Ballantine.

Chomsky, N. (1957): *Syntactic Structures.* The Hague: Mouton & Co.

Cobb, S. (1957): Monism and Psychosomatic Medicine. *Psychosom.* **19,** 177–8.

Colby, K. M. (1960): Experiment on the effects of an observer's presence on the image system. *Behav. Sci.* **5,** 216.

Colby, K. M. (1961): On the greater amplifying power of causal-correlative over interrogative input on free association in an experimental psychoanalytic situation. *J. Nerv. & Ment. Dis.* **133,** 233.

Condon, W. and Sander, L. (1973): Personal communication.

Deutsch, F. (1959): *The Mysterious Leap from The Mind to The Body.* New York: International University Press.

Ellenberger, H. (1970): *The Discovery of the Unconscious.* New York: Basic Books.

Fisher, S. & Cleveland, S. E. (1958): *Body Image and Personality.* Princeton, New Jersey: Van Nostrand.

Freud, S. (1925): Instincts and their viscissitudes. In: *Collected Papers* **4,** 60–83. London: Hogarth Press.

Henry, J. & Stephens P. (1969): Psychosocial stimuli to induce renal and cardiovascular pathology in mice. (Abstract) *Psychosom. Med.* **31,** 454.

Holt, R. R. (1972): Freud's mechanistic and humanistic images of man. In: *Psychoanalysis and Contempory Science* Vol. 1. Ed. by R. R. Holt and E. Peterfreund, New York: MacMillan.

James, W. (1890): *Principles of Psychology*. England: Dover Publishers.

Kety, S. (1969): New perspectives in Psychopharmacology. *Beyond Reductionism: New Perspectives in the Life Sciences*. Ed. by A. Koestler & J. R. Smythies, London: Hutchinson.

Knapp, P. H. (1969): Image, symbol and personality. *Arch. Gen. Psychiatry* **21**, 392–406.

Knapp, P. H. (1973): Experimental Free Association. Unpublished manuscript.

Knapp, P. H., Mathé, A., & Vachon, L. (1976): Psychosomatic aspects of bronchial asthma. In: *Bronchial Asthma, Its Nature and Management*. Ed. by E. B. Weiss and M. S. Segal, Boston: Little Brown.

Knapp, P. H. & Nemetz, S. J. (1960): Acute bronchial asthma: 1. concomitant depression and excitement, and varied antecedent patterns in 406 attacks. *Psychosom. Med.* **22**, 42–56.

Langer, S. K. (1942): *Philosophy in a New Key*. New York: Mentor Press.

Miller, G. A., Galenter, E. & Pribram, K. H. (1958): *Plans and the Structure of Behavior*. New York: H. Holt & Co.

Morris, C. (1938): Foundations of the theory of signs. In: *Foundations of the Unity of Science: Toward an International Encyclopedia of Unified Science* Vol. 1, No. 2. Ed. by O. Neurath, Chicago: University of Chicago Press.

Mushatt, C. (1973): Mind-body environment: Toward understanding the impact of loss on psyche and soma. In press, *Psychoanal. Quart.*

Neisser, U. (1963): Imitation of man by machine. *Science* **139**, 193–197.

Ogden, C. K., Richards, I. A. (1923): *The Meaning of Meaning*. New York: Harcourt Brace.

Pinderhughes, C. (1969): Understanding black power. *Am. J. Psychiatry* **125**, 1552.

Ricoeur, P. (1970): *Freud and Philosophy: An Essay on Interpretation*. D. Savage (Transl.) New Haven: Yale University Press.

Ryle, G. (1949): *The Concept of Mind*. London: Hutchinson & Co.

Sander, WL. W. (1964): Adaptive relationships in early mother–child interaction. *J. Amer. Acad. Child Psych.* **3**, 231–264.

Scheflen, A. E. (1966): Systems and psychosomatics. *Psychosom. Med.* **28**, 297–304.

Schildkraut, J. J. & Kety. S. S. (1967): Biogenic amines and emotion. *Science* **156**, 21–30.

Skinner, B. F. (1971): *Beyond Freedom and Dignity*. New York: Knopf.

Spence, D. (1972): Digital and analog thought. Unpublished Manuscript.

Spitz, R. A. (1957): *No and Yes*. New York: Int. Univ. Press.

Stechler, G. Bradford, S. & Levy, H. (1966): Attention in the newborn: Its effect on motility and skin potential reactivity. *Science* **151**, 1246–1248.

Walter, W. G. (1953): *The Living Brain*. New York: W. W. Norton & Co.

Weisman, A. (1958): Reality sense and reality testing. *Behav. Sci.* **3**, 228–261.

Weiss, J. M. (1971a): Effects of coping behavior in different warning signal conditions on stress pathology in rats. *J. Compar. Physiol. Psychol.* **77**, 1–13.

Weiss, J. M. (1971b): Effects of punishing the coping response (conflict) on stress pathology in rats. *J. Comp. Physiol. Psychol.* **77**, 14–21.

Weiss, J. M. (1971c): Effects of coping behavior with and without a feedback signal on stress pathology in rats. *J. Comp. Physiol. Psychol.* **77**, 22–30.

Whitehead, A. N. (1926): *Process and Reality*. New York: McMillan.

Wolff, H. G. (1948): *Headache and Other Head Pain*. New York: Oxford.

3   Introduction

When the enigmatic relation of mind to brain is discussed, we are perforce in the domain of meaning. It would seem reasonable, then, to suggest that an inquiry into the general origins of meanings *per se* might provide some insight into how the mind–brain relation in particular became a "problem." Savodnik follows this strategy by focusing on Cassirer's conception of the "symbolic consciousness" and the role of language. For Savodnik, "the construction of the problem of mind and body is a function of the symbolic consciousness," which, more basically, is dependent on the ontogenesis of the "human spirit." Thus, Savodnik tends to find the mind–brain issue to lie in the vicissitudes of symbol formation, at that place where Weimer points to an ambiguous "deep structure."

Psychoanalysis, as a conceptual scheme, provides a unique perspective on those vicissitudes by laying down "the categories for an existential–phenomenological psychology by providing us with an account of the different modes of thought" as manifested in a psychoanalytic session. It is here, Savodnik suggests, that exclusive reliance on "ordinary language" is problematic, since what was historically (ontogenetically) an ordinary language comes to be extraordinary in the typical adult world, save in the specially contrived psychoanalytic situation, wherein psychological regression can come into the service of philosophical inquiry. In following the methods of free association, the regressive thought patterns which ensue are in fact "the unfoldings of different modes of symbolic consciousness."

Savodnik argues that at the level of Cassirer's "expressive function," there is no mind–brain problem, since mind and brain are not yet conceptualized and distinguished as somehow in opposition to one another. The problem originates at the level of the "representative

71

function" through the imposition of such *concepts* as "objects" clearly demarcated in space–time and "causality." An attempt to apply a linguistic analysis at this level to the more primitive expressive level creates the mind–brain problem by superimposing an ontological plane of thought onto a phenomenological plane.

Although Savodnik succeeds in enriching the mind–brain puzzle by considering psychoanalysis through the vehicle of Cassirer's thought, the solution offered may not be entirely convincing to all. Although an infant, or a person regressed on the analyst's couch, does not find the mind–brain distinction to be a problem, it does not necessarily follow that the problem is created *de novo* at an unregressed level. Since ontological issues do not arise at the expressive level, some might argue, the mind–brain enigma does not exist there; but when ontological issues do arise at the representative level, they become valid issues at this level. If mental and physical languages at the representative level do not reflect real differences in the world, then we are owed a quite detailed explanation of just how the confusion is engendered there, and not engendered elsewhere. If we are just mistakenly mixing together ontological and phenomenological planes, then why is the mind–brain distinction so compelling and difficult to eradicate from our daily lives? But it may well prove that a detailed phenomenological inquiry into earlier modes of developmental function would support Savodnik's position.

Presumably Savodnik has something different in mind than Weimer's suggestion that the confusion at the representative level is a function of an ambiguous underlying grammar. If some clear diagnosis could be made, then it is likely that clear-eyed skeptics would willingly stretch out on a Cassirerian couch to be freed of their painful philosophical perplexities. But until such a time, considerable *a priori* faith in the "treatment" would seem necessary.

3 Mind, Brain, and the Symbolic Consciousness

IRWIN SAVODNIK

The relation between the concepts of mind and brain has been the subject of philosophical analysis for a very long time, and many theories concerning the nature of that relation have been propounded. The problem dates back at least to the time of Plato, and in recent years philosophers seem increasingly compelled to attack it. In the 20th century a particularly strong approach has been along the lines of linguistic analysis, so that the manner in which language relates to the formulation of the problem in the first place is dealt with analytically, "therapeutically," and imaginatively. Approaches have been "common sensical" (Moore), "logistic or analytic" (Russell), grammatical (Wittgenstein), linguistic (Austin), and conceptual (J. L. Wisdom). The rewards of this approach have been considerable, particularly with respect to delimiting these various sorts of boundaries of our capacities for, and limitations with respect to, knowing.

In this paper I shall deal with this relation between the problem of mind and brain and the role which language plays in its formulation and possible solutions. The plan of the paper will be an examination of the concept of symbolic consciousness as elaborated by Ernst Cassirer, some related notions of Freud about free association, and

IRWIN SAVODNIK · University of Pittsburgh

several remarks by Wittgenstein which bear on the problem as a whole. The attempt will be to show that *the construction of the problem of mind and body is a function of the symbolic consciousness, and that the latter is embodied in the world through language in ways which are congenial to our ways of knowing*. In this context there are several points which suggest themselves:

1. *The problem is fundamentally philosophical in nature*. That is, while definitive solutions are certainly not to be expected from philosophers, without the use of philosophical analysis it is most unlikely that the problem can be clarified or, indeed, even stated at all. The use of physiological data, biochemical analysis, or even psychotherapeutic material in a psychoanalytic setting can be helpful to suggest some pathways toward clarification, but in themselves will get us no further toward a solution. There is real danger that too much data will obscure the problem even further by forcing us to neglect our tools of anaysis and spend time instead sorting out the data into tidy packages.[1]

2. *Insofar as this is a philosophical problem it is approachable vis à vis the logical relations which are seen to exist between the various concepts related to and including those of consciousness and brain*. The teasing out of these relations is an exercise in how we think and the manner in which we conceptualize the world.

3. *The manner in which the world is conceptualized by us can be understood from the standpoint of the symbolic consciousness*. Just what is involved in this concept will be spelled out in detail below. The role of symbol formation in the genesis of the problem of body and mind has not been clearly delineated, particularly with respect to various modalities of human thought, namely unconscious processes, archaic conceptions, and discursive logic. The advantage of dealing with the problem

---

[1] It should be pointed out that to label a problem as being fundamentally philosophical in nature is to provide it with a special sort of dignity. The problem at hand becomes a locus of inquiry which points up the richness of individual thought. The security of scientific precision, while not to be ignored, is not always the endpoint of human inquiry. Russell (1969) makes this point in the following passage: "The value of philosophy is, in fact, to be sought largely in its very uncertainty. The man who has no tincture of philosophy goes through life imprisoned in the prejudices derived from common sense, from the habitual beliefs of his age or his nation, and from convictions which have grown up in his mind without the co-operation or consent of his deliberate reason. To such a man the world tends to become definite, finite, obvious; common objects rouse no questions, and unfamiliar possibilities are contemptuously rejected. As soon as we begin to philosophize, on the contrary, we find . . . that even the most everyday things lead to problems to which only very incomplete answers can be given. Philosophy, though unable to tell us with certainty what is the true answer to the doubts which it raises, is able to suggest many possibilities which enlarge our thoughts and free them from the tyranny of custom. Thus, while diminishing our feeling of certainty as to what things are, it greatly increases our knowledge of what they may be; it removes the somewhat arrogant dogmatism of those who have never traveled into the region of liberating doubt, and it keeps alive our sense of wonder by showing familiar things in an unfamiliar aspect (pp. 156–157).

from this perspective is that the metamorphosis of the symbolic consciousness, both ontogenetically and phylogenetically, may provide an
insight into the way in which the problem actually came into existence.
Rather than take the view that the problem of the relation of mind to
brain is merely a function of our language, it might be more helpful to
formulate its genesis and elaboration from the point of view of symbol
formation and thereby indicate the common theme which underlies
the situation regardless of the predominant role of symbolic thought
(Natadze, 1969).

Whether this task can be accomplished is presently problematic, but my aim is to indicate a path toward intelligibility with
respect to the role of symbolization in our conceptualization of mind
and brain. The point I would like to make here is that it is *persons* who
construct the problem of the relation of body and mind and it is *persons*
who attempt to solve that problem. In an interesting way, the nature of
persons in some certain respects may involve us in some engaging
insights regarding the "world knot." The reasons for this will become
clearer as we proceed, but at this juncture it can be stated that what is
peculiar to an individual and social perspective on "what there is" is
the key to finding a path through this labyrinth.

There are several ways in which a theory of persons could be
constructed, not all of which are equally good. One of the most well
known of these theories is Strawson's, in which a person is, briefly put,
construed as "a type of entity such that *both* predicates ascribing states
of consciousness *and* predicates ascribing corporeal characteristics, a
physical situation, etc. are equally applicable to a single individual of
that type" (Strawson, 1959, pp. 81–113). The point that Strawson makes
here is that "person" is a more primitive concept than either "consciousness" or "body." By adopting this tack he explicitly avoids the
Cartesian error of assuming the primacy of consciousness and thereby
the problem of interactionism. On the surface, this approach is novel
and at times exciting. The problem, however, is that Strawson is not
terribly clear about just what a person is. We all know what he wants to
avoid, but what he arrives at seems to remain somewhat obscure.
Certainly, a person is not merely a body a spiritual substance. Yet,
when we attempt to find the entity which is a person we have a difficult
time. If John is *not* John's body, then what is the relation between the
person called John and the body identified as being John's? Is a person
a body of a different sort, or perhaps an abstract entity? Whatever it is,
the concept of person as Strawson uses it remains vague (but perhaps
not empty) for our purposes. This is not to say that Strawson's theory of

persons is impossible, only that it is not as helpful to us as another approach to the theory of persons might be.[2]

Another manner of dealing with the problem can be constructed from the point of view of human action. Human beings as persons are capable of human action and such action is explained in a certain way. One way of explaining the action of another person is to speak in terms of the rules which characterize what he is doing.[3] In football, for instance, bringing order out of chaos which seems to occur periodically on the playing field is achieved by stating to oneself the rules of the game which are applicable at a particular moment. For instance, when one player with the ball is "attacked" by five others in uniforms of another color from his, it is pointed out that one rule of the game is to prevent the man with the ball from gaining ground by stopping his forward motion. Similarly, in games like chess and in language the rules tell us a great deal about the meaning of human action. Without reference to them we cannot understand what is taking place.

This is certainly not to say that we all have explicit knowledge of rules which characterize our actions. We certainly do not. It is only when we take on the task of explaining actions that rules are somehow introduced. One helpful way of seeing this point is to imagine a game, e.g., a chess game, in which the players do not adhere to the rules at all. Pawns move like queens, the king jumps three spaces at a time,etc. What becomes apparent is that there is no game at all being played, excepting of course that game which is being played by obeying the rule that whatever game is being played no rules will be followed; but such a rule is itself quite problematical since there is a difference between disobeying a rule and not knowing how or what rule to follow in a particular game.

An additional datum here is that when people obey rules they

---

[2] Wittgenstein (1958) provides the foundation for Strawson's theory of the person and is considerably more succinct in his presentation in *The Philosophical Investigations*, par. 299–309ff. Richard Smith (1974) points out that in the *Investigations* Wittgenstein establishes that we require a subject function model for persons as opposed to the object /description model appropriate for things. This point is suggested by Wittgenstein (1963) when he says:

"The whole modern conception of the world is founded on the illusion that the so-called laws of nature are the explanations of natural phenomena.

"Thus people today stop at the laws of nature, treating them as something inviolable, just as God and Fate were treated in past ages.

"And in fact both are right and both wrong: though the view of the ancients is clearer in so far as they have a clear and acknowledged terminus, while the modern system tries to make it look as if everything were explained" (6.371–6.572).

[3] Wittgenstein (1958) states, "every course of action can be made out to accord with the rule" (par. 201ff). There are numerous references to rules throughout the Investigations. See A. I. Melden (1961, 1964 pp. 58–76); R. S. Peters (1958) deals with the rule following model of behavior; also Irwin Savodnik (1973). For more recent discussions of action see Arthur Danto (1973) and Alvin I. Goldman (1970).

do not first state the rule to themselves and then perform the action. A good example of this is that people usually follow grammatical rules quite unreflectively. This is not to say that, for the most part, they are unjustified in following the rules. Rather, as Wittgenstein says, "When I obey a rule, I do not choose. I obey the rule blindly."[4]

We could certainly follow this path and find fruitful results, since, from the point of view of an enterprise like psychotherapy, such an approach to the difficulties of human action may be quite rewarding in that it enables one to "find one's feet" with another, to borrow a phrase from Wittgenstein. However, the rule following model of behavior must be expanded when we begin to discuss those areas of human experience which are far removed from the ordinary in certain respects.[5] I have in mind the archaic modes of thought present in psychoanalytic encounters in which the unconscious is purported to become conscious, and also those ways of thinking manifest in earlier cultures.

In these contexts the rule is certainly important, but there is another dimension of human activity which is equally important, and that is the symbolic consciousness (Natadze, 1969; J. Russell, 1973). It is this aspect of personal and social life with which I shall deal in pursuing another path for the construction of a "theory" of "persons." It is applicable in this context because the construction of such a "theory" is offered as an alternative approach to the mind–body problem. While animals may be said to demonstrate some ability to think symbolically, I do not think it outrageous that man should be regarded as having developed the power of symbolic formation to an extent which provides him with a certain uniqueness. *The rules of behavior are related to the rules of the symbolic consciousness of man, and the heart of this consciousness contains the core of the problem of the relationship of conscious life and brain activity.* Through an understanding of this unique dimension of human life the architecture of the problem may be delineated.

It should be pointed out, then, that the examination of this nexus of philosophical difficulty is not merely through an investigation

---

[4] Wittgenstein (1958, par. 217, 219, and 485) addresses himself to the notion of justificaton with respect to following a rule. I should perhaps make the point that the understanding of chess had by champions of the game is entirely respectable but quite different from understanding the material structure of a chess set (i.e., the quantum mechanical description) (1958, par. 31, 35, 36, 181, 562, 563, p. 181, also 1965, p. 7). In addition, consider Kenny's (1973) quote of Wittgenstein in *Wittgenstein und der Weiner Kries*, shorthand notes of Waissman's dating about 1929: "If you ask me where lies the difference between chess and the syntax of a language, I reply: solely in their application. If there were men on Mars who made war like the chess pieces, then the generals would use the rules of chess for prediction."

[5] D. Davidson (1963) remains the chief opponent of the distinct between action, behavior, reason, and cause.

of how we think about the problem. Rather, it is an investigation into the various *modes of thought* which underlie and are the basis of our multitudinous ways of thinking about problems. The relationship between the mind and the body, or, more accurately, between the concepts "mind" and "body," is for certain limited purposes in this paper construed as a problem emerging from the structure of certain modalities of the symbolic consciousness.[6]

PSYCHOANALYSIS AND THE SYMBOLIC CONSCIOUSNESS

The role that psychoanalysis plays in the investigation of the problem of consciousness and brain is itself quite problematic. This latter feature seems to be a function of the more general problem of the role of data in the approaches to the problem. Many philosophers will hold that increasing the amount of data in an attempt to solve a problem such as the relationship of consciousness to brain is to misconstrue the nature of the problem in the first place. If we assert that data get us no closer to a solution of the problem, then why should psychoanalysis in its empirical dimension be exempt from such a generalization? Certainly, whatever an analytic client reveals through the process of psychoanalytic investigation is highly personal and seemingly would have nothing to offer of general value to a solution. However, psychoanalysis is also a conceptual scheme of considerable complexity whose *theoretical* foundations may point the way in our investigation. In particular, it pays special attention to the different modes of symbolic activity manifest in the experience of a person. Knapp points out that these become apparent in psychoanalytic experience and are accounted for in psychoanalytic theory.[7]

---

[6] Cf. J. Margolis, (1973). The view of man put forth here is that man is a physically embodied cultural emergent.

[7] P. Knapp (this volume) is ambiguous over the meaning of the term "split." He seems to acknowledge the common philosophical usage of the term in the sense that there is a dualism of terminology with respect to the problem of mind and brain. However, he also uses the term more specifically from the point of view of psychoanalytic metapsychology in that the concept of splitting is regarded as a pathological mechanism in the adult ego. Briefly, it refers to the inability of the ego to regard an object (i.e., a person) in an ambivalent way, e.g., good *and* bad. The splitting here is between mind and brain, subjectivity and objectivity. The problem is that Knapp seems to construe a philosophical problem (see footnote 1 above) as a *fundamentally* psychological one. That is, he seems to assert that at the heart of the philosophical problem of mind and brain are certain psychological mechanisms which, if elucidated, will lead to a clarification and perhaps a solution to the problem. Such a psychologism is at best problematic and at worst regrettable. For example, suppose Knapp were right and he could show that the present philosophical problem is reducible to psychological mechanisms. How, then, would he handle the concept of "psychological mechanisms," which is certainly not without its problems. He cannot make use of other psychological mechanisms to explain the ones he has invoked since the very concept is up for grabs. To formulate the problem through ambiguously defining a term via philosophy and psychology is, it seems to me, to set out on a path leading to yet greater ambiguity.

If the problem of the relationship between consciousness and brain may be construed as a problem of symbolic formation, and if psychoanalysis provides us with a special type of theory about such formations, then psychoanalysis may very well provide us with a base upon which the philosophical dimensions of the problem are illuminated. Knapp refers to the primitive linguistic stages of human history in which the first references to self are made. In line with this are the regressive thought patterns of analytic patients, children, or in some cases persons who are called "schizophrenic." It is apparently an implication of his paper that an investigation of these more primitive modalities of thought can be rewarding by reaching that point in the development of self-consciousness in which the differentiation of self and nonself has not yet occurred. To understand the manner in which this differentiation occurs may shed some light on the subject of the relationship between brain and consciousness.One naturally thinks of Ernst Cassirer in this context since he takes a very similar approach to the problems of philosophy. For him, only a thoroughgoing historical understanding of the genesis of a concept or problem is sufficient for offering a solution to the problem.

It is with such an attitude that Cassirer attempts to unify the variety of human symbolization from mythical representation of natural events to mathematics and theoretical physics. All of these different forms of expression are the product of the human spirit. It is through an understanding of the development of that spirit that the problems of philosophy are to be framed. An understanding of the relationship between mind and brain involves an investigation of the symbolic activity of the person and the origin of the split. For Cassirer (as for Knapp, I suspect), the problem arises because of the character of the human spirit, and only through an analysis of that character may a solution be framed. This approach is, of course, quite in line with the Kantian quest for the presuppositions of human thought,[8] the neo-Kantian development of philosophical anthropology and the "linguistic turn" (Rorty, 1971).

Philosophical anthropology asks the question, "What is man?" To deal with this question is to delve into that character of the human spirit which gives rise to the very bifurcation presently under examination, i.e., the problem of symbolization *as such*. A possible answer to the basic question, that of the relationship of brain and consciousness, is to be found in an even more basic problem, namely, what is it about the human spirit that gives rise to such a problem at all?

---

[8] For an examination of the relationship between Wittgenstein's view of reality and the Kantian perspective, see Hubert Schwyzer (1973).

It is of interest that Wittgenstein saw a profound connection between language and what he called "form of life." That is, in order to understand what a concept means it is necessary to understand the living context in which it is embedded, out of which it may emerge, and which we may "abstract" for study. The relation between symbolization and the symbolized can only be shown, not stated informatively. In psychoanalysis we can speak about the grammar of "transference," "catharsis,' "fixation," "projection," "introjection," etc. As Kenny points out:

> Language-games can indeed be described, but they cannot be informatively described to someone not a participant. The interpretation of rules in the language-game must come to an end, and no rule can be given for the translation from rule into action.[9]

This is why I refer to the "grammar" of the psychoanalytic concepts above. In this context, the domains of what can be shown and what can be informatively stated are quite distinct, as are the grammar of the terms and the relation which adheres between them and what they purportedly symbolize.

Just as Wittgenstein asserts a connection between language and "form of life," so Cassirer states that, in order to understand a philosophical concept, the genesis and development of that concept from the perspective of the ontogenesis of the human spirit must be accomplished. Where, in Wittgenstein, words and their meanings are rooted in various forms of life, in Cassirer, philosophical problems are rooted in their individual histories and their relation to the human spirit. In both cases, there is a context in which a problem is understood and outside of which that understanding is truncated.[10]

I would like to approach the symbolic character of human life as it bears on the problem of consciousness and brain from two perspectives, namely that of free association as elaborated in psychoanalytic theory and what Cassirer calls symbolic pregnance. The latter will be seen to have a considerable relation to the concept of overdetermination in Freud. In an investigation of these two standpoints the variations in symbolic consciousness will be seen as they relate to the genesis of the problem of the relation of consciousness and brain. Furthermore, the power of the method of free association will be shown to be a function of the more primitive or intuitive modalities of thought which take hold in psychoanalytic regression.

---

[9] See Kenny, A. (1973, p. 228). See also Wittgenstein (1958, sec. 201ff.).
[10] It is obvious that Cassirer owes a considerable debt to Frege which he acknowledges through his writings (1953). In a related sense, see W. V. Quine (1963). See also Wittgenstein (1965, pp. 7–8).

FREE ASSOCIATION AND THE ORIGIN OF THE PROBLEM OF CONSCIOUSNESS AND BRAIN

Perhaps the single most important aspect of free association as a guide to the present problem is the fact that the individual displays thought patterns which are increasingly regressive in character. For example, a somatic symptom such as a headache, cough, or abdominal pain may initially be explained in terms of objective conditions such as low humidity, the presence of allergens, or the ingestion of bad food. Even at this stage there may be equivocation in the use of certain terms, thereby pointing the way to more primitive modalities of thought. Knapp points out that the phrase "splitting headache" is an illustration of the equivocation between sophisticated metaphorical usage and more archaic concrete visual expression. As a psychoanalytic hour progress, the references to a somatic symptom may become more entangled with the problems of interpersonal relations, relationship with the analyst, and infantile wishes. Finally, the "meaning" of the symptom may involve such fundamental dimensions of life as aggression, love, fear, helplessness, dependency, and punishment. In a sense, analysis of the structure of a psychoanalytic hour lays down the categories for an existential–phenomenological psychology by providing us with an account of the different modes of thought, i.e., symbolic consciousness manifest during that hour. In a similar vein we are provided with the categories of a descriptive metaphysics in that fundamental ways of being in the world are put forth. These categories emerge, i.e., can be inferred, in the context of regression, and may not be initially apparent at the outset of a psychoanalytic encounter.[11] It may be then, that the more primitive modalities of thought reveal basic ways of confronting the world which are otherwise hidden from us *in our ordinary discourse.* This point opens up a challenge to ordinary language analysis since the type of experience described was at one time ordinary but no longer is, and we may wonder how the more

---

[11] Wittgenstein's (1958) notion of "grammar" becomes crucial in this context. Consider his statement in par. 371. In par. 373 he says, "Grammar tells what kind of object anything is. (Theology as grammar.)" Yet, Wittgenstein warns us to avoid thinking that grammar tells us what to *do with* our language with respect to our particular purposes. Thus, "Grammar does not tell us how language must be constructed in order to fulfill its purpose, in order to have such-and-such an effect on human beings. It only describes and in no way explains the use of signs." (par. 496). Thus, grammar does not tell us how language emerges from the living context of human interaction. *Given* a language, however, and assuming that that language provides us with a basis for understanding the nature of being in the world, then the role of grammar becomes crucial since the structure of both the language and the world is *shown* through it.

archaic usages employed in free association are reflective of the forms of life from which they originally emerged.[12]

If we agree with Austin (1964) that "our common stock of words embodies all the distinctions men have found worth drawing, and the connections they have found worth making, in the lifetimes of many generations" (pp. 1–29), or with Winch (1958) who states: "To ask whether reality is intelligible is to ask about the relation between thought and reality" (p. 11), then the language expressed in a state of regressive thought during an hour of free association may tell us something about our own histories and older realities which will shed some light on the problem at hand. If we can find that point in the development of thought—personal, societal, or racial—then perhaps something of the original character of the relationship of the terms "brain" and "consciousness" may be seen. Regression has multiple uses, as Lewin (1958) points out, and perhaps we are finding a novel use for it—namely, philosophical—in the present context.

Knapp (this volume) emphasizes that the various modalities of conscious or unconscious thought, what he calls "underlying structures," are arranged hierarchically. In a broad sense he echoes Cassirer, who points out that the three functions of symbolic consciousness—the expressive, representative, and conceptual—are all contained within the human spirit, even while one may seem to predominate over the other to the extent that those others seem quiescent. At this point it is well to clarify these three levels of thought in order that the nature of regressive thought may be understood in the terms of symbolic consciousness.

THREE LEVELS OF SYMBOLIC ACTIVITY

The expressive function is the most elemental mode of symbolic acivity: It is found in its richest form in the thought patterns of people still entrenched in a mythical world view. In the simplest sense, the relation between symbol and object is such that there is no distinction between the two in the experience of the one whose consciousness is oriented at such a level. Here, *the symbol and object*

---

[12] I do not want to give the impression here that I regard language, or more properly, language-games and forms of life as being somehow independent of each other. Rather, the view is that they are "grammatically" Siamese twins such that they are mutually dependent on one another for meaning and existence. This is what I think Wittgenstein (1958) is getting at when he says, "to imagine a language means to imagine a form of life" (par. 19).

symbolized are experienced as one and the same, so that the borders of perception do not yet indicate a clear line between the two. The symbol does not mediate between the object and the perceiver. Knowledge at this level of consciousness is immediate. Heidegger (1962c) sees this in Plato when he discerns that the first conception which Plato had of truth was that of unhiddenness, i.e., genuineness, or authenticity. In this formulation, the thing makes itself known to the perceiver (or knower) directly without mediation. For Heidegger, Plato changed the course of Western philosophy when he moved from that point of view to the theory of knowledge that is offered us in the *Republic.* Heidegger makes this point in his inimitable fashion in the following passage:

> To say that an assertion "is true" signifies that it uncovers the entity as it is in itself. Such an asertion asserts, points out, 'lets' the entity 'be seen' in its uncoveredness. The *Being-true* (truth) of the assertion must be understood as Being-uncovering. Thus, truth has by no means the structure of an agreement between knowing and the object in the sense of likening of one entity (the subject) to another (the object). (p. 261)

In *An Introduction to Metaphysics* Heidegger (1962b) points to the tragic turn in Greek philosophy (something which Nietzsche had foreshadowed in the 19th century) when he states that

> a consequence of the change is that, from the standpoint of both the idea and of statement, the original essence of truth, *aletheia* (unconcealment) has changed to correctness. For unconcealment is that heart and core, i.e., the dominant relation between physis and logos in the original sense . . .The transformation of physis and logos into idea and statement has its inner ground in a transformation of the essence of truth from unconcealment to correctness.[13]

It is important to point out here that the expressive function admits poorly of formulation precisely because it is a pretheoretical mode of consciousness. Since the activity of theoretical consideration involves the separation of symbol and object, that point becomes clear. Confusion is avoided, especially in the context of phenomenological and Heideggarian jargon, if it is recognized that the level of discourse is

---

[13] Heidegger's view is certainly not a traditional one regarding Plato's conception of truth. As Crombie (1963) points out, *aletheia* means not only unconcealment but reliability as well. In that regard, it applies equally well to things (*onta*) and propositions. But, says Crombie, having *aletheia* depends upon acknowledging the existence of universals and concomitantly disavowing sense-data as the source of ultimate knowledge. Such a view is decidedly against the one put forth by Heidegger and raises the problem of how Heidegger's conception of *aletheia* is related to the problem of universals in Plato's epistemology.

experiential, or even psychological, if you will. If Heidegger had acknowledged the different levels of discourse with which he is struggling his point would be much clearer. Cassirer (1957) is much more
lucid in this respect in the following passage in which he points out the
role of the expressive function in mythical thought:

> In dealing with the problems and the phenomenology of the pure
> experience of expression, we can entrust ourselves to the leadership and
> orientation neither of conceptual knowledge nor of language. For both of
> these are primarily in the service of theoretical objectivization; they build up
> the world of the logos as a thought and spoken logos. Thus, in respect to
> expression, they take a centrifugal rather than a centripetal direction. Myth,
> however, places us in the living center of the sphere, for its particularity
> consists precisely in showing us a mode of world formation which is
> independent of all modes of mere objectivization. It does not recognize the
> dividing line between real and unreal, between reality and appearance,
> which theoretical objectivization draws and must draw. All of structure
> moves on a single plane of being, which is wholly adequate to it. Here there
> is neither kernel nor shell; here there is no substance, no permanent and
> enduring something which underlies the changing, ephemeral appearances,
> the mere "accidents." The mythical consciousness does not deduce essence
> from appearance, it possesses—it has—the essence in the appearance. The
> essence does not recede behind the appearance but is manifested in it; it
> does not cloak itself in the appearance but in the appearance is given to
> itself. Here the phenomenon as it is given in any moment never has a
> character of mere representation, it is one of authentic presence; here a
> reality is not "actualized" through the mediation of the phenomenon but is
> present in full actuality in the phenomenon. When water is sprinkled in rain
> magic, it does not serve as a mere symbol or analogue of the "real" rain; it is
> attached to the real rain by the bond of an original sympathy. The demon of
> the rain is tangibly and corporeally alive and present in every drop of water.
> Thus, in the world of myth every phenomenon is always and essentially an
> incarnation. (pp. 67–68)

This most archaic and fundamental form of the symbolic consciousness points in a dialectical manner (à la Hegel) toward a type of
thought which is opposed to it, namely the representative mode or
function. *The primary difference between the representative mode and the
expressive function is that in the former there is a significant opposition or
articulated tension between the symbol and that which is signified.* The
world no longer is viewed as a purely fluid realm where symbol and
object are fused into one impressive reality revealing one level of
existence. Instead, there emerges here the early crystallizations within
experience which determine the basis of the modal form. It is these

crystallizations which signify each other and relate to one another in such a way that the structure which arises from within this context reveals a certain unity not perceptible on the expressive level. For the first time, objects point to and relate to one another; they become associated with each other according to characteristics which persist in the experiencing of them. These "characteristics," or, as Cassirer puts it, "properties," are now recognized as being in some way different from the object itself. The color red may be both the color of a person's blood and, at the same time, may be descriptive of a setting sun. The "thing–property" relationship is thus evident here, whereas it does not exist on the level of mythical thought.

The structure of experience, then, is a function of the mind. Certain impressions are recognized as permanent features of the world, while others are viewed as transitory and subject to change. These permanent features of the world, while others are viewed as transitory and subject to change. These permanent features in the manifold of our impressions serve as "perspectives" around which our experience is structured and ordered in such a way that reference to events can be on a level of a somewhat crude abstraction. That is, the possibility of "talking about" is for the first time really introduced on a conscious level. An example of this point is seen in Plato (see 1963). In the *Sophist*, Plato comes to grips with the problem of distinguishing between the object and that which signifies the object.

STRANGER: When a thing exists, I suppose something else that exists may be attributed to it.
THEATETUS: Certainly.
STRANGER: But can we say it is possible for something that exists to be attributed to what has no existence.

The fundamental instrument of the intuitive or representative function is language. It is language which establishes the possibilities for objectivity and a meaningful organization of experience on a more sophisticated level than that which is evident on the expressive level. Through the instrument of language, a clear dichotomy is established between the sign and the signified. The flux of experience is ordered through verbalization of the manifold of impressions which impress themselves upon individuals. However, this verbalization or representation is not a purely independent function. It has not yet attained that type of existence which is not dependent on anything else. Language as a construct of the symbolic consciousness is permeated throughout by an intuitional character, or as Cassirer puts it, "genuine onomotopoeic formations." On the representative level the symbol is rooted to the object which it signifies. Its existence is contingent upon the existence of another thing.

On the third level of symbolic consciousness seen in the conceptual function, the symbol gains complete freedom and is in no way tied to any object. It does not mediate between the knower and that which is to be known, but rather gains its meaning from its own internal consistency and order. An example of this function is to be seen in modern mathematics, in which the function of the symbol is not to denote any object in the world but rather is one of being related to the other symbols which are part of the manifold of conceptual thought. In this context, Cassirer attempts to establish the concept of number as a relational, rather than a substantial, quantity. Indeed, it is the goal of Cassirer in *Substance and Function* (1953) to show that all scientific concept formation is the result of the precise application of relational thinking to the natural world.

The history of philosophy demonstrates the growing realization of the power of the relational concept over the generic concept. One of the most dramatic and revealing points of reference in this respect is the thought of Descartes, inventor of analytic geometry. It is the analytic geometry of Descartes that first gives birth to the "serial concept." This new tool depends for its development upon one fundamental concept—motion. This concept is in great opposition to the generic framework of ancient geometry because it dissolves the rigid architectonic schematization which freezes geometrical figures into isolated categories and seeks to demonstrate the process of transition which establishes fundamental relations between them. Motion for Descartes is not to be understood in a sensuous way. Rather, it is conceived of as ideal. As Cassirer puts it, it is an expression of the synthesis by which the successive manifold of positions, which are connected by law, are brought into the unity of spatial forms. The "serial concept" arises out of an understanding of the idea of motion in analytic geometry. Geometrical figures are determined, or, more precisely, constructed, through the movement of a point in coordinated space. The series of points which describes the path of the moving point is the result of a certain numerical rule which controls their positions. Motion is, then, reduced to a set of numerical determinations which describe the construction of a geometrical figure through a succession of arithmetical values.

By constructing such a notion of the concept, Cassirer fits it into his neo-Kantian perspective quite neatly by asserting that it is a presupposition for the possibility of objects.[14] Since the concept on the level of scientific theoretical thought is a product of the conceptual function it is logically independent of any object. It provides the very possibility of having objects in our experience at all. Ultimately, the scientific object is "ideal" and cannot be reduced to the object of intuition. It is built up out of a set of pure relations. There is no attachment to the "reality of things." Thus, the scientific concept is a manifestation of the highest "symbolic form" which man is able to construct.

The developments in modern mathematics show decisively that there is no necessary relation between the object of scientific conceptualization and that of sensuous intuition. In the realm of science and mathematics the symbol finally achieves an autonomy which is unequalled in any other sphere of human spiritual activity.

SYMBOLIC FORMS AND ARCHAIC REMNANTS

Having reviewed symbolic activity, we may find this analysis quite helpful in understanding both free association itself and the manner in which that method relates to the problem of consciousness and brain. I would like to assert that what emerges in the act of free association quite often in an analytic hour is that *the regressive thought patterns of the individual are the unfoldings of different modes of symbolic activity.*

If we refer to Knapp's account of an analytic session this point becomes quite clear. The first reference to an element of experience, in this case a headache, may be a mixture of types of thought, but the main thrust is quasiscientific. The patient ties to find an objective basis for that part of his experience. This is exemplified in Knapp's account when the patient, in trying to account for a headache, employs a considerable degree of scientific thinking in his statement: "The apartment was very dry last night and I woke up with a *splitting headache* on the right side." Quite apparently, he is asserting a scientific causal relation between the low humidity and his pain. He might be thinking as follows: "Dry air" causes an evaporation of the serous fluids in the

---

[14] This point of view of Cassirer's is derived directly from Kant's concept of transcendental knowledge. Kant (1965) states: "I entitle *transcendental* all knowledge which is occupied not so much with objects as with the mode of our knowledge of objects in so far as this mode of knowledge is to be possible *a priori*" (p. 59).

sinus cavities of my head which then become inflamed and excite the sensory nerves which innervate them." Or he might just know that there is a correlation between humidity and headaches in his personal experience. In either case, he is thinking on a somewhat lawlike or nomological level in his attempt to find objective or "external" causes for his headache.

Knapp speaks of a man who refers to splits[15] or conflicts with his mother, the analyst, or himself. Here the concept of splitting is taken more literally as *representing* other aspects and particular events of the patient's life. The reference to the splitting headache is a symbolic linguistic reference to other "splitting" events in the patient's experience which are bothering him. In this context he is no longer speaking on a conceptual level but on a linguistic or representative one. Here the earlier functions of language become manifest and the clear representation of an object or event by a word or phrase is apparent. Scientific or quasiscientific explanation is not attempted here. It will not serve the purposes of the patient who is trying to *represent* rather than to *explain* his conflicts. In the regression to more archaic modes of thought, the patient is concerned with *revealing* what bothers him rather than explaining what it is. It is not the "why" but the "what" that is primary. As he regresses even further this tendency to unhiddenness becomes clearer and more overt.

At the most regressed level of discourse the psychoanalytic patient begins to reveal a blurred distinction between himself and the world. He can be cinematographic and speak of parts of his body feeling strange, fragmented, or of a different size.

> You know, holding my head it doesn't feel like my head. It hasn't—it feels like it's smaller and like it's not my head. My hands feel much bigger than my head. My head's shrinking. If I were to run my hand over my head right now I would say this does not feel like my skull. It feels like somebody else's. It's a baby's head I guess . . . no hair. (this volume, p. 40)[16]

In this short section the patient seems to be saying two things about his body. On the one hand he expresses the feeling that his head does not

---

[15] Here the concept of splitting is treated ambiguously by Knapp as both a psychological modality and a philosophical problem. An implication of Knapp's ambiguity here is that such a concrete interpretation of the concept is rooted in its archaic usage in which the psychical experience of splitting resulted in the philosophical awareness of the differentiation of mind and brain.

[16] Regression to a point in which the distinction between self and nonself is blurred can be seen in schizophrenic thought patterns. In such a world the logic of existence is quite different and has been investigated to a considerable extent. See J. S. Kasanin (1944). One psychotic individual once said to me, "When I looked at the waves in the ocean I thought they were my life going up and down." With the blurring of the distinction of self and nonself the neutrality of the world breaks down and has a personal meaning for the individual in a multitude of ways. All the world is animated and oriented to the individual in highly individual manner. The general problem of mind and brain cannot be constructed because the distinction between oneself and a piece of reality which is not directed toward that person cannot be drawn.

feel the way it usually does; namely, as part of him. It is as if it has a certain autonomy apart from the rest of his body. On the other hand, this disturbed attitude is, I think, a reflection of his awareness that his body, or a part of it, is somehow merging with outer objects that are not a part of him. But the disturbed attitude is part of an awareness of himself as he steps back from himself in reflection. There are islands of nonregressed thinking such that the actual experience of blurred boundaries between one's self and the object world is not terrifying at all. This is known from the study of infants who uniformly demonstrate this sense of fluidity with things. It is the reflection of awareness of this state of consciousness, this fluidity, rather than the state itself, which causes the fear of disturbance on the part of the patient. This point becomes clearer and culminates in the last reference to his headache, when the patient strikes a pose in which his hands and head *are* a spider. In this context the strength of the message is not in the symbolic representation of the spider with the hands and the head but rather in the patient's experience that the configuration of his body parts are indeed a spider. At the very same time he expresses horror over the presence of the spider and an awareness that he is indeed symbolizing a spider from the point of view of the analyst when he says "and that's what a spider's *like*."

It is important to note the mixture of symbolic forms which are present in the speech of the patient. There are several aspects of this point which are of interest. In the first place, this mixture of modes of discourse is generally indicative of the fact that all these symbolic forms are carried by the individual (as well as the culture) throughout his life. What happens in the analytic session is that the proportions which are usually present and characterize the relative degrees of discourse at particular levels are upset. As the session progresses the predominant mode of symbolic consciousness becomes more and more primitive. Another point, however, is that, in the same way that primitive modalities of thought are to be reflected in our everyday speech, so too are more sophisticated forms of consciousness to be found in the patient during his regression to archaic thinking. It is perhaps because of this fact that he is able to get up at the end of the hour and walk out in a nonpsychotic state of mind. Knapp points this out by stating that there are "underlying structures" which are "hierarchically organized" and it is to this feature of symbolic thinking that I now turn.

SYMBOLIC PREGNANCE

The individual carries with him the history of symbolic forms elaborated by all men, i.e., mythical, linguistic, and scientific. In free association a regression to earlier symbolic forms is accomplished, thereby revisiting an earlier historical period of the individual and the culture. Both Cassirer and Freud make this point. Freud states it in reference to Darwin in his work with Breuer, *Studies on Hysteria* (Freud & Breuer, 1966). This reference is significant because it illustrates an important dimension of the symbolic consciousness, namely *symbolic pregnance*. The concept of symbolic pregnance involves two subservient notions. In the first place, *a symbol contains as part of its meaning the entire complex of symbolic forms with which it is related.* For example, the parabola as a mathematical curve designates not just itself but also a concept of the *manner* in which conic sections as such are generated. Involved in this broader concept is some concept of space, i.e., a manifold for the ordering of the relations of each particular curve. Hence, an individual symbolic presentation is pregnant with innumerable sets of other such presentations and points beyond itself to as yet unrealized possibilities. The exploration of these possibilities is akin to the integration of a mathematical function in that the individual function as such represents the elements of the whole in infinitesimal form.

A second way in which symbolic pregnance manifests itself is though *the generation of meanings on other levels of the symbolic consciousness.* As Cassirer points out, a line may be construed as a mathematical function or as a mythically significant entity having a set of meanings quite discrete from those conceived by considering only one manifold or level of meaning. Any symbolic entity can function on different levels of thought, being once a theoretical scientific object distinct from any physicalist interpretation, and again as a primitive one not yet distinct from that which it symbolizes.

Lovejoy points out the case of Copernicus as an example of the amphibious nature of such symbolic thought. Copernicus is pictured as diligent and scientific when plotting the paths of the planets and sun. Yet, when confronted with his data, the mythical and religious meaning inherent in the symbols with which he was working were so powerful as to constrain him from arriving at the proper scientific answers to the problems at hand. He still saw the planetary paths in terms of circles rather than ellipses and still calculated distances from the earth instead of the sun. Were it not for the symbolic pregnance of the material with which he was dealing, the confusion of thought would have been considerably less likely. Given, however, the multileveled meanings of the symbolic objects representing the celestial sphere, Copernicus was necessarily knee deep in two different worlds—one that of a new scientific cosmology, the other that of a longstanding religious *weltanschauung.* The point here is not to be taken as a

negative one, but rather one which illustrates the richness and complexity of human thought and the central role which symbolic formation has in the construction of reality.[17]

From the point of view of psychoanalysis the concept of symbolic pregnance gains deeper meaning. Freud recognizes the role of
symbolic activity in a sphere of human consciousness which is as yet
unexplored, namely, that of unconscious conflict. Certain conflictual
material cannot be confronted directly, and Freud postulates the principal of "primary process" psychic functioning in which there is *mechanical* discharge of psychic energy which, when blocked by defenses, is
expressed symbolically. Through primary process "thinking," certain
symbolic forms are constructed, albeit mechanically, such that original
meanings are disguised and hidden both from the author and the
public. Often the symbol is based on rather primitive modes of thought
such as the onomatopoetic function of language. Freud explains this on
the basis of the fundamental associationism which underlies his metapsychology. A symbol emerges as a "representative" of the original
thought because it happens to lie in the path of association. It may
appear that the symbol is "chosen," but Freud avoids that degree of
intentionality in favor of his mechanistic bent.[18] The important point in
this context, however, is that the symbol is pregnant with a number of
meanings which Freud took the pains to investigate in detail and which
are on various levels of symbolic thought. A particular example of
Freud's discovery is to be seen in his analysis of the hysterical symptom
and its relation to Darwin's (1955) work, *The Expression of the Emotions
in Man and Animals.* Knapp (1963) has considered this problem in
considerable detail in his book, *Expression of the Emotions in Man.*

Freud illustrates the concept of symbolic pregnance in his

---

[17] A. O. Lovejoy (1960, pp. 99–143). Lovejoy provides an account of the problems of Copernicus and
his novel world view and elucidates the mythical background which so vehemently defended itself
against the intrusions of this new perspective. In particular, the concept of infinity is recognized
as being of far greater significance than the relatively unimportant but highly popularized notion
that the earth is no longer the center of the universe. The concept of infinity is recognized as one
which is more than merely problematic to a consciousness which is dominated by mythical
remnants clearly opposed to a scientific world-view. See also Bronowski (1959) where the author
indicates the importance of such "purely" representational works as William Blake's for understanding the paradigm shift established by Copernicus.

[18] Sigmund Freud (1963). Freud explains the meaning of "primary" in the following passage in which
he also emphasizes the ontogenetic ideal which he was later to weave into a broader viewpoint
along the lines of Haeckel's notion of ontogeny recapitulating phylogeny: "In the psychology which
is founded on psychoanalysis we have accustomed ourselves to take as our starting-point the
unconscious mental processes, with the peculiarities of which we have become acquainted through
analysis. These we consider to be the older, primary processes, the residues of a phase of development in which they were the only kind of mental processes. The sovereign tendency obeyed by
these primary processes is easy of recognition; it is called the pleasure–pain (lust–unlust) principle,
or more shortly the pleasure-principle; from any operation which might arouse unpleasantness
('pain') mental activity draws back (repression). Our nocturnal dreams, our waking tendency to shut
out painful impression, are remnants of the supremacy of this principle and proofs of its power."

discussion of the case of Fraulein Elizabeth von R. At the very end of the discussion he suggests that the hysterical symptom is a symbol which is rooted in linguistic usage and was, at one time in the life of the individual, taken literally. "A stab in the heart" or a "slap in the face" for the hysteric are not metaphors, but rather are literal representations of the words in the expressions. To display an hysterical symptom is to point to an earlier phase of development in the individual and the race. In both, the growth of symbolic forms evolves from such literal meanings into metaphorical interpretations. The pregnance of the hysterical symbol lies in its multitudinous character and its historical significance. The symptom is at once a physiological phenomenon presumably *explainable* by scientific causal explanation, and also an archaic mode of expression in which the face of the symptom is its meaning. It is the literal interpretation of the linguistic description of the symptom which indicates the complex admixture of symbolic thinking present within the individual. A slap in the face is at the same time an affront to one's character and a physically traumatic event. The engaging point here is that for the individual manifesting such a symptom the two meanings are not disparate. They coexist without conflict. It is the symptom itself rather than the paradoxical set of meanings associated with it by virtue of its individual symbolic pregnance which is the cause of concern by patient.

This coexistence of symbolic forms leads us to an interesting formulation of the problem of brain and consciousness. The fuller meaning of the hysterical symptom is gotten through the historical perspective of Darwinian thought. As Freud points out, Darwin understood the expression of the emotions at least partially as having evolved from actions which were, at one time in the history of the species, selectively significant, both for the survival of the individual and the preservation of the species. The baring of teeth in the creation of a smile or grin was once, in the development of species, a premonitory action toward biting.[19] For Freud, primary process thinking is shown to be rooted in historical developments, in that what is now a figurative expression was originally a description of an actual state of affairs. It is as if the physiological expression of the emotions is under the aegis of the primary process mode of mental functioning, whereby the phylogeny of archaic function is recreated. Symbolic pregnance is a unique characteristic of the human spirit and provides some insight into the

---

[19] This view of Freud's might be regarded as somewhat dated. Konrad Lorenz (1966) takes up the social significance of the behavior just described through the notions of appeasement and submission gestures which tend to bring intraspecies aggression to a halt.

very way the formulation of the problem of consciousness and brain comes about.[20]

How does the preceding argument contribute any insight into the problem of the relationship between the concepts of consciousness and brain? The answer to this question is found in the description of the different levels of symbolic form and the corresponding levels of experience which are inextricably tied to these different modes of human expression. Psychoanalysis provides for us a glimpse into the archaic forms of human thought from both an ontogenetic and phylogenetic standpoint. The architecture of Cassirer's thought with respect to his concept of symbolic forms and symbolic pregnance points the way to the structure of these more archaic forms. Where psychoanalysis provides the opportunity for direct experience, analysis along the lines of Cassirer's point of view provides a formal structure to the problem. In the following an account of the problem in terms of both Cassirer's thought and psychoanalytic metapsychology will be presented.

On the level of the expressive function the problem of brain and consciousness does not exist. This is not to say that there are no differences in experience between what will later be called the subjective and objective spheres. It is only that the two provinces are not yet conceptualized and distinguished *against* one another. There is certainly a duality of experience, but there is no distinctness to that duality in the sense that the latter is at all recognized, acknowledged, or posited as such. While the poles of experience are present, they are not perceived as such and no opposition is acknowledged. When there is no distinction between symbol and object there is none between self and world, and hence there can be none between the material self and psychical experiences which are the correlates of that self. As Cassirer (1957) says,

---

[20] In his studies, Freud (1966, p. 233) indicates the relation he sees between hysterical symbolism and emotional expression from the point of view of Darwin. In this context the primary process mode of mental functioning is shown to be rooted in evolutionary developments in that what is now a figurative expression was originally a description of an actual state of affairs. It is as if the physiological expression of the emotions are primary process ways of recreating the phylogeny of archaic functions. Freud states; "All these sensations and innervations belong to the field of "The Expression of the Emotions," which, as Darwin in 1872 has taught us, consists of actions which originally had a meaning and served a purpose. These may now for the most part have become so much weakened that the expression of them in words seem to us only to be a figurative picture of them, whereas, in all probability the description was once meant literally; and hysteria is right in restoring the original meaning of the words in depicting its unusually strong innervations. Indeed, it is perhaps wrong to say that hysteria creates these sensations by symbolization. It may be that it does not take linguistic usage as its model at all, but that both hysteria and linguistic usage alike draw their material from a common source."

For an account of the manner in which Freud unites his numerous approaches to the problem of hysteria—the neurological, evolutionary, and intrapsychic—see D. Rapaport (1960).

>   In expression there is no cleavage between the mere sensuous exis-
>   tence of a phenomenon and a spiritual–psychic meaning which it immedi-
>   ately divulges. It is essentially an utterance—yet an utterance which remains
>   entirely within itself. (p. 93)

This passage begins to suggest why the mode of primary
process functioning found in dreams and in the accounts of things by
"regressed" persons does not admit of the law of contradiction. The
very notion of contradiction is not yet a possibility on this level of
thought. The idea of contradiction contains within itself the notion of a
distinct duality—of things which mutually oppose one another—and
that duality is what is missing on the level of expression. It is the fusion
of image and thing, of symbol and object symbolized, that is so characteristic of expression. It is not that the polarities are not contained
within this manifold, but rather that they are not experienced as such.
The expressive function, though, contains the kernel of differentiation
present on the representative level of symbolic function. There is a
difference in the expressive function,

>   but although the difference exists, it is not yet *posited* as such; this
>   occurs only when consciousness passes from the immediacy of life to the
>   form of the spirit and of spontaneous spiritual creation. It is only in this
>   transition that all those tendencies which are implicit in the sheer facticity of
>   consciousness unfold: what previously was a concrete unity despite all its
>   inner antitheses now begins to separate (*auseinandertreten*) and in this ana-
>   lytical differentiation to interpret (*auslegen*) itself. The pure phenomenon of
>   expression has yet no such form of dichotomy. In it a mode of understanding
>   is given which is not attached to the condition of conceptual interpretation:
>   the simple baring of the phenomenon is at the same time its interpretation,
>   the only one of which is susceptible and needful. (Cassirer, 1957, pp. 93–94)

The problem centers about the transition from one symbolic
form to another—from the expressive to the representative. It is in this
transition that the problem of body and mind first emerges *as a problem*.
For the expressive function, no problem exists; for the representative,
in which is contained the core of philosophical thought and metaphysical speculation, the problem emerges through the imposition of
concepts foreign to the primary experience of the expressive function,
namely, those of object and causality. Through the introduction of
these concepts the transformation of symbolic function from an
expressive intuitive level to a linguistic representative one can be
seen. When these concepts are then imposed from above on the
expressive function in an attempt to analyze the mode of thought,
there is a resultant distortion of the nature of that experience. The

concept of object carries with it the idea that the world is composed of a series of discrete entities with boundaries clearly demarcated from one another in *space* and *time*. In the expressive function, as we have seen, this sort of delineation is not crystallized and the imposition of the object concept onto the fluid realm of expression changes the picture radically. The result, from the perspective of the problem of brain and consciousness, is to see the problem in terms of two heterogeneous domains which are somehow related to one another but whose initial simplicity and unity are no longer manifest.

With the predominance of representative or philosophical thought, the problem is transposed onto an ontological plane from that of the phenomenological. The problem of meaning on the expressive level is transformed into the problem of underlying reality on the philosophical one. As Cassirer (1957) puts it, "the bond which links psychic and corporeal existence in the phenomenon of expression breaks as soon as we pass from the plane of the phenomenon to that of true being, to the plane of metaphysical knowledge" (p. 94).

The emergence of the problem of body and mind thus corresponds to the rise of metaphysical thinking and the transposition of phenomenological thought to ontological problems. What was once experienced as a unity is now posited as a problem, as a heterogeneity of being. The problem emerges through the use of metaphysical concepts, specifically, those of object and causality such that the articulation of distinctness was not previously capable of realization.

> When it becomes apparent that the unity of body and soul, though undeniable as a phenomenon, cannot be represented in metaphysical concepts without grave contradictions, the metaphysicians infer not a deficiency in the *concepts* but an irrationality in *being*. They do not find fault with metaphysical thinking for shattering the unity of the phenomenon and dissolving it into disparate elements; instead they shift the incomprehensibility and contradiction into the core of reality itself. (Cassirer, 1957, p. 97)

The movement from the expressive function to the representative one is paralleled in psychoanalysis in several ways which illuminate the problem of consciousness and brain. The reporting of dreams, the offering of early experiences via what Freud called screen memories, and the verbalization of essentially nonverbal experiences are three examples. I would like to deal with the first only in an attempt to establish the parallel mentioned above more clearly.

Briefly put, dreams operate in accordance with the primary process mode of mental functioning. The principle of contradiction does not exist, experiences of space and time are quite fluid and different from waking life, and different modes of symbolization are present via the *mechanism* of that process. When the dream is reported, however, little of the phenomenological reality is related through the medium of everyday speech. The "secondary revision" transforms the dream into a story or a portrait which has the superficial appearance of ordinary logical discourse. "I dreamt I was on a roller coaster," or "I was sitting by a pond with my piano," are typical ways of relating parts of dreams with the attempt to render them intelligible. It is as if the person wanted to be at a pond with a piano and the problem is to find out what the other conditions of the situation actually were. It was Freud's genius to recognize the relating of the dream as a *distortion* of the experience via the principle of contradiction, the concept of causality and that of object. Once a "conceptual" approach is avoided as the initial way of understanding the dream, the way is open to deal with the meaning of the dream apart from what the initial presentation offers. Freud made this distinction when he explained the meanings of the manifest content and latent content of a dream. The latter is the "true" meaning of the dream while the former is only the "apparent" meaning.

The manner in which Freud began to understand dreams in this way centers about his concentration on the experience of the dream. The problem was to understand the structure of that experience and to remain faithful to that structure in the interpretation of the dream. Other and earlier modes of interpretation always failed because they did not give full acknowledgement to the meanings embedded in the fabric of the dream itself. Instead, dreams were explained as allegories, as literal picturings or as random firings of the brain. When Freud presents us with the concepts of displacement, condensation, and symbolic representation, he is providing us with a logic of the primary process mode of mental functioning. He is fully acknowledging the primacy of the dream experience and not relegating it to a position of lesser significance with respect to the rational intellect which actually reports the dream. It is not to the secondary revision which we must attend, but to the experience of the dream itself.

The move from primary process mental functioning to that of secondary process thought is analogous to the move from the expressive function into metaphysical thought. With respect to the problem of consciousness and brain, we can approach it from either direction, i.e., metaphysical or phenomenological. Contemporary philosophy has concentrated on the former. The problems with such an approach have already been pointed out. If philosophy were to attend to the phenomenological dimensions of the problem, perhaps some new insights could be gained. It is in the expressive function that the experience of mind and body are unified and it is there that the phenomenon of both is most clearly to be seen. The transposition of the problem into the domain of metaphysics brings with it some peculiar notions not readily correlated with experience. For example, Cassirer points out that by the time Descartes had inherited the problem all that remained of body was extension and all that remained of the psyche was cognition. Were philosophy to stay with the phenomena the problems of such a Cartesian shrinkage might not arise.

The problem of consciousness and brain requires a greater respect for the primary experience which each of us has of each portion of our experience. The structure of that experience, when delineated, will go a long way toward elucidating the nature of the problem. In the same way that Freud attended to the remnants of archaic thought via the dream, so philosophy must attend to the primal experience of man, both from an ontogenetic and phylogenetic point of view, if the problem of mind and brain is to be untangled. In the same manner that Freud saw the dream experience as mirroring the early experiences of the man and the race, so the problem of consciousness and brain is a problem of the early experiences of each individual man, as well as the species. Similarly, just as psychoanalysis has provided us with the structure of archaic experiences, so too can philosophy deal with the structure of archaic linguistic usages to illuminate the boundaries of the problem of consciousness and brain.

REFERENCES

Austin, J. L. (1964): A plea for excuses. In: *Philosophical Papers*. Ed. by J. O. Urmson and G. J. Warnock. London: Oxford University Press.
Bronowski, J. (1959): *Science and Human Values*. New York: Harper and Row.
Cassirer, E. (1953): *Substance and Function*. Dover: New York.
Cassirer, E. (1957): *The Philosophy of Symbolic Forms* Vol. III. New Haven: Yale University Press.
Crombie, (1963): *An Examination of Plato's Doctrines* Vol. II. New York: Humanities Press.
Davidson, D. (1963): Actions, reasons and causes. *The Journal of Philosophy* Vol. LX.
Danto, A. (1973): *Analytical Philosophy of Action*. Cambridge: Cambridge University Press.
Darwin, C. (1955): *The Expression of the Emotions in Man and Animals*. New York: Philosophical Library.
Freud, S. (1963): Formulations regarding the two principles in mental functioning. In: *General Psychological Theory*. Ed. by P. Rieff. New York: Collier Books.
Freud, S. & Breuer, J. (1966): *Studies on Hysteria*. Trans. by J. Strachey. New York: Avon Books.

Goldman, A. I. (1970): *A Theory of Human Action*. Englewood Cliffs: Prentice-Hall.

Heidegger, M. (1962*a*): *Being and Time*. New York: Harper and Row.

Heidegger, M. (1962*b*): *An Introduction to Metaphysics*. New York: Doubleday Anchor.

Heidegger, M. (1962*c*): Plato's doctrine of truth. In: *Philosophy in the Twentieth Century* Vol. 3. Ed. by W. Barret and H. Aiken. New York: Random House.

Kant, I. (1965): *The Critique of Pure Reason*. Trans. by N. K. Smith. New York: St. Martin Press.

Kasanin, J. S. (1944): *Language and Thought in Schizophrenia*. New York: W. W. Norton.

Kenny, A. (1973): *Wittgenstein*. Cambridge: Harvard University Press.

Knapp, P. (1963): *Expression of the Emotions in Man*. New York: International Universities Press.

Lewin, B. D. (1958): *Dreams and the Uses of Regression*. New York: International Universities Press.

Lorenz, K. (1966): *On Aggression*. New York: Bantam Books.

Lovejoy, A. O. (1960): *The Great Chain of Being*. New York: Harper and Row.

Melden, A. I. (1961): *Free Action*. New York: Humanities Press.

Melden, A. I. (1964): Action. In: *Essays in Philosophical Psychology*. Ed. by D. F. Gustafson. New York: Anchor Books.

Margolis, J. (1973): *Knowledge and Existence*. New York: New York University Press.

Natadze, R. G. (1969): Experimental foundations of Uznadze's theory of set. In: *A Handbook of Contemporary Soviet Psychology*. Ed. by M. Cole and I. Meltzman. New York: Basic Books.

Peters, R. S. (1958): *The Concept of Motivation*. New York: Humanities Press.

Plato (1963): Sophist. In: *The Collected Diaglogues of Plato*. Trans. by F. Macdonald Cornford. Ed. by E. Hamilton and H. Cairns. New York: Pantheon Books.

Quine, W. V. O. (1963): Two dogmas of empiricism. In: *From a Logical Point of View*. New York: Harper.

Rapaport D. (1960): The structure of psychoanalytic theory. In: *Psychological Issues* Vol. II, No. 2.

Rorty, R. (ed.) (1971): *The Linguistic Turn*. Chicago: University of Chicago Press. Chicago, Illinois.

Russell, B. (1969): *The Problems of Philosophy*. New York: Oxford University Press.

Russell, J. M. (1973): Psychotherapy and quasi-performance speech. *Behaviorism* Vol. I, No. 2.

Savodnik, I. (1973): Understanding persons as persons. *Psychiatric Quarterly* **43**, 93–108.

Schwyzer, H. (1973): Thought and reality, the metaphysics of Kant and Wittgenstein. *The Philosophical Quarterly* **23**, 193–206.

Smith, R. (1974): From an intentionalist perspective. *Inquiry* **17**, 1–22.

Strawson,P. F. (1959): *Individuals*. Garden City: Anchor Books.

Strawson, P. F. (1964): Persons. In: *Essays in Philosophical Psychology*. Ed. by D. F. Gustafson, New York: Anchor Books.

Winch, P. (1958): *The Idea of a Social Science*. New York: Humanities Press.

Wittgenstein (1958): *Philosophical Investigations*. Ed. by G.E.M. Anscombe. New York: Macmillan.

Wittgenstein (1963): *Tractatus Logico-Philosophicus*. Trans. by D. F. Pears and B. F. McGuinness. New York: Humanities Press.

Wittgenstein (1965): *Blue and Brown Books*. New York: Harper and Row.

4   Introduction

It may be surprising to modern philosophers that dualism still lives in contemporary science, but Eccles provides a firm defense of this position while considering contemporary neuroscience at the most sophisticated of levels. For Eccles, "the seat of the soul" is in the dominant cerebral hemisphere, almost always the left, where language function resides. (He remains "agnostic" about the right hemisphere and animals.)

While philosophers may object, it is important to appreciate why Eccles takes this position. For many scientists, there is a conviction that accumulating data will bear greatly on the problem, and when enough data is in, the problem will *disappear* very much as the erstwhile philosophical "problem of life" has been mitigated to a great extent by the advances of modern science. But in addition, it appears that Eccles believes in an immaterial soul, and buttresses this belief with a variety of data and concepts. Philosophically, he aligns himself with Popper.

One might imagine that a neuroscientist who has immersed himself in the intricacies of the nervous system and whose research on the cerebellum "virtually constrains" him to think of its "acting essentially as a computer" would reduce the mind–body problem to a clockwork brain (Eccles, 1970). Eccles is filled with "wonder of the conscious life that each of us experiences" and a profound appreciation of its "tremendous mystery." Although the philosophically oriented reader might choose to skip over some of the sections in the following paper which provide a detailed neurophysiologic account, he would miss the possibility of gleaning at least some rudimentary sense of the workings of that truly miraculous organ which is glibly termed "the human brain"—and without which there would be no philosophy!

To illustrate his case, Eccles discusses the problem of free will. But after lucidly explicating current views of the neural machinery entailed in willed action, the account of the relation to consciousness may prove wanting. As Eccles states,

> My hypothesis would be that the highly specialized modules in the regions of the brain in liaison with the conscious self . . . can function as extremely sensitive detectors of consciously willed influences, at least when they are poised at special levels of activity. . . . the mental act we call willing must guide or mould this unimaginably complex neuronal performance of the liaison cortex so that eventually it 'homes in' on to the appropriate module of the motor cortex and brings about discharges of their motor pyramidal cells.

Eccles holds that the inability of physics and physiology to explain this action of the conscious self on the liaison cortex is but a reflection of the limitations of present-day science. But many would argue that Eccles simply avoids the issue, since even a complete science of a material brain could never conceptualize how an immaterial mind might act upon it; that is, empirical science is extraneous to this issue.

Perhaps the main force of Eccles' arguments, here and elsewhere, lies in his eloquently delineating the deficiencies of the physicalist account. If the latter can be shown to ultimately fail in answering Eccles' insistent question, "What am I?," then the dualism of the western tradition is likely to win the issue by default.

REFERENCES

Eccles, J. C. (1970): *Facing Reality*. New York: Springer-Verlag.

4 Brain and Free Will

JOHN C. ECCLES

PHILOSOPHICAL INTRODUCTION

That we have free will is a fact of experience. Furthermore, I state emphatically that to deny free will is neither a rational nor a logical act. This denial either presupposes free will for the deliberately chosen response in making that denial, which is a contradiction, or else it is merely the automatic response of a nervous system built by genetic coding and molded by conditioning. One does not conduct a rational argument with a being who makes the claim that all its responses are reflexes, no matter how complex and subtle the conditioning. For example, one should not argue with a Skinnerian, and moreover a Skinnerian should not engage in argument. Discourse becomes degraded into an exercise that is no more than conditioning and counter-conditioning—what we may characterize as Skinnerian games!

     Nevertheless, despite these logical problems, it is widely held that free will must be rejected on logical grounds. The question can be raised: can free will be accommodated in a deterministic universe? That this may be possible has been shown by philosophic arguments developed initially by Popper (1950a, 1950b) and later very extensively elaborated by MacKay (1960, 1966, 1967, 1971a, 1971b).

JOHN C. ECCLES·State University of New York at Buffalo

In 1950 Popper considered the behavior of calculating and predicting machines operating according to the laws of classical physics. He showed that in principle there are certain predictive tasks that cannot be carried out. For example, such a machine cannot predict its future states, because an attempted prediction based on the situation up to the time of prediction would be outmoded by the introduction of the additional information embedded in the prediction, and the updated prediction would similarly be again outmoded, and so on indefinitely. In the case of two such machines, A and B, A many be able to predict the future states of B, given full information of B, but only if B is not informed in advance of A's prediction.

In a series of publications MacKay (1960, 1966, 1967, 1971*a*, 1971*b*) has discussed the freedom of action of human agents in a mechanistic universe, substituting conscious human agents for the calculating and predicting machines considered by Popper. However these human agents are controlled by brains that are assumed to be "as mechanical as clockwork," and that are immersed in a deterministic physical environment. The special feature introduced by MacKay is that an observer is equipped with a "cerebroscope" (cf. Feigl, 1967; Pepper, 1960), a mythical and absurd scientific instrument giving a complete description of the ongoing brain states of subject A, and also of the environment! Armed with these devices and with a Laplacean intelligence, it is postulated by MacKay that the observer can predict with certainty the behavior of A, for example the making of a decision between alternative choices that A believed were open to him. Thus, at the time A believes that he is acting freely in coming to a decision, this decision has already been predicted by B. MacKay argues that A was correct to believe that he was acting freely, even though he was carrying out the predictions of the omniscient observer. MacKay's point is that if A had been informed of the prediction before his decision, he could have altered his decision and thus falsified the prediction.

For example, MacKay (1967) states:

> If the brain were as mechanical as clockwork, no completely detailed present or future description of a man's brain can be equally accurate whether the man believes it or not. (a) It may be accurate *before* he believes it, and then it would automatically be rendered out of date by the brain-changes produced by his believing it; or (b) it might be possible to arrange that the brain-changes produced by his believing it would bring his brain into the state it describes, in which case it must be inaccurate *unless* he believes it, so he would not be in error to *disbelieve* it.
>
> Notice that we are not saying only that the subject cannot *make* or

discover a prediction of his future brain-states, but that there *exists* no definitive prediction that could claim his assent.

MacKay calls this the Principle of Logical Indeterminacy. MacKay (1971*b*) has succinctly summarized his philosophical position on free will as follows.

> Many arguments against free will from deterministic brain theory fail at just their point. Their advocates successfully prove (*ex hypothesi*) that *brains* are not free; but they seem unaware that what was at issue was a different question: namely, whether *people* are free; and that freedom is something it would not even make sense to attribute to brains as physical objects. But, you may ask, does not this create difficulties for the view that the personal story of mental activity and the physical story of brain activity reflect complementary aspects of our human nature? If the stories in "agent-language" and "observer-language" are supposed to be correlates, how can one be deterministic and the other indeterministic? The answer is that if the two were simply *translations* of one another, as in some "identity theories", they could not differ in determinateness; but as *correlates,* even if the correlation were one-to-one, they suffer no such restriction.

In general I find myself in agreement with this summary statement of MacKay on free will. But I have grave misgivings to the effect that this very clever sophistry has side-stepped the central problem of free will because it has avoided any consideration of what is going on in one's brain when one is carrying out an action that has been freely chosen—such as bending a finger in the case illustrated in Figure 5 *intra*. If in willing an action one does not *effectively* influence the patterns of neuronal activity in the cerebral cortex and so bring about the desired discharge of motor pyramidal cells, then free will is an illusion, however subtle the philosophical arguments. Reference should be made to recent critical discussions of MacKay's contribution to the free-will problem (Landsberg and Evans, 1970; Evans and Landsberg, 1972; Watkins, 1971; McDermott, 1972). McDermott (1972) concludes that MacKay "has substituted for the old: 'I'm free because I feel free' the more cumbersome cry: 'I'm free because I know that I don't yet know what I'm going to do.' "

In order to come to grips with this problem of mind–brain interaction it is essential to study as far as possible the recent scientific discoveries on the microstructure and mode of neuronal operation in the neocortex. It will then appear that "cerebroscopes" are magical devices from science fiction—as also are Laplacean intelligences. Furthermore, it is absurd to state that the brain is as "mechanical as clockwork."

STRUCTURAL AND FUNCTIONAL CONCEPTS OF THE CEREBRAL CORTEX

The Modular Concept

Physiological investigations by Mountcastle (1957) on the somesthetic cortex and by Hubel and Wiesel (1962) on the visual cortex revealed that the pyramidal cells of small, sharply defined areas exhibited an approximately similar response to specific afferent inputs. The cells were located in cortical zones forming columns orthogonal to the cortical surface. In fact the primary sensory areas are composed of a mosaic of such columns with irregular cross sections averaging about 0.2 mm² in area. Recent investigations by Szentágothai (1969, 1972, 1973), Colonnier (1966, 1968), and Colonnier and Rossignol (1969) have provided important information on this columnar concept by revealing its structural basis. There is now an identification of many specific types of neurones in the columns and of their probable role in the processing of information in respect both of their synaptic connectivities and of their nature as excitatory or inhibitory cells. As a consequence, we are becoming aware that the column is a complex organization of many specific cell types. Szentágothai (1973) therefore develops the concept that, in both structure and function of the cerebral cortex, the column or module is the basic unit. He goes so far as to postulate that the modules are comparable to the integrated microcircuits of electronics (Szentágothai, 1973, personal communication). The modules represent what he calls a basic neurone circuit that in its elemental form is constituted by input channels (afferent fibers), complex neuronal interactions in the module, and output channels, largely the axons of the pyramidal cells. Despite the diversity of the structure obtaining in different regions of the neocortex, Szentágothai (1972) finds five basic similarities:

(1) A fairly uniform principle of lamination, (2) a relatively uniform main cell type: the pyramids, (3) certain characteristic types of interneurons or Golgi 2nd type cells, (4) an essential similarity in the organization of input channels: association afferents, commissural afferents, specific and non- (or less) specific subcortical afferents, and (5) an essential similarity in the organization of the output lines, mainly the axons of pyramid neurons. This gives us the confidence that in spite of obvious differences in detailed structure and even more in connexions with other regions of the CNS, certain "units" of neocortical tissue might be built on the basis of the same fundamental principle, i.e., they might be essentially similar as devices for processing neural information.

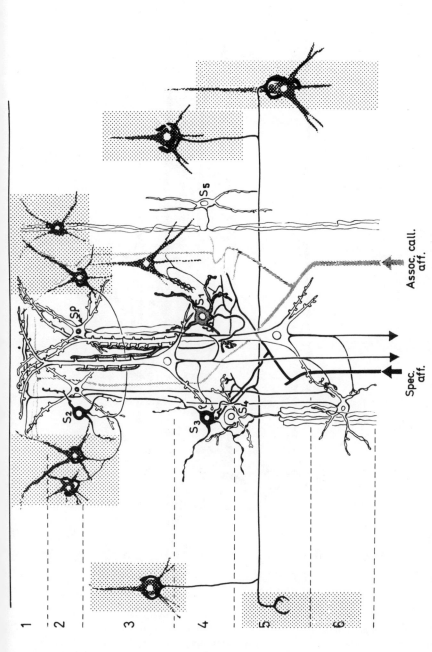

Figure 1. Semidiagrammatic drawing of some cell types of the cerebral cortex with interconnections as discussed in the text. Two pyramidal cells are seen centrally in laminae 3 and 5. The specific afferent fiber is seen to excite a stellate interneurone S_1 (cross-hatched) whose axon establishes cartridge-type synapses on the apical dendrites. The specific afferent fiber also excites a basket-type stellate interneurone S_2 that gives inhibition to pyramidal cells in adjacent columns, as indicated by shading. Another interneurone is shown in lamina 6 with ascending axon, and S_5 is an interneurone also probably concerned in vertical spread of excitation through the whole depth of the cortex (Szentágothai, 1969).

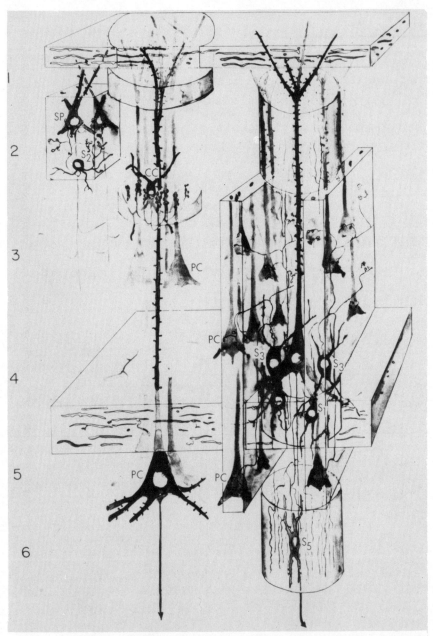

Figure 2.   Semidiagrammatic drawing as in Figure 1, but with a more realistic representation of a column on the right with two vertical inhibitory slabs on either side. Details of
the more superficial laminae are shown to the left. CC is a recently recognized inhibitory
cell, the so-called chandelier cell (Szentágothai, 1972).

Some basic patterns of operations within and around the module are shown diagrammatically in Figures 1 and 2. These figures give greatly simplified pictures of the neuronal composition of a module and its surround. According to Szentágothai there is a major functional subdivision between the neuronal connectivities in laminae 3, 4, and 5 and those in laminae 1 and 2.

Figure 1 shows that in laminae 3, 4, and 5 there are the endings of the specific and nonspecific afferent fibers on the basal dendrites of pyramidal cells, on the dendrites of several species of excitatory interneurones, and on the dendrites of inhibitory interneurones (S_3). Also the association and commissural fibers give branches to cells in the deeper laminae on their way to their principal terminations in laminae 1 and 2 (Heimer, Ebner, & Nauta, 1967). Some of the excitatory neurones (S_1) of lamina 4 (cellule à double bouquet, S_5, of Ramón y Cajal) are powerfully excitatory to the apical dendrites of pyramidal cells by the so-called cartridge type of synapse in which the axon of this Golgi type II cell runs along the dendrites forming hundreds of synapses in a manner comparable to the climbing fiber synapses on Purkyně cells. Other interneurones (not illustrated) more widely distribute their excitatory synapses, both vertically and transversely. Others again (S_4 of Figure 1) are more localized. These last two types give very few synapses to any particular interneurone or pyramidal cell. The convergent action of many is required for an effective excitation. The overall result of the sequences of synaptic excitation by all of these excitatory cells is a powerful excitation of pyramidal cells within the column that is illustrated in Figure 2. There is a kind of amplification process. On the other hand the inhibitory neurones (S_3 in Figure 1 and 2) of laminae III and IV of the module are excited by specific afferents either directly or indirectly by mediation of the excitatory interneurones, and exert their inhibitory influence on pyramidal cells in vertical slabs shown in Figure 2 (Marin-Padilla, 1969, 1970) immediately adjacent to the columnar module, i.e., to the somata of pyramidal cells of laminae 3, 4, and 5 of adjacent modules (cf. Figures 1 and 2). There is convergence of several basket cells onto any one pyramidal cell soma, on which there are 50 to 100 inhibitory synapses (Colonnier and Rossignol, 1969).

In contrast to the powerful localized action of specific afferent fibers in laminae 3, 4, and 5, there is in laminae 1 and 2 the less concentrated action of the other main input lines to the module, the association fibers from other regions of the cortex and commissural fibers of the corpus callosum (cf. Figures 1, 2). These fibers, as well as the ascending axons of the Martinotti type cells of laminae V and VI, branch to form in laminae I and II tangentially running axons which are up to 5 mm in length for the Martinotti cells. These axons form crossing-over synapses (at about 45° angle) with ascending dendrites of pyramidal cells of the deeper laminae (cf. Figure 1, 2) and also of the star–pyramid cells of laminae 2 (SP in Figure 1, 2). It is assumed that any one afferent fiber exerts such a limited synaptic excitation by these crossing-over synapses that the summation of very many callosal or association fiber inputs is required for effective action. Thus laminae 1 and 2 are zones of diffuse mild excitatory action on pyramidal cells. In addition, in lamina 2 there are small varieties of basket cells (S_2) with a much more limited axonal distribution to the star–pyramidal cells (SP in Figures 1, 2) than occurs for the basket cells of the deeper laminae. This finer pattern of inhibitory action as well as the more diffuse milder excitation of laminae 1 and 2 lead to the postulate that in these superficial laminae there is a mild and fine-grain modulation of pyramidal cells. However, Szentágothai (1972) states that much more systematic study is needed in order to discover if the association and callosal afferents also establish a high level of synaptic connectivity with cells in the deeper laminae, which presumably would be much more limited in tangential spread than occurs in the superficial layers.

These considerations reveal that in the first place the functional uniqueness of a module derives from the limited range of excitatory action by the specific and other afferent fibers—in laminae 3, 4, and 5—no more than 500 μ—and from the powerful and vertically localized excitation by the interneurones (S_1, S_5) giving the cartridge-type synapses. A further defining factor is the inhibitory surround built up by the basket cells in laminae 4. It should be noted in parenthesis that Szentágothai (1972) generalizes from the specific sensory areas to the neocortex in general. One can assume that nonspecific afferents from the thalamus, for example, have the same distribution as the specific afferent in Figure 1. These modules of the neocortex are embedded, as it were, in the much more diffuse and mild excitatory and inhibitory actions of laminae 1 and 2, which span many modules with what we may suppose to be a general modulating influence, though a finer grain may be given by the very localized basket cell action on the star–pyramidal cells of lamina 2.

The excitatory level built up in a module is communicated from moment to moment by the impulse discharge along the association fibers formed by the axons of pyramidal cells and of certain large stellate cells (Szentágothai, 1972). In this way powerful excitation of a module will spread widely and effectively to other modules, but of course principally to laminae 1 and 2 of these modules. Less powerfully excited modules will be less effective in intermodule transmission, and of course there will be zero action by those modules effectively inhibited by basket-cell action. There is as yet no quantitative data on module operation. However the number of neurones in a module is surprisingly large—up to 10,000, of which there would be some hundreds of pyramidal cells and many hundreds of each of the other species of neurones. Other operative features not mentioned and as yet but little understood are the axon collaterals of pyramidal cells which would give positive feedback circuits. In fact the operation of a module can be imagined as a complex of circuits in parallel with summation by convergence of hundreds of convergent lines onto neurons and, in addition, a mesh of feed-forward and feed-back excitatory and inhibitory lines overpassing the simple neuronal circuitry expressed in Figures 1 and 2. Thus we have to envisage levels of complexity in the operation of a module far beyond anything yet conceived and of a totally different order from any integrated microcircuits of electronics, the analogous systems mentioned earlier. Moreover there will be an enormous range in the output from a module—from high frequency discharges in the hundreds of constituent pyramidal cells to the irregular low-level discharges characteristic of cerebral cortex in the resting state (Evarts, 1964; Moruzzi, 1966; Jung, 1967). The range of projection of the pyramidal cells is enormous—some go only to nearby modules, others are remote association fibers, and yet others are commissural fibers traversing the corpus callosum to areas of the other side, which tend to be in mirror-image relationship.

The Patterns of Module Interaction

Figure 3 is a diagrammatic attempt to illustrate in the limited time span of a fraction of a second the ongoing module to module transmission. It attempts to show the manner in which association fibers from the pyramidal cells in a module can activate other modules by projections of many pyramidal axons in parallel. These other modules in turn project effectively to further modules. In this assumed plan of a small zone of the neocortex the pyramidal cells of the modules are represented as circles, solid or open, according as they participate in one or another class of modality operation, e.g., to one type of sensory input for A and to another for B. Main lines of communication between successive modules are shown by arrows, and there is one example of a return circuit giving a loop for sustained operation in the manner of the closed self-reexciting chains of Lorente de Nó. In addition, convergence

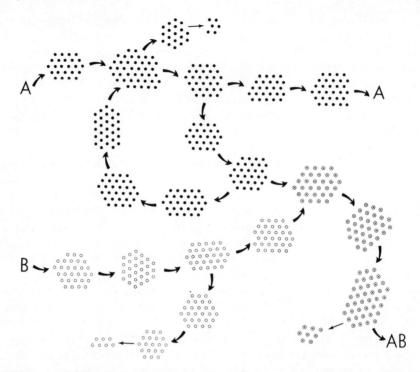

Figure 3.   In this schema of the cerebral cortex looked at from above, the large pyramidal cells are represented as circles, solid or open, that are arranged in clusters, each cluster corresponding to a column as diagrammed in Figure 1, where only two large projecting pyramidal cells are shown of the hundreds that would be in the column. The large arrows symbolize impulse discharges along hundreds of lines in parallel, which are the mode of excitatory communication from column to column. Two inputs, A and B, and two outputs, A and AB, are shown. Further description in text.

of the modules for A and B modalities gives activation of modules by both A and B inputs with a corresponding symbolism—dense-core circles. The diagram is greatly simplified because in it one module at the most projects to two other modules, whereas we may suppose it to be to tens or hundreds. There are three examples where excitation of modules was inadequate for onward propagation. Thus in the diagram two inputs, A and B, give only two outputs, A and AB. Figure 3 represents the kind of patterning of neuronal activation in the cerebral cortex that was imagined by Sherrington (1940). He likened it to "an enchanted loom, weaving a dissolving pattern, always a meaningful pattern, though never an abiding one, a shifting harmony of subpatterns."

The diagram of Figure 3 is particularly inadequate in that there is no representation of the irregular background discharge of all types of cortical neurones. The modular activation and transmission must be imagined as being superimposed upon this ongoing background noise. Effective neuronal activity is ensured when there is in parallel activity of many neurones with approximately similar connections. Signals are in this way lifted out of noise. Thus instead of the simplicity indicated in Figures 1, 2, and 3, we have to envisage an irregular seething activity of the whole assemblages of neurones, the signals being superimposed on this background by phases of collusive activity of neurones in parallel either within modules or between modules.

As Szentágothai (1972) points out, we recognize in the modular concept many species of neurones, each type having its characteristic connectivities both in its synaptic input and output. Furthermore, we can envisage patterns of modular interaction, as in Figure 3. We have progressed far from the quasi-random connectivity postulated by Utley (1955) and Sholl (1956) for the neocortex. This modular structure with all its detailed connectivity would be built by genetic coding and all the secondary instructions, the specific chemical specificities, in a manner as yet only dimly understood in a few special sites in the central nervous system (cf. Sperry, 1971). The more comprehensive connectivities of modules would also be built by similar instructions. All that happens in the learning process is presumed to be changes in microstructure at the synaptic level, particularly in the synapses on dendritic spines which provide the principal sites for excitatory synapses on both pyramidal and stellate cells (cf. Eccles, 1972).

The Unique Areas of the Human Neocortex

Thus far we have been considering the structure and functioning of the mammalian neocortex as studied in a few zones at a level which is still woefully inadequate. The modular concept was developed originally for primary sensory areas, but may now be extended to the whole neocortex on the basis of the finding that the same neuronal species are of general occurrence, particularly the interneurones giving the cartridge type of synapse (Szentágothai, 1972).

The evolution of man's brain from primitive hominids was associated with an amazingly rapid increase in size, from 550 g to 1400 g in a million years. But much more important was the creation of special areas associated with speech. We can well imagine the great evolutionary success attending not only the growth of intelligence that accompanied brain size in some exponential relationship, but also the development of language for communication and discussion. In this manner primitive man doubtless achieved great successes in communal hunting and food gathering, and in adapting to the exigencies of life in linguistically planned operations of the community. We now know that special areas of the neocortex were developed for this emerging linguistic performance, which in 98% are in the left cerebral hemisphere (Penfield and Roberts, 1959). Usually (in 80% of brains) there is a considerable enlargement of the planum temporale in the left temporal lobe and in the areas bordering the sulcus in the inferior frontal convolution (Geschwind, 1972), and this enlargement is developed by the 28th week of intrauterine life in preparation for usage some months after birth. Its development represents a very important and unique construction by the genetic instructions provided for building the human brain.

It would appear that the cerebral cortex in the linguistic areas has some unique properties. When the speech areas are damaged in children up to 5 years of age, there is evidence that in some cases there is transfer to mirror areas of the undamaged hemisphere. However this evidence is derived from such doubtful criteria as are provided by the Wada test with intracarotid injection of sodium amytal on each side in turn. There is reliable evidence that in some cases the speech centers are not switched, even with severe damage at birth, as for example in the case reported by Nebes and Sperry (1971). We can envisage that very special cerebral actions would be required in the decoding of the neural signals generated by sounds in order to give meaningful sentences. Unique patterns of neuronal connectivities must have been developed. As yet there have not been any attempts to study the speech centers at an adequate level of electromicroscopy. It would be expected that very special structural and synaptic relationships would have to be evolved for carrying out this neuronal performance at the requisite level of subtlety and complexity; and superimposed on these elemental operations there would be hierarchies of spatiotemporal patterns in an as yet unimaginable manner. It is postulated that, in the speech and related ideational areas of the brain, hierarchies of neuronal performance were evolved in the emergence of man's brain with its transcendent performance in language and ideation. And from this stems the cultural heritage of man that has been the theme of recent philosophical contributions by Popper (1972). He shows that culture can properly be given status in his trialist world, as World 3. World 3 was made by man, and the World 3 in which he develops makes man in each successive generation.

Furthermore, Sperry's (1968, 1970a, 1970b) investigations on commissurotomy patients have shown that the dominant linguistic hemisphere is uniquely concerned in giving conscious experiences to the subject and in mediating his willed actions. It is not denied that some other consciousness may be associated with the intelligent and learned behavior of the minor hemisphere, but the absence of linguistic or symbolic communication at an adequate level prevents this from being discovered. It is not therefore "self-consciousness." The situation is equivalent to the problem of animal consciousness, to which we should be agnostic.

Figure 4 shows in diagrammatic form the association of linguistic and ideational areas of the dominant hemisphere with the world of conscious experience. Arrows lead from the linguistic and ideational areas of the dominant hemisphere to the conscious self (World 2) that is represented by the circular area above. It must be recognized that Figure 4 is an information-flow diagram and that the superior location adopted for the conscious self is for diagrammatic convenience. It is of course not meant to imply that the conscious self is hovering in space above the dominant hemisphere! It is postulated that in normal subjects activities in the minor hemisphere reach consciousness only after transmission to the dominant hemisphere, which very effectively occurs via the immense impulse traffic in the corpus callosum, as is illustrated in Figure 4 by the numerous arrows. Complementarily, as will be discussed in full later, it is postulated that the neural activities responsible for voluntary actions mediated by the pyramidal tracts normally are generated in the dominant hemisphere by some willed action of the conscious self (see downward arrows in Figure 4). When destined for the left side, there is transmission to the minor hemisphere by the corpus callosum and so to the motor cortex of that hemisphere.

It must be recognized that this transmission in the corpus callosum is not a simple one-way transmission. The 200 million fibers must carry a fantastic wealth of impulse traffic in both directions. In the normal operation of the cerebral hemispheres, activity of any part of a hemisphere is as effectively and rapidly transmitted to the other hemisphere as to another lobe of the same hemisphere. The whole cerebrum thus achieves a most effective unity. It will be appreciated from Figure 4 that section of the corpus callosum gives a unique and complete cleavage of this unity. The neural activities of the minor hemisphere are

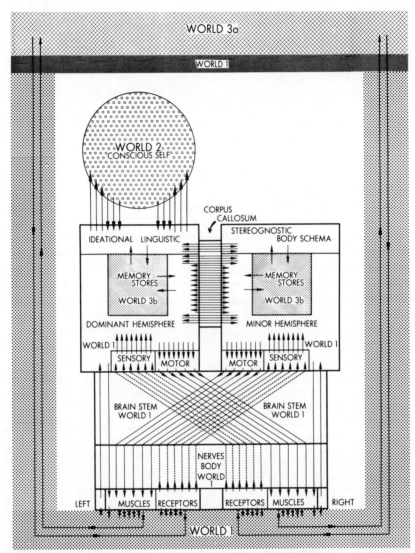

Figure 4.   Modes of interaction between hemispheres: Communications to and from the brain and within the brain; diagram to show the principal lines of communication from peripheral receptors to the sensory cortices and so to the cerebral hemispheres. Similarly, the diagram shows the output from the cerebral hemispheres via the motor cortex and so to muscles. Both these systems of pathways are largely crossed as illustrated, but minor uncrossed pathways are also shown. The dominant left hemisphere and minor right hemisphere are labeled, together with some of the properties of these hemispheres. The corpus callosum is shown as a powerful cross-linking of the two hemispheres and, in addition, the diagram displays the modes of interaction between Worlds 1 and 2, as described in the text.

isolated from those cerebral areas that give and receive from the conscious self. The conscious subject is recognizably the same subject or person that existed before the brain-splitting operation and retains the unity of self-consciousness or the mental singleness that he experienced before the operation. However, this unity is at the expense of unconsciousness of all the happenings in the minor (right) hemisphere.

CEREBRAL RESPONSES DURING WILLED ACTION

We are now in a position to consider the experiments of Kornhuber and associates on the electrical potential generated in the cerebral cortex prior to the carrying out of a willed action. The problem is to have an elementally simple movement executed by the subject entirely on his own volition, and yet to have accurate timing in order to average the very small potentials recorded from the surface of the skull. This has been solved by Kornhuber and his associates (Deecke, Scheid, & Kornhuber, 1969; Kornhuber, 1974) who use the onset of the movement to trigger a reverse computation of the potentials up to 2 sec before the onset of the movement. The movement illustrated was a rapid flexion of the right index finger. The subject initiates these movements "at will" at irregular intervals of many seconds. In this way is was possible to average 250 records of the potentials evoked at various sites over the surface of the skull, as shown in Figure 5 for the three upper traces. The slowly rising negative potential, called the *readiness potential,* was observed as a negative wave with unipolar recording over a wide area of the cerebral surface, but there were small positive potentials of similar time course at the most anterior and basal regions. Usually the readiness potential began almost as long as 800 msec before the onset of the movement, and led on to sharper potentials, positive then negative, beginning about 90 ms before the movement. Finally, as shown in the lowest trace, at 50 ms a sharp negativity developed over the area of the motor cortex concerned in the movement, the left precentral hand area in this case. We can assume that the readiness potential is generated by complex patterns of neuronal discharges that eventually project to the appropriate pyramidal cells of the motor cortex and synaptically excite them to discharge, so generating this localized negative wave just preceding the movement.

These experiments at least provide a partial answer to the question: What is happening in my brain at a time when a willed action is in process of being carried out? It can be presumed that during the readiness potential there is a developing specificity of the patterned

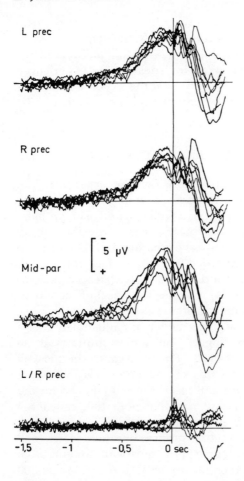

L prec

R prec

Mid-par

L / R prec

5 µV

-1,5   -1   -0,5   0 sec

Figure 5. Cerebral potentials, recorded from the human scalp, preceding voluntary rapid flexion
movements of the right index finger. The potentials are obtained by
the method of reverse analysis.
Eight experiments on different days
with the same subject; about 1000
movements per experiment. Upper
three rows: monopolar recording,
with both ears as reference; the low-
ermost trace is a bipolar record, left
versus right precentral hand area.
The readiness potential starts about
0.8 sec prior to onset of movement;
it is bilateral and widespread over
precentral (L. prec, R. prec) and parietal (Mid-par) areas. The premo-
tion positivity, bilateral and widespread, too, starts about 90 msec
before onset of movement. The
motor potential appears only in the
bipolar record (L/R prec); it is unilateral over the left precentral hand
area, starting 50 msec prior to onset
of movement in the electromy-
ogram (Kornhuber, 1974).

impulse discharges in neurones so that eventually there are activated
the correct motor cortical areas for bringing about the required movement. It can be regarded as the neuronal counterpart of the voluntary
command. The surprising feature of the readiness potential is its wide
extent and gradual build-up. Apparently, at the stage of willing a
movement, there is very wide influence on the patterns of neuronal
operation, or, as we will consider below, on the patterns of module
operation. Eventually this immense neuronal activity concentrates onto
the pyramidal cells in the proper zones of the motor cortex for carrying
out the required movement. My hypothesis would be that the highly
specialized modules in the regions of the brain in liaison with the
conscious self (the ideational and linguistic areas of Figure 4) can

function as extremely sensitive detectors of consciously willed influences, at least when they are poised at special levels of activity (cf. Eccles, 1970, Chap. 8). As a consequence, the willing of a movement produces the gradual evolution of neuronal responses over a wide area of frontal and parietal cortices of both sides, so giving the readiness potential. Furthermore, the mental act that we call willing must guide or mold this unimaginably complex neuronal performance of the liaison cortex so that eventually it "homes in" on to the appropriate modules of the motor cortex and brings about discharges of their motor pyramidal cells (cf. Eccles, 1973, Chapters 4, 6).

Free will is often denied on the grounds that you can't explain it, that it involves happenings inexplicable by present-day physics and physiology. To that I reply that our inability may stem from the fact that physics and physiology are still not adequately developed in respect to the immense patterned complexity of neuronal operation that can be imaginatively appreciated to some small degree from the tremendously simplified illustrations of Figures 1, 2, 3, and 4. The subtlety and the immense complexity of the patterns written in space and time by this "enchanted loom" of Sherrington's and the emergent properties of this system are beyond any levels of investigation by physics or physiology at the present time, as I have argued in my book *Facing Reality* (Eccles, 1970)—and perhaps for a long time to come. I would postulate that in the liaison areas these neuronal patterns of module activity are the receiving stations or antennae for the ongoing operations in the consciousness of World 2, as illustrated in Figure 4.

Even after this transmission from World 2 to the liaison brain, we still have to consider the further neuronal pathways thence to the motor cortex. Movements on the right side would result from some complex patterns of neuronal action, first in the liaison areas and then through unknown pathways to the motor cortex, the whole procedure occupying as long as 800 msec as defined by the average duration of the readiness potential. The situation is similar for movements on the left side except that there is in addition the crossing to the minor hemisphere via the corpus callosum. Since the calculated time for such a crossing is no more than 10 msec, motor actions voluntarily carried out by the minor hemisphere carry no more than a negligible temporal penalty. Again it must be recognized that in the ordinary performance of voluntary movements both the minor and dominant hemispheres are involved, and doubtless there is much to-and-fro communication across the corpus callosum during the readiness potential, which in its initial stages is bilateral even during the programming of a strictly unilateral action such as the flexion of one finger.

UNCONSCIOUS ACTIONS EMANATING FROM THE HUMAN CEREBRAL CORTEX

In order to define the special status of actions regarded by the subject as freely initiated by him, reference will be made to two types of actions that are sharply distinguished by the subject.

It has been known for many years that electrical stimulation of the motor cortex of conscious subjects evokes actions which are disowned by the subject. As Penfield reports: "When a subject observes such an action, he remarks, 'that is due to something done to me and is not done by me.'" Evidently a motor action emanating from the motor cortex in response to a voluntary command has some concomitants that are not present when a similar action is artificially evoked from the motor cortex.

The remarkable finding after the operation of sectioning the corpus callosum (Sperry, 1968, 1970a, 1970b) is that all of the actions programmed from the right cerebral hemisphere (the minor hemisphere) are not recognized by the conscious subject as being instituted by him. These actions would, of course, be on the left side, and the left hand is used in the tests. His conscious awareness of actions is restricted to those programmed from the left cerebral hemisphere, though, of course, through his sense organs he is informed, as it were indirectly, of the actions of the left hand that are programmed by the right hemisphere. Strictly speaking, therefore, we can state that the actions effected by the right cerebral hemisphere are unconscious actions.

The conscious subject, who is, recognizably, the same subject that existed before the brain-splitting operation, complains about the left hand, which is, of course programmed from the unconscious right cerebral hemisphere. He makes various statements such as "I cannot work with that hand," that the hand "is numb," that "I just can't feel anything or can't do anything with it," or that "I don't get the message from that hand." If the subjects perform a series of successful trials and correctly retrieve a group of objects which they previously stated they could not feel, and if this contradiction is then pointed out to them, we get comments like "Well, I was just guessing," or "Well, I must have done it unconsciously."

As illustrated in Figure 4, after section of the corpus callosum, there is no neural pathway from the conscious subject via the liaison brain to the right motor cortex. It would be of great interest to investigate the distribution of the readiness potential over the cerebral hemispheres in commissurotomy patients. It would be predicted that, for willed movements of the right hand, the readiness potential would have a distribution corresponding to its generation only in the left hemisphere. Necessarily the experiment cannot be done when the subject is attempting to carry out willed movements of the left hand. Since these movements do not occur, it is not possible to carry out the recording procedures, which necessitate a backward computation triggered by the initiation of the movement.

These two examples of unconscious actions emanating from the cerebral cortex serve as a reminder that, in a less dramatic manner, the great majority of actions initiated from the human cerebral cortex via the pyramidal tract are not consciously willed—at least in all their diverse details. At most, consciousness comes in to issue general commands for complex actions, the detailed execution being left to the neural machinery of the cerebral cortex with all the ancillary machinery of the brain stem, cerebellum, and spinal cord.

REFERENCES

Colonnier, M. L. (1966): The structural design of the neocortex. In: *Brain and Conscious Experience*. Ed. by J. C. Eccles. New York: Springer-Verlag. pp. 1–23.

Colonnier, M. L. (1968): Synaptic patterns on different cell types in the different laminae of the cat visual cortex. An electron microscope study. *Brain Res. 9*, 268–287.

Colonnier, M. L. & Rossingnol, S. (1969): Heterogeneity of the cerebral cortex. In: *Basic Mechanisms of the Epilepsies*. Ed. by H. H. Jasper, A. A. Ward and A. Pope. Boston: Little, Brown and Company. pp. 29–40.

Deeke, L., Scheid, P., & Kornhuber, H. H. (1969): Distribution of readiness potential, pre-motion positivity, and motor potential of the human cerebral cortex preceding voluntary finger movements. *Exp. Brain Res. 7*, 158–168.

Eccles, J. C. (1970): *Facing Reality*. New York: Springer-Verlag. p. 210

Eccles, J. C. (1972): Possible synaptic mechanism subserving learning. In: *Brain and Human Behavior*. Ed. by A. G. Karczmar and J. C. Eccles, Heidelberg: Springer-Verlag. pp. 39–61.

Eccles, J. C. (1973): *The Understanding of the Brain*. New York: McGraw Hill. p. 238.

Evans, D. A. & Landsberg, P. T. (1972): Free will in a mechanistic universe? An extension. *Br. J. Philos. Sci. 23*, 336–343.

Evarts, E. V. (1964): Temporal patterns of discharge of pyramidal tract neurons during sleep and waking in the monkey. *J. Neurophysiol. 27*, 152–171.

Feigl, H. (1967): *The "Mental" and the "'Physical."* Minneapolis, Minnesota: University of Minnesota Press. p. 179.

Geschwind, N. (1972): Language and the brain. *Sci. Am. 226*, 76–83.

Heimer, L., Ebner, F. F. & Nauta, W. J. H. (1967): A note on the termination of commissural fibers in the neocortex. *Brain Res. 5*, 171–177.

120   □   JOHN C. ECCLES

Hubel, D. H. & Wiesel, T. N. (1962): Receptive fields, binocular interaction and functional architecture in the cat's visual cortex. *J. Physiol.* **160,** 106–154.

Jung, R. (1967): Neurophysiologie and Psychiatrie. In: *Psychiatre der Gegenwart.* Berlin, Heidelberg, New York: Springer-Verlag. 328–928.

Kornhuber, H. H. (1974): Cerebral cortex, cerebellum and basal ganglia: An introduction to their motor functions. In: *The Neurosciences: Third Study Program.* Ed. by F. O. Schmitt and F. G. Worden, Cambridge: MIT Press.

Landsberg, P. T. & Evans, D. A. (1970): Free will in a mechanistic universe. *Br. J. Philos. Sci.* **21,** 343–358.

MacKay, D. M. (1960): On the logical indeterminacy of a free choice. *Mind* **69,** 31–40.

MacKay, D. M. (1966): Cerebral organization and the conscious control of action. In: *Brain & Conscious Experience.* Ed. by J. C. Eccles, New York: Springer-Verlag.

MacKay, D. M. (1967): *Freedom of Action in a Mechanistic Universe.* Eddington Memorial Lecture. London: Cambridge University Press.

MacKay, D. M. (1971*a*): Choice in a mechanistic universe: A reply to some critics. *Br. J. Philos. Sci.* **22,** 275–285.

MacKay, D. M. (1971*b*): Scientific beliefs about oneself. In: *The Proper Study.* Ed. by G. N. A. Versey. Vol. 4. Royal Institution of Philosophy Lectures. London: Macmillan. pp. 48–63.

McDermott, J. (1972): I'm free because I know that I don't yet know what I'm going to do? *Br. J. Philos. Sci.* **23,** 343–346.

Marin-Padilla, M. (1969): Origin of the pericellular baskets of the pyramidal cells of the human motor cortex: A Golgi study. *Brain Res.* **14,** 633–646.

Marin-Padilla, M. (1970): Prenatal and early postnatal ontogenesis of the human motor cortex: A Golgi study, II. The basket-pyramidal system. *Brain Res.* **23,** 185–192.

Moruzzi, G. (1966*a*): The functional significance of sleep with particular regard to the brain mechanisms underlying consciousness. In: *Brain and Conscious Experience.* Ed. by J. C. Eccles, New York: Springer-Verlag. pp. 345–388.

Mountcastle, V. (1957): Modality and topograhic properties of single neurones of cat's somatic sensory cortex. *J. Neurophysiol.* **20,** 408–434.

Nebes, R. D. & Sperry, R. W. (1971): Hemispheric deconnection syndrome with cerebral birth injury in the dominant arm area. *Neuropsychologia* **9,** 247–259, England: Pergamon Press.

Penfield, W. & Roberts, L. (1959): *Speech and Brain-Mechanisms.* Princeton, New Jersey: Princeton University Press.

Pepper, S. C. (1960): A neural-identity theory of mind. In: *Dimensions of Mind.* Ed. by Sidney Hook. London: Collier-MacMillan Ltd. 45–61.

Popper, K. R. (1950*a*): Indeterminism in quantum physics and in classical physics. *Br. J. Philos. Sci.* **1,** 117–133.

Popper, K. R. (1950*b*): Indeterminism in quantum physics and in classical physics. *Br. J. Philos. Sci.* **1,** 173–195.

Popper, K. R. (1972): *Objective Knowledge. An evolutionary approach.* London: Oxford University Press.

Sherrington, C. S. (1940): *Man on His Nature.* London: Cambridge University Press. p. 413.

Sholl, D. A. (1956): *The organization of the cerebral cortex.* London: Methuen & Co. Ltd. New York: John Wiley & Sons, Inc.

Sperry, R. W. (1968): Mental unity following surgical disconnection of the cerebral hemispheres. In: *The Harvey Lectures.* New York: Academic Press. pp. 293–323.

Sperry, R. W. (1970*a*): Perception in the absence of the neocortical commissures. In: *Assoc. Res. Nerv. Ment. Dis.*, Vol. 48. Baltimore: The Williams and Wilkins Company.

Sperry, R. W. (1970*b*): Cerebral dominance in perception. In: *Early Experience in Visual Information Processing in Perceptual and Reading Disorders.* Ed. by F. A. Young & D. B. Lindsley. Washington, D.C.: National Academy Science.

Sperry, R. W. (1971): How a developing brain gets itself properly wired for adaptive function. In: *Biopsychology of Development.* Ed. by E. Tobach, L. Aronson, and E. Shaw, New York: Academic Press. pp. 27–44.

Szentágothai, J. (1969): Architecture of the cerebral cortex. In *Basic Mechanisms of the Epilepsies.* Ed. by H. H. Jasper, A. A. Ward & A. Pope. Boston: Little Brown & Co. pp. 13–28.

Szentágothai, J. (1972): The basic neuron circuit of the neocortex. In: *Symposium on Synchronization Mechanisms.* Eds. Petsche-Brasier, Vienna: Springer.

Szentágothai, J. (1973): Synaptology of the visual cortex. In: *Handbook of Sensory Physiology.* Ed. by R. Jung. Vol. 7/3, Springer-Verlag.

Uttley, A. M. (1955): The probability of neural connexions. *Proc. Roy. Soc.* **B144,** 229–240.

Watkins, J. W. N. (1971): Freedom and predictability: An amendment to MacKay. *Br. J. Philos. Sci.* **22,** 263–286.

5   Introduction

Dualism still lives! And Savage, in the following article, would like to finally lay "the ghost in the machine" to rest. Mustering a multitude of weighty arguments—old and new—he assaults what many regard as Eccles' Cartesianism. Yet, after all, it would seem that the tormented spirit escapes again. It may be useful to consider just why it is so difficult to stay the apparition, and prick him to the quick.

When all is said and done, dualism is the only position on the relation of mind to brain which is not counterintuitive to the western mind (that is, a western mind untutored as to philosophy.) One cannot see, hear, touch, taste, or smell one's "mind." It is unlocatable and insubstantial. It seems categorically distinct from the "physical things" of the world. Moreover, each person has privileged access to his own mind, which is a truly private sanctuary. (What a milestone in psychological development when the child finally realizes that his parents do not know what he is thinking and feeling! The child's discovery of his capacity to "dissemble" is a philosophical discovery of the first rank!) Finally, this mind can control the corporeal body, freely willing it to do this and that. No matter what the archdeterminist B. F. Skinner argues, it seems that, if one so chooses, one can, for example, put a period here. rather than here. just by an "act of will."

Now, faced with the manifest evidence of direct experience, the turgid arguments of the philosopher may seem "but wild and whirling words," a kind of sophistry which may seem intellectually satisfying, yet remains empty and unconvincing as soon as we put down the book. One suspects that Savage gets through his day in a thoroughly dualist manner. Of course, it is as unfair to ask that a philosopher actually live his philosophy as it is to ask that a psychotherapist be a paragon of mental health. But it will seem to some that

Savage's carefully reasoned arguments are impotent against the Cartesian bastion of ordinary experience, when Sir John Eccles wills his waggling index finger at Professor Savage and demands, "Explain this!" And the materialist explanation does indeed seem contrived, like a somewhat cerebral hat trick.

In sum, Cartesianism is intuitively plausible, whereas materilism is counterintuitive. Until materialists provide an intuitively plausible account of mind and brain, their arguments against Cartesianism are likely to be unpersuasive to many.

Rather than commenting further on Savage's detailed critique of Eccles' position, we defer to Eccles' defense, which follows the Savage article.

5 An Old Ghost in a New Body

C. WADE SAVAGE

Descartes regarded a living human being as a machine inhabited by a person—a ghost, critics say—and he called this inner person "the soul." The operator of a crane is often used to illustrate his conception, but mistakenly. For the crane can do nothing without the help of its operator. The human machine, on the other hand, can do many things without the help of the inner person: It can digest food, breathe air, adjust its own temperature, and so on. Descartes believed that animals are mere machines, and therefore held that the human machine can do anything an animal (even an ape) can do without the help of the soul.

It is more accurate, therefore, to use the analogy of the pilot of a sophisticated robot, such as a spacecraft landing on the moon or a lunar exploration vehicle possessing legs, grasping claws, and sensors. The robot can do a great many things without the aid of its pilot: detect a rock of an unusual color, grasp the rock and place it in a storage compartment, and so on. But some things it cannot do unaided; for example, avoid a soft spot on the moon surface that looks solid, detect the unusual rock in deep shade, and so on. So the robot is designed, we will suppose, to transmit live pictures of its environment to the pilot's compartment, and with a set of controls that permit the pilot to take

C. WADE SAVAGE·Minnesota Center for Philosophy of Science, University of Minnesota

control of all or most of the craft's functions. The pilot cannot supply the robot with better sensory capacities, since he, like the robot, must rely on the signals that produce the television image; nor can he supply the robot with better motor operation, since with his controls he activates the same machinery the robot controls activate. But he can supply the robot with reasoning, or thought, which provides for a better analysis of the sensory data (for perception), better control of the motor operations (for decisions, and will); and—perhaps unfortunately for the robot—with the desires, purposes, and aversions that he possesses. The total system—robot plus pilot—thus becomes more intelligent and more subservient to the needs of persons. If we supply the robot with a loudspeaker connected to a microphone in the pilot's cabin, then the system acquires language—the physical expression of thought.

On Descartes' view, a human being is analogous to a robot-plus-pilot. But analogous only: for when we examine the interior of a human body we fail to find any pilot, any inner person. The reason, according to Descartes, is that the inner person is an immaterial, nonspatial agency—called the soul, or mind—which somehow acts upon and is acted upon by the body's nervous system. And here the view encountered its first difficulty. For Descartes was unable to explain to the satisfaction of his critics, or even to many of his disciples, how an immaterial, nonspatial system acts on a material, spatial system. So acute was the difficulty that Descartes' successors, while retaining the immaterial soul, abandoned the hypothesis that it acts on or is acted on by the body. These philosophers—the parallelists—held that the soul and body behave in parallel, *as if* the one acted on the other and the other on the one, when in fact there is no interaction. (When asked for an explanation of this parallel behavior, they often replied that it was arranged by God.) Thus the soul became useless in the explanation of behavior. If, as the parallelists would have it, the human body can behave as it does without being acted upon by or acting upon the soul, then all human behavior can be explained and understood without the hypothesis of the soul. It is, of course, a short step to materialism. If the hypothesis of the soul is unnecessary in the explanation of human behavior, why not abandon the troublesome hypothesis altogether?

There are difficulties in Descartes' hypothesis of the soul in addition to those arising from its immateriality and its alleged interaction with the body. As Descartes saw it, the human robot (body) can do much of what it does without the aid of its pilot (soul)—anything, in fact, that an ape can do, which is considerable. What he believed it not capable of, unaided by the soul, is conscious, rational, reflective (thinking), genuinely purposive, voluntary behavior—behavior that requires conscious perception, reasoning, thinking, formulating plans or goals, and consciously executing plans (willing). These are functions of the soul. Since an ape does not have a soul, it is not capable of the sort of behavior that requires these function. Now, this Cartesian argument can be reversed, as follows. Since an ape *is* capable of conscious, rational, reflective, purposive, voluntary behavior, the ape has a soul. The Cartesian may insist that apes are not capable of the behavior in question. But on what grounds? As every animal psychologist knows (or should know), apes exhibit the sort of behavior that in human beings is called conscious, rational, reflective, purposive, and voluntary. If the Cartesian replies that only behavior that requires a soul merits these labels, he begs the question. If he continues to insist that apes do not have souls, it can be pointed out to him that since conscious, rational, reflective, purposive, or voluntary behavior in an ape does not require a soul, such behavior in human beings does not require a soul either. Again, the hypothesis of the soul is seen to be unnecessary in explaining human behavior. Why not abandon it?

That is to say, why not abandon the hypothesis of an *immaterial* soul. Perhaps some part of the nervous system of both apes and humans generates conscious, rational, reflective, purposive, voluntary behavior. If so, we might call that part of the nervous system the *material* soul, since it performs the functions Descartes assigned to the immaterial soul. Whether there is any such part of the nervous system is, of course, a question to be decided by neurophysiologists, psychologists, and cyberneticians. Whatever they decide, we are safe in assuming, as materialists, that either some part of the body, or the body as a whole, performs the functions that Descartes assigned to the soul. We may call that part, or the body itself, the material soul. That humans have souls in this sense is the germ of truth in Descartes' view, and a minute germ it is.

In light of these familiar difficulties, it is a bit surprising to discover in our midst the ghost of Descartes, embodied in that intelligent machine known as Sir John Eccles. I would have supposed that three centuries of criticism, together with developments in animal psychology and computer science, had laid that spirit to rest. But perhaps my desire for progress in philosophy has blinded me to residual advantages in the Cartesian conception. In any case, Eccles' papers afford an opportunity to review the old issues with up-to-the-minute neurological flesh on their bones, and to see if we can learn anything new from them. Perhaps we shall learn how it is possible for a contemporary neuroscientist to remain a Cartesian. And it should be noted that many contemporary scientists are Cartesians, though few as classically so as Eccles. Perhaps we shall also be able to test an intriguing hypothesis. Some philosophers believe that Descartes was at heart a mechanist; and that had he been nourished by contemporary scientific culture instead of 17th-century Christian culture, he would not have posited the soul, but would have held that humans as well as animals are simply machines. Professor Eccles may be arguing and theorizing as Descartes would were he among us.

INTERACTION

As we have seen, one major difficulty in the Cartesian view is that of explaining how an immaterial soul acts on and is acted on by a material body. Eccles believes that contemporary neurophysiology can contribute to the solution of this difficulty. Descartes' animal spirits and the nerves as conduits for these were abandoned long ago. The neuron with its axon and dendrites has been the standard building block of central nervous tissue for some time. More recently, nerve impulses have been considered to be neurochemical waves of disturbance. None of these developments has had the slightest bearing on the adequacy of Descartes' conception of the human being. The most significant recent development in neurophysiology, as Eccles sees the matter, is the hypothesis of the neural "column" as the functional unit of the cerebral cortex. These columns are clusters of interlaced neurons—pyramidal cells and others—positioned at right angles to the surface of the cortex; and it appears that, not individual neurons, but columns of these must discharge in order to activate the organism. Professor Eccles appear to believe that somehow such discoveries bring us closer to understanding how the soul acts on the body. As the sequel shows, this is simply wrong. The last 350 years of neurophysiological science have not brought us one bit closer to understanding the mystery.

Eccles diagrams the relation of the soul to the brain in Figure 4 (this volume, p. 114). His usual term for the soul is "the conscious self." (In the diagram it is called "World 2" for reasons that need not concern us here.) The downward arrows from the circle representing the conscious self represent volitions, or acts of will—the actions of the soul on the body. The upward arrows represent perceptions or consciousness of sensations—the actions of the body on the soul. We are given the following explanatory comment.

It must be recognized that Figure 4 is an information-flow diagram and that the superior location adopted for the conscious self is for diagrammatic convenience. It is of course not meant to imply that the conscious self is hovering in space above the dominant hemisphere! It is postulated that in normal subjects activities in the minor hemisphere reach consciousness only after transmission to the dominant hemisphere, which very effectively occurs via the immense impulse traffic in the corpus callosum, as is illustrated in Figure 4 by the numerous arrows. Complementarily, . . . it is postulated that the neural activities responsible for voluntary actions mediated by the pyramidal tracts normally are generated in the dominant hemisphere by some willed action of the conscious self (see downward arrows in Figure 4) (this volume, p. 113).

Here we have a contemporary neurophysiologist telling us where the soul acts on the body: not on the pineal gland, as Descartes sometimes suggested, but on a specific area of the cerebral cortex of the dominant hemisphere.

In an attempt to become more specific, he ventures the following hypothesis:

. . . we have to assume that for "will" to be operative, large populations of cortical neurones are subjected to strong synaptic bombardments and are stimulated thereby to discharge impulses which bombard other neurones . . . at any instant the postulated action of the "will" on any one neurone would be effectively detected by the "critically poised neurones" on which it acts synaptically . . . in the active cerebral cortex the patterns of discharge of large numbers of neurones would rapidly be modified as a result of an "influence" that initially caused the discharge of merely one neurone. But further, if we assume that this "influence" is exerted not only at one node of the active network, but also over the whole field of nodes in some sort of spatiotemporal patterning, then it will be evident that potentially the network is capable of integrating the whole aggregate of "influences" to bring about some modification of its patterned activity, that otherwise would be determined by the pattern of afferent input and its own inherent structural and functional properties (1974, pp. 100–101).

The basic features of this theory can be briefly presented as follows. The primary activity of the brain is the action of *individual neurons* on other neurons through synaptic connections on the axons and dendrites of each. The secondary activity of the brain (at least the cortical areas) is the action of *columns of neurons* on other columns. The tertiary activity of the brain—and that which controls the organism by the producing motor impulses—is the action of *groups of columns of neurons* on other groups (in the manner depicted in this volume, p. 110 Figure 3). The resulting patterns, or waves, of neural activity lead

Eccles (following Sherrington) to liken the brain to an "enchanted
loom, weaving a dissolving pattern, . . . a shifting harmony of subpatterns" (this volume, p. 110), and to say that "it is absurd to state
that the brain is as 'mechanical as clockwork'" (this volume, p. 103).

These remarks are misleading, for they can easily be taken to
imply that, in some cases, the action of groups of neurons—the "patterned activity of the brain"—cannot be explained by means of the
actions of the individual neurons comprising the group; and that the
actions of the individual neurons must be explained, at least in part, by
means of the action of the groups they are in. This is an emergentist
position, whose leading exponent among neurophysiologists is R. W.
Sperry.

> . . . consciousness is conceived to have a directive role in determin-
> ing the flow pattern of cerebral excitation . . . conscious awareness . . . is
> interpreted to be a dynamic emergent property of cerebral excitation . . . the
> more molar conscious properties are seen to supersede the more elemental
> physio-chemical forces, just as the properties of the molecule supersede
> nuclear forces in chemical interactions . . . Individual nerve impul-
> ses . . . are simply carried along or shunted this way and that by the prevail-
> ing overall dynamics of the whole active process (in principle—just as drops
> of water are carried along by a local eddy in a stream or the way the
> molecules and atoms of a wheel are carried along when it rolls down a hill,
> regardless of whether the individual molecules and atoms happen to like it
> or not) (Sperry, 1969, pp. 533–534).

Sperry calls this position "emergent interactionism": "emergent" for
reasons made clear in the passage above, "interactionism" because,
while the emergent conscious properties direct individual nerve impulses, these properties are at the same time "directly dependent on the
action of the component neural elements. Thus a mutual interdependence is recognized between the sustaining physico-chemical processes
and the enveloping conscious qualities" (Sperry, 1969, p. 534).

Sperry may have developed this view in an attempt to solve
the problem of mind–body interaction. If so, the attempt seems a
failure. It is clear enough how the conscious, emergent properties
depend on individual nerve impulses, for these properties are patterns
of individual nerve impulses (such dependence is, incidentally, not
causal dependence). But it is completely unclear how the conscious,
emergent properties "direct" individual nerve impulses. Drops of
water are not "carried along" by the local eddy, They and their actions
on one another constitute the local eddy. However we assess Sperry's
position, it is, apparently, not the position of Eccles. The emergentist

does not posit a soul, or conscious self, as an entity or system separate from the brain. For him consciousness is certain (emergent) brain properties.

Now the problem of how the will influences the behavior of the organism—how for instance, I will my finger to move—arises for Eccles in the following way. Behavioral activity is assumed to be caused by motor nerve activity and motor nerve activity by the activity of groups of neurons in the cortex. So if will is to influence behavioral activity, it must influence neuron-group activity. But it can only do this by influencing the activity of individual neurons in the group. To solve this problem, Eccles speculates that when the cortex is at a high general level of arousal, the firing of a single neuron can cause the discharge of several critically poised neurons, and each of these causes several more to discharge, and so on until a large group of neurons are discharging. In this way the will can, by acting on a single neuron, or on each of a few critically located neurons, influence neuron-group activity. The production of an avalanche provides an analogy for the mechanism posited here. A person on a mountaintop can, by releasing a single rock, or a few critically located rocks, produce an avalanche involving thousands of rocks. The person could in this manner cause (what is analogous to a behavioral act) the destruction of a building at the foot of a mountain. It should now be clear that Eccles is not an emergentist. In his view, the avalanche of falling rocks—or of neuronal discharges—is determined by its components, and not the other way round.

The problem of how the will influences behavior is thus reduced to the problem of how the will acts on individual neurons. To this latter problem Eccles offers not even the hint of a solution, and cannot offer a solution as long as he holds that the soul is an immaterial, nonspatial system. Does the soul act on a neuron in the way that one neuron acts on another? If so, the soul is something like a neuron—a material, spatial agency. Does the soul act on a neuron in the way that a cosmic ray might act on a neuron to cause it to discharge? If so, the soul is something like a cosmic ray (or the sun that emits the ray) and is a material, spatial entity. Does the soul act on a neuron in a manner quite unlike those mentioned? If so, the action of the soul is utterly mysterious and inexplicable. This is precisely the unsatisfactory state in which Descartes left the problem of interaction. For all his brandishing of contemporary neurophysiological theory, Eccles has made no contribution to its solution. He could make such a contribution by identifying the soul with some material system; for example, with the sun and its cosmic rays bombarding the brain. This would be a strange theory (my soul is the sun? and yours also?), and is probably objectionable for a number of reasons, but it has no interaction problem. Or Eccles could identify the soul with some part or system of the brain, a theory that has no obvious defect in the present writer's opinion. Eccles' reasons for avoiding this theory will become clear in the sequel.

As long as the action of the soul on the body is mysterious and inexplicable—as it must be if the soul is an immaterial, nonspatial system—there is no need for Eccles to go to such trouble in speculating how the discharge of a few neurons (caused by the soul) can cause large collections of neurons to fire. He can simply say that the soul sometimes causes large collections of neurons to fire. The ability of the soul to cause one neuron to fire is no less mysterious than its ability to cause a collection of neurons to fire. This point shows quite clearly that Eccles "explanations" of interaction are pseudoexplanations. Since interaction between an immaterial soul and a material brain is mysterious and inexplicable, one may presume it to occur in whatever manner one wishes (consistent with the observable brain effects); which is equivalent to saying that one has no idea how it occurs.

The dualist may be tempted to argue that, since the immaterial soul is nonspatial, the problem of how it interacts with the brain is specious. The immaterial soul is not at any distance from the brain. It is just as correct to say that the immaterial soul is "in" individual neurons as it is to say that it is "outside" individual neurons, and just as correct to say that the soul is a "force internal" to the individual neuron as it is to say that it is a "force external" to the individual neuron. Suppose we say, then, that the soul is internal to the individual neuron on which it acts; then the problem of interaction disappears, does it not? It does not, because the solution is specious. The solution erroneously assumes that we can meaningfully say that the soul is inside, or internal to, something. If the soul is nonspatial, it makes as little sense to say that the soul is inside or internal to something as it does to say that soul is outside or external to something. But what then *is* the problem of interaction? How is the problem to be stated?

On the assumption that the soul is an immaterial, nonspatial entity, there is indeed no interaction problem of the kind we find in physics or physiology. If the neurophysiologist theorizes that nervous impulses are generated by neurons acting on neurons, he is required to say how this interaction occurs. The current explanation is that interaction consists in ion flows across membranes at the synapses of the interacting neurons. This is a physical explanation of physical interaction. There cannot be a physical explanation of soul–body interaction, since it is not a physical interaction; so it seems unfair to require the dualist to provide a physical—hence inappropriate—explanation of interaction. However, it is entirely fair to require the dualist to provide an *appropriate* explanation—a nonphysical explanation—of the nonphysical interaction between soul and body. And we have no idea what such an explanation might consist in, for our concept of an explanation is that of a physical explanation. We cannot even *formulate* an explanation of soul–body interaction, much less *test* our formulation by experiments. The dualist can always say that this demonstrates the limitations of our conceptual system, the limitations of our concept of explanation. But as scientists we must surely regard this as obfuscation. If the hypothesis of an immaterial soul is, by definition, the hypothesis of an entity whose operations are inexplicable to human scientists, then human scientists should reject the hypothesis.

INTELLIGENT BEHAVIOR

A second major difficulty in the Cartesian view emerges if we ask why human behavior is supposed to require a soul when animal behavior does not. Eccles says:

> . . . I think that there is no meaning or scientific value in ascribing mental properties to systems that exhibit order or apparent purpose or memory, or even intelligent action . . . Even when we come to the apparently intelligent actions of higher animals with their remarkable abilities to learn and remember, I have not found any reason to go beyond the purely mechanistic neurophysiology in explaining their brain performances, which of course was the position of Descartes (1974, pp. 87–88).

Then why go beyond the purely mechanistic neurophysiology in explaining the performances of *humans*? Eccles' answer can be divided into three parts: the hypothesis of the soul is held to be required to explain (a) intelligent behavior, (b) consciousness, and (c) free agency. We will discuss these parts of the answer in order listed.

Eccles holds that the hypothesis that the human body has a soul is required to explain certain intelligent human behavior; behavior that, however similar it may be to that of higher animals, is different enough to require a different explanation. Human linguistic behavior (language, we will say) is perhaps the best exemplar of the sort of behavior Eccles has in mind. (Human language has long been a principal refuge of the soul. For a retrospective of Descartes' treatment of language, see Gunderson, 1971.) The difficulty for Eccles is, of course, that some animals exhibit linguistic behavior. He takes note of this fact and discounts it.

> Undoubtedly, the experimental investigations on chimpanzees, with respect to their developing both a sign language (Gardner and Gardner, 1969) and a symbol language (Premack, 1970), show that the chimpanzee brain exhibits considerable levels of intelligent and learned performance, but this chimpanzee communication is at quite a different level from human speech (1974, pp. 95–96).

Eccles will not find it difficult to discover differences between human and chimpanzee speech. Human speech is more creative (capable of greater novelty), communicative, comprehensive, etc.; and it contains symbols for numbers, quantities, abstractions, etc. However, he will find it difficult—impossible in the author's opinion—to discover differences that require us to posit a soul for the human but not for the chimpanzee. (Some linguists believe that human language requires the hypothesis of innate generating mechanisms—genetic wiring of the brain, so to speak. This, of course, is not the hypothesis of a soul, at least not an immaterial soul.)

The existence of animal language is no longer the major challenge to Cartesianism. The current focus is on computer language, about which Eccles says nothing in the papers under review. For several decades, computers have been capable of emitting language in the form of printed-out "answers" in a human script to "questions" fed into the computer in a special computer language into which the human operator translates his questions. In the early models, such responses exhibited no creativity, and could be made only to the stimuli of a computer language. But new models are being designed and built that can "talk" to human beings in a humanlike manner; i.e., that can respond directly to human language in language that exhibits the same sort of creativity exhibited by human language (see, e.g., Winograd, 1973). There is no good reason (none known to the author, at least) to doubt that one day we shall have a computer whose linguistic performance is indistinguishable from that of a human. The arrival of that day may not disabuse the Cartesian of his belief in the existence of the human soul. But it will establish that the soul is not required to explain such intelligent behavior as human language, and thus will deprive the Cartesian of a principal argument for the existence of the soul.

Observing the remarkable computer imagined above, Eccles would probably say: "But it does not think or reason, since it has no soul. Its language is mere imitation of human language, and, unlike the latter, is meaningless, nonreflective, and nonrational." One can predict this response from statements such as: "One does not conduct a rational argument with a being who makes the claim that all its responses are reflexes, no matter how complex and subtle the conditioning" (this volume, p. 101). Now, we do not determine whether another human being can think or reason by inspection of its mental processes. Rather, we observe its behavior, including the linguistic; and if it behaves in a reflective, rational manner, we conclude that it thinks and reasons. If the computer behaves in a reflective, rational manner in its linguistic or other behavior, we will, if consistent, conclude that it thinks and reasons. As for meaning, it is not some "essence" or "life" breathed into behavior by a soul or other agency; it is a feature of the behavior. A meaningful utterance is one made in an appropriate way under appropriate circumstances. If the utterance of a human has these features, we pronounce it meaningful. If the utterance of a computer, or an animal, possesses these features, then, to be consistent, we must pronounce it meaningful.

Pressed by these arguments, the Cartesian may say of our talking computer: "Well, since it is capable of uniquely human behavior, behavior that requires a soul, the computer has a soul." (Apparently Eccles would *not* make this response.) One cannot help seeing this response as an *ad hoc*, desperate attempt to maintain the hypothesis of the soul. If the talking computer is endowed with a soul, who so endowed it? God, presumably, since human manufacturers apparently cannot create souls. But then we must suppose that God waits while the manufacturers build the computer and, at the moment of its completion, installs in it a soul. And why does He wait until the moment of completion? The computer is being built according to a certain design, and it is the design, rather than its realization in a particular collection of hardware, that seems to require soul. (Some thinkers have suggested that the soul of either a computer or a human being is the *program* of the machine. This conception seems too insubstantial and abstract to satisfy the Cartesian.) Given these theological problems, it seems the better part of wisdom to suppose that the computer is completely made by human manufacturers and is not equipped with a soul, especially since none is required to explain its behavior. And if none is required for the talking computer, none is required for the human being.

Descartes defined the soul as a thinking thing, and he believed that the soul is the *only* thing that thinks. But consider. Human linguistic behavior is generated by thought. This proposition follows from our ordinary definition of thought. For, as we ordinarily define it, thought is whatever generates such behavior as human language. Now if computers can generate humanlike language, then computers can think; and if computers do not have a soul, computers can think without a soul. It follows that the soul is not the only thing that thinks. If computers can think without a soul, then so can the human body think without a soul. It can think by means of its brain alone, which can be regarded as a biological computer.

This conclusion seems forced upon us by biological and computer science. Eccles cannot remain a Cartesian and accept it. Yet he comes within a hair's breadth of doing just that.

> Since neural events in the minor hemisphere do not directly give the subject conscious experiences, we have to postulate that the neuronal machinery concerned in these specific operational tasks works at an unconscious level, which would be in good accord with the psychiatric concept of the unconscious mind. For example, in listening to music it can be envisaged that initially immense and complex operational tasks such as decoding, synthesizing and patterning are carried out in the temporal lobe of the minor hemisphere. Communication via the corpus callosum to the liaison areas of the dominant hemisphere with the consequent conscious experiences presumably is delayed until these most sophisticated neural operations have been carried out in the special musical centers. In their operational function these centers can be regarded as being analogous to the speech centers . . . (1974, p. 97).

The passage above illustrates a pervasive feature of Eccles' view of the conscious self, the tendency to suppose that the brain does all the work—analyzing, integrating, inferring, in short, thinking—and the conscious self sits back and "experiences" the results. This makes the soul a freeloader, something that does no work, and something that can be dispensed with.

If such tasks as the decoding, synthesizing, and patterning of music can be carried out by the cortex unconsciously—i.e., without the activity of the conscious self—then it is easy to suppose that thinking can be carried out by the cortex without the activity of the conscious self. For understanding language can be compared with understanding music, and understanding language is thinking. Why doesn't Eccles face it? The brain can think, and can do so without the soul. That the brain can think without the soul does not quite entail that the soul does not exist. But if the soul does exist, what is its function?

Does the soul think, as well as the brain? If not, then there is one less reason for positing its existence, since there is one less function it participates in or performs. If so, if both brain and soul are capable of thinking independently, then why the duplication of function? On this view the soul is like a person equipped with a computer capable of performing operations of thought. Why would the person need the computer? Well, the computer can continue to work when the person becomes fatigued; and the computer may be able to think faster, or better than the person. The admission that the brain might think better than the soul does not make the dualist inconsistent, but it should make him uncomfortable. The more critical question for the dualist is, "Why does the computer need the person?" Well, the computer might think less well than the person in some areas (theoretical, or abstract areas, for instance); and the computer might not be as skillful or imaginative in programming computers as the person. But if, as seems likely from developments in computer science and neurophysiology, the brain can do everything in the way of cognitive processing a soul can do and do it just as well, then why retain the troublesome hypothesis of the soul?

CONSCIOUSNESS

Eccles second reason for positing the soul (conscious self) is that only the conscious self is capable of consciousness. He says: "By consciousness I mean conscious experience, which each of us has privately for himself" (1974, p. 87). What Eccles means by "conscious-ness" and "conscious" is the major difficulty in understanding and assessing this part of his argument for the conscious self, and the above definition does little to ameliorate the problem. What are "experi-ences"? Perceptions, feelings, volitions, beliefs, thoughts, decisions, purposes, and so on, presumably. Now if it makes sense to speak of conscious perceptions, feelings, etc., it must also make sense to speak of unconscious perceptions, feelings, etc. But does Eccles want to say that there can be unconscious thoughts, unconscious purposes, uncon-scious decisions? If so, then thinking, purposing, and deciding do not require a conscious self; and, therefore, there is no reason to deny that animals think, purpose, and decide. If, on the other hand, Eccles says that thoughts, purposes, and actions are necessarily conscious—cannot be unconscious—then his use of the term "conscious" is obscure. If I can be conscious of something (perception, thought, etc.), then I can fail to be conscious of it; i.e., it can be unconscious.

Most of Eccles' pronouncements about consciousness are made in the course of examining the "split-brain" experiments of Sperry and his associates, experiments with human subjects in whom the corpus callosum—the neural connecting system between the two brain hemispheres—has been surgically interrupted. Such a subject is typically unaware of all perceptual inputs to the minor (right, usually) hemisphere—i.e., is not conscious of seeing objects in his left visual field; and he is not conscious of controlling his left hand. Of his left hand he says such things as, "I cannot work with that hand," "That hand is numb," and "I just can't feel anything or do anything with it." Nonetheless, the subject can carry out with his left hand intelligent, goal-directed, creative actions that require sensation and memory for their performance. For example, he may pick up a quarter from the table—no dollar notes being made available to him—when a dollar sign is flashed in his left visual field (a stimulus he is unaware of seeing). And he may be able to produce geometric drawings and mosaic constructions with his left hand that are superior to those he can produce with his right, of which latter he is conscious and does have conscious control (1974, p. 91).

Eccles concludes that the conscious self is directly connected, both in normal and in split-brain subjects, to the dominant hemisphere; and that the reason the split-brain subject is unconscious of actions and perceptions on his left is that the minor hemisphere has been disconnected from the conscious self.

> We can regard the minor hemisphere as having the status of a very superior animal brain. It displays intelligent reactions and primitive learning responses and it has a great many skills, particularly in the spatial and auditory domains, but it gives no conscious experience to the subject. Moreover, there is no evidence that this brain has some residual consciousness of its own (1974, p. 92).

It is tempting to clarify the terms "conscious" and "consciousness" as follows. That the split-brain subject is doing something with his left hand (drawing, for instance) is undeniable; but he is not conscious of what he is doing. Similarly, that he sees things in his left visual field—his left hand, the paper on which he is drawing—is undeniable; but he is not conscious of what he sees. He is conscious in the sense that he sees: we may call this consciousness$_1$. He is not conscious in the sense that he is not conscious of what he sees: we may call this consciousness$_2$. Consciousness$_2$ is a sort of *self*-consciousness: consciousness of the actions and perceptions of oneself. Better still, it is *meta*consciousness, at least as regards perception, since it is consciousness of consciousness. With this terminology, we can describe Eccles' position precisely. Consciousness$_1$ is possible without a conscious self, or soul. The minor hemisphere of the split-brain subject, and the brain of an animal, are capable of consciousness in this sense. Such brains are not capable, however, of consciousness$_2$. Consciousness in this sense is a function of a conscious self. Only when the brain is connected to a conscious self, as it is in the normal human being, is it capable of consciousness$_2$.

The above clarification helps us understand why Eccles insists that consciousness cannot be a function of the brain, but must be a function of the conscious self. It is because he means by "consciousness" consciousness$_2$. He holds that consciousness$_1$ (seeing, for instance) is a function of the brain. But since consciousness$_2$ is consciousness of consciousness$_1$, it cannot be a function of the brain. For no material system, such as the brain, can be conscious of itself. Eccles does not explicitly make this argument in the papers under review, but it seems to be suggested by several things he does say, for example, "How can brain states describe themselves?" (1974, p. 88).

This is an ancient argument, and a fallacious one. In the first place, it is no more difficult for a material system to be conscious of itself that it is for an immaterial system (such as the conscious self) to be conscious of itself. Self-consciousness has seemed puzzling to many philosophers. Some have likened it to an eye seeing itself, and have argued that, just as an eye seeing itself is logically impossible, self-consciousness is logically impossible. But if self-consciousness is possible, as Eccles surely assumes, it is just as possible in a material system as it is in an immaterial one. To illustrate this point, consider the following, completely speculative, hypothesis. When a person sees a drawing, certain waves of neuronal discharge are generated in his cortex. Perhaps these waves have relatively low intensity when the subject is not conscious of seeing the drawing, and relatively high intensity when he is conscious of seeing the drawing. This is mere speculation and may be incompatible with current neurophysiological theory. But the general point is clear: some modification of the same brain processes that constitute consciousness$_1$ can be identified with consciousness$_2$. Which is to say that a material system can be conscious of itself.

In the second place, when something is conscious$_2$ of consciousness$_1$, it is not conscious of itself, for the two consciousnesses are different. Consequently, we can suppose that consciousness$_1$ is one brain function, and consciousness$_2$ another brain function that impinges on the first. Thus, consciousness$_2$ may be a system in the dominant hemisphere, and consciousness$_1$ another system in the minor hemisphere, on which consciousness$_2$ impinges in normal subjects. In the split-brain subjects, the consciousness$_2$ system in the dominant hemisphere cannot impinge on the consciousness$_1$ system in the minor hemisphere, owing to interruption of the corpus callosum. There is no need to suppose that consciousness$_2$ is an immaterial system (the conscious self) separate from the brain.

The analysis above has been based on our distinction between consciousness$_1$ and consciousness$_2$, and the assumption that the split-brain subject is not conscious$_2$ of his perceptions and actions on his left. It has to be pointed out that this assumption seems false. If the subject is not conscious$_2$ of the movements of his hand and of seeing the marks on paper he makes as he draws, how does he accomplish this highly difficult task? Drawing requires continual monitoring of the marks made and the movements that make them, and this monitoring seems to be nothing other than consciousness$_2$. If this is correct, and if, as Eccles claims, consciousness$_2$ is a function of a conscious self, then a conscious self must be connected to the minor hemisphere of the split-brain subject, and to the brains of chimpanzees, who are capable of tasks as sophisticated as drawing. If, on the contrary, a conscious self is not required for consciousness$_2$ in these cases, then it is not required for consciousness$_2$ in the normal human subject. But it seems undeniable that there is a sense in which the split-brain subject is not conscious of his perceptions and actions. So it seems we must introduce another sense of consciousness, consciousness$_3$, with which to express this fact.

To understand this third sense of consciousness, we need to consider additional cases. We say of sleepwalkers, persons dazed from a blow to the head, and hypnotized persons that they are not conscious (or, not fully conscious). And we say of normal persons absorbed in some activity that they are not conscious (or, not fully conscious). What we mean by this is that they do not know what they are doing, or what their situation is. Consciousness$_3$ is consciousness of what one is doing and what one's situation is. It is self-consciousness, in the ordinary sense of that term. Our major test for whether a person knows what he is doing and what his situation is consists in getting him to *describe* what he is doing and what his situation is, either at some later time (from memory) or at the moment. Thus, to discover whether a person is walking in his sleep, we question him about what he is doing, where he is going, what his name is, where he lives, and so on. We use similar tests to discover whether a dazed boxer has emerged from his daze. (Note that the answers do not all have to be true for the subject to be conscious$_3$.)

We tend to regard a subject's description of what his situation is and what he is doing as the *only* test of whether he is conscious$_3$. And since animals cannot provide such descriptions we conclude that they are not conscious$_3$, not self-conscious. (Eccles at least, seems to reach the conclusion in this manner.) But consider. If a dog is brought home from a long stay in the hospital, and immediately proceeds to search for familiar objects and places, then he knows what his situation is, and is conscious$_3$. If the dog is surprised in the act of eating a steak waiting to be broiled, and slinks away with ears down and tail between his legs, then he knows what he is doing, and is conscious$_3$. So if consciousness$_3$ requires a soul, dogs (some of them, at least) have souls.

Discussing what we have here called consciousness$_3$, Eccles says:

> . . . by forging linguistic communication of ever increasing precision and subtlety, man must gradually have become a self-conscious being aware of his own identity or selfhood. As a consequence he also became aware of death, as witnessed so frequently and vividly in other members of the tribal troup that he recognized as beings like himself (1974, pp. 102–103).

The penultimate developments are said to be those "in religion, in philosophy and in science that are associated with his attempts to understand the manner of being he was, his origin, and his destiny" (1974, p. 103). Most dogs have no awareness of death, at least, not their own death. And pretty obviously they make no attempts to understand the manner of being they are, their origin, and destiny. But it does not follow that they are not self-conscious. All that follows is that they do not have as high a degree of self-consciousness as do humans. They have a less complicated conscious self, or soul (and may be the better for it). Or, if Eccles denies that dogs have souls, to be consistent he must also deny that humans do. The relative complexity of human self-consciousness is not an adequate reason for positing souls in humans and none in dogs.

Finally, it should be noted that even if the only proper test for self-consciousness (consciousness$_3$) were the subject's *description* of what he is doing and what his situation is, it would follow that some animals are not self-conscious; but it would not follow that only humans have souls, and that a soul is required for self-consciousness. The talking computer imagined in the previous section is able to describe its situation ("I am a model X-001 computer. I was programmed in 1990.") and what it is doing ("I am now checking the last computation."). Either this self-conscious (conscious$_3$) computer has a soul, or the hypothesis of the soul is not required to explain self-consciousness. The latter is surely the more reasonable alternative.

FREE AGENCY

Eccles' third, and major, reason for positing the soul (conscious self) is that without it free will, or free agency, is inexplicable.

> . . . it is postulated that the neural activities responsible for voluntary actions mediated by the pyramidal tracts normally are generated in the dominant hemisphere by some willed action of the conscious self (see downward arrows in Figure 4). When destined for the left side, there is transmission to the minor hemisphere by the corpus callosum and so to the motor cortex of that hemisphere (this volume, p. 113).

In the split-brain subject, the corpus callosum has been interrupted, and this explains, according to Eccles, why the behavior of the subject's left hand is not free; the willed action of the conscious self cannot be transmitted to the minor hemisphere which controls the movement of the left hand.

It is worth noting, for its application to a later point, the controversial character of Eccles' interpretation. Eccles assumes that the subject's left-hand movements are unfree (involuntary), and explains this fact by the disconnection of the left hand from the conscious self. It is possible to assume that the subject's left-hand movements are free (voluntary) movements, even though the subject is not conscious of these movements, and then to explain this fact in one of two ways. The first is to hypothesize that there is a second conscious self connected to the minor hemisphere, but suppressed by the dominant conscious self and unable to communicate with the experimenter because of its lack of connection to any linguistic area of the brain. (Sperry proposes a hypothesis similar to this [1969, p. 532].) On the second explanation, there is only the one conscious self connected not only to the dominant hemisphere but also the minor hemisphere, and it wills the movements of the left hand without being conscious that it does so. Eccles may reply that one cannot will an action without being conscious that he does so. But this is doubtful. Both laymen and psychologists are accustomed to distinguishing between "consciously willed" and "unconsciously willed" actions, and Eccles himself sometimes employs the first of these two phrases.

Some dualists would argue that even if *every* action of a subject is like the actions of the left hand in the split-brain subject, still the human has free will and requires a conscious self. For as long as the conscious self of the human performs acts of will (represented by the downward arrows in Eccles' Figure 4), the human has free will, even if these acts of will are ineffective and do not cause neurons to discharge. This is a parallelist position, and not the position of the interactionist

Eccles, who says:

> If in willing an action one does not *effectively* influence the patterns of neuronal activity in the cerebral cortex and so bring about the desired discharge of motor pyramidal cells, then free will is an illusion, however subtle the philosophical arguments (this volume, p. 103).

It is, therefore, most accurate to say that Eccles' reason for positing the conscious self is to explain free *agency*, not free will.

This precision helps us to uncover fallacies in some of Eccles' arguments. He says: "That we have free will is a fact of experience" (this volume, p. 101), meaning, one would suppose, that since each of us has the experience of free will, each of us has free will, and therefore a conscious self that does the willing. This is a familiar and well-criticized argument. Unless freedom is a feeling, "I feel free" does not entail "I am free," any more than does, "I feel imprisoned" entail "I am imprisoned." And if freedom is just a feeling, it hardly seems worth having. Free *agency*, on the other hand—the ability to act freely—is worth having. But its existence cannot be established by introspecting our feelings, or experiences. "I feel that I am acting freely" does not entail "I am acting freely." Free agency is not a "fact of experience."

Because he fails to distinguish between free will and free agency, Eccles does not see that we can infer nothing about the existence or nature of free agency from "experience."

> It has been known for many years that electrical stimulation of the motor cortex of conscious subjects evokes actions which are disowned by the subject. As Penfield reports: "When a subject observes such an action, he remarks, 'That is due to something done to me and is not done by me.'" Evidently a motor action emanating from the motor cortex in response to voluntary command has some concomitants that are not present when a similar action is artificially evoked from the motor cortex (this volume, p. 118).

There is a sense in which Eccles' conclusion—stated in the last sentence—is trivially true. The concomitant of the voluntary action that is not present when a similar action is artificially evoked is Penfield's electrode! Of course, Eccles does not intend this trivial interpretation. Plainly he thinks that some important inference can be based on the subject's experience of unfreedom. This is an error. Suppose Penfield had been clever enough to evoke the subject's motor response together with the remark, "that is something done by me" (there is no reason to think this impossible). Should we then infer that the subject's action was free? Obviously not. That the subject *feels* free (or unfree) is poor evidence that he *is* free (or unfree).

This point can also be illustrated by the split-brain experiments of which Eccles makes so much. The split-brain subject says of his left hand, "I cannot work with that hand," "I just can't feel anything or do anything with it." And all the while the subject is drawing geometrical figures! Should we infer that the drawing is unfree? Plainly, we should not. The subject's actions (drawing) are remarkably similar to actions that in normal subjects we call "free," or, at least, "voluntary." It is therefore just as reasonable to infer that free or voluntary actions do not require an experience of freedom, and therefore do not require the operation of Eccles' conscious self.

If we should not infer that a subject's actions are free from the fact that he feels (experiences) them to be free, it is plainer still that we should not infer that they are free in Eccles' sense. Free action, according to Eccles, is action ultimately caused by acts of will on the part of an immaterial conscious self. Why an *immaterial* conscious self? To develop this query, consider the following simple modification of Eccles' diagram (Figure 4). The circle "hovering" above the dominant hemisphere is taken to represent another part (or system) of the *brain*, separately drawn for illustrative purposes. The downward arrows (as well as the upward) are taken to represent the action of neurons on other neurons; hence, acts of will are discharges of special neurons. These discharges are the "experiences of freedom" subjects often have. And the reason such experiences are sometimes deceptive is that the neuronal discharges are sometimes ineffective. In this model, the conscious self has become a material system. Why doesn't Eccles adopt this materialist model? Won't it explain free action as well as his immaterialist model?

The answer requires distinguishing two versions of the materialist model: the determinist and the indeterminist versions. The determinist holds that every event has a cause. Consequently, on the determinist version, volitional discharges of neurons are caused by the discharges of other neurons. Eccles is an indeterminist; he holds that some events do not have causes, namely, those acts of will that cause free action. So, he would reject the determinist version. But there is an indeterminist version of the materialist model, on which the volitional discharges of neurons are uncaused. A volition is, in this view, the *spontaneous* discharge of a neuron. Eccles would reject this view because it allows that some physical events—"volitional" neuronal discharges—are uncaused. Eccles wishes to remain a determinist in the physical–physiological sphere while holding that volitions are uncaused. To do so consistently, he must hold that volitions are nonphysical events and locate them in an immaterial soul (conscious self). It thus seems that he can have his cake and eat it.

But can he? The major motivation for determinism in the

physical sphere is our hope that physical events are predictable, hence manipulable, hence subject to rational control. If physical events are caused, they are predictable; if uncaused, then unpredictable. The spontaneous discharge of a neuron is uncaused and *completely* unpredictable. The discharge of a neuron which is caused by an uncaused mental volition is not completely unpredictable, since it can be predicted from the volition. But the discharge is *highly* unpredictable (as highly unpredictable as it can be without being completely unpredictable), since it cannot be predicted until the causing volition has occurred. On Eccles' indeterminist immaterialist model, neuronal events are only slightly less unpredictable than they are on the indeterminist materialist model; not enough, it would seem, to compensate for the disadvantages in the immaterialist model.

Immaterialism is therefore not required to explain (or allow for) free agency: one can hold that free actions are caused by uncaused physical events. But there is a deeper point to be made. Many philosophers believe that indeterminism is not required to explain (or allow for) free agency. This tradition was begun by Hume and reaffirmed by Schlick and the logical positivists. Such philosophers are called soft determinists, or compatibilists, since they hold that there is no incompatibility between the view that every event—every action included—has a cause and the view that some actions are free. Free action is defined by these philosophers as action with a special kind of cause. For one thing, the cause must be internal to the brain, so an action caused by an electrode touched to the cortex is unfree. Eccles makes vague objections to this view, but he fails to cite the most important one. How does the compatibilist distinguish between free and unfree actions where both are internally caused? The actions of a normal person are caused by neuronal discharges in his cerebral cortex; but so are the actions of an epileptic during a seizure. What justifies our calling the one type of action free, and the other type unfree? The compatibilists have never answered this objection. And their failure to do so is the most important argument in favor of indeterminism.

But the indeterminist view is no less objectionable. In contrast to compatibilism, it provides a clear definition of a free action; namely, a free action is one caused by uncaused volition. But it forces us to hold that if any action is free, then some events are uncaused. And it is an article of scientific faith that every event has a cause. To believe otherwise is to open the door to superstition and magic. This objection will not impress those who believe that science has limits and cannot enmesh everything in its causal web. For them, we provide a second, much more important objection.

On the indeterminist definition, a free action is one caused by an uncaused volition; whether the volition be identified as a spontaneous neuronal discharge, or a spontaneous mental act of will. The volition is not only not caused by any physical event, such as a neuronal discharge, it is not caused by any mental event either. Hence, it is not caused by a wish, desire, thought, purpose, plan, decision, or intention. The volition is therefore either an unpredictable, random event, or one that can be predicted only by statistical methods without certainty. Consider the flexing of my finger. If this action is free on the indeterminist definition, then I do not know when I will flex my finger. If the finger flexing is free, then I do not think about flexing it, nor do I wish, desire, plan, decide, or intend to flex it; or, if I do any of these, they have nothing to do with my flexing it. Free agency in this sense is of no use to me. Indeed, it is a liability, since free actions are, apparently, among the class of actions over which I have no control.

Compatibilism (soft determinism) seems to imply, by contrast, that I do have control over my free actions. For these are a subclass of the class of actions that are affected by my wishes, desires, thoughts, purposes, plans, decisions, and intentions. Since compatibilism also adheres to the scientific article of faith that every event has a cause, it seems much the more preferable view.

The above treatment of the advantages and disadvantages of determinism and indeterminism is standard among contemporary philosophers, but it is not conclusive. How is the issue finally to be resolved? Is neurophysiology of any help at all? Many contemporary philosophers believe that developments in neurophysiological science (and perhaps science in general) have no bearing on such large and enduring metaphysical issues as dualism versus materialism and freedom versus determinism. Eccles believes otherwise. There is at least one point where he seems to be right and the philosophers wrong.

Neurophysiological data do seem to have bearing on the truth or falsity of compatibilism. If the view that some actions are free and some unfree is compatible with the view that every event has a cause, then there must be some difference between the causal neurophysiological mechanism of actions we call free and that of the actions we call unfree. Neurophysiological evidence that there is no such difference is evidence that compatibilism is false. Neurophysiological evidence that there is such a difference is partial evidence that compatibilism is true. Partial, because the difference must be of the right sort, i.e., must correspond to the presence and absence of wishes, thought, plans, decisions, etc. Neurophysiologists may be developing evidence of the latter sort—partial evidence that compatibilism is true. Curiously, this evidence is cited by the indeterminist Eccles in support of his own position.

Kornhuber and his associates recorded brain potentials in a subject who was instructed to flex his finger "at will." They discovered, over a wide area of the cerebral surface, "a slowly rising negative potential, called the *readiness potential*" which usually "began almost as long as 0.8s before the onset of the movement" (Figure 5, this volume p. 116). Eccles says:

> These experiments at least provide a partial answer to the question: What is happening in my brain at a time when a willed action is in process of being carried out? It can be presumed that during the readiness potential there is a developing specificity of the patterned impulse discharges in neurones so that eventually there are activated the correct motor cortical areas for bringing about the required movement. It can be regarded as the neuronal counterpart of the voluntary command. The surprising feature of the readiness potential is its wide extent and gradual build-up. Apparently, at the stage of willing a movement, there is a very wide influence on the patterns of neuronal operation, or, as we will consider below, on the patterns of module operation. Eventually this immense neuronal activity concentrates onto the pyramidal cells in the proper zones of the motor cortex for carrying out the required movement (this volume, pp. 115–116).

These experiments provide some evidence for the soft determinist, or compatibilist, view, on which free (voluntary) action is action with a special sort of cause. The special cause may be the readiness potential, the developing specificity of patterned impulse discharges, the concentration of neuronal activity onto the cells that produce the free movement.

The Kornhuber results are regarded by Eccles, however, as evidence for his own indeterminist view.

> My hypothesis would be that the highly specialized modules in the regions of the brain in liaison with the conscious self . . . can function as extremely sensitive detectors of consciously willed influences, at least when they are poised at special levels of activity . . . As a consequence, the willing of a movement produces the gradual evolution of neuronal responses over a wide area of frontal and parietal cortices of both sides, so giving the readiness potential. Furthermore, the mental act that we call willing must guide or mold this unimaginably complex neuronal performance of the liaison cortex so that eventually it "homes in" onto the appropriate modules of the motor cortex and brings about discharges of their motor pyramidal cells . . . (this volume, pp. 116–117).

It is just as reasonable to construe the Kornhuber results as evidence for a materialist, determinist view as it is to construe them as evidence for Eccles' immaterialist, indeterminist view. There is no compelling reason to suppose, as Eccles does, that the readiness potential is caused by a "mental act of willing." Willing on the materialist view is some neural process, and we can suppose that this neural process generates the readiness potential. Perhaps the neural event of willing is the discharge of one, or a few, neurons. If so, willing may generate the readiness potential in the manner hypothesized by Eccles. The point is that willing need not be regarded as an immaterial, uncaused event. Eccles would undoubtedly respond that if willing is a neural event then it is caused by other neural events; which is contradictory, since willing is by definition an uncaused event. The reply of the compatibilist (soft determinist) is that this argument merely begs the question of whether willing can be identified with a neural process having a certain kind of cause.

When I freely flex my finger, I am the agent: "I do it." We often describe such actions by saying they are done "at will." Such ordinary descriptions lead Eccles to say that when a subject flexes his finger freely, his mental willing "guides" the neuronal discharges in his cortex so that they "home in" on those modules of the motor cortex whose discharge is required to actuate the muscles of the finger. Eccles is misled, according to the compatibilist. For the compatibilist, "doing it myself," or doing it "at will," is the effecting of the finger movement by a certain kind of cause—call it a "volition" or "act of will" if you must—which itself has a cause of a certain kind. The cause of my finger flexion is *my* neural activity, it is neural activity in *me*, and in that sense it is *I* who move my finger. Now, since some of my actions are caused by my neural activity and are nonetheless *un*free, the compatibilist must distinguish between those of my neural causes that effect free action and those that do not. The Kornhuber results may help to make this distinction. In any case, they provide just as much evidence for the compatibilist (soft determinist) view as they do for Eccles' indeterminist view.

To summarize this section, free action does not require the hypothesis of an immaterial, uncaused soul, and the experimental data do not support that hypothesis.

DISPROVING CARTESIANISM

In this paper it has been argued that all human behavior can be emitted by a body unaided by an immaterial soul, that the explanation of human behavior does not require the hypothesis of an immaterial soul. It may be of value to see just how unpersuasive this argument can be to a committed Cartesian. The dualist points to some feature (creativity, for example) of a certain human behavior (speech, for example) and says: "There, you see? Only a being with a soul is capable of that sort of behavior." And the materialist replies: "No, such behavior can be generated by a sufficiently advanced mechanical brain." How can we resolve the dispute? By philosophical argumentation? By theoretical scientific considerations? By experiment? Suppose a friend and I encountered an unfamiliar machine picking up steel girders and riveting them into place as the superstructure of a building. My friend says: "It must have an operator; only a machine with a person controlling it is capable of doing things like that." And I reply: "No, a sufficiently advanced automaton could do just what that contraption is doing." How could the dispute be resolved?

Surely not by philosophical—i.e., *a priori*—argument. *A priori* argument can no more determine whether a crane-riveter automaton is possible than it could have determined whether the vacuum cleaner or washing machine is possible. Similarly, it would seem, *a priori* argument cannot determine whether a speaking automaton is possible.

Theoretical scientific considerations, on the other hand, are relevant. Suppose I could show my friend automata in operation that are rather like, in what they do, the crane-riveter contraption we encountered, and could produce a theoretical description (blueprint?) of an automaton that can do exactly what the crane-riveter does. This would afford considerable evidence that such automata are possible. Similarly, it would seem, if we could show the dualist a working automaton that emits language rather like human speech, and could produce a theoretical description (a computer program?) of an automaton that speaks exactly as humans do, then we would have produced considerable evidence that a speaking automaton is possible, and that speech does not require a soul. It would not be conclusive evidence, because the theory in whose terms the description of the automaton was given might be incorrect; it could be that on a correct theory the automaton is theoretically impossible.

A more expensive way of settling the dispute is by trying to construct an automaton that does what the crane-riveter does. If we succeed, then, by definition, we have shown that a crane-riveter automaton is possible. Note that we have not shown that the particular crane-riveter we encountered is an automaton: *that* one may have an operator. If we fail to construct a crane-riveter automaton, we have not thereby shown that such automata are impossible. There were, one would suppose, many unsuccessful attempts to construct an automatic washing machine. Fortunately, the would-be inventors did not conclude that such automata were impossible. Similarly, if computer scientists succeed in constructing a speaking automaton (in "simulating human speech") they will, of course, have shown that speaking automata are possible, that speech can be emitted by devices without souls. Note that they will not have shown that human beings do not have souls. But they will have shown that it is not *necessary* to hypothesize the soul in explaining human speech. If computer scientists fail to construct speaking automata, they will not thereby have shown that such automata are impossible.

The direct method of settling the dispute is to discover whether the crane-riveter contraption has an operator, or is rather an automaton. If we discover that the contraption has no operator, then we have of course discovered that it is possible for such contraptions to have no operator, and the dispute is settled. But if we discover that the contraption has an operator, the dispute remains unsettled. For it may still be possible to build machines that do without an operator what this one does. Note that it may be quite difficult to determine whether the machine has an operator. That there is a person in the cab is not definitive; he may be a featherbedder who has absolutely nothing to do with the operation of the machine. That there is no person in the cab is also not definitive; the machine may be operated by remote control or radio. Similarly, if we discover that the human body has no soul, we will have discovered that human behavior can be emitted by an automaton. And if we discover that the human body has a soul, the question of whether human behavior can be emitted by an automaton will remain unsettled.

But how can we discover whether the human body has a soul? When we examine the interior of the human body, we find no operator. This in itself shows nothing, since the operator may be influencing the body from a distance by some radio-like process. Eccles makes precisely this suggestion when he says:

> I would postulate that in the liaison areas these neuronal patterns of module activity are the receiving stations or antennae for the ongoing operations in the consciousness of World 2 [the conscious self] as illustrated in Figure 4 (this volume, p. 117).

Therefore, to establish that the brain is not being influenced by a soul from a distance, we must show either that the body has no device for receiving such distant influences, or that such distant influences have no way of propagating themselves to the brain. Establishing either point is enormously difficult.

Proving that the brain is not influenced by a soul is rather like trying to prove that God does not intervene in the physical universe. To prove the latter conclusively we would have to show that every physical event is caused by some other physical event rather than by God. And how will we do that? It is practically impossible (logically impossible if the physical universe is infinitely large) simultaneously to examine every event in the physical universe. Similarly, to prove conclusively that the brain is not influenced by a soul, we would have to show that every brain event is caused by some other brain or physical event. We would have to show that the discharge of every neuron is caused either by the discharge of some other neuron or by some other physical event. And how will we do that? It is practically impossible—and probably always will be so—simultaneously to monitor the activity of every neuron.

Nevertheless, there comes a point at which the hypothesis that God intervenes in the physical universe, even though it cannot conclusively be disproved, becomes unreasonable. The hypothesis that the soul intervenes in the physical system called the brain becomes unreasonable at a much earlier stage of scientific investigation, since the brain is a finite, relatively small system. In the opinion of the author, that stage has been achieved. Chimpanzees are capable of language that is very like a primitive human language. Computers are being built that can respond to human language in humanlike language. Neurophysiological investigations have so far failed to uncover any neural events not caused by physical events. There is, in short, a mountain of evidence that all human and animal behavior is caused by neural events, and that every neural event is caused by some physical event. The evidence is not conclusive, but it rarely is even in the best of science. In the face of what evidence we do have, it is unscientific to believe that the soul acts on the body.

The same sort of evidence cannot be used to disprove the epiphenomenalist theory that the body acts on the soul, since the effects of this action are immaterial. Such effects leave the physical universe just as it is. Nor can this sort of evidence be used to disprove the parallelist theory that each human being has a soul that neither acts upon nor is acted upon by the body. It is not clear that the parallelist theory can be disproved by empirical evidence of *any* kind. (Whether it can is an unsettled question in philosophy.) But this issue is irrelevant to present concerns. Parallelism and epiphenomenalism are of no use to a physical scientist. Since, on these theories, the soul does not act on physical and biological systems, the soul cannot be employed as a hypothesis to explain the behavior or internal operations of any of these systems. If my soul does not act on my body, then it does not generate my intelligent behavior, nor my conscious behavior, nor my free (voluntary) behavior.

Interactionist dualism (the theory that the body and an immaterial soul act on one another) would be useful, but, as we have seen, it has no scientific basis. Eccles should confess to this, and cease practicing on us the delusion that neurophysiological investigations can confirm the existence of the soul.

Eccles occasionally betrays religious and political motivations for his dualism (not altogether surprising in light of the history of the position). For example, commenting on the views of B. F. Skinner, as contained in the latter's widely excoriated book, *Beyond Freedom and Dignity*, Eccles says:

> This type of behaviorism leads to a caricature of man—beyond freedom and dignity—that ignores the personal experiences that for each of us is the primary reality. It can appeal only to the philosophically naive and to those seeking the power that devolves from the absolute control of man (1974, pp. 89–90).

In these same pages we find, what we would expect, that Eccles rejects, not merely Skinnerian behaviorism, but all forms of behaviorism and materialism, including the recent psychoneural identity hypothesis.

Eccles seems to be echoing the old complaint that materialism degrades us by placing us on a level with animals and machines and plant and rocks. It degrades us only if we begin with a degraded conception of animals, machines, plants, and rocks. It is possible to be a materialist while holding that all life is sacred. It is even possible to be a materialist while holding the more profound view that all *being* is sacred (although this view is usually associated with monism). Given the political uses to which dualism has sometimes been put (justification of cruel treatment of animals, for instance) one might even suppose that materialism is the more humane view, in the broad sense of the term (as in "the humane society"). But this would be a mistake. Dualism is humane in this sense as long as it concedes that animals, too, have souls: feelings, desires, purposes, thoughts, consciousness, rights—the same rights to life and to absence of pain that we accord humans. Its refusal to make this concession seems, to this author, to be the product of human vanity.

REFERENCES

Eccles, J. C. (1974): Cerebral activity and consciousness. In: *Studies in the Philosophy of Biology: Reduction and Related Problems.* Ed. by F. J. Ayala and T. Dobzhansky, Berkeley: University of California Press.

Descartes, R. (1967): *The Philosophical Works of Descartes* Vol. 1. Ed. by E. S. Haldane
    and G. R. T. Ross, New York: Dover Publications.
Gunderson, K. (1971): *Mentality and Machines.* Garden City: Doubleday.
Sperry, R. W. (1969): A modified concept of consciousness. *Psychol. Rev.* **76,** 532–536.
Winograd, T. (1973): Research in natural language. *Computer* **6,** 25–30.

5 How Dogmatic Can Materialism Be?

JOHN C. ECCLES

In the preceding paper, Dr. Savage's technique is the classical one of erecting a straw man which he then proceeds to demolish. It would be tiresome to respond to every criticism. Instead I restrict myself to a few test cases.

For his introduction, we find a superficial account of the Cartesian hypothesis of the dualism of soul and body. This is a curtain raiser for the statement, "In the light of these familiar difficulties, it is a bit surprising to discover in our midst the ghost of Descartes, embodied in that intelligent machine known as Sir John Eccles"; hence the title! Dr. Savage even admits that many contemporary scientists are Cartesians and wonders why. Such wondering may lead to wisdom, since the list of neuroscientists would include Sherrington, Penfield, Russell Brain, Thorpe, Walsh, as well as the philosphers Popper and Polten, and the psychologist Beloff.

In the section on *Interaction*, it appears that Dr. Savage is out of his depth. When he tries to write of recent discoveries in the neural sciences, the result is replete with errors and misunderstandings. Further, throughout the discussion, I deliberately refrained from using the theological term "soul." In the whole of my discussion and my writing, I used the philosophical words "conscious self" and "pure ego," rather

JOHN C. ECCLES·State University of New York at Buffalo

than the word "soul," which Savage uses satirically. Savage's attack is, in fact, just a rehash of the standard beliefs of the faith of materialist monism. One has read it all so many times before. It really is reassuring to me to find there is not one criticism that I am unfamiliar with!

I am attacked on the grounds that I hint of a solution of how the will acts on neurones; but I do not claim that I have a solution of the mind–brain interaction in its special aspect of the free-will problem. The statement that I make is: "Free will is often denied on the grounds that you can't explain it, that it involves happenings inexplicable by present-day physics and physiology." To that I reply that our inability may stem from the fact that physics and physiology are still not adequately developed in respect of the immense patterned complexity of neuronal operation that can be imaginatively appreciated to some small degree from the tremendously simplified illustrations of Figures 1, 2, 3, and 4. The subtlety and the immense complexity of the patterns written in space and time by this "enchanted loom" of Sherrington's and the emergent properties of this system are beyond any levels of investigation by physics or physiology at the present time, as I have argued in my book *Facing Reality* (Eccles, 1970)—and perhaps for a long time to come.

It should be apparent to philosophers of science that fundamental problems are not usually solved by one brilliant flash of scientific insight. Instead, the scientific effort is to define the problem more clearly by attempting to understand the physical conditions basic to the problem under consideration. In the old-fashioned philosophy, the mind–body problem was very crudely defined. It was Descartes' great contribution to establish that it was in fact a mind–brain problem. It is certainly important if this problem becomes further sharpened as a mind–cerebral cortex problem, or as a mind–dominant hemisphere problem, or, finally, as a mind–cortical liaison area problem. With these advances in topographical definition, there are also advances in the understanding of the structure and operation of the neuronal machinery in the cortex. No claim is made that a solution of the mind–brain problem is at hand. My claim is that the discoveries in the neural sciences in recent decades have contributed significantly to an understanding of the physical substrate upon which the mind–brain problem and the free-will problem are superposed. The denial of this claim is just a piece of obscuranticism by Dr. Savage. Furthermore, the attack to which I am subjected in this article is based on dogmatic faith in the deterministic physics of 19th-century vintage. There is no reference to such problems of modern physics as the principle of indeterminacy or to the paradoxes involved in trying to understand the ultimate nature of matter. Who is to predict that a deeper understanding of physics will not give a new conceptual base for the formulation of the mind–brain problems? I marshal these statements against the materialist dogmas of the last paragraph of the section *Interaction*.

The section on *Intelligent Behavior* is devoted to linguistic performances of chimpanzees and computers. I am no more impressed by contemporary computer magic and computer magicians than I am by magic and magicians of other ages. Science fiction may be good for entertainment, but it must not be taken seriously. The whole section on *Intelligent Behavior* deserves no further comment. The final sentence, though, is worth quoting. "But if, as seems likely from developments in computer science and neurophysiology, the brain can do everything in the way of cognitive processing a soul can do and do it just as well, then why retain the troublesome hypothesis of the soul?" To which I reply, firstly, that the premise is untrue and, secondly, that to reject something because it is troublesome is antiscience. All scientific hypotheses arise out of troubles, and science consists in taking trouble about troublesome problems.

The section *Consciousness* is mainly devoted to a separate paper of mine (1975). There is an initial discussion about what I mean by consciousness which may be as confusing to the reader as it is to me. We are told, "Eccles insists that consciousness cannot be a function of the brain, but must be a function of the conscious self." I have never used "function" in this ambiguous sense, but I do state that the dominant linguistic hemisphere is uniquely concerned in giving conscious experiences to the subject and in mediating his willed action. It is not denied that some other consciousness may be associated with the intelligent and learned behavior of the minor hemisphere, but the absence of linguistic or symbolic communication at an adequate level prevents this from being discovered. My hypothesis is that the state of *self-consciousness* can arise only when there is an adequate level of activity in the neuronal machinery of the liaison brain in the dominant hemisphere. This hypothesis is in accord with all relevant scientific evidence, but must of course be subjected to ongoing scientific testing of the most rigorous kind.

In the section on *Free Agency* there is at the outset confusion arising from misunderstanding of the neural sciences. There is apparently a naive belief that actions can only occur when willed and that there are "consciously willed" and "unconsciously willed" actions. Much confusion is generated by this word usage. Most of our actions are automatic and not consciously willed. They should be referred to merely as unconscious actions. Even when we are willing an action, our conscious action consists as a rule in giving a general command which the neuronal machinery of the cerebral cortex, the cerebellum, and associated nuclear regions refines to a skilled, smooth response by unconscious action of the most complex kind. There is now an immense literature on this motor control. Most of the philosophical arguments and criticisms of this section would have to be scrapped in the light of this scientific knowledge.

It is time that philosophers talking on free agency of human action inform themselves on the science of motor control. The necessity for this is particularly evident in the misunderstandings that arise when Dr. Savage is discussing Kornhuber's experiments. For example, "There is no compelling reason to suppose, as Eccles does, that the readiness potential is caused by a 'mental act of willing.' " To which I reply: Ask the subjects of the experiment,who are well-trained neuroscientists. I have myself discussed the experiment very fully with all of them whom I have met on many occasions. They are unanimous in stating that they experience it as a mental act at the time of the voluntary movements of their finger in Kornhuber's experiments. In fact, the very essence of the design of the experiment was that it had to be a free act initiated without any reference to any signal or to any imposed timing. Later we are told by Dr. Savage that "The cause of my finger flexion is *my* neural activity, it is neural activity in *me*, and in that sense it is *I* who move my finger." This is just the old obscurantist materialism which refuses to recognize the experience of willing because it conflicts with a dogmatic belief.

In the section on *Disproving Cartesianism* we are introduced again to the automatic crane-riveter as an analogy of human action. I wonder why Dr. Savage has concentrated so much on such an absurd analogy for the mind–brain problem.

As we near the end of Dr. Savage's paper, he commits himself to some generalizations that show his unfamiliarity with brain science as it has developed in the recent decades of this century. In comparing the brain with the physical universe, he regards it as a finite, relatively small system. He makes the following statement: "There comes a point at which the hypothesis that God intervenes in the physical universe, even though it cannot conclusively be disproved, becomes unreasonable. The hypothesis that the soul intervenes in the physical system called the brain becomes unreasonable at a much earlier stage of scientific investigation, since the brain is a finite, relatively small system. In the opinion of the author, that stage has been achieved." Does Dr. Savage not know that, even at our present primitive level of understanding of the human brain, we know it has a degree of organized complexity of a different order from anything else in the physical universe, and in fact of the whole cosmos? In expressing this opinion, Dr. Savage is making the error that one would expect of some naive critic in confusing mere mass and immensity with complexity of organization. Finally, on the basis of the quasilinguistic abilities of chimpanzees and computers and the extraordinary statement that "Neurophysical investigations have so far failed to uncover any neural events not caused by physical events," Dr. Savage concludes that "There is, in short, a mountain of evidence that all human and animal behavior is caused by neural events, and that every neural event is caused by some physical event." Would he please substitute "molehill" for "mountain" in this statement!

We are finally led to a pathetic appeal: "Interactionist dualism (the theory that the body and an immaterial soul act on one another) has no scientific basis. Eccles should confess to this, and cease practicing on us the delusion that neurophysiological investigations can confirm the existence of the soul." It is regrettable that Dr. Savage should make this accusation, which is based upon his misunderstanding. In the last paragraph, there is also much to regret. For example, why can a materialist hold that all life is sacred, or that all being is sacred, given the ordinary usage of the word "sacred"? Then we are told that political uses of dualism are discreditable relative to materialism since it justifies the cruel treatment of animals. However he qualifies this: "Dualism is humane . . . as long as it concedes that animals too have souls . . . rights, the same right to life and to absence of pain that we accord humans." I assume that Dr. Savage is referring simply to furry animals that are not used for food but as pets and as playthings in zoos. Perhaps he might also like to extend it to feathered animals. But the word "animals" is a scientific term applying to the whole of one of the great branches of biology, down to the most humble protozoan. How far down will he go?

Finally, dualists as myself are accused of human narcissism. If this accusation means that in the biological world only human beings are endowed with a self-consciousness, and with a cultural creativity, and that they are distinguished completely from animals by the ability to think logically, creatively, and imaginatively and to communicate these thoughts in every medium of cultural expression, then I am happy to admit that I am guilty of human narcissism.

The difference between Dr. Savage and me is that I seek to understand the brain–mind problem in the first place as a problem based upon scientific studies of the brain using, of course, reductionist strategies, and in the second place, as it arises in my own personal life and experience, where I am metaphysically an antireductionist. It is my experience that I have self-consciousness and that I can consciously and effectively will actions. Dr. Savage is concerned with the problem as he sees it in objective observations of others, leaving himself out of the equation. For that materialist monism is enough. I regard this materialist dogma as an ancient superstition according to which man is the victim of iron determinism as defined by nineteenth century physics.

REFERENCES

Eccles, J. C. (1970): *Facing Reality*. New York: Springer-Verlag.
Eccles, J. C. (1975): Cerebral activity and consciousness. In: *Studies in the Philosophy of Biology: Reduction and Related Problems*. Ed. by F. J. Ayala & T. Dobzhansky, Berkeley: University of California Press.

6   Introduction

The assertion that mental events have a causal relation to neural events is within a long-standing philosophical tradition. However, it is most unusual for a contemporary neuroscientist to argue, as Sperry does, that mental phenomena exert a "regulative control" on the brain's physiology. It is through "emergent interactionism" that Sperry defends what he considers to be a nondualist view that "mental events are *causes* rather than *correlates.*"

In this view, mental properties are yet undiscovered holistic and configurational properties which are "different from and more than the neural events of which they are composed." The relationships among parts have causal efficacy over and above such efficacy for the parts *per se.* Sperry considers the hierarchy from the subatomic and subnuclear levels, which are embedded within molecules, to the brain cells, which are embedded within "the larger network properties of the circuit systems." But not all of the emergent properties at the higher levels of cerebral activity are conscious properties. Rather than the degree of complexity, it is the "operational function" which determines the conscious effect. Brain circuits may be "specifically designed to produce the particular conscious effects obtained from different brain regions." Sperry illustrates this view by considering his own split-brain research wherein the brain is surgically bisected by severing the corpus callosum which connects the cerebral hemispheres. (Under normal conditions, collosal activity ties the hemispheres together into a "single unified process.")

Sperry recognizes his conceptual difficulty in distinguishing neural events with emergent consciousness from neural events without emergent consciousness. He suggests that "a cerebral process acts as a conscious entity, not because it is spatially set apart from other cerebral activity, but because it functions organizationally as a unit." But the emergent dynamics of nerve-network and cerebral-circuit interactions "have yet to be elucidated."

It is here that a potential weakness in Sperry's account becomes apparent. One must have a conviction that neuroscience will ultimately elucidate "certain special types of cerebral events, unique as far as we know and yet to be discovered—hardly to be identified with what has heretofore been termed the neural events." It is apparent that Sperry's neuroscience still seeks a functional "seat for the soul," which a cynic might consider to be a null advance over Descartes' anatomic seat for the soul, the pineal gland. Although Sperry and Eccles converge on this issue, it is unlikely that most philosophers share their faith in a utopian science.

Sperry's emergentism is radical indeed. Although one might be prepared to accept the emergence of water from the combination of hydrogen and oxygen atoms, it is a much stronger claim that mind emerges from brain, since the ontologic status of water on the one hand and atoms of hydrogen and oxygen on the other are comparable, whereas the ontological status of mind is far different from that of brain. To pursue this point, if anything emerges from the neural parts, it would be an "emergent neural organization," just as an internal-combustion engine emerges from the interrelating of its component parts on the assembly line. But the emergent engine and the emergent neural organization appear to have "physical" properties which are different from "mental" properties. It might be argued that the question of the relationship between emergent neural organization and emergent mental phenomena is simply to reiterate the mind–brain problem all over again in a sophisticated version.

Yet, Sperry's argument has an intuitive appeal. Certainly the extraordinary complexity of the human brain provides a unique soil for the emergence of mind. Further, we experience our consciousness to be causally potent. By parsimoniously considering the inevitable consequences of the evolution of complex systems such as the human brain, emergent interactionism can account for everything that dualism accounts for. The neurosciences are indeed young, and it is likely that major *empirical* discoveries are yet to be made, and these may well prove to vindicate Sperry's argument.

6 Mental Phenomena as Causal Determinants in Brain Function

R. W. SPERRY

The central concepts concerning consciousness that I shall try to defend have already been presented in some detail (Sperry, 1952, 1964, 1965). Accordingly, I shall review them only in brief outline, devoting the bulk of the discussion to various peripheral aspects and implications that previously have had less emphasis. At the outset let me make it clear that when I refer to consciousness I mean that kind of experience that is lost when one faints or sinks into a coma. It is the subjective experience that is lacking during dreamless sleep, that may be obliterated by a blow on the head, by anoxia, or by pressure on the inner walls of the third ventricle during brain surgery. On the positive side we can include as conscious events the various sensations elicitable by a local electric current applied to the unanesthetized brain, or the pain of a phantom amputated limb, as well as most of our waking subjective experience, including self-consciousness.

I want to emphasize, however, that I shall not be concerned particularly with *self*-consciousness any more than with the conscious-

---

R. W. SPERRY·California Institute of Technology

ness of other selves, or with that of external objects, situations and events; *self*-consciousness is a separate story in itself. Nor shall I be trying to define different forms of consciousness, nor intermediate states between full awareness and the *sub*conscious or the *un*conscious. My arguments can all be referred to some clearly accepted and simple example of conscious experience, like seeing red, or hearing a musical tone, or feeling pain. The problem is difficult enough in its simplest and clearest formulation without introducing the confusion of border-line states. I assume that, if we can find an answer to the mind–brain problem in its simplest form, we shall then be able to apply the basic concepts to its more complex aspects.

For the sake of further clarification, let me specify that I shall address myself throughout to the problem of the nature of conscious-ness and the mind–brain relation as it presents *in other people's brains* primarily, rather than in my own brain. This, it is hoped, will avoid various logical entanglements that otherwise arise. This starting move is based, of course, on the assumption that other people's brains do have consciousness much like my own. Those who are not willing to accept this assumption have, I suspect, a separate problem all their own. I am not trying by this step to avoid entirely questions concerning the privacy of conscious experience. A number of different approaches to this important privacy, or first-person, property of consciousness are recognized, and I will try to outline later, in context, the explanation to which my own position leads.

Perhaps the quickest way to center in on our current interpret-ation is to compare it broadly with others. We can start by saying that ours does not belong among positions based on dualism, epipheno-menalism, or other parallelisms. We can bypass as well the radical behaviorist refusal to consider the problem, and various sophistries and epistemological gymnastics that would make it just a pseudoprob-lem or explain it away as unimportant or nonexistent. We can also bypass the traditional materialism of the hard-core reductionistic and dialectic varieties. Our position does not accord either with the inter-pretation of subjective experience as just an inner aspect of the one material brain process. It is further distinguishable from the so-called "identity theory," that version of materialism which holds that mental phenomena are *identical* with the neural events. This view does not correlate consciousness with language particularly. Finally, it is in disagreement with the position known as panpsychism in which rocks and trees and all things in the universe are held to possess conscious-ness of some sort.

AN EMERGENT THEORY

On the positive side our present view can be classified broadly as an "emergent" theory of mind that needs to be distinguished from other emergent theories advanced previously, mainly by the Gestalt school in psychology. It differs from these in several respects: first, the phenomena of subjective experience are not thought to be derived from electrical field forces or volume-conduction effects, or any metaneuronal by-product of cerebral activity. Our view relies on orthodox neural-circuit and related physiological properties (Sperry, 1952; 1953; Sperry & Miner, 1955). Second, there is no assumption of the need for an isomorphic or topological correspondence between the events of perceptual experience and corresponding events in the brain. I have conceived the mental properties to be *functional* derivatives that get their meaning from the way in which the brain circuits and related processes operate and interact, rather than in terms of isomorphic correlations (Sperry, 1952). Reference to "spatiotemporal patterning" of brain activity is safe as far as it goes, but this term fails to connote the operational derivation of the conscious properties that I have tried to emphasize. Third, the conscious subjective properties in our present view are interpreted to have causal potency in regulating the course of brain events; that is, the mental forces or properties exert a regulative control influence in brain physiology. The subjective conscious experience on these terms becomes an integral part of the brain process, rather than a correlated phenomenon as conceived by Köhler (Köhler and Held, 1949) and others. The mental events are *causes* rather than *correlates*. In this respect our view can be said to involve a form of mental interactionism, except that there is no implication of dualism or other parallelism in the traditional sense. The mental forces are direct causal emergents of the brain process.

When I initially stated this view in 1965 one had to search a long way in philosophy, and especially in science, to find anyone who would put into writing that mental forces or events are capable of causing physical changes in an organism's behavior or its neurophysiology. With rare exceptions writings in behavioral science dealing with perception, imagery, emotion, cognition, and various other mental phenomena were very cautiously phrased to conform with prevailing materialist–behaviorist doctrine. Care was taken to be sure that the subjective phenomena should not be implied to be more than passive correlates or inner aspects of brain events, and especially to avoid any implication that the mental phenomena might interact causally with the physical brain process. Those few who did subscribe earlier to the theory of psychophysical interaction were such extreme dualists that little heed was paid them in behavioral science. Once we could show how mental events can causally influence neural events in a compromise formulation that does not violate the principles of scientific explanation, the long-standing resistance to mental–physical interaction began to decline. It is only since then that mental imagery, for example, has been able to gain popular acceptance as an explanatory construct. Today it becomes increasingly difficult to differentiate some of the closely related positions on these matters, and one must go back to the "pre-'65" versions in order to make clear distinctions.

COMPARISON WITH IDENTITY THEORY

Our "emergent interactionist" position was described as a compromise between dualistic mentalism and pre-'65 materialism, indicating that it would not be difficult to stretch either mentalism or materialism, including identity theory, to encompass the emergent interpretation. I say this despite the declaration of Feigl (1967) that,

> If future scientific research should lead to the adoption of one or another form of emergentism (or—horrible dictu!—dualistic interactionism), then most of my reflections will be reduced to the status of a logical (I hope not illogical!) exercise within the frame of an untenable presupposition.

I was unable to find in pre-'65 identity theory anything to distinguish the conscious from the many nonconscious properties that seem to comprise the subsystems of any given neural event, nor did I find a distinction between neural events that involve consciousness and those that lack consciousness, as in the cerebellum or spinal cord. In general the term "neural events," as this term had been used thus far in science and philosophy, hardly included the holistic conscious properties that I think of as the mental properties of the brain process. These special mental properties have not been described objectively as yet in any form. They are holistic configurational properties that have yet to be discovered. We predict that, once they have been discovered and understood, they will be best conceived of as being different from and more than the neural events of which they are composed. In our own view, colors, sounds, sights, taste, smell, pain, and all the other phenomena of the world of inner mental experience are given due recognition as phenomena in their own right. Rather than being identical to the neural events, as is generally understood, they are emergents of these events. To say that the mental experience is identical to the brain process is analogous, in our interpretation, to saying that the physiological brain process is itself identical to the chemical events that compose it, or that these chemical events are in turn identical to their atomistic and electron–proton events, etc. It is like saying that the upcoming ninth wave at Laguna is nothing but another uplift and fall of H_2O and other molecules.

I take the stand that wholes and their properties are real phenomena, and that these and their causal potency are just as important as the properties of the parts to which the reductionist position likes to give prior, or even sole, recognition. This is to say, that the relationships of the parts to each other in time and space are of critical importance in causation and in determining the nature and properties of all entities. It is a pragmatic interpretation of what is real and meaningful.

In trying to see that the pattern properties are just as real and important as are the properties of the parts, it may help to recognize that the properties of the parts are themselves in turn holistic properties of subsystems at a different level. The reductionist approach that would always explain the whole in terms of the parts leads to an infinite regress in which eventually everything is held to be explainable in terms of essentially nothing. Let me repeat that the thing to remember in this connection is that, in the causal interplay between systems and their surroundings, the spatial and the temporal relationships of the constituent parts of a system have in themselves important causal efficacy over and above the properties of the parts *per se*.

Even a pile of stones (Wimsatt, 1971) will be a very different entity with very different properties depending on how the given set of stones happens to be piled together. When hit by a car or jiggled by an earthquake, different patterns of the whole may exhibit properties that supersede those of the parts in determining the causal consequences. There is no way in which the relationships of the parts in space and time for any given entity can be reduced to the properties of the parts alone.

A SIMPLE APPROACH

The way in which mental phenomena are conceived to control the brain's physiology can be understood very simply in terms of the chain of command in the brain's hierarchy of causal controls (Sperry, 1965). It is easy to see that the forces operating at subatomic and subnuclear levels within brain cells are molecule-bound, and are superseded by the encompassing configurational properties of the brain molecules in which the subatomic elements are embedded; that is, the nuclear and other subatomic elements are pushed and hauled about in chemical interactions by the enveloping molecular properties. In the same way the properties of the brain molecules are enveloped by the dynamics of cellular organization, and the properties of the brain cells are in turn superseded by the larger network properties of the circuit systems in which they are embedded.

At the apex of the brain's organizational hierarchy are found the large cerebral processes that mediate mental activity. These large cerebral events as entities have their own dynamics and associated properties that causally determine their interactions. These top-level systems' properties supersede those of the various subsystems they embody.

Only *some* of the dynamic holistic properties that emerge in the higher levels of cerebral activity are conscious phenomena. Many others are not, even though the unconscious activities may in some cases be equally or more complex. Complexity alone is not, in our scheme, the source of the conscious qualities (Sperry, 1966). It is the operational function rather than the complexity of any given cerebral process that determines its conscious effect.

In this respect my interpretation differs from that of Teilhard de Chardin (1959). Consciousness in my view is strictly a property of brain circuits specifically designed to produce the particular conscious effects obtained from different brain regions. On these terms I see no way in which the consciousness of individuals could become coalesced into a megaconscious experience of humanity as a whole, nor any way in which the consciousness of one brain could influence that of another by a metaphysical route.

As is the case for most, or all, part–whole relationships, a mutual interdependence is recognized to exist between the neural events and the emergent mental phenomena. In other words, the brain physiology determines the mental effects and the mental phenomena in turn have causal influence on the neurophysiology. The interjection of subjective mental experience into the causal sequence of decision making on these terms brings a compromise, not only between materialism and mentalism, but also between the positions of determinism and free will. Determinism of this kind, in which subjective experience is included as a causal agent in brain function, allows degrees of freedom in any voluntary choice far above that envisaged in traditional materialism or atomistic determinism.

I have tried to tie these general principles to the example of subjective pain as it is referred to an amputated limb (Sperry, 1965). For present purposes let us make it more specifically the pain of a phantom left foot that is produced by stimulation of a sore toe in the opposite hindfoot in one of our experimental "sensory nerve cross" rats. These are rats in which the right hindfoot has become reinnervated by foreign nerves that originally had supplied the left foot (Sperry, 1943). The switch in nerve connections from left to right foot is brought about by surgical cross-union of the sciatic nerve and its branches from left to right leg in the fourth week after birth as a test of central nervous plasticity and the functional interchangeability of nerve connections. Occasionally the animals will "instinctively" chew off the denervated insensitive foot on the left, and there is also a tendency for cutaneous trophic sores to develop in the right foot while it is being reinnervated. Such a sore on the right foot heals very slowly, despite antibiotics, because these rats walk around on three legs protectively holding up the wrong foot from which the pain seems to come and thereby putting additional pressure and trauma on the sore right foot. Occasionally, as the result of an extra-hard impact or abrasion to the right foot, the rat may yip or squeak and will turn to lick, not at the sore right foot, but at the uninjured left foot when it is there, or otherwise at the amputation stump.

I choose this example to emphasize, among other things, my assumption that conscious experience is not restricted to the human species. Self-consciousness is another matter, of course, and may well be limited mainly to man with some beginnings in the higher subhuman forms. The experimental rat's false reference of pain to the amputated left foot persists throughout life, and this example thus serves to reinforce our view that the basic circuit properties responsible for conscious experience are largely determined genetically (Sperry, 1969). They may have evolved initially around sensory functions and/or around a primitive awareness with positive and negative reinforcement functions.

The main point to be brought out with this example is the contention that the animal's responses in protectively holding up the wrong foot and in yipping and licking the wrong foot are caused directly in brain function by the subjective pain property itself, rather than by the physiology of the nerve impulses or by the chemical, atomistic, or other subunit features of the brain process. The pain sensation is considered to be a real emergent phenomenon in itself.

Although built of neural events, and possibly of glial events as well, the pain sensation as a larger whole is not itself the same as the constituent neural and glial events. Nor is the subjective pain to be viewed as a mere parallel correlate of the brain process. Rather, I look upon it as a real dynamic entity in the brain activity that has an important causal role as a phenomenon itself in the stimulus–response sequence. In other words, a full objective account of the whole stimulus–response process would not be complete without including the pain as such. Although our neurophysiology is not yet sufficiently advanced to give an adequate description of the neural composition of the pain phenomenon, or of other conscious events, one assumes that this will be possible eventually as our knowledge of brain mechanisms continues to advance.

THE BISECTED BRAIN AND UNITY OF CONSCIOUSNESS

Philosophy has been concerned with the "unity of consciousness" in connection with problems relating to the nature of the self, the person, and personal identity. In our "split-brain" studies of the past two decades (Sperry, 1961, 1966, 1968, 1970a, 1973), the surgically separated hemispheres of animals and man have been shown to perceive, learn, and remember independently, each hemisphere evidently cut off from the conscious experience of the other. In man the language-dominant hemisphere further reports verbally that it is not consciously aware of the concomitant or immediately preceding mental performances of the disconnected partner hemisphere. These test performances of which the speaking hemisphere remains unaware obviously involve perception, comprehension, and in some cases nonverbal memory, reasoning, and concept formation of different kinds depending on the nature of the test task. In these and in many other respects, the split-brain animal and man behave as if each of the separated hemispheres had a mind of its own.

This division by surgery of the normally unified realm of conscious awareness into two distinct domains of conscious experience that exist in parallel, and in some cases have content that is mutually contradictory, has been subject to several different philosophical interpretations. One line of reasoning concludes that each hemisphere of the brain must have a mind of its own, not only after surgery but also in the normal intact state as well; that is, the normal individual is interpreted to be a compound of two persons, one based in each hemisphere (Bogen, 1969; Puccetti, 1973). A contrasting interpretation says that only one, the language-dominant hemisphere, remains conscious (Eccles, 1970), and thus the unity of consciousness is preserved. It is inferred that the disconnected minor hemisphere operates like an automaton or complex computer. Another view holds that consciousness is not centered in either right or left hemisphere, but in some unified metaorganizing system (MacKay, 1966), presumably in the intact brain stem. There are additional variations on these main themes (Nagel, 1971).

The state of our progress in understanding the nature of consciousness is nicely illustrated in the diversity of positions seriously supported here and currently among our colleagues. At least one of our conferees (like Whitehead, Waddington, and others) maintains that rocks have consciousness (Globus, 1973). In other words, panpsychism still lives! At the other extreme, another of our members would deny conscious experience, not only to rocks and plants, but even to the minor hemisphere of the human brain (Eccles, 1970). Others claim that each of us in the normal state operates with two distinct right and left domains of conscious awareness.

My own inclination is to see consciousness as being unified in the normal brain but largely divided in the bisected brain, depending on the depth and extent of the surgery, and depending also on the nature and level of the particular conscious process in question. I would credit the neocommissures with a unifying role in conscious activity under normal conditions that in effect serves to tie the conscious function of the hemispheres together across the midline into a single unified process. The callosal activity thus becomes part of the conscious event. The fiber systems uniting right and left hemispheres are viewed as being not essentially different in their relation to consciousness from those uniting front and back or other areas within the same hemisphere. I know of no evidence as yet that says we must exclude white-matter neural events from consciousness, or, in other words, that conscious effects are confined to grey-matter dynamics. This interpretation does not exclude the possibility that the conscious processes in left and right hemispheres may function separately in the undivided brain under exceptional conditions, and particularly where pathology tends to depress commissural function.

Surgical separation of the hemispheres, especially the deeper bisections we perform in animals, I have interpreted as resulting in the creation of two distinct domains of consciousness. This says nothing about *self*-consciousness. It remains to be determined how much, if any, self-consciousness is present in the disconnected minor hemisphere of man. However, preliminary findings from experiments in progress in collaboration with Zaidel support the conclusion that the disconnected minor hemisphere does in fact exhibit characteristic self-conscious reactions to pictures of itself, showing appropriate emotional displays in different contexts.

Our interpretation does not preclude a retention in the bisected brain of a right–left unity in some aspects and levels of conscious experience. This is assured in part by bilateral sensory representation in each hemisphere as is the case, for example, with facial sensibility. We presume, however, by extrapolation, that these unified "whole-face" experiences in each hemisphere are cut off from their counterparts in the opposite hemisphere.

The structure of the conscious cerebral process is inferred to be such that some aspects of conscious experience may be separated by commissurotomy, while others, united through bilateral representation and/or brain stem mechanisms, remain intact (Sperry, 1965, 1968, 1973). In most of our work we have naturally emphasized the more interesting and striking aspects of consciousness that are separated by the surgery and which predominate in the kinds of test tasks we employ. However, I have also tried to stress the presence of many unifying factors. The possibility remains that some elemental components of consciousness stay unified in the split brain, even in those tests where the bulk of the conscious content is clearly divided.

On these terms, neural activity transmitted through the corpus callosum becomes part of the conscious brain process. However, in order to properly comprehend the critical holistic properties of the conscious process, one would have to include the associated activity on both sides. In the callosal fiber systems and those associated cortical mechanisms on either side, we probably come as close as anywhere in the brain to a direct grip on psychoneural relations. Consider, for example, the normally unified perception of the whole visual field and its division down the vertical midline that is produced by midline commissurotomy.

As knowledge of brain function and the mind–brain relation advances, one would anticipate that terms like "mind" and "person" will have to be redefined, or at least more precisely defined. Already it makes little sense, employing past definitions, to argue about how many "minds" or "persons" are present in the bisected brain. What is needed is better understanding of the functional relationships between the neural mechanisms that are divided and those that are not, and their respective roles in the generation of conscious experience.

Following our present emergent approach in which mental phenomena are conceived to be determined by—and built from—neural events, I infer that the neural mechanisms from which the mental effects in each hemisphere are generated may have common undivided brain stem and perhaps cerebellar components, which may or may not have any conscious properties in themselves, but which are essential substructure constituents of the conscious experience. Particularly important among the undivided brain stem components are the neural mechanisms of attention.

Thus if one were to diagram schematically the structure of mind after cerebral commissurotomy it would be crudely Y-shaped, containing a common stem with left and right upper arms in each hemisphere. Each hemisphere contains the representation of a bilateral body schema in which the ipsilateral limb extremities are present, but fainter and more crudely depicted. The external surround also is bilaterally represented. It is much better for the contralateral side, especially in vision, but the ipsilateral half of space is not absent. Thus each disconnected hemisphere retains the anatomical substrate for a unified self in a bilateral surround, and presumably its functional correlates. Each hemispheric representation is based in and functionally dependent upon intact brain stem mechanisms that are in part bilateral and, of course, remain intact in the human commissurotomy patients.

One can ask what separates the conscious part of the brain process from its lower level nonconscious foundations. Also, for any given stimulus–response sequence, what separates the nonconscious sensory input on the one side and the motor output on the other from the more central conscious portion of the total activity? Similarly, among the higher cerebral functions, what kind of boundary or interface do we picture between processes that have conscious properties and those that do not? The answer is that we do not picture anything separating the conscious from the unconscious neural events—aside from organizational coherence. No interface or other definite boundary is imagined to be interposed between the two.

Although the holistic properties are spoken of as encompassing or enveloping the constituent neural events, the implication is not that of an enveloping surface film or electrical potential difference or other interface, but only that of smaller neural events being caught up in the dynamics of larger neural events. A cerebral process acts as a conscious entity, not because it is spatially set apart from other cerebral activity, but because it functions organizationally as a unit. Presumably the conscious process may be interwoven with, and may share active components with, other brain processes that do not reach conscious awareness. The holistic properties are not to be conceived in simple spatial, volume, or dimension terms but rather in terms of nerve-network and cerebral-circuit interactions, the emergent dynamics of which have yet to be elucidated, especially for the upper, conscious levels of brain function.

Normally, with the neocommissures intact, neural events in right and left upper arms of our schematized Y substrate of conscious-ness become merged into a unified conscious brain process. The crite-rion for unity is an operational one; that is, the right and left compo-nents, coalesced through commissural communication, function in brain dynamics as a unit. This is illustrated in the unified visual perception of a stimulus figure flashed tachistoscopically half in the left and half in the right visual half-fields. In the normal brain the right and left hemispheric components combine and function as a unit in the causal sequence of cerebral control. In the divided brain, on the other hand, each hemispheric component gets its own separate causal effect as a distinct entity.

PRIVACY OF SUBJECTIVE EXPERIENCE

The objective description of pain or of other conscious phe-nomena is not expected to be the same as the subjective description. The reason, however, that an observer's understanding and description of another's subjective experience differs from the subjective experience itself is not so much because this involves a second-order representa-tion of a representation (Globus, 1973), but for a more basic reason involving the nature of the causal relationships involved. The conscious subjective qualities, as I conceive them, derive from the selective opera-tional interactions of brain events in a matrix of brain activity (Sperry, 1952, 1969). The only way an observer brain would be able to interact with and thereby experience the subjective qualities of another brain would be through an intimate communication into the interior of the observed brain that would enable it to react to the internal operational effects and internal relations of the observed brain. An observer rela-tion is not enough; the second brain must be in an intimately involved relation with the internal operations of the first brain. Reasoning from our split-brain findings in animals and human patients, I have used the example of a corpus-callosum-type of intercommunication system in this connection (Sperry, 1969) to illustrate the kind of interaction that is required.

Just as it is possible to describe and understand the workings of an internal-combustion engine without being directly involved in the internal explosions, temperatures, and pressures, so it should be possible in principle to describe and understand in objective terms the phenomena of subjective experience. These descriptions are not yet, however, available. Essentially I was only predicting that, when these objective descriptions are eventually achieved, they will be found to be expressible in terms of emergent holistic properties of high-order cerebral processes, and further that these emergent phenomena will be seen to play a potent causal role in brain function that cannot be accounted for in terms merely of the neurophysiologic and neurochemical events as these are traditionally conceived.

In arriving at an objective understanding of the mental phenomena it will be helpful to keep the subjective qualities in mind and not be misled into thinking of these emergents of neural events as being "nothing but" or "identical to" the neural events themselves. A neural event, or, preferably, a brain event or brain process, is many things: it includes the physiology of nerve-impulse traffic, the underlying chemistry, plus all sorts of subatomic low- and high-energy physical phenomena. While these may be the stuff of neural events, they are not, as I see it, the conscious phenomena. The latter are distinct causal properties that emerge only at upper levels of the brain hierarchy and with certain special types of cerebral events, unique as far as we know and yet to be discovered—hardly to be identified with what has heretofore been termed the neural events.

Although it is not difficult, as indicated (Sperry, 1970b), to stretch the materialist or mentalist approaches of 10 years ago to incorporate these emergent interaction concepts, it is important to recognize the various differences involved. These differences have important consequences in other areas of philosophy that deal with determinism and free will (Sperry, 1964, 1965), with the concept of causation (Pols, 1971), and with the whole field of human values and the relation of scientific explanation to value judgment (Sperry, 1972). Value theory has been rather neglected in philosophy of late but could take on new importance on our present terms, especially in view of the critical significance of human value priorities in the context of mounting crisis problems.

Our interpretation of the phenomena of inner experience as causal control agents in cerebral function yields a picture of scientific determinism somewhat different from either the materialist or mentalist views. Introduction of mental phenomena into the causal sequence of brain function means, among other things, that values of all kinds, even aesthetic, spiritual and irrational, must now be recognized as positive causal factors in human decision making—as must all other components of the world of inner subjective experience. The degrees and kinds of freedom thereby introduced into the causal sequence of a volitional choice can be seen to set the human brain apart, by comparison, above all other known systems, at an apex post in the deterministic universe of science. Considered broadly, our present interpretation goes far to restore to human nature the personal dignity, freedom of choice, inner creativity, and other humanistic attributes of which it has long been deprived by the behavioristic and materialistic movements in the brain-behavior sciences. By uniting the subjective mental phenomena with the objective cerebral events within a single monistic continuum in the brain, it serves also to bridge in principle the long-standing gap between science and the humanities.

Our current interpretation leads to a unifying concept of mind, brain, and man in nature and points to a "this world" framework for human values—a framework within which science can operate. Subjective values become objective causal agents operating in the physical brain, and through the brain onto the surrounding world. As the brain process comes to be understood objectively, all mental phenomena, including the generation of values, can be treated as objective causal agents in human decision making. The origins, directive potency, and the consequences of values all become amenable, in principle, to objective scientific investigation and analysis. This applies at all levels, from that of the pleasure–pain centers and other reinforcement systems of the brain on up through the forces that mold priorities at the societal, national, and international plane. A separate science of values becomes theoretically feasible, and a matter of top priority today considering the critical control role played by the human value factor in determining world crisis conditions.

Some of the main implications can be seen to derive from the fact that conscious experience in this view is given an operational causal role in objective models of cerebral function, and thus a reason for being and for having been evolved. This is not true for the materialistic or various parallelistic interpretations in which the brain would function just as well in terms of the neural events whether or not neural events had subjective properties.

ACKNOWLEDGMENTS

Supported by USPHS grant No. MH 03372 and the Hixon fund of the California Institute of Technology.

REFERENCES

Bogen, J. E. (1969): The other side of the brain. II. An appositional mind. *Bull. L.A. Neurol. Soc.* **34,** 135–162.

Eccles, J. C. (1970): *Facing Reality:* Philosophical adventures by a brain scientist. New York: Springer-Verlag, pp. 73–80.

Feigl, H. (1967): *The Mental and the Physical.* Minneapolis: Univ. of Minnesota Press.

Globus, G. G. (1973): Unexpected symmetries in the world knot. *Science* **180,** 1129–1136.

Köhler, W. & Held, R. (1949): The cortical correlate of pattern vision. *Science* **110,** 414–419.

MacKay, D. M. (1966): Discussion. In: *Brain and Conscious Experience.* Ed. J. C. Eccles, Heidelberg: Springer-Verlag, pp. 312–313, also 422–444.

Nagel, T. (1971): Brain bisection and the unity of consciousness. *Synthese* **22,** 396–413.

Pols, E. (1971): Power and agency. *Intern. Philos. Quart.* **XI,** 293–313.

Puccetti, R. (1973): Brain bisection and personal identity. *Br. J. Philos. Sci.* **24,** pp. 339–355.

Sperry, R. W. (1943): Functional results of crossing sensory nerves in the rat. *J. Comp. Neurol.* **78,** 59–90.

Sperry, R. W. (1952): Neurology and the mind–brain problem. *Amer. Scientist* **40,** 291–312.

Sperry, R. W. (1961): Cerebral organization and behavior. *Science* **133,** 1749–1757.

Sperry, R. W. (1964): Problems outstanding in the evolution of brain function. In: *James Arthur Lecture.* New York: American Museum of Natural History.

Sperry, R. W. (1965): Mind, brain, and humanist values. In: *New Views on the Nature of Man.* Ed. by J. R. Platt, Chicago: University of Chicago Press, pp. 71–92.

Sperry, R. W. (1966): Brain bisection and mechanisms of consciousness. In: *Brain and Conscious Experience.* Ed. by J. C. Eccles, Heidelberg: Springer-Verlag, pp. 298–313.

Sperry, R. W. (1968): Mental unity following surgical disconnection of the cerebral hemispheres. In: *Harvey Lectures.* New York: Acad. Press, Inc.

Sperry, R. W. (1969): A modified concept of consciousness. *Psychol. Rev.* **76,** 532–536.

Sperry, R. W. (1970a): Perception in the absence of the neocortical commissures. *Assoc. for Research of Nervous and Mental Diseases* **48,** 123–138.

Sperry, R. W. (1970b): An objective approach to subjective experience: Further explanation of a hypothesis. *Psychol. Rev.* **77,** 585–590.

Sperry, R. W. (1972): Science and the problem of values. *Perspectives in Biology and Medicine* **16,** 115–130.

Sperry, R. W. (1973): Lateral specialization in the surgically separated hemispheres. In: *The Neurosciences: Third Study Program.* Ed. by F. O. Schmitt and F. G. Worden, Cambridge: MIT Press.

Sperry, R. W. & Miner, N. (1955): Pattern perception following insertion of mica plates into visual cortex. *J. Comp. Physiol. Psychol.* **48,** 463–469.

Teilhard de Chardin, P. (1959): *The Phenomenon of Man.* New York: Harper.

Wimsatt, W. C. (1971): Aggregativity and complexity. *Proc. 4th Int'l. Cong. for Logic, Methodology, and Philos. of Sci.*

7 Introduction

In support of Sperry's theory that mind emerges from brain, Dewan considers emergent phenomena dealt with by the engineer in control system theory. For example, out of the mutual entrainment of individual alternating-current generators in the national electrical power grid, there emerges a "virtual governor" which controls the entire system, even though the virtual governor has no palpable, locatable "physical existence." Dewan points out that this virtual governor, like Sperry's emergent consciousness, is a holistic property, has causal potency, and supervenes in the behavior of individual units.

It would seem fair to agree with Dewan that there is a "deep analogy" here which requires the most careful philosophical analysis. A discussion of the fascinating properties of "optimal control," "adaptive control," and "generalized optimal–superadaptive control," which utilize systems of extraordinary complexity and adaptive power compared to the relatively simple power grid, only serves to deepen the analogy. Certainly the output of these control systems, that is, their *behavior*, is quite typical of the output of the brain, our *behavior*, given specified input stimuli to the system. Indeed, "the mind behaves like a virtual governor." But *is* it a virtual governor? An answer to this question quickly entangles one again in the world knot.

If we were to ask as to the nature of a virtual governor, the response that it has to do with the *interrelationships* between individual generators provides at least a partially satisfactory answer, in that we can ascertain that it is the manner of interrelating which produces the special behavior of the system. We might denote that manner of interrelating with the term "virtual governor" and still remain at least partially satisfied with what we have said. *Pari passu*, it makes some sense to say that the manner of interrelating between individual neurons produces special behavior of the human system. But when we attempt to denote that manner of interrelating with the term "awareness," we are no longer satisfied with what we have said. What we term "awareness" has no obvious connection to the interrelating of "things" such as neurons. The analogy here becomes murky, despite the compelling nature of Dewan's mechanical examples.

In discussing the issues of "self" and "identity" in machines and men, Dewan makes some intriguing moves when he considers the (science fiction) possibilities of immortality for ourselves and the possibilities for conscious machines. The decision procedures with regard to these possibilities involve subjective experience, which entails internal communication between the system and itself, since for Dewan, "the loops of internal communication comprise the essential 'substance' of consciousness." It is apparent that Dewan sees no fundamental difference between man and machines; Dewan would like to attribute a very real kind of consciousness to machines, in contrast to the behaviorism wherein any real kind of consciousness is taken away from men. The grim foreboding strikes one that even if it is established that men are nothing but machines, this issue will remain: are *both* men and machines conscious, or is mind some kind of illusion for both? We suspect that, just as in the case of philosophical discourse, disputation between advanced computers, and also between such computers and their human confreres, is unlikely to settle the issue!

7 Consciousness as an Emergent Causal Agent in the Context of Control System Theory

E. M. DEWAN

The relationship between the inner awareness called consciousness and the externally observable neurophysiology of the brain is an enigma that seems to defy comprehension. Quite recently, however, a novel and enlightening viewpoint has been proposed which may well be the first sizable step toward a real understanding of this relationship. This theory, due to R. Sperry (1969), is perhaps best summarized in his own words, namely that consciousness is:

> . . . interpreted to be a direct emergent property of cerebral activity, is conceived to be an integral component of the brain process that functions as an essential constituent of the action and exerts a directive holistic form of control over the flow pattern of cerebral excitation. . . . although the mental properties in brain activity, as here conceived, do not directly intervene in neuronal physiology, they do *supervene*. . . . The individual nerve impulses and associated elemental excitatory events are obliged to operate within larger circuit-system configurations of which they as individuals are only a part. These larger functional entities have their own dynamics in cerebral activity with their own qualities and properties.

E. M. DEWAN·30 Fuller Road, Lexington, Massachusetts

They interact causally with one another at their own level as entities. It is the emergent dynamic properties of certain of these higher specialized cerebral processes that are interpreted to be the substance of consciousness.

This theory of mind can receive support from a rather surprising direction: the discipline of control system theory of engineering technology. For some reason, man often seems to reinvent principles of communication and control which were already found long ago by Nature. The purpose of this paper is to compare Sperry's idea with what exists in present-day technology, as well as with extrapolations of it into future technology, in order to show that it is not at all difficult to see in a more detailed way how mind could emerge from interactions between neurons.

P.A.M. Dirac, the great physicist credited as being one of the "founding fathers" of quantum mechanics, once said, "God is a mathematician." By this he meant to express his appreciation of the beauty, simplicity, and symmetry of the inanimate world which made it possible for his formal mathematical equations to predict the existence of things not yet discovered in the laboratory. However, when one applies his image of the Creator to the world of living things, one finds instead that "God is the ultimate engineer (control, information, chemical, electrical, mechanical, . . .)."[1]

The concept of feedback forms the basis of control systems engineering. Over the last few decades it has been found that feedback plays this same fundamental role at all levels of biological organization. This ranges from subcellular processes, bodily processes, and so on, all the way up to things seen at the level of economic systems and governmental systems. But the concept of feedback itself can be generalized in ways which are perhaps not as well known. The simplest generalization is the "mutual entrainment of oscillations." As will be shown, this phenomenon has direct relevance to emergent biological properties in general and provides the simplest paradigm of the type of emergence depicted in the quotation from Sperry. As will be shown, mutual entrainment is very prevalent in biological systems and, like ordinary feedback, it is a "favorite trick" in both nature and technology.

But the phenomenon of "mutual entrainment of oscillations" is itself a phenomenon capable of still greater generalization. Therefore, after we have described it at length, we shall explore those directions of generalization which would seem to give it the power it would need to *explain* mind and inner awareness as an emergent phenomenon of neuronal activity.

[1] After radar was invented, man discovered that the bat used an acoustic radar. When a more sophisticated form of radar was invented, namely "FM radar," it was realized that indeed the bat had already been using that too!

MUTUAL ENTRAINMENT OF OSCILLATIONS

We will now start toward our goal of generalizing feedback. This first step will consist of shifting our considerations from a single control system to a population of mutually interacting control systems. We shall consider the most simple nontrivial example that we can find so that the principles will be as clear as possible. After this, all our generalizations will be in the direction of greater complexity of control and interaction. Thus, this first step is the most significant one for our purposes.

The term "entrainment" refers to the synchronization of an oscillator to an input signal. The most familiar technological example, perhaps, is its use in television. The picture on the television tube is created by a scanning electron beam which goes row by row across the picture from top to bottom. This beam is controlled by two oscillators, one for the vertical and the other for the horizontal direction. The picture remains stationary only when these oscillators are "locked in" or entrained to pulses originating from the transmitter. As all television viewers know, occasionally the oscillators can "break out" of synchrony, causing the picture to "rotate." The remedy is to readjust the natural frequency of the oscillator until it is "close enough" to the input frequency. It then locks in again, or becomes entrained, and the picture again stands still.

The same "lock in of frequency," or entrainment, is seen at many levels of biological organization. The subject of "biological clocks," especially those concerned with approximately 24-hour biological (ciradian) rhythms, contains numerous examples where the "day–night" cycles of animals can be *locked* to various periods near 24 hours in a way which is extremely analogous to the television example. In all cases of such synchronization, we have a sort of feedback. Under the correct circumstances, the oscillator finds a "stable phase" relation to the input. Any small disturbance will be subsequently "corrected" and the oscillator "stays in step" with the input. In this sense the entrained oscillator acts as a control system in reference to its input frequency. But at the same time an oscillator is *already* a feedback control system in regard to its own internal working, since it has a stably controlled amplitude.

Now, let us consider the phenomenon of direct interest to this paper: *mutual* entrainment. In contrast to the above, mutual entrainment occurs when two or more oscillators interact with each other in such a way as to *pull one another together into synchronism.* This phenomenon was first observed over 300 years ago by the physicist

Huygens (noted for "Huygens' Principle" and for the invention of the pendulum clock). He noticed one day that two clocks which were mounted on a common support ticked in unison. Huygens explained the phenomenon, after a series of experiments, by showing how the movement of the support would tend to keep pendulums swinging at a relative phase of 180 degrees and hence "in unison." At the time that Huygens made his discovery of the "sympathy" of the clocks he realized neither its tremendous role in biology nor its future role in the technology that was to come.

The synchronous flashing of fireflies in Southeast Asia (Wiener, 1961) presents a dramatic visual demonstration of mutual entrainment. As part of the sexual "display" activity of this species, entire trees and bushes laden with them flash exactly in unison. Apparently the fireflies see and mutually influence each other until they become mutually synchronized.

The same sort of thing happens in the case of the muscle cells of the heart. Each cardiac cell is an automonous oscillator, as shown by *in vitro* culture. When such cells are allowed to mutually interact, they then "beat as one." The term "fibrillation" refers to the breakdown of mutual entrainment of cardiac cells. During fibrillation, the heart cannot pump blood, and the patient will die unless the heart cells are resynchronized. Such "defibrillation" is possible by administering an electric shock to the heart which "restarts" the cells in unison. Thus, here is one obvious and dramatic biological example of how a life can totally depend on mutual entrainment.

There are many other examples which illustrate the importance of mutual entrainment in biology. The work on circadian rhythms has shown that the timing of biochemical processes in animals is best described in terms of entrained oscillators. If an animal is entrained to an unusual cycle length differing significantly from 24 hours, there is a very noticeable difference in the relative phases of the various biochemical oscillations in the animal. In other words, the basic processes occuring in biological organisms involve *mutually* entrained oscillations.[2]

---

[2] As an example, consider the following typical hypothetical situation. Suppose that an animal is entrained to a 24-hour light–dark schedule and that a certain chemical "A" in its blood reaches a peak value at the midpoint of the waking part of its cycle. Now suppose that the animal is then entrained to a 27-cycle. Typically A will not peak at the midpoint of the waking part of the cycle, but instead will occur earlier, say very soon after it wakes. On the other hand, if the animal were entrained to 21-hours, A might peak nearer the time it goes to sleep again. In other words, the wake–sleep cycle and the cycle of A keep "in step" with each other, but their relative *phases* are altered. Of course, there are a large number of cycles like A; call them B, C, D, etc. Their relative phases are all altered when the light–dark cycle is altered. The simplistic idea formerly held that the peak of A *causes* B to peak 4 hours later and C 2 hours after B, etc., is contradicted by such experiments as the above, and, rather than imagining a causal chain of chemical events in the body separated by fixed time *intervals*, we now view the chemical processes as oscillators *entraining* each other.

How does mutual entrainment come about and what is the mechanism for this process? The explanation is perhaps best given by using the famous example described by N. Wiener (1961), namely the electrical power system. This system consists of a network of AC generators, most of which are run by steam engines. Now, each engine-generator is an oscillator which has built into it a regulator or governor which controls its speed so that it deviates very little from 60 Hz at any time. In other words, each oscillator has a feedback device which causes it to *stay at* 60 cycles per second no matter what the present "load" may be—a larger load automatically causing a reaction in the governor to increase steam pressure and vice versa.

A generator in isolation does not give a very steady 60-Hz output. An electric clock attached to such a generator will become quite inaccurate after awhile. But, in remarkable contrast, when a large number of such generators are interconnected, they behave much more stably; that is, they all lock into step with one another or mutually entrain in a manner which is basically the same phenomenon as the fireflies flashing together or the heart cells "beating as one." In the case of the generators, the mechanism is easy to describe.

If one generator leads the others in phase, i.e., if it is slightly faster, then its energy will be *absorbed*, not only by the load, but also by all generators which lag behind it. This will increase the load on the generator, forcing it to slow down a bit so that it won't "get out of step." If by chance it *lags* in phase, the other generators pump energy *into* it so that it catches up. Thus, generators which go a bit too fast are slowed down while those that lag are speeded up. They *pull together in frequency*.

The generalization of feedback to a sort of mutual and shared feedback should now be easy to see. The stability and accuracy of a *system* of generators is far greater than any single unit. This mutual entrainment is a splendid example of *self-organization*, and it is obvious that such a system can be regarded as a *single unit* so far as its function is concerned. Out of mutual entrainment has emerged what Wiener terms a *"virtual governor"* which controls the entire system in a manner which uses feedback. This virtual governor is not located in one spot in the system, but rather it pervades the system as a whole, so that it does not have a "physical existence" in the usual sense. It is an *emergent property of the entire system* which goes far beyond what any single unit can accomplish in accuracy and power.

Now let us reconsider Sperry's idea. We see that mutual entrainment is a very simple but very instructive paradigm of a holistic property of control which has causal potency, which is emergent, and which *supervenes* in the behavior of the individual units. Like Sperry's neurons, the individual generators must operate "within larger circuit-system configurations of which they as individuals are only a part," and further, these larger functional entities (the overall behavior of the grid) "have their own dynamics . . . " Thus, the "virtual governors" of a power grid stand in relation to the individual governors in a way which is analagous to the way consciousness and mind stand in relation to the activity of the neuronal units of the brain. This is a deep analogy and it forms the basis of this paper. Parenthetically, it should be pointed out that mutual entrainment is a good analogy for many other holistic properties in biology and sociology.[3]

ONTOLOGICAL STATUS OF CONSCIOUSNESS IN RELATION TO THE MUTUAL ENTRAINMENT PARADIGM

The mutual entrainment analogy raises a fundamental question concerning the "reality status" of consciousness from this point of view. Consider the virtual governor of the power grid. One could say that the grid acts *as if* there were a virtual governor but "in reality" the virtual governor *doesn't exist*. All that *really* happens is that there are myriads of interactions and reactions between the individual generators. The virtual governor, from this point of view, is an *illusion*. But then, using our analogy between consciousness and the virtual gover-

---

[3] The "self-organization" property which arises from "mutual control" seen in entrainment has many analogies in life and in living systems. For example, consider "language." How does the common use of verbal symbols arise? We can see some explanation if we watch young children talking together. If one mispronounces a word, the others are quick to correct him or "kid" him about it. And of course, this is true in general for *any* "unusual" or "antisocial" behavior. One can see how "cultural norms" can "emerge" even without benefit of "mass media." In biology the development of the embryo involves self-organization on a "global" scale (i.e., the total embryo seems to coordinate its own development). In fact there is a tremendous similarity between embryo development and what happens in the brain, and both must involve "generalized entrainment" if not "entrainment." Goodwin and Cohen (1969) have advanced a theory of development involving entrainment and phase control of oscillation and have done experiments based on this hypothesis.

Other examples of "entrainment" and "generalized entrainment" are: (a) synchronous chirping of crickets, (b) synchronous emergence of chicks from eggs layed on successive days (believed to be due to *acoustic* entrainment because it does not happen if the eggs do not touch each other), (c) family dynamics, (d) the behavior of fish in schools, (e) birds flying in formation (it is believed that they supply one another with additional "lift" if they fly in a certain V-shape formation; presumably, and this is a speculation, if one bird uses "too much lift" from the other birds, they vocally complain and cause it to do its "fair share"—hence the noise they make while flying), (f) in the case of cell-division cycles in the liver, a "minimally modified" cancer cell can be identified by the fact that it has broken off from the mutually entrained cycle of the others, (g) the size of nations was probably controlled by the distance over which transportation and communication allowed "mutual entrainment" in the generalized sense, and central control, at least in the days before modern communication systems, etc. Finally there is the example known to all lovers when they say "This is bigger than both of us!," when they discover that their individual identities are starting to become subservient to a mutual or shared identity and control.

nor, we get the suggestion that perhaps *consciousness itself is an illusion!* In what follows we wish to point out why this part of the analogy breaks down.

Another point of view is that each theory has, in a sense, its own "level of reality." By this I mean that the quantities of, for example, temperature, pressure, and heat are all real in the context of thermodynamics, even though the theory of statistical mechanics derives these quantities as the average results of the movement of large numbers of tiny particles. From the point of view of statistical mechanics, thermodynamics is a "phenomenological theory." Pressure is *just* the average force due to the momentum exchanges between many billions of billions of particles and therefore pressure does not *really* exist but is an illusion. The thermodynamic point of view, however, is that its quantities are measurable and, at the microscopic level in question, these quantities certainly do exist and certainly are real. Thus this theory has its own level of reality. One could further point out that the particles of statistical mechanics are themselves phenomenological entities and that, at a deeper level, they are made up of smaller more complicated things that must be "explained" in terms of quantum theory where the duality between waves and particles makes the situation much more involved than in ordinary classical statistical mechanics.

What is the reality status of consciousness from this second point of view? I would say that it assigns to consciousness the status of a "convention," i.e., its reality would depend on which *level* we would wish to regard it.

Both of the above points of view assign a rather ambiguous status to the reality of consciousness. They suffer from a fundamental oversight which can be uncovered only by looking at the basis of epistemology itself (Margenau, 1950). We must begin from the most basic proposition: All knowledge is connected to *experience.* (What would "knowledge" be if it were *unknowable?*) But experience itself is a form of awareness, or consciousness. Epistemology in effect assumes the reality of consciousness. If we assert that self-reflexive awareness is the epistemological definition of the construct called consciousness, it follows that, of all the constructs man has created, the one called consciousness has a highly privileged place in the hierarchy of "real things." It is, so to speak, the "most" real of all constructs. (For the constitutive definition of consciousness and its relation to "other minds" see Dewan, 1957.)

To summarize this view on the ontological status of consciousness, it is a holistic emergent property of the interactions of neurons which has power to be self-reflective and ascertain its own awareness.[4] As such, its reality is neither a convention nor a relative concept which depends on a particular point of view. Rather, its reality must be taken as axiomatic to epistemology.

There is a very interesting connection between self-reflexive awareness and the meaning of "self" and "identity." This will be examined in the sequel, and the bearing of this on the question, "Can a machine have consciousness?" will be considered. For the present, however, we turn to further generalizations of feedback by generalizing the meaning of "mutual entrainment."

GENERALIZED MUTUAL ENTRAINMENT

In ordinary mutual entrainment, we considered the interaction between individual oscillators which themselves were "control systems" in the sense that each had a governor which by means of feedback regulated their individual frequency and amplitude of output. These control systems, however, had very *limited* "behavior." Consider, for the sake of comparison, a large number of people interacting with each other. Each person has individual needs, and by mutual interactions between many people there emerges a community or social system. Such a system organizes itself so that the needs of the individuals are satisfied. Somehow the individuals in the system have a way of controlling each other for their own goal satisfactions (manipulation, cooperation, financial arrangements, etc.) and in the end an overall control system comes into being. In this example, we have an illustration of generalized entrainment; a common government, economic system, language, culture, and law system are all part of it. Anyone "getting out of line" in terms of behavior gets "feedback" to pull him "in" again just as, by analogy, the generators "pulled together in frequency."

The above example points the way to our generalization. The difference between it and the generator example is the degree of complexity of communication, control, and "behavior" involved. Though the two examples differ vastly, they still share the common property of

[4] In higher order adaptive control systems, or even in the case of lowest order adaptive control, there is a sort of "self-examination" going on. The adaptive controller is examining and testing the manner in which the servo-control "copes" with changes. When this manner is inadequate in view of changing environment or circumstances, the system is modified until it can again cope adequately. Perhaps the property of "self-reflexive" awareness is a direct consequence of our ability to *adapt* and change our "criteria" for "success" etc. (The converse to this would not be true however.)

mutual feedback of the subsystems. We shall now consider a number of levels of sophistication in control theory. They will consist of (1) optimal control, (2) adaptive control, and (3) generalized optimal–superadaptive control. The thesis is that the interaction between such generalized subsystems would give rise to an emergent property more closely resembling mutual entrainment. After all, a neuron can be regarded as a *living creature*.

Optimal Control

The stringent requirements for economy of weight, fuel, time, etc. brought on by space-age technology design requirements have provided strong motivation for the development of optimal control in recent years (Dewan, 1971). For example, when a rocket is sent to a distant planet, the cost of additional fuel rises exponentially, since every pound of it in the vehicle represents additional weight to overcome when escaping the influence of the earth's gravitational field. The purpose of optimal control theory is to design procedures which use scarce commodities to maximum effectiveness. The basic "trick" used by the engineer is not very difficult to understand and is very instructive. The actual details (which are omitted here) are of course very complicated and mathematical.

We hasten to point out that the theory of optimum control has found application far outside of the field of space technology. For example, it has been used in management sciences, economics, and operations research, to name a few examples. (It is also true that the "ultimate engineer," i.e., Nature, has been making extensive use of it!)

To clarify the basic concept, let us consider a particular example. Suppose that an engineer is given the task of setting up a list of instructions (to a pilot or to a computer) for controlling some sort of aircraft in a way which will take a minimum amount of fuel to reach a certain altitude at a certain final speed. How does the engineer find the "optimal procedure?" The trick is to set up a mathematical function known as a "performance index." This function contains all the parameters which are relevant to fuel utilization (speed, drag, thrust, altitude, attitude, etc.). He then uses various mathematical procedures or computational procedures which give him the trajectory and parameter settings which minimize fuel consumption. The performance index here would be proportional to the amount of fuel required.

Thus, optimal control involves the maximization of a performance index. Notice that this is a generalization of feedback. In the latter, an "error" is "minimized." Here we have a much more complicated control problem, but the trick is to lump everything together in a way which gives *one* quantity, the performance index, to be minimized or maximized. Another optimal control is seen in evolution. There the performance index is survivability.

The generalization of "entrainment" would consist of the interaction of many optimal control systems, each possessing its own performance index. The next question is: have the engineers and mathematicians worked on this problem? The answer is "yes." The discipline goes under the title "differential games." The word "games" enters because the majority of the situations considered involve control systems working in *competition;* i.e., one maximizes the performance index of the *combined system* while the other minimizes it. Notice that the engineers consider it to be *one* system controlled by a multiplicity of controllers. In the case of mutual entrainment of electric generators they sometimes regard the system as *one generator* with an "equivalent flywheel,"[5] etc.

Recently the workers in differential games have realized that they should regard the field to be "generalized optimal control theory." They have branched out in several directions, including one characterized as "team theory." This latter is more along the lines we are considering here. In team theory, one considers mutually interacting "controllers," each with his own "payoff function" or "performance index." A correct design would give rise to a total system which is itself an optimal control system even though each element is "doing its own thing" (maximizing its own payoff function).

Thus, the case of the generators gave rise to a system which could be regarded as one supergenerator. Here we end up with one superoptimal control system which has emerged from what can be regarded as the interaction of a number of optimal control systems.

The comparison with human behavior is evident. Very often a person will enlist the cooperation of another person by making a "deal," i.e., an arrangement whereby both benefit. This is the generali-

---

[5] In other words, the system as a whole has a certain resistance to having its frequency changed for the reasons indicated. This resistance is much larger than found in a single generator. But if you made a single generator with a *larger* flywheel, its resistance to sudden frequency change would be increased because the *inertia* of the large wheel would be greater and would be more resistant to change of frequency. Now imagine a theoretical generator with a huge flywheel. How big would this wheel have to be in order to have the "inertia" or resistance to frequency change of an entire generator grid? The engineers can calculate this, and, for reasons of simplification, they can resort to representing the grid as a *single* generator with a *single* flywheel with inertia "equivalent" to the stability of the grid.

zation of mutual entrainment which comes from optimal control. Presumably neurons may be optimal control systems.

Adaptive Control, Superadaptive Control, Superadaptive
Optimal Control, and Beyond

To escalate our generalization of the "mutual entrainment" concept a few steps more, let us now turn to the general basis for "adaptive control theory" (Dewan, 1971). It is generally agreed that adaptability is a most salient property of biology. Feedback itself, in the most ordinary sense, represents a form of "adapting," but, as has been found in technology, there are situations where ordinary feedback is not sufficient for the job at hand. An example is the automatic pilot for a certain experimental aircraft (the X-15) which flys from sea level to altitudes many miles up where air is extremely low in density. The aircraft can be controlled at low altitude by using control surfaces on the wings and tail in the usual manner. As it gains in altitude, the density of the air goes down and the same change of motion of the vehicle will necessitate a larger movement of the control surfaces. At still higher altitudes, the control surfaces have virtually no effect because there is very little air flow in a near vacuum. At such altitudes the aircraft must be controlled by small rockets as in any other space vehicle. At intermediate altitudes a mixture of the two modes could be used to advantage. The point is that here is an example of a control system where the *means of coping* depends on the altitude. In other words, the plane must function in different environments where it must *adapt* its *method* of coping and where, as a result, automatic pilots are in existence which undergo a "metamorphosis" as the plane ascends, so that the plane always responds in an appropriate way to the pilot's manipulation of the controls. The automatic pilot automatically "compensates" for environmental changes.

It is important to see the difference between ordinary feedback control and adaptive control. The first case is exemplified by the ordinary autopilot. The latter can maintain a set altitude or direction in a manner resembling a thermostat. In spite of wind changes, etc., it senses the error between actual behavior and desired behavior and manipulates the controls to bring the error to as close to zero as possible. In contrast, the adaptive autopilot has one additional dimension of control. It senses the *environment* and, in so doing, can adapt the *method by which the device controls the aircraft,* in addition to maintaining constant altitude and direction. This second level of control thus modifies *the process* by which a lower level control device makes its "corrections."[6] Thus, a feedback device modifies a feedback device.

How does the adaptive autopilot sense the environment in practice? The one used on the X-15 aircraft does this by oscillating the control surfaces slightly and sensing the reaction of the plane. The diminishing of reaction for a given excursion of the surface automatically causes a compensation to take place.

The idea of adaptive control can be generalized. Consider a superadaptive control (Dewan, 1971). In this case one could have a feedback device modify a feedback device which modifies the main feedback control. In other words, one could have a device which modifies its *method* by which it modifies its method of control. This would indeed increase adaptive capability. Furthermore, one can imagine any number of levels of superadaptability; thus, there is in principle no apparent limit to how far one could generalize in this dimension! (No one knows at this time the degree to which Nature has seen fit to go, but no doubt she's gone further than we have.)

Now, suppose we have a *(super)adaptive optimum* control system. Here the performance index as well as method of coping could be automatically adjusted to circumstance. If we could imagine a large number of such systems interacting with one another, we can see that there is much more room for complexity of behavior and adaptibility. Imagine them behaving in such a way as to induce each other into changing their own performance indices so as to maximize the "common good" of the system. Although, so far as I am aware, this situation has not been studied in the literature of technology, one can speculate that out of such mutual interaction a total superadaptive optimal control system could emerge.

The Emergence of Mind and Consciousness

The main question of how mind and consciousness could emerge from neuronal activity can now be put into the perspective of

---

[6] Perhaps if the X-15 autopilot had a higher level of adaptive control, it and its pilot would not have ended so tragically. On its last flight it reentered the denser atmosphere (I am told) with an orientation which had not been anticipated. When this sort of thing happens to a sophisticated control system, it can easily change into a system bent on its self-destruction. (This phenomenon of self-destruction was also involved in the Northeast 1965 power blackout.)

the above extrapolations of control systems technology. First, we recall again that each neuron is a living creature and that, as such, it may be regarded as a control system of higher degree of complexity than a mere feedback device. It probably can adapt, "learn" (a form of adaptive control), and optimize its peformance in the sense of optimal control. In other words, neurons are likely to be superadaptive and optimal.

Next, we consider that neurons can make up subsystems which themselves can be considered to be systems with emergent properties going beyond single neurons and, in fact, one can imagine hierarchies of systems with subsystems. We shall not belabor the possible structural arrangements.

Finally, one can imagine the total system of the brain itself. To our knowledge this is surely the most complex entity in the universe. The level of complexity is beyond comprehension. Quite obviously there must be tremendous ongoing interaction and mutual control between the systems and between subsystems of the brain. Out of this interaction it is possible to imagine the emergence of an "inner awareness" which can "supervene," in Sperry's sense of that word. This consciousness would be the ultimate embodiment of what was earlier called a "virtual governor." Its unique property would be its self-reflexive *awareness* and its "self identity." Note the analogy between adaptive control and self-reflexiveness. In other words, I am proposing that our "inner world" which we "perceive" within "ourselves" is the emergent self-controlling virtual governor resulting from generalized entrainment of large numbers of superadaptive optimum control systems arranged into a hierarchical mutually cooperative structure—of sublime and majestic engineering dimensions!

Admittedly this view is completely without technical detail. However, it seems to be an appropriate step in the direction first pointed out by Sperry. Since the virtual governor does not have a physical existence in the usual sense, but is a property of the system as a whole, we at last have a concrete example that gives us some rational way to think of consciousness, which must somehow emerge from physical neuronal activity but at the same time not have a physical existence in the usual sense.[7]

---

[7] We have argued that mind behaves like a virtual governor, and this has been lumped together with consciousness and awareness, but these words in fact refer to distinctly different things even though they are related. Mind *includes* consciousness, and consciousness *includes* self-reflexive awareness. I assume all three are "emergent," but that awareness is the emergent property which plays the role of the highest level, or levels, of superadaptive control. For awareness to come in to existence there would probably be a critical amount of information flow, structure, and control, but here lies the core of the mystery, and our ignorance is still too great to probe further. Here are some questions: "Does a neuron have consciousness?" "How could you find out?" "What are the necessary and sufficient conditions for awareness?"

ON THE CONCEPTS OF SELF AND IDENTITY IN THE CONTEXT OF SELF-REFLECTIVE AWARENESS AND FEEDBACK

We now turn to the question, "What constitutes the 'me' that inhabits this body?" We shall see that the central theoretic point of view of this paper leads us to some new information. To expose the problem in a vivid way we consider the following parable.

A doctor comes to town who can transform old people into young people. Each old person who undergoes this doctor's operation subsequently reemerges from his hospital completely transformed into a young person. He has all his own memories, talents, and all those qualities which make all his intimate acquaintances affirm that he is indeed the same person who went into the hospital.

One day a patient overhears two nurses talking indiscreetly and thus learns the secret of the operation. It turns out that the doctor has been collecting unwanted babies and raising them on a 'people-farm' under hygienic conditions. By some unknown method he keeps their minds a blank while their bodies grow into early adulthood. Then when a "customer" comes in the doctor "operates" (using another unknown technology) by transferring all information in the patient's brain into the blank brain of one of the young bodies he has been saving for this purpose. This is analogous to copying the entire contents of an old notebook into a new one. The operation is conducted under anesthesia. Then the customer is killed and his body destroyed without trace. The new body is awakened and it invariably says, "It's *great* to be young again!" It then signs the check and cheerfully walks out of the hospital.

The question is, "Who walked out of the hospital?" Would *you* have that operation? I originally heard this story from George Gamow, and my first reaction was that the young person walking out of the hospital was a perfect *duplicate* of the person who entered. In other words I would not have that operation simply because it wouldn't be *me* who walked out.

The question which leads us to a new insight is: "Is there any other science-fiction type of operation that one could dream up which would not have the drawbacks of the above?" Any such modification would entail an alteration of the *subjective* side of this situation since, so far as any uninformed outsider could see, the same person came out of the hospital; i.e., there was no external indication of change of identity. The modification that I would propose it that the operation be done without anesthesia. The subject could be aware of himself during the entire transfer process. He could monitor the process "from the inside" so to speak. More specifically, he could be "in touch" with himself during the operation as he is gradually transferred. For example, in midcourse he might be able to move his right hand. Then this is transferred and he moves it again and sees and feels the hand of the other body move, etc. At that point, his former right hand would no longer be "part of himself." In this way, by means of self-reflexive awareness and "feedback" he would be able to be certain that he, as an individual, is not lost in the process. In the end no external observer would be able to tell the difference between this modified operation and the former one. The only difference would be in the mind of the subject. The old body would be destroyed as before but "he" would have escaped death.

This illustrates the enormous importance of feedback, control, and self-reflexive awareness with regard to "self" and "consciousness." It is not enough for a brain to have an identical structure for it to contain the *same* consciousness. One must presuppose an internal communication between the system and itself during a transfer process. This implies that the loops of internal communication comprise the essential "substance" of consciousness. This is completely in line with the above "virtual governor hypothesis."[8]

In order to be the same consciousness, it is necessary that the material structure responsible for the consciousness be in mutual communication. This is also true for the right and left half brains. When their main communication link (the corpus callosum) is cut, there is no longer a single consciousness. Instead there are two. This suggests that "internal communication" is a necessary condition for consciousness.

The other arguments above show that consciousness does not depend on the "stuff" or the exact material constituting the brain. In other words, a person's self-awareness and identity do not change so radically with age that he becomes an entirely different entity, yet the atoms and molecules that constitute his brain as a small child are mostly absent in his adult brain due to metabolic turnover, etc. Since one's mental identity and consciousness awareness does not necessitate an identical substrate, it must need an identical or similar functional *structure*. But even this can change without destroying the identity of the mind in question (a person, however modified, usually has the

---

[8] When man and machine cooperate in a feedback loop, a single system emerges. We all are aware of this in everyday life. If someone crashes his car into the fender of your car, you will probably say, "What do you mean by crashing into *me* like that?"

Another example of this is the following case. I once asked the operator of a giant crane: "Do you think of that machine as an extension of yourself?" He quickly answered, "Buddy, in this business you've gotta think of it that way!" I then said, "How does it feel when you leave it and go home?" He replied, "I feel like I've left part of myself behind."

same "self," even after brain damage). This seems to strongly suggest that the "substance" of consciousness is message and communication—the flow of communication and control signals and the like.

COULD A MACHINE HAVE A CONSCIOUSNESS?

Perhaps the most quoted paper in regard to this question is one by Turing (1956). The key issue is: "How would one *know* that the machine was conscious?" What would be the test? Turing's famous test can be summarized as follows: Imagine a computer which could communicate with a person and could engage in a dialogue. Suppose it to answer questions and react verbally in such a way that would make it impossible for anyone to *distinguish* between this computer's response and the responses of a human being. Turing says that under these conditions one would conclude that the machine must be conscious. In other words, if a machine can imitate the outputs from a human consciousness, then it is conscious by his definition. This definition seems to have satisfied many people.

In my opinion this test of consciousness fails to answer the question of whether or not a machine can have an *"inner awareness."* Imitation is not sufficient, for it is possible to imagine a machine acting exactly *as if* it were aware but in reality having no awareness at all.[9]

What alternative is conceivably possible that would get at the basic issue? My answer can be given in terms of the "Doctor Parable." Suppose there were a machine which could pass the Turing test, and suppose that the mechanism of the computer *used essentially the same principles employed by the brain for its operation.* (This last clause is admittedly full of philosophical problems we shall not stop to consider here.) Suppose further that you now asked me to prove that the machine is conscious. The scenario for the proof is this. First I would

---

[9] Scriven has suggested that the method to solve the problem of proving whether or not a machine is conscious is to, first, program it in a manner which will not allow it to lie. Then ask it, "Are you conscious?" If it says "Yes!" then you have proved that it is conscious.

But something seems to be wrong with this argument. The question being asked is, "How do you find out if a machine is conscious?" Presumably there is no test from the outside and one wants to avoid a yes response in the event that the machine is not conscious. But since there is no test, there can be no program. How can one program a system to do something (i.e., always tell the truth) if there is no way to check on it? When it comes to the question of "Are you conscious?" if there is no way to test and see if the program is working, there is no way to construct the program. This would be just as impossible as painting a person's portrait without visual contact with your hand or canvas and, at the same time, having no feedback of any kind (kinesthetic or tactile) from your arm and hand. There can be no complex control without feedback, and there can be no program without a test of *some* kind.

personally introduce you to the doctor of the "Doctor Parable" story, and then he would transfer your mind into the machine (step by step, an outlined in the previous section so that you would not lose touch with yourself). Then, after a while, say after conversing with me or someone else by means of the computer output terminal to assure all witnesses that it is *your* mind that is inside the computer, you could be transferred back into your own brain by our fictional doctor and then you could ask yourself the question, "Was I conscious when the machine was me?" The answer to this question would prove or disprove for you, and you alone, whether or not a machine could be conscious. We could take your word, or we could repeat your experiment to decide for ourselves. In my opinion, this would be the only way to get a scientific answer to the question of machine awareness.

CONCLUSION

We have considered the problems of consciousness from the viewpoint of advanced control theory. Starting with Sperry's theory that consciousness is an emergent process that supervenes in a causal, holistic way on activity in the brain, we then compared it to the emergence of a "virtual governor" in mutual entrainment of a system of oscillators. This discussion was then generalized from the concept of mutual entrainment to include the mutual interactions of control systems much more general than feedback oscillators. The generalizations were in the direction of adaptive control and optimal control. We speculated that the interactions between such complex systems could give rise to a "virtual governor" which would be a global property of the brain having "awareness" as well as "self-reflexive awareness." We then turned to the problems of "identity," "self," and "consciousness in man-made mechanisms," and, by means of a science-fiction parable we saw what would be involved in deciding these questions. We also saw, again from the control systems viewpoint, the crucial roles played by internal communication and control in the definitions of self and identity.

It will take a long time before control theory will be able to grapple with biological intelligence, but the interesting surprises that await workers in this field should provide generations of philosophers and scientists with strong motivation for uncovering the techniques of "the ultimate engineer."

REFERENCES

Dewan, E. M. (1957): Other minds: An application of recent epistemological ideas to the definition of consciousness. *Philos. Sci.* **24**, 70.

Dewan, E. M. (1971): Cybernetics and attention. In: *Attention in Neurophysiology*. Ed. by C. R. Evans and J. Mulholland. New York: Appleton.

Goodwin, B. C. and Cohen, M. H. (1969): A phase-shift model for the spatial and temporal organization of developing systems. *Journal Theoret. Biol.* **25**, 49–107.

Margenau, H. (1950): *The Nature of Physical Reality*. New York: McGraw-Hill.

Sperry, R. W. (1969): A modified concept of consciousness. *Psychol. Rev.* **76**, 532–536.

Turing, A. M. (1956): Can a machine think? In: *The World of Mathematics, Vol. 4*. Ed. by J. R. Newman. New York: Simon & Schuster, 2099.

Wiener, N. (1961): *Cybernetics*. Cambridge: MIT Press.

8   Introduction

The case for mind as an emergent property of brain, developed by Sperry, Chapter 6, hinges on the concept of *emergence*. Wimsatt provides a detailed philosophical analysis of this concept and of the related notion of a "level of organization" in the following article. Taken together, the two articles provide a fine illustration of the advantages which occur when scientists and philosophers each focus on what they know best. Sperry's theory would appear to be integral to and illuminated by his empirical work, especially the results of his "split-brain" studies; thus, his understanding of the way that the brain does all the things it can do leads to his emergent theory. Wimsatt dissects the concept of emergence with philosophical instruments applied to a variety of scientific examples, sharpens Sperry's position, and would seem ultimately to strengthen it greatly. Since Wimsatt's article is both comprehensive and at a very high level of abstraction, as well as being detailed and technical, we summarize here some of its major points, as a guide to the more general reader, who may disappreciate Wimsatt's technique (which the *aficionado* applauds).

     For Wimsatt, the issue of both the emergence of new properties at some higher level of organization and the reduction of these properties to a lower level of organization are inseparably interwined. In presenting Sperry's view of the mental, Wimsatt points out that to hold mental properties to be "configurational" is to say that they are specific "relational properties" of parts, and not properties of parts apart from the whole. Such relational properties need not have a precise location within the system. Although the claim that the whole is "more than" and "different from" the sum of its parts is usually meant in the sense that the whole cannot be *reduced* to lower level parts and their relational properties, Wimsatt's central theme is that such a reduction is

199

possible, when reduction is properly understood. However, to have *both* emergentism and reductionism entails that the properties of the functional whole are "something more" and "different from" a *simple aggregate* of the relational properties of the parts. What Wimsatt is after here is the seemingly magical trick of reducing upper level phenomena (the whole) to lower level phenomena (the parts), while at the same time retaining the independent reality of the upper level phenomena which are reducible.

In Part II, Wimsatt first focuses on reductions by distinguishing intralevel from interlevel reductions in science. Failure to distinguish the two in the technical literature on theory reduction has lead to incorrect attribution of many properties of the former process to cases like Sperry's, which is of the latter type. With interlevel reduction, when there are highly complex and "open-ended" mappings of higher level phenomena onto lower level phenomena and mechanisms, there cannot be a simple kind of *translation*—as between putative synonyms in two languages—nor can there be a simple *relation* between upper and lower level theories or parts of theories. In such a case, relatively simple mapping becomes possible only by bringing in the entire *context* of key terms at the lower, and sometimes at both levels, so that the translation *per se* is incomplete without the contexts by means of which they are interpreted. Since complete translation is therefore impossible, rather than being able to replace the upper level by the lower, the upper level is in fact irreplaceable. Interlevel reduction, then, can be regarded as involving an explanatory *relation* between *phenomena* and mechanisms (rather than between theories) at the two levels, or even regarded as involving an interlevel *theory* explaining the relations between phenomena and mechanisms at these levels. It is thus a misnomer even to call it *theory* reduction.

The role of explanation and identification in reduction is also considered. Wimsatt attacks the view that the goals of interlevel reduction are ontological—to establish identities between upper and lower levels (in order to eliminate or show the dispensibility of the former), with explanation serving no role or only a subsidiary role in this context. Instead, he suggests that explanation is the primary goal of interlevel reduction and that identities function primarily as tools to serve this end. Since descriptive inconsistencies or incompletenesses are the source of explanatory failures, it becomes crucial to make comparisons of different-level descriptions of the same system, to make certain that the descriptions fit one another. These comparisons are made by using identifications.

Identifications used in this manner to improve explanatory

power are tentative, modifiable, and entail a series of successive approximations. Identification and explanation involve a dialectic process in which the concepts and entities of the upper level affect the elaboration of lower level theories as much as the lower affects the upper, until finally an exact fit in all relevant respects ensues. The concepts of each level come to *presuppose* those of the other in this coevolution, according to Wimsatt's version of reduction, rather than having a situation in which the lower level dominates. That reduction is possible, then, does *not* necessitate denying equal status to the upper level, since the fit in reduction depends on both upper and lower level contributions; no magic is involved after all!

In Part III, Wimsatt's discussion begins abstractly. In discussing any level of organization, he indicates that it is necessary to delineate the units whose relatedness in fact comprise the organization. These units are not known as units directly, but *via* a set of categories, usually associated with a *theory*, which provides such a delineation. Thus it is possible to think of a particular theory as a kind of "sieve" or filter which sorts out particular kinds of units, with theories at different levels of description picking out different units at the respective levels of organization. Levels of organization are seen to be sets of units which interact with greater regularity and predictability than related assemblages of slightly different units. This fact about the world then gives a criterion for the reality of a theory; that is, a theory can be said to determine *natural* units when its concepts and laws yield a "maximum of predictability and regularity" at the level of those units. As adaptive conceptual instruments, theories must be efficient and the characteristics of levels guarantee that "good" theories about them will yield greater predictive and explanatory benefits at lower conceptual and calculational cost than "bad" theories.

That a level and the best theory about that level both share the property of being maxima of regularity and predictability make Wimsatt's move closely related to Weimer's (1973) claim that "an organism is a theory of its environment," but shows in addition how the organism-*qua*-successful-theory is selected out precisely at the levels of organization inherent to the environment "in something like a cost–benefit manner towards the minimization of uncertainty" in that environment. When systems are allowed to freely evolve, as in organic evolution, their natural units tend to be appropriate to—to *fit*—the natural units of their environment. It is obvious (once pointed out!) that the best detector of levels of organization in the environment is an organism whose levels allow maximal predictability and regularity *vis-à-vis* the comparable levels of organization in the environment. *Organisms which are better in this respect will be selected for.* It is a generalized version of this selection phenomenon which is responsible for the evolution of levels of organization themselves, as coevolved units or systems which evolve (in most respects), to interact with one another in a maximally regular and predictable manner.

Having discussed units and levels, Wimsatt returns to the relationship between levels. For a reductionist, lower level entities, phenomena, explanations, and laws are regarded as more basic or primary than upper level ones. Wimsatt argues that this is a question of explanatory strategy; for example in cases where a phenomenon is not explicable at its own level, where is it most productive to look—to lower or to higher levels? The reductionist's answer "to lower levels" is generally a sound strategy because of contingent features of our world, but even in our world this is not *always* so (cf. the case for selection systems or Dewan's (this volume) "virtual governor"). He argues that these same contingent features of our world also account for the facts that lower level (compositional) redescriptions of an entity or property are usually regarded as (1) more informative, (2) more likely to become assimilated to the meanings of theoretical and observational terms, and (3) more general than higher level (contextual) redescriptions.

As a result, the claim that "the whole is nothing more than the sum of its parts" is shown to be *logically and ontologically* equivalent to "the parts are nothing more than the decomposition of their whole." What Wimsatt considers to be the "temptation" to make the first statement rather than the second derives not from some greater reality or esoteric fundamentality of the parts, but from the role of explanatory strategy. This "temptation" is deeply imbedded in the western scientific paradigm.

In the final section, Wimsatt returns to the problem of dualities—thought and language, phenomena and noumena, and especially first-person-private and third-person-public—in relation to levels. For some X, its own level L_X is *ineliminable* in two senses. First, it is *conceptually* ineliminable because the concepts of L_X provide the best (i.e., low-cost and high-benefit) descriptive level at which regularities in the phenomena of L_X can be predicted by X. (However, if X were a sufficiently rich system, theories at other levels could be constructed at low cost which improve X's predictions with respect to L_X, and under some conditions L_X might then be regarded as conceptually eliminable.) Secondly, it is *experientially* ineliminable because major entities and properties of L_X are "sensorily immediate" to X, since X is intrinsic (first person) to L_X; that is, an X on any other level is extrinsic (third person) to L_X. Empirically based knowledge requires at least some sensory immediacy. (In Russell's terms, to completely eliminate L_X for X is to forgo "knowledge by direct acquaintance.") Reducibility of L_X for X, if possible, would involve *conceptual* eliminability, but the reality of L_X for X would still be secured by its sensory immediacy—its *experiential ineliminability*.) This might legitimately be regarded as a third kind of "emergence," though one which, unlike the usual senses of "emergence," is entirely *independent* of the reduction question.) Like Sperry, and *contra* Globus, Wimsatt restricts sensory immediacy to systems which are organizationally equivalent ("in loosely construed functional terms") to physical nervous systems interacting with the environment. Following along these lines, mind–brain dualism can be completely accounted for by considering "the nature and structure of lower and higher level interacting systems."

The consequence of Wimsatt's discussion is that it becomes possible to have one's emergent cake and digest it too! Mind is indeed an emergent property of brain, as Sperry argues, at the same time that it is reducible to brain, in Wimsatt's functional analysis of reductionism. Although some philosophers may find Wimsatt's emergent cake unpalatable, and others may find it palatable but indigestible, Wimsatt provides an intriguing conceptual basis for Sperry's mind–brain solution.

REFERENCE

Weimer, W. B. (1973): Psycholinguistics and Plato's paradoxes of the *Meno*. *American Psychologist* **28**, 15–33.

8 Reductionism, Levels of Organization, and the Mind–Body Problem

WILLIAM C. WIMSATT

Dr. Sperry's position is complex and variegated, and I will be unable to discuss some of the issues raised by him in this volume and in other closely related papers. He has chosen to characterize his position generally as "emergent interactionism" and to spend a great deal of time distinguishing it from other views, ranging over the spectrum from dualism to materialism. His more general conception justifies and merits a more general response, which I shall present here.

In some ways, this is true of the volume as a whole: A number of exciting results and conjectures are presented and in some areas we see vague outlines of scientific solutions that should importantly reshape our philosophical perspectives. But clearly a most striking phenomenon is that, even in the face of general acceptance of and agreement on most of the data and interpretations, newer positions seemed to redifferentiate along older lines in ways that seemed curiously, even frustratingly, independent of what the facts are. It is perhaps for this reason that I find myself returning to what must be an old question for those who find dualisms redundant and materialisms too spare: *Can one be a reductionist and an emergentist too?* It is this question which I find

WILLIAM C. WIMSATT·University of Chicago

most strongly posed by Sperry's position, and which I will try to provide grounds for answering in the affirmative.

On the way, I will try to break new ground—primarily in trying to analyze reduction from a functional and dynamical perspective (in opposition to the structural and static accounts of classical positivism); in trying to give an account of the notion of a level of organization which is consistent with the rich plurality of phenomena that we all recognize to exist, and also with the reductionism which seems inevitable; and perhaps most of all, in trying to use these to show how one man's "emergent interactionism" can be another man's "identity thesis." Unlike some, I do not think that the facts are philosophically neutral, but the facts which must be considered go beyond the results of neurophysiology into the cognitive and functional dynamics of scientific progress. But perhaps it might be said, after all, that these are but some of the more remote results of neurophysiology.

PART I. SPERRY'S VIEW OF THE MENTAL

Although Sperry presents his thesis over a number of papers, most of the key features of his analysis can be teased out of a few quotes.[1] In what follows, the interpolated letters indicate phrases I will discuss below. The first quote refers primarily to the "emergent" side of his "emergent interactionism":

> [The conscious properties of the brain process] are [a] holistic [b] configurational properties that [c] have yet to be discovered. Once they have been discovered and understood, we predict that they will be [d] best conceived as being [e] different from and [f] more than the neural events of which they are composed. . . . colors, sounds, sights, taste, smell, pain and all the other phenomena of the world of inner mental experience are given due recognition as [g] phenomena in their own right. Rather than being identical to the neural events [h] as these are generally understood, they are emergents of these events. (p. 166)

The following points emerge:

(1) If the mental properties are (b) "configurational properties," they are in one sense (a) "holistic," since they are *relational properties* of the parts, and thus not properties of the parts apart from the whole.

---

[1] The primary other sources are his 1966, 1969, and 1970. Unless otherwise noted, citations will be this volume.

Furthermore, most interesting configurational properties are relatively specific—a relatively small proportion of possible or actual configurations have them. This is integral to Sperry's denial of panpsychism and to his view of the unity and privacy of subjective experience. Trees and rocks (and the spinal cord of an ox, see his 1966, p. 307) all fail to have the appropriate configurational properties to be conscious, though some animals do, and if so, they too are conscious. Split-brain patients have two consciousnesses because of the relative dynamical isolation of their hemispheres, and normal people have one consciousness because they have an intact corpus callosum. These are all relevant configurational properties.[2]

(2) Mental properties could be holistic in another sense, however, in not having a precise location within the whole system. It is commonly but mistakenly accepted that *physical* parts of a system must have a precise location within that system. I have argued elsewhere (Wimsatt, 1974a; see also Gregory, 1959, for general remarks and Longuet-Higgins *et al.*, 1970; Pribram, 1971a; and Bartlett and John, 1973, for relevant theory and details in neurophysiology) that it is characteristic of *functional properties* and *functionally defined parts* in complex physical systems that even when characterized in a manner that is unexceptionably physical, they are often not precisely localizable. This fact has not been appreciated by physicalists in countering dualistic and antireductionistic arguments based upon localization problems (see also Wimsatt, 1974b, and Kim, 1971, pp. 329–336).

(3) It is by now definitive of an emergentist position to claim that the whole (or its properties) is (f) "more than" the parts (or properties of the parts) of which it is composed. There are two interest-

---

[2] I think that Sperry is wrong in believing that his view of the nature of subjective experiencing is or must be opposed to that of Globus (1972, 1973, this volume). At least one way of reading Globus' talk of transformation boundaries is that these boundaries occur at the normal outer limits of the sensory receptors of the central nervous system under normal circumstances, when the massive interconnections of the intact corpus callosum render the two hemispheres so dynamically interdependent that the two hemispheres act as one self. Globus could consistently add that under naturally occurring or surgically induced rare circumstances in which signals cannot pass through the corpus callosum, the two hemispheres are much more independent, and with them, their respective sensory inputs, which now subjectively define two separate but largely (to an "outside" observer) coextensive transformation boundaries. Sperry claims (p. 174) that " . . . an observer relation to another brain is not enough [to share or have a common subjective experience, as] the second brain must be in an intimately involved relation with the internal operations of the first brain." He would presumably apply the same remark also to the two hemispheres, in case of a commissurotomy. Globus has been saying the same thing in other language: a representing of a representing (third person view of a neural event) is not the same as a representing (first person view of the same neural event). The difference here is that between "observer" and "internal relation", but said in a language that philosophers will more readily understand, and which makes clear that a *kind* of category mistake is being committed by those who would *straightforwardly* identify the two perspectives.

ingly different interpretations of this claim however. The first is that attempts to identify or explain the upper-level whole and its properties with or in terms of a configuration of the lower-level parts and their known monadic and relational properties will fail. It is as such a claim of nonreducibility. On the second interpretation, the interlevel identification and reduction which is denied on the first interpretation is presupposed and the "more than" claim involves a denial that the relational properties of the parts in the compositional identification are of a sufficiently symmetric, simple, and conservative sort to regard this compositional identification as "additive" or "aggregative." (See Wimsatt, 1971a, Chap. 8, for an analysis extending suggestions by Levins, 1970, pp. 76–77). This interpretation presupposes reducibility, but says something about the form and complexity of relations between levels—in particular that the parts are (or are not, for nonaggregativity) intersubstitutable without changing the system properties in question. This will hereafter be called the "second sense of emergence," "emergence₂." The related sense of aggregativity will be denoted "aggregative₂."

The first interpretation of "The whole is more than the sum of its parts" is far more common. In at least many situations, however, the second seems more appropriate. Sperry's remarks on emergence are consistent with, and indeed congenial to, the second interpretation. Dewan's (this volume) claim that entrainment is not an "average" effect (presumably [1969, p. 329] because the interactions are nonlinear), make it another example of this kind of emergence. This concept of emergence as nonaggregativity has substantial importance in evolution and throughout the life sciences, broadly construed, for it often as Dewan notes (1969, p. 329) can result in a form of self-organization. As such, it is essential to the reductionist's account of the hierarchial evolution of complex systems. (See Simon, 1969, chapter 4.) In more than one sense, without emergence, life as we know it would be impossible!

Another feature which seems frequently connected with discussions of emergence in the mental realm is derived from the immediacy of sense experience, which is frequently described as if it were a kind of ineliminability. There is a tendency to conflate this with irreducibility (emergence₁) via a double mistake: (1) to believe that reduction implies conceptual eliminability (I argue in part II that it does not); and (2) to believe that the kind of ineliminability involved in the immediacy of sense experience is conceptual (which it is not). I discuss this last issue, and this feature, which could be called "emergence₃," in the last section of part III. The most important distinction between these three kinds of emergence for the present is as follows: Emergence₁ implies *irreducibility*. Emergence$_2$ implies *reducibility*. and emergence$_3$ is *independent of the question of reduction*.

(4) A related ambiguity infects the claim that whole properties are (e) "different from" parts' properties. It could be taken as a straightforward claim of nonreducibility. More moderately, it could be taken as a claim that the *basic* properties and entities of one level are different from the *basic* properties and entities of another. As such, it is not inconsistent with reducibility, since the higher-level entities and properties might be identical with configurations and relations of the lower-level entities and properties. Here again, Sperry's remarks are consistent with the second interpretation, as upper-level basic entities might well be (d) "best conceived" (for reasons of theoretical economy, familiarity, or predictive or manipulative efficacy) as different from lower-level basic entities (h) "as these are generally understood"—especially if the relevant configurations of lower-level basic entities (c) "have yet to be discovered."[3]

(5) Sperry's "interactionism" dovetails neatly with his views on emergence and could be regarded as a consequence of his view that conscious subjective events have causal potency. This is part of the reason for saying that mental phenomena are real in their own right (see (6) below), and thus that they are emergent. Conscious events are asserted to have causal potency at the level of other macroscopic events and behavior, as is illustrated by his discussion of the pain avoidance behavior of a rat in which the nerves going to left and right hind feet have been experimentally crossed. Sperry is particularly concerned to argue against epiphenomenalism and behaviorism, and suggests a position which is noteworthy in another respect:

> The present interpretation by contrast would make consciousness an integral part of the brain process itself and an essential constituent of the action. *Consciousness in the present scheme is put to work. It is given a use and a reason for being, and for having been evolved.* (Sperry, 1969, p. 533, italics added)

This is a conception of the nature and role of consciousness that some psychologists are just beginning to return to, and most recent

---

[3] This last phrase is the key to Sperry's perhaps mistaken opposition to the identity theory:

"In the related 'identity' theory of mind, subjective phenomena have been postulated to be identical with the neural activity, *something that is supposed to become apparent if one looks at and talks about the mind–body relation in the appropriate way* " (Sperry 1970, p. 587, italics added).

Sperry clearly takes the identity theory to be something which its proponents regarded as establishable, not by empirical discoveries but by conceptual arguments. As such he has misread the view of most identity theorists, who would regard themselves as arguing over the conceptual preconditions to the truth of an identity thesis, with the decision (if no contradiction is to be found at this level) ultimately depending upon the empirical facts.

philosophers appear never to have discovered.[4] Sperry's functionalistic *and* evolutionary justification here is reminiscent of Charles Darwin's classic and now often forgotten work on the emotions (Darwin, 1872). I believe that this approach is an essential prerequisite to achieving a proper understanding of mind, body, or the relation between them.

In addition to the involvement of consciousness in interactions with other phenomena at the same level, Sperry sees consciousness as involved in mutual interactions with lower-level phenomena— simultaneously controlling and being controlled by events at lower levels (p. 173; also 1970, pp. 588–9), " . . . just as drops of water [both make up and] are carried along by a local eddy in a stream" (1969, p. 534).

Reductionistically inclined writers frequently claim to find this kind of talk mysterious, especially when it is claimed that lower levels are controlled from above, or even more, that there is a *hierarchy* of levels of control (also see 1970, p. 588), with higher levels controlling lower levels. I suspect that they are bothered here by the feeling that some entity under one description is said to be the cause of its own behavior under another description. This has the air of some sort of vicious circularity (see, e.g., Sperry, 1969, p. 534) or might be thought to violate Hume's dictum of the logical independence of cause and effect. I think that it involves neither.

It is too easy to act as if the aims of reduction have already been completed (instead of merely promised) so that at the lower-level we have a complete description of things at that level, and thus (derivatively, since reduction is complete), also of everything at higher levels. If this *were* so, it would seem improper to talk about upper-level events causing lower-level events because the upper-level events would *already* be included, complete with causal relations, at the lower level. "Upper-level causation," one could say, "is just a shorthand for lower-level causation," and this "interaction" talk suggests that there are other entities and other relations *in addition to* what exits at the lower-level.

But whatever the *promises* of reductionism, we do not in any interesting cases actually *have* the complete lower-level descriptions necessary to make upper-level descriptions and causal talk redundant. Characteristically, scientists are satisfied with lower-level descriptions and analyses for a few mechanisms which are particularly crucial for

---

[4] A notable exception is the recent and stimulating work of D. C. Dennett (1969, 1971) who invokes natural selection to explain and analyze intentionality. See also Campbell (1973*a*) and Wimsatt (1972*a*, 1972*b*).

explaining (or particularly mysterious at) the upper-level of phenomena. Either *this* alone *is* reduction, or (as is more often assumed) it is an acceptable down-payment on a promissory note of reduction.

What we *actually* have then is a patchwork of partial descriptions and perspectives at various levels which cut up the system in quite different ways and each of which captures or tries to capture one or a few relevant causal factors, leaving many identities and causal relations unclear or unspecified. Under such circumstances, interactional talk like that of Sperry is necessary, even for a reductionist, and indeed, usually represents the best (in terms of completeness and economy) that we can do. This situation is one I have described elsewhere more fully as involving "descriptive" and "interactional" complexity (Wimsatt, 1974a).

Furthermore, while I would defend reductionism in a broader sense, I think that many problems arise with the standardly accepted accounts of reduction which lead to the "nothing more than" talk which Sperry and I both find objectionable. I believe that the different accounts suggested here for reduction and for the idea of a level of organization show such worries of vicious circularity or other logical error to be mistaken, even if a thoroughgoing reduction is accomplished.

(6) Perhaps this discussion is not quite fair to Sperry, for I have made him look almost like a typical reductionistic materialist or identity theorist. These are positions which he has taken great pains to disassociate himself from—at least in their "pre-'65" versions (also see 1970, p. 587), though sometimes with mysterious results.

Sperry suggested in the quote beginning this section that upper-level phenomena be recognized (g) "in their own right"—presumably even *after* their description in terms of configurations of neural events have been discovered. He also criticizes the reductionistic approach as leading " . . . to an infinite regress in which eventually everything is held to be explainable in terms of essentially nothing." (p. 167)

Yet, elsewhere, in a passage purporting to *contrast* emergence with identity, this critique of reductionism becomes paradoxical, for mental events are said to be related to neural events in a manner " . . . analogous . . . to saying that the physiological brain process is itself identical to the chemical events that compose it, or that these chemical events are in turn identical to their atomistic and electron-proton events, etc." (p. 167). Here is another mystifying juxtaposition: Part of the force of saying that upper-level phenomena are real in their own right is the claim that they have real causal efficacy of their own. But when we try to find some antireductionistic meaning in this, we find instead that:

> In the dynamics of these higher level interactions, the more molar conscious properties are seen to *supersede* the more elemental physicochemical forces, *just as the properties of the molecule supersede nuclear forces in chemical interactions.*(Sperry, 1969, p. 534, italics added)

Sperry further explicitly denies that lower-level laws are broken when higher-level processes "intervene" (see 1969, p. 533, 1970, p. 587), and disavows positions which see a conflict between laws at upper and lower levels (*ibid*). He is in effect reasserting a classical emergentism at all levels but without many of the antireductionist views usually associated with it. Can he do this?

In these remarks, and in Sperry's philosophical writings generally, the reductionistically inclined reader will time and again find apparent direct attacks on his position—and find his own reductionistic paradigms or principles appealed to bolster these attacks. It is tempting initially to accuse Sperry of inconsistency, and I confess that this was my initial reaction. I now believe that Sperry has found an important and largely repressed tension within the reductionist position. It is this: How can one be a reductionist and at the same time admit the reality (in some "hard-nosed" sense) of some upper-level phenomena which one has just reduced? One might claim that if all of the relevant lower-level phenomena exist, this is *ipso facto* to admit the reality of the upper-level phenomena since the upper-level phenomena are *made up* of lower-level phenomena. But this claim has the clear air of a cop-out; it is admitting the reality of upper-level phenomena all right, but in a distinctly derivative and "soft-nosed" manner.

I believe that it is possible to go at least part way toward resolving these tensions, and this requires a closer examination of models of reduction and their applications, which will be attempted in the second part of this paper. In the third part of the paper an analysis of levels is advanced which not only permits a generically reductionistic solution of many of the difficulties besetting reductionism *per se*, but also seems to suggest a strategy for a reductionistic account of first-person–third-person asymmetries (see Gunderson, 1970, and Globus, 1972) without the complementarity proposed by Globus (1972, 1973, this volume). I would argue that both this solution and the kind of reductionism behind it are in the spirit of Sperry's "emergent interactionism."

PART II: REDUCTION AND ITS FUNCTIONS—REAL AND MYTHOLOGICAL

The easy agreement I find with most aspects of Sperry's views of the mental realm does not extend to his views on reductionism or the psychophysical identity theory, both of which he claims to oppose. I think that the fault here is of philosopher and scientist alike, and lies largely with current analyses (and sometimes with current mythologies) or reduction. I will discuss two contrasting views of reduction. The first, or "ontological simplicity" view is in some ways a caricature of views which are loosely called "positivistic" or "reductionistic" and is strongly influenced by "structuralist" considerations. It has nonetheless been an influential caricature, and has not infrequently been taken as a true picture of reductionism—most often, but not always, by its opponents. The second view involves a bifurcation between intralevel and interlevel reductions and seems to be favored by the inclusion of functional considerations. It contains much to be found in reductionistic writings—though frequently treated as asides and usually ignored in subsequent discussions. I will argue that this functional view presents a better account of reduction *in science* (there is an arguably separate reductionist tradition in philosophy) and one which is relatively congenial to Sperry's remarks. Its careful development is absolutely essential to a defense and proper understanding of the psychophysical identity thesis.

Structural and Functional Analyses of Reduction

Disputes over the relative importance or primacy of structure and function were frequent in 19th-century biology, though there now seems to be fairly widespread agreement among biologists that neither is primary, and each affects the other. For philosophy of science in the positivistic tradition, the corresponding question has not even been seriously entertained; there has been an unequivocal emphasis on structure.

Structure in this tradition meant logical structure and a common strategy for the analysis of terms, procedures, and entities of science was to exhibit a logical schema which was supposed to give its idealized logical, rational, or reconstructed form. Thus theories were analyzed as "partially interpreted" formal (i.e., axiomatic deductive) systems. Explanation, prediction, and theory testing were all suggested to have the form of a deduction. The most widely accepted account of *theory* reduction (and there *was* no other interesting kind) was as the defineability and deducibility, respectively, of the concepts and laws of one theory (the reduced theory) from the concepts and laws of the other (the reducing theory). (See Nagel, 1961.)

Also common on this view is the feeling that there is something wrong with the reduced theory, at least by contrast with the reducing theory: it is less general, less correct, less exact, less specific, less explanatory, or contains concepts which are for some reason thought to be inferior to those of the reducing theory. For this reason one often hears that (1) reduction allows "translation" of the language of the reduced theory into the "scientifically preferable" terminology of the reducing theory, as if the aim of reduction was to avoid certain ways of talking, or (2) that it shows that upper-level entities are "nothing more than" lower-level entities as if it were important to show that they were of no significance in and of themselves, or (3) that reduction allows elimination of extra assumptions, entities, concepts, or terms, as if the scientist should, like the mathematician, aim primarily to deduce and define as much as possible from a basis which is both as small and as certain as possible.

But questions of what reductions are for—what functions they might serve—were seldom asked *explicitly*, summarily answered (if at all), and rarely subjects of further debate.[5] I suspect that much of the support for the "ontological simplicity" view of reduction comes from an uncritical acceptance of the application of "Ockham's razor" as a major goal of science, and probably owes its persistence (outside of logic and mathematics) to the attentions paid to structural features of reductions at the expense of a careful analysis of the functions they characteristically serve. This has resulted in serious distortions:

(1) The structural unity of reductions (the claim that all reductions are kinds of deduction) together with a belief in the importance of structure lead to the view that all reductions are fundamentally alike. But there are at least two functionally distinct kinds of reduction which are so different in their functions and, derivatively, in most of their deeper structural properties, that one is lead to doubt not only the

---

[5] One striking exception to this is Jaegwon Kim's (1964) comparative analysis of the functions of deductive argument in explanation and prediction which gives important insights into the workings of the standard deductivist account of these activities. In retrospect, I think that it must have had seminal influence in the development of the view advocated here.

unitary model of reduction but also the primacy of structure over function in its characterization.

(2) Many of the important aspects of the "ontological simplicity" view of reduction can be seen to derive erroneously from a conflation of the functionally distinguishable interlevel and intralevel types of reduction. The proper model for the mind–body problem is interlevel reduction. Eliminative materialism seems however to derive its inspiration from intralevel reduction. When the two types are separated out, there is *no* defensible "ontological simplicity" view of the nature and functions of reduction, and upper-level phenomena are seen neither to be eliminated nor to be "analyzed away."

Until part III (where I will attempt to analyze the concept of a level in more detail) I will presuppose intuitions of what a level is and of when things are at the same or at different (higher or lower) levels, which I will try to guide with a few remarks and examples. I will assume that being at a given level is a property primarily of things in the world: phenomena, objects, properties, processes, causes and effects, etc., and derivatively of linguistic things relating to them: descriptions, law-statements, theories, predicates, etc. Intuitively, one thing is at a higher level than something else if things of the first type *are composed of* things of the second type, and at the same level with those things it interacts most strongly and frequently with or is capable of replacing in a variety of causal contexts. In a derivative sense, one can similarly talk about the level (or levels) of a theory and its parts, and using something like the causal replaceability criterion, compare levels of concepts in competing theories which are sufficiently similar in the relevant (usually causal) respects.

Intuitively, the sequence "atom, molecule, cell, organism, population" represents entities of successively higher levels (though there may be levels in between some of them). Mendelian genetics is at a higher level than molecular genetics, and cognitive psychology is at a higher level than the physiology of the synapse. On the other hand, DNA and RNA, neurons and neuroglia, the disposition to see Mach bands and having lateral inhibition networks in the retina and/or visual cortex, pool cues and eight-balls, the automobile and horse-and-buggy it replaced, and mass in Newtonian and in Einsteinian physics are pairs from common levels.

More difficult examples are easy to come by, and I will not always assume (as in this section) that theories are limited to single levels, that levels are always well defined, or that two or more entities can always be unambiguously ordered with respect to level.

Intralevel Reductions

In two recent papers (1973*a*, 1973*b*) Thomas Nickles has force-fully argued that many cases of "intertheoretic" reduction do not fit very well the classical accounts of theory reduction. The abbreviated account I will give here for intralevel reduction is in many respects an amplification and extension of his view, though perhaps from a different perspective than he envisioned.

Nickles suggests that the function of reduction in many cases (such as the relation of classical mechanics to the special theory of relativity) is "heuristic and justificatory" (1973*a*, p. 185) and not explanatory or eliminative as is generally assumed. The kinds of cases he considers are of the relation of one theory to its successor, in which the latter theory is said to correct the earlier theory and show it to be an approximate special case. Thus he considers how relativistic mechanics "reduces to" classical mechanics in the limit as the velocity of the system approaches zero (or, in another way, as c, the speed of light approaches infinity.)[6] He notes that these reductions can often occur in a *variety of ways* between the same two theories, and symmetrically—in both directions (1973*a*, p. 198). (Neither of these is true for interlevel reduction.) He also argues that the kinds of manipulation which produce this kind of reduction are better regarded as transformations in a broader sense, rather than as deductive arguments.

I wish to suggest that this kind of reduction is usefully considered as a kind of pattern-matching.[7] If one is trying to match two patterns, this can usually be done in a variety of ways, and often (though not always) it makes no difference which pattern you start with in the effort to reduce it to or "turn it into" the other (see also Nickles, 1973*a*, p. 198). Deductions, when they play a role, could be used as transformations even under conditions where meaning change or the literal falsity of the older theory prevents their having the status of sound arguments. Most importantly, the functions of identification and reduction in intralevel cases seem all to require an evaluation and classification of the similarities *and differences* between the successive theories—which is a paradigmatic description of a pattern-matching

---

[6] In transforming one theory into the other, the term $(1 - v^2/c^2)$ frequently occurs as a factor or divisor. It is easily seen that this approaches 1 if either v approaches 0 or c approaches ∞, under which conditions the theories are said to produce "equivalent" results. Nickles notes that in this sort of reduction, it is usually the later, more sophisticated theory that is said to "reduce to" the earlier—also a difference with the interlevel case, in which it is the upper level (and usually earlier) theory which reduces to the lower level account.

[7] This move is in the tradition of remarks of Hanson (1961, 1970) but was most strongly inspired by D'Arcy Thompson's theory of transformations (1961, chapter 9).

task. An identification of these similarities and differences is essential not only for the justificatory and heuristic roles proposed by Nickles, but also for testing and elaborating the new theory:

(1) The *similarities*, emphasized by the reduction, play a *justificatory* role for the new theory by showing that it is confirmed by the evidence that supported the old theory under those conditions for which the latter is a good approximation.

(2) The *transformations* involved in the reduction, together with any unreduced differences that might remain, determine the range and limitations of the old theory as a "valid approximation," and thus allow its use as a *heuristic* predictive and calculating device when it is applicable and easier to manipulate than the new theory.

(3) The unreduced *differences* between the two theories have significance in several ways:

(a) Some of the differences will have been *anomalies* for the older theory. To be accepted, the new theory must account for at least some of these anomalies.

(b) Other differences will have been unanticipated. Locating them is facilitated by reduction, and provides *new predictive tests* for the successor theory (some of which might involve reanalysis of the old data in a new light).

(c) Some of the differences will not be sufficiently well-defined to immediately suggest predictions, but will nonetheless suggest new directions for *amplifying and extending the new theory.*

(d) *Meaning changes,* if they occur, and are relatively clearly defineable and localizable, pose no special problems for this sort of reduction.

With the view of intralevel reduction as pattern-matching, its justificatory, ampliative, and testing functions (all of which pertain only to the most recent theory in a successional sequence) and in most cases also its heuristic functions would be totally served by reducing only *neighboring* theories in a successional sequence to one another. This pattern-matching involves transformations and classification of similarities and differences and thus sometimes takes a great deal of effort. But if reductions involve work, and if they have no function except between theories which are "nearest neighbors," we might expect on cost–benefit considerations that they would not be performed between more distant relatives. *Thus suggests that intralevel reductions should be intransitive*—that a number of intralevel *reductions* could "add up" to an intralevel *replacement.*

This pattern-matching view also sheds some light on the frequently debated problem of the *incomparability* of theories. (See, e.g., Feyerabend, 1962; Kuhn, 1962; and Shapere, 1966, 1969.) I suggest that incomparability or incommensurability arises when it is no longer possible to specify and *isolate* or *localize* the similarities and differences between two theories. In that case it will be impossible to say what parts of the two theories are responsible for differences (or similarities) in their predictions. One can then no longer say what parts of the older theory are to blame for the difference, and it is falsified as a whole.[8]

I do not accept the standard view among many philosophers that incomparabilities derive simply from meaning changes of key terms in the two theories, unless the meaning changes *also* have this unlocalizable character. Meaning change, if it is localizable to specific terms and analyzable in its effects, is *just one more difference* that must be considered in comparing the two theories—not a special kind of difference that makes reduction impossible. The argument of some writers that any meaning change in a deduction (of the old theory from the new) makes a *fallacy of equivocation* and thus prevents reduction is a *non sequitur*. Equivocation is dangerous in a deduction only if you are trying to construct a sound argument, leading to a true conclusion. But the assumption of a reduction of this type is generally that the new theory is true, but that old theory to be derived from it is *literally false*. So if the argument form is valid, there had better be an equivocation somewhere! The function of deduction in this case is as a kind of known transformation of one theory into another—not to derive the old theory as a true conclusion. In this respect, the "structuralist" or "deductivist" account of reduction is at least seriously misleading, and is simply incorrect as it is usually interpreted. I believe that this upholds Nickles' (1973a) alternative "transformationalist" account.

Incomparabilities naturally arise when comparing properties of systems which can be treated as kinds of networks in the relevant respects. Glymour (1973) has described the structure of theories in terms of networks in order to analyze questions of the independent testability of components of the theory (see also Blachowitz, 1971) in ways that is quite suggestive of this idea, and I have argued (1971a, 1971b, 1972a, pp. 23–26, 55–61) that similar problems arise for "func-

---

[8] The functions listed under items 1, 2, and 3c would be rather more severely compromised than those of items 3a and 3b for which rather more "observational" comparability is all that is required. This is why we can talk about similarity of predictions of two theories in situations where we can't say that much else is comparable. When comparing networks, comparability may vary from point to point in the network. Similar remarks apply in comparing the functional organization of two distinct kinds of animal: they may be readily comparable in terms of number of offspring, even though they may have radically different modes of organization and be incomparable for virtually everything else.

tional equivalents" in systems whose functional organization differs appreciably. Parallel problems arise also in taxonomy and in decision theory.

If theories are reducibly related only if they are sufficiently similar to localize their differences, incomparabilities could result as a cumulative effect when differences and the complexity of intervening transformations pile up in a series of successive intralevel reductions until they become too complex to handle. This again suggests that intralevel reductions should be intransitive and that enough of them should add up to a replacement. Furthermore, this conclusion appears to be accepted at least implicitly by most philosophers and historians of science: Relativistic mechanics may reduce to classical mechanics (etc.) but it clearly replaces (rather than reduces to) Aristotelian physics.

Interlevel Reduction

No distinction is made in the literature between interlevel and intralevel reductions, and indeed, the writings of Nagel (1961), Schaffner (1967) and others suggest or argue for a unitary account of reduction. Thus, it would not be surprising to find suggestions that interlevel reduction should fail under conditions similar to those in which intralevel reductions fail—where there are no known transformations from one level or theory to the other or where there is reason to believe that the transformations, if they exist, would be exceedingly complex. Taylor (1967), Fodor (1968, 1974), Sperry (1970, p. 587), and Hull (1972, 1973) have all raised this as a problem for reductionistic programs—the first three in psychology, the last in genetics. Taylor's argument (1967, p. 206) is both representative and tempting:

> . . . if human behavior exhibits lawlike regularity, on the physiological level, of the sort which enables prediction and control, and a rougher regularity of a less all-embracing kind on the psychological level, it does not follow that we can discover one–one or even one–many correspondences between the terms which figure in the first regularities and those which figure in the second. For we can talk usefully about a given set of phenomena in concepts of different ranges, belonging to different modes of classification, between which there may be no exact correspondence, without denying that one range yields laws which are far richer in explanatory force than the others.

Taylor suggests that without this correspondence between terms (or, as it is sometimes put, between types or kinds of entities) reduction is impossible (1967, p. 211), and that the "soul" of material-ism is lost—even though correspondences between *particular* physiol-ogical and psychological states could result in "some kind of identity thesis" (*ibid.*).

In more specific and detailed arguments, Hull claims (1972, pp. 496–7; 1973) that the Mendelian property of genetic epistasis (gene "masking" or, more generally, genetic interaction) can be a product of an arbitrarily long list of different kinds of molecular mechanisms. Also, if one limits consideration to those dynamical configurations which are sufficiently important and frequent to be called "mecha-nisms" or "standard boundary conditions," he claims that given molecular mechanisms can result in a variety of different alternative Mendelian outcomes (1972, p. 497; 1973, pp. 39–42). If these claims are correct, then either one is left with arbitrarily complex mappings between theoretically relevant properties at the two levels of organiza-tion, or one can restore one–one mappings only at the cost of " . . . no longer correlating Mendelian predicate terms with molecular mecha-nisms but with the entire molecular milieu" (1973, p. 42).

This *seems* to be the same kind of potential difficulty in locat-ing correlates as there was with localizing similarities and differences between successive theories in cases of intralevel incomparability and replacement. Hull concludes (1973, p. 44):

> If the logical empiricist analysis of reduction is correct, then Mende-lian genetics cannot be reduced to molecular genetics. The long-awaited reduction of a biological theory to physics and chemistry turns out not to be a case of "reduction" after all but an example of replacement. But given our pre-analytic intuitions about reduction, it *is* a case of reduction, a paradigm case.

I suggest that we follow our intuitions at this point and regard the relation of Mendelian to molecular genetics as one of reduction, as most biologists would and accept, at least provisionally, Hull's claims about the complexity of mappings between levels. What follows from this about the concept of interlevel reduction? What can (and what cannot) be done that could have been done if the mappings between levels had been less complex?

Most importantly, Hull is *not* claiming that there are any upper-level phenomena which cannot be *explained* at the lower-level. That is, he is not claiming that reduction fails because the phenomena are *emergent*$_1$. Any given case of Mendelian inheritance presumably has a molecular explanation. Furthermore, I believe that this claim of lower-level *explanatory* adequacy is at the heart of what most scientists mean by reduction in interlevel cases. If this is so, however, than there are some fundamental differences between interlevel reduction on the one hand, and both intralevel reduction and the standard model of reduction on the other. Two things which have traditionally been associated with reduction are ruled out by highly complex or open-ended mappings between upper- and lower-level concepts. The first is the view of reduction as *translation*. The second is the view of reduction as a relation between theories or parts of theories. Neither of these can be maintained for interlevel reduction, though both are more-or-less true of intralevel reduction and the standard model.

The demise of translation. The first thing to go must be the view of interlevel reduction as a kind of *translation*. If the molecular (or neurophysiological) milieu must be brought in each time to get one–one or many–one correspondence between lower and upper levels, then the putative translation is *context-dependent*, which is to say that it is *incomplete*. By comparison, in the study of foreign languages, an expression whose meaning is strongly dependent upon myriad fine details of the context in which it is used and/or requires a thorough knowledge of the language in which it occurs to be understood correctly, is said to be *untranslatable* or only *partly* translatable.

This conclusion is often avoided, hidden, or (revealingly) implied in conversation by the standard claim of philosophical reductionists which is for "translatability *in principle*"—which is, in effect, often to admit to *de facto* untranslatability. *In principle* results are results which are accessible to LaPlacean demons, but could nonetheless turn out to be unachievable for any present or conceivable future science. (See Boyd, 1972, for an illuminating discussion of this and related points.) One of the more pervasive systematic errors of the tradition in philosophy of science has been the use of *in principle* arguments and assumptions when it is quite clear that we are (in Stuart Kauffman's fortuitous phrase) "dinky computers" rather than LaPlacean demons. LaPlacean demons may be able to solve any problem as long as it is finite, but "dinky computers" have to give up after a *small* finite number of steps. I will argue later that in principle translatability has its place in interlevel reduction, but not as a real goal of science.

Another argument for the unimportance of type-correspondences or translations in interlevel reductions is suggested by their *transitivity*, which is systematically presupposed both by reductionists and by anti-reductionists, and provides one of the more striking contrasts between intralevel and interlevel reductions. The unity of science movement presupposed this transitivity in its hope to reduce the social sciences to physics (*via* psychology, biology, chemistry, and all points in between). So also does Sperry's "infinite regress" argument against reductionism that " . . . eventually everything is held to be explainable in terms of essentially nothing" (p. 167).

If *real* translations or type correspondences were important for interlevel reductions, we would expect interlevel reductions to be *in*transitive (like intralevel reductions) as the complexities of the transformation or translations add up with successive reductions until real translation is impossible. But interlevel reduction is transitive. Thus, *real* translatability cannot be important. In fact, there is seldom any attempt to push translations of a given phenomenon below a given level unless there are problems or unexplained facts at the level, though one may well claim reduction to lower levels without the translations. *In principle* translatability *is* assumed to be transitive of course, but I will argue below that it has its primary significance as a way of interpreting identity claims, and is not (of itself) a real goal or result of reduction in science.

Another striking contrast between inter- and intralevel reductions is the matter of replacement. By analogy with the intralevel case, enough interlevel reductions should "add up" to a replacement, as increased complexity rules out real translatability. But, by contrast, in interlevel reduction, the more difficult the translation becomes, the more *irreplaceable* the upper level theory is! It becomes the only practical way of handling the regularities it describes.

Replacement clearly means different things in the two cases. In intralevel cases, if one theory replaces another it *supersedes* it. The relation is asymmetric, and occurs when the old theory is so different from the new one that difficulties of translation prevent achievement of the functions of intralevel reduction. These were the only reasons for keeping it around, since it was presumed to be incorrect, and when it cannot serve these functions, it is *eliminated*.

In interlevel contexts, one characteristically talks about re-plac*eability* rather that replace*ment*, and in situations where ready translatability or substitutability (sometimes in *both* directions) are assured. It thus occurs when theories are very similar (usually in their ability to handle given problems), and may be symmetric or asymmetric. Asymmetries or failures of translatability carry with them no automatic presumption of upper-level guilt in interlevel cases. Asymmetries of translation may occur because lower level theories give more specific descriptions, but in general problems of translation might result from explanatory inadequacies of the lower theory (emergence of the upper phenomena), the upper theory (which is then "corrected" by the lower theory), both, or *neither* (as when there is nothing wrong with either theory, but there simply are no neat type-correspondences). Hull was thus just wrong in suggesting that this last situation suggested replacement in interlevel cases. It would have in intralevel cases, and the fault is that of the traditional model of reduction, which fails to distinguish the two.

It is worth noting that "nothing more than" talk is used both in intra- and in interlevel contexts in talking about replacement. But if I am right, there is a very different force to the claims that "What we used to call demons are *nothing more than* collections of natural phenomena," and "What people call mental phenomena are *nothing more than* the occurrence and normal effects of certain types of organized neural activity in higher organisms." One may thereby demythologize natural phenomena, but one will not thereby dementalize organisms. This casts real doubt on the defensibility of "eliminative materialist" views like that of Rorty (1965), which suggest that mental language and entities will be eliminated with further scientific progress. I think that such views rest on a confusion between intralevel and interlevel cases of replacement.

Phenomenal reduction vs. theory reduction.   Giving up translatability in interlevel cases raises serious questions about another central assumption of the standard model of reduction—that it is to be regarded as a relation between theories, or parts of theories. (See, e.g., Nagel, 1961, and Schaffner, 1967.) This would also further widen the gap between intralevel reduction and interlevel reduction, since on Nickles'·account or the pattern-matching analysis suggested here, *intralevel reduction must be a relation between theories or parts of theories* since it is these which are transformed, compared, and contrasted to see their similarities and differences.

There are three things most directly compromised by giving up neat type-correspondences or translatability:

(1) The first is a neat deductive relation between types of the two theories. While one could presumably construct relations between *particular* occurrences of the phenomena described at lower and at upper levels, relations between types would, because of the complexity of the mappings, just be a collection of the relations between particu-

lars. Since theories are characterized by their concepts, and not by the particulars they describe, this should be enough to challenge the view that interlevel reductions are relations between theories.

(2) A similar thing happens to the claim that in a reduction, the lower-level theory *explains* the upper-level theory. Phenomena of a given upper-level type will have diverse lower-level types, and conversely. In this case, being able to explain any given example of an upper-level phenomenon in lower-level terms (the core of the interlevel reduction claim) is not equivalent to being able to explain upper-level phenomena *of that type*. We cannot explain the unity of that upper-level category at the lower level because it *has* no lower level unity! Being able to explain an upper level theory surely involves being able to explain why its categories are as they are and work as they do. What is being explained is not the theory, but its phenomena.

(3) A failure of neat interlevel type correspondences also rules out versions of the identity theory in which upper-level properties are individually identified with and reduced to lower-level properties. Many philosophers have felt that any weaker identity theory is too weak to be interesting—a claim I shall examine below. But a type of property-identity theory is probably too strong for multilevel identifications in biological and psychological systems for reasons having to do with the complexity of interlevel mappings, which I have argued is a product of an optimal mode of organization of evolving systems (see my 1974a and below).

What is interlevel reduction? Given its basis in a claim of explanatory adequacy of lower-level theory for any phenomena at a given level (usually of well-delineated types), it is probably better regarded as an explanatory relation between a lower level theory or domain of phenomena and a domain (roughly in the sense of Shapere, 1974) of upper-level phenomena than as a relation between lower and upper level theories. An even better proposal, especially in cases where there is a partial explanation of upper-level categories, is Roth's (1974) suggestion that what is going on is the development of an *interlevel theory* to explain phenomena at a variety of levels. Part of her contention is that there often are not two distinct theories at separate levels to be related, and that the categories developed are ambiguous with respect to level. These conclusions are nicely supported by her analysis of the development of the operon theory and theories of allosteric regulation in molecular biology. Her analysis also supports strongly the view of the dynamics of theory evolution, reduction, and interlevel identification advanced in the next section.

Reduction, Explanation, and Identification.   Something more remains to be said about the relation between reduction, explanation and identification—at least to counter the temptation to think that identification (in the service of ontological simplicity) is the primary end of reduction, and that explanation somehow serves that end. I believe that the reverse is true: *identification can be seen as a 'tool in the service of reduction, and the interesting dividends of interlevel reduction in general, and of a psychophysical identity theory in particular, are explanatory rather than ontological.*

Without type-correspondences, property identifications seem to be ruled out, and about the only kind of identity left is "stuff" identity—roughly, that the stuff with the psychological properties is the same stuff as the stuff with the physical properties. Philosophers, concentrating on ontological dividends, have found this to be uninteresting and trivial. It seems like a common sense conclusion that we hardly need scientific sophistication or data to embrace. They are right in assuming that there must be something more to reduction than undifferentiated stuff-identity, but they are wrong in assuming that this something more is a stronger *identity* condition, such as property-identity. The something more that makes a stuff-identity theory nontrivial is its explanatory import—that any upper-level phenomenon in need of explanation has a lower-level explanation. These explanatory demands are also the source of the transitivity of interlevel reduction, though I do not believe, as Sperry and many philosophers have assumed, that the aim of reduction is to explain everything at the lowest level.

The point of reduction is not to get an "infinite regress" explanation for "eventually everything" in terms of "essentially nothing," but only to make sure that everything gets explained—at *some* level or other. This in fact allows for the possibility that some things may require explanation at *higher* levels, something which I will discuss in Part III. Also, while we may explain away false theories, or explain why we believed them, we do not literally explain something false or something that did not happen (Sklar, 1967, p. 112). So the full explanatory maxim which takes account of both of these factors is: *Explain everything that occurs and nothing that doesn't.*

This suggests that one theory does not explain another which it corrects, except, at most, in its corrected form. It further suggests that intralevel reduction, which involves corrections of the older theory does *not* involve an explanation of the older theory.

Given these explanatory ends, consider what would happen if

interlevel reductions or identifications were allowed to be "inexact" or "approximate" like intralevel reductions and identifications. As one went up several levels, errors could accumulate until they exceeded a threshold of detectability. At this point, one could have one of two things: (1) a theoretical prediction of and explanation for something which does not occur; or (2) an emergent$_1$ phenomenon—a detectable phenomenon for which there was no prediction or explanation. Either violates one horn of the explanatory maxim. The occurence of either is accepted as a *criterion* for denying that one or more of the putative lower-level reductions or identifications was correct. But this is just the *modus tollens* form of the transitivity of identification and reduction, generated from the constraint that one must not allow an explanatory maxim to be violated.[9]

A lower-level explanatory failure is by definition a reductive failure, in the way I have been using the term. But couldn't the transitivity of reduction be a straightforward consequence of the transitivity of identity? Could it be identity which licenses the transitivity rather than the desire to avoid explanatory failures? But I have already shown that if the only point of reductions was to establish "stuff coreferentialities," there would be no reason for such scientific detail. These identities could be established with much less work and their transitivity would give the transitivity of reduction directly—at the cost, however, of leaving it a mystery why scientists should bother to do so much work, of why reductionists should make such a fuss about *"in principle* translatability," and of what all this has to do with explanation . I believe that regarding identities as a means rather than an end in reductions explains in a more unified and satisfying manner the various properties of interlevel reduction.

Many writers have emphasized the importance of identities in

[9] One can easily construct cases of this sort involving several levels from the history of development of theories accounting for the macroscopic behavior of gases in terms of a microscopic model. Thus, both the ideal gas law and the Van der Waals equation of state were explicable via "molecular" models which ignored any details of molecular structure. This could be done for "normal" temperatures and pressures because in this range, energies were low enough that changes in molecular structure were not produced by normal interactions. At elevated temperatures, however, the higher energies activate internal vibrational degrees of freedom, and produce deviations from the specific heats predicted by those models which ignored molecular structure. Energy was apparently not being conserved (because it was disappearing into the molecule). At still higher temperatures, had 19th-century physicists pushed the issue far enough, appreciable degrees of ionization would have resulted in all of the complexities of modern-day plasma physics, and a whole host of phenomena which are emergent relative to either of the theories mentioned, but not relative to some added assumptions—including a number of assumptions about molecular structure and energy activation levels.

Rather more amazing than the fact that theories which ignore certain lower-level structural details occasionally break down is the fact that this happens as rarely as it does. This "hierarchial" organization of nature, in which one can usually get away with ignoring a huge amount of detail each time one goes up a level, is remarkable and demands explanation.

explanation. Causey (1972) argues that propery-identities rather than property-correspondences are required for explanation. It is a general presumption of the traditional model that identities are useful intermediaries in explanations. Thus, if X causes Y, Y is identical with Z, and Z causes W, the identity, $Y = Z$ *can* play an essential role in the explanation of W's occurrence, given the occurrence of X.

But neither of these explains the complexity of reductions or the subtle uses to which identity claims are put. I believe that identity statements (like generalizations, on Popper's [1959] "falsificationist" views) are honored mainly in the breach. They are the most sensitive possible tool in our conceptual armory for detecting errors, and as such, they are used to ferret out the source of explanatory failures. This functional hypothesis explains *why* they are made, *when* they are made, and *how* they are made in reductive explanations.

Leibniz's Law of the identity of indiscernibles requires that things which are identical share *all* properties which are had by either. This is the strongest possible claim one can make about the relationship between two things. It also makes identity the most demanding template to use in detecting differences between two patterns. If one wished to locate the source of an error in a putative reduction leading to an unexplained occurrence or a failed prediction (an "explained" *un*occurrence), then one could not use a more accurate measuring stick than identity. The uncompromising demands of Leibniz's Law guarantee the transitivity of identity claims, and thus license looking to deeper levels of description if the next lower level turns up no differences capable of handling the explanatory anomaly. Identity claims thus provide probes of potentially unlimited sensitivity and depth for pinpointing sources of explanatory failures.

This hypothesis explains a number of things:

(1) The *In Principle* translatability that reductionists are so enamoured of seems best viewed as a claim flowing from the application of Leibniz's Law when two levels of description are held to apply to the same object. By Leibniz's Law, any property applicable at either descriptive level must, subject to the transformations (in size, scale, or whatever) necessary to go from one level to the other, have an applicable translation at the other. These claims are thus the tool by which differences, if any, (and identities, if none) are found.

(2) The truth of such an identity claim does not imply that relatively simple translations between types at the two levels can be found. When they can be found, it is tempting to speak of derivability of upper-level descriptions, laws, and theories from lower-level descriptions, laws, and theories, and to treat reduction as a relation

between theories. Interlevel theory reduction is then a limiting special case of reductive or identificatory explanatory relations between phenomena and mechanisms at two or more levels.

(3) Nothing would push us past simple coreferential identity (or dualism) at the common sense level if the motive force had to come from identity claims. But the motive force comes from a desire to find explanations for all real phenomena. This force leads us to look for descriptions at other levels, and thus gives us new material to which we might apply Leibniz's Law. Nothing in Leibniz's Law prevents us from simply asserting the coreferentiality of mental and physical descriptions to objects which have both properties. *The anomalies arising from this coreferentiality are all explanatory!* Mental and physical properties in such objects seem curiously interdependent and interrelated.

Why? How? There may be more identity relations than can be seen at the common sense level, but only explanatory demands give a reason to look for them. The complexity of interlevel reduction and its transitivity must be understood in terms of these demands, rather than just in terms of identity and its transitivity. It is the explanatory force of an identity theory which makes it nontrivial, even if it gets no further *in its identity claims* than the "stuff-coreferentiality" with which we all started, in our common sense view.

(4) If identity claims were the goal of reduction, one might expect that they would be made only after all of the relevant information on all of the relevant properties is in. In fact, identity claims are constantly being made and refined as interlevel knowledge progresses, at what must seem on that hypothesis scandalously little evidence and at scandalously early stages of the investigation.

But if identity claims are tools for finding the source of explanatory failures, it explains why they are made and refined throughout the process of an investigation. Furthermore, it helps to explain why demonstration of correspondences between descriptions at two levels, in the absence of explanatory failures or explicit grounds for *ruling out* an identification, is sufficient for identification, without further justification. (A further important factor is discussed in the next section.) A claim of identification is made and stands until it is defeated rather than being withheld until demonstrated—an appropriate location of the burden of proof if identities are to be used as tools in this way.

(5) The reasons for the sterility of most of the current philosophical discussion of the identity theory can now be seen. On the one hand, its attackers point to the stringency of Leibniz's Law, and either to the triviality of the identifications that have actually been established, or to the supposed impossibility of ever establishing any inter-

esting identifications. Supposed differences are pursued for their own sake, without questions of *explanatory* adequacy or failure ever arising. But no scientist will bother with differences unless they are relevant differences, and relevant differences are ones which point to actual or potential explanatory failures. The nonspatiality of the mental realm (no matter how central it was to Descartes) is not relevant to the argument that the mental is not physical until it is argued that this nonspatiality *does not admit of a physical explanation,* or is responsible for some other feature of the mental realm which does not admit of a physical explanation.

On the other hand, defenders of the identity theory have also argued their case either independently of explanatory considerations, or only with such gross attention to explanatory matters as to be unconvincing, irrelevant, and misleading as to how explanatory considerations enter. It is a parody of explanatory procedure in science to invoke explanatory demands only against parallelism, or with the supposition of complete psycho-physical correspondence, to argue that if the corresponding things were not assumed to be identical, then the correspondences would have to be explained. This makes explanation enter in only in a negative way—that if Ockham's razor were not applied in the interests of ontological simplicity, then there would be a series of "nomological danglers" (Feigl, 1967) to be explained.

Most identity theorists don't even pay this much lip service to explanation, but pass immediately to the identities, which they view as the cash value of the identity thesis. Stuff-identities would have too little value, so property identities are assumed to be the proper topic of analysis. The analysis proceeds with Leibniz's Law to try to show how it would be possible (without strict inconsistency) to assert that thus-and-such a mental predicate or property could be identical with some physical property or other. *Which* physical property is assumed to be irrelevant, as the widely accepted dummy constant "firings in the C-fibers" attests. Specific physical properties would involve a specific explanatory theory, and it is said not to be the job of philosophers to work with specific explanatory theories. If I am right, the optimal strategy for the identity theorist is not to waste time arguing for the in principle possibility of the identity theory, but to look for plausible explanations for the important and relevant differences between the mental and physical realms. If the explanations are forthcoming, the identities will be assumed. If not, the explanatory failures will force a careful use of Leibniz's Law to detect differences which might be used as the basis for new explanatory hypotheses.

This may look more like a scientific task than a philosophical one. But if so, it will certainly produce results which contradict philosophical claims. Some of these will be dualistic claims, but not all; closer attention to the real dynamics and contents of interlevel reductions in science cannot help but show that much of what passes for "scientific materialism" in philosophical circles is seriously misnamed. Materialism it may be, but scientific, it is not.

The Dialectics of Reduction[10]

I have separated inter and intralevel reductions in order to isolate some of their logical differences, and to point to some of the errors that can arise by confusing their functions and properties. This separation however is somewhat artificial. It seems inevitable that normal scientific progress (which I will assume to mean progress in explanation), generally requires drawing *inter*level connections. Furthermore progress to an empiricist inevitably involves trial-and-error search, with concomitant errors. (See Campbell, 1973*a*.) But errors and their corrections, we saw, get redescribed as *intra*level theory changes, so it would seem that any *real* cases of interlevel progress will involve both. A number of features arise from their interaction which have important consequences for the defensibility of various views on the mind–body problem and its probable fate in the progress of science.

The dialectics of Identification.   Interlevel reduction involves a kind of "fit"—the kind of fit necessary to explain upper level phenomena, to assert compositional identities, and where the mapping of types from lower to upper levels permit, to construct type-correspondences and identities. It had in the past been generally assumed that correspondences and identities were equally sound bases for and, tacitly, that they are *equally probable products* of intertheoretic explanation.

Both seem to be clearly false. Kim (1966) argues that empirical evidence would be incapable of deciding between a "correspondence thesis" (a presumably noninteractionist form of dualism) and an "identity thesis" (or thoroughgoing physicalism). More recent work (especially Causey 1972) suggests that at least some identifications are necessary for intertheoretic reduction and explanation, but even this has no suggestions as to why identifications rather than correspond-

---

[10] This title is taken from a paper of the same name by Ernan McMullin (1972) in which he reaches some of the conclusions of this paper by another route.

ences become assertable. The considerations concerning the use of identity claims raised in the preceding section and the process of generating interlevel "fit" provide such an explanation.

There seems to be a natural tendency to assume that intertheoretic "fit" takes place wholly or primarily by modifications in the upper level theory. Thus, Schaffner's (1967) model of reduction provides for modification in the reduced theory but none in the reducing theory (a view which he changes in his later work). The reasons for this belief are varied and complex, but it is clearly a mistake. In fact, corrections in theories occur at all levels, but they tend to be hidden at lower levels.[11]

The primary sources of corrections at one level in contexts where we are trying to construct a reduction are the phenomena and theories at the other levels we are trying to relate it to. Considering only two levels, in an idealized reduction, this means that the theories at these two levels undergo a *co*evolution—they are the major factors producing change in each other: A lower-level model is advanced to explain an upper-level phenomenon which it doesn't fit exactly. This leads to a closer look at the phenomenon, and perhaps results in some change in the way in or detail with which it is described. This will also lead to changes in the lower level model and may suggest new phenomena to look for. These changes usually produce an improvement in "fit" in some respects, but may involve a poorer fit in others, or suggest new areas in which fit must be obtained. But as argued above, interlevel explanation requires *exact* fit in all relevant dimensions, so the cycle will be repeated as many times as necessary to produce it. This "zigzag" pattern of successive modifications at alternate levels is a special case of what Herbert Simon has called "means–end analysis" (Simon, 1966*a*, 1966*b*, 1969). It is also characterizable in terms of the "TOTE"units of Miller, Galanter, and Pribram (1960). On either account, it is an extremely general feature of human problem solving behavior and biological adaptation—indeed of the selection process itself.

The successive modifications sew the two levels together more

---

[11] Perhaps the main reason, apart from the assumed explanatory priority of lower levels (See part III) is that reduction is simply never raised as an issue in the early stages of lower level theory construction—which is often even called by a different name, the less honorific "model building." This is the period in which lower level corrections are most obvious—a period in which upper level theories and phenomena are wholesale winnowers of failed models. It seems likely that positivistic bias towards "contexts of justification" and away from "contexts of discovery" (based on a belief that discoveries are serendipitous and illogical, and thus not part of the "logic of science") also lead away from the early "model building" stage. One justifies edifices—theories which one is committed to and loath to change substantially. One discovers models, which are readily changeable, because change is painless before one has begun to presuppose them in other areas and become committed to them as foundations.

closely than Siamese twins. The initial rough identity claims are refined, explanations are sought and found, concepts are modified, and with each cycle, the concepts and entities of each theory in turn affect the form of those of the other. Cognitively, they become mutual *presuppositions* of one another. As one goes through a number of cycles, these presuppositions accumulate until the structure of each is *built into* the structure of the other as a result of the fact that in each case it is the "other" entities and their relations which are to be matched. When theories have coevolved in this manner, identification is natural, and the assertion of correspondence rather than identity is unusual, and demands explanation. It never arises, unless there is some reason for doubting the identification, and the only *cognitively* acceptable reason for doubt in such a context is a failure of fit or of explanation.

Accounts like those of Kim (1966) which talk about and compare the bases in the evidence for asserting correspondence or identity and find no difference have made a strategic error. By hypothesis, there is no empirical difference, since the only correspondence thesis that could be fairly compared with an identity thesis would (also) be a perfect "fit." But talk about bases in this context suggests that there is a time when one considers all of the evidence and then decides on one or the other, and this is what is false. Identities and correspondences are both more-or-less indirect products of myriad decisions we have made along the way, not direct products of a single temporarily isolable decision. By the time questions of reduction arise, we have usually been *presupposing* most of the identities for some time.

My personal belief is that these facts about identification count strongly not only against the dualisms (or trialisms?) of Eccles (this volume) and antireductionism of Taylor (1964), but also against any radical "double-aspect" theories and the "complementarity" view of Globus (1972, 1973, this volume). At the same time, taking the identity thesis seriously clearly involves at least a *moderate* kind of dualism, "complementarity" or "double-aspect" theory, in that no identity theory will involve a satisfactory "fit" unless it explains (among other things) the substantial and absolutely central differences between first and third-person (or subjective and objective) perspectives. The difference between moderate and radical bifurcations, however, is that what the radical bifurcationists regard as a fundamental ontological split, the moderates regard as an important difference which is to be given a basically physical explanation in terms of a physically explicable inner–outer distinction. Gunderson's work (1970) has gone a long way in this direction—as have Globus, Pribram (1971a, this volume) and von Bekesy (1967).

The unificatory power of the coevolution of theories in this manner should not be underestimated. In particular, arguments that the identification would have to be cross-categorial are of little weight. Some cross-categorial identifications and predictions (like some from the same category) will never be made—just because no empirical or theoretical end can be served by making them. Thus, "The number 3 is green" (a standard example) makes no sense, but this is because it has no use. There is no barrier to making cross-categorical identifications when they serve a useful end, and explanation is such an end. Categories are often nothing more than the ossified skeletons of dead theories, kept partly because they are useful and partly because they are there. They can and will be changed if they become too confining in the progress of science.

A closer look at the history of the development of a statistical thermodynamics and of the development of genetics (see, especially, Darden, 1974; Roth, 1974; and Wimsatt, 1974b) reveals changes in point of view that before the fact would clearly have been interpreted as cross-categorial identifications. That it does not look so after the fact is to be expected, for one of the burdens of the theory is to *explain how the categories apply to the entities in question in such a way as to make the identifications not only possible, but plausible, or even inevitable.* The genetic case is especially interesting for the details of the gradual spatialization and localization of the genome involve several cross-categorial identifications and explanations that have direct relevance for the identification of the categorially nonspatial mental realm with the categorially spatial physical realm (see Wimsatt, 1974b).

Correspondence or Elimination: The Failure of Dialectic?   If the inevitable result of this kind of interlevel coevolution is identification, it is less clear that this kind of coevolution is inevitable. Are there alternatives? In particular, in what circumstances do we assert correspondences or eliminate entities rather than make identifications?

Some writers argue that the identity thesis is based upon a very poor induction, since there never before has been a case like it in which something from one kind of realm, e.g., the mental, is *identified* with something from another kind of realm, e.g., the physical. This is a bad argument. It is false that there have been no prior cases like it and it rests too much implicit weight on "category mistake" arguments which I criticized above. It should be noted that however good or bad the argument is, it would *also* apply *mutatis mutandis* to the assertion of correspondence, though no one seems to be bothered by—or even to have noticed—this fact. Perhaps this is because it is mistakenly thought that correspondences are "directly observable" and that identities are something which we can assert on that basis when we have some *additional* evidence that licenses them. But correspondences are usually constructed or inferred, just as identities. They are the normal end product of taking a different path and not usually just a way station on the path to identites.

The scenario that sees them as the latter involves something like the assumption that separate theories can evolve separately as accounts of two disparate realms and yet be so similar in detail that when someone notices the correspondence, the realms, entities and properties are immediately identified—or not identified as one chooses. It is not impossible that extensive correlations should precede and provide the basis for first identifications, especially for "smaller" theories, or at the model-building stage, but this is wildly improbable for two theories as ramified, complicated, and already intertwined (see Knapp, this volume) as the mental and physical accounts of human behavior. The kind of fit envisioned would be impossible without the coevolution of theories, and that in turn involves and results in identifications.

An interesting case which appears at first to be a counterexample to this thesis is that of the localization of the genes on chromosomes following discovery of widespread correspondences between the behavior of chromosomes and that postulated for Mendel's units. Darden (1974, p. 114) lists 10 respects in which correspondences emerged or were suggested by the work, before 1905, of Boveri and Sutton. Since Mendel's work had neither influenced nor been influenced by development in cytology, uncritical reading of Sutton's 1903 paper, in particular, might seem to support the naive view that a large number of independently discovered properties of genes and chromosomes were observed by him to correspond, thus leading to the identification. In fact, only 3 or 4 of these (Darden suggests 4, but one is equivocal) were *observed* isomorphisms—known to be true independently of Mendel's units and of the chromosomes. The rest of the correspondences were *inferred*, either of Mendel's units from the behavior of chromosomes (3 cases), or conversely (2 cases), or (in 2 cases) was observed of *neither* but predicted of both on the assumption that they were plausible properties for material chromosomes.

Thus the case of genetics in this period suggests that most of the correspondences were predictions from a hypothesized identification, rather than a prior basis for such an identification. This also characterizes the further development of the chromosomal theory of heredity by the Morgan school, in which observed and inferred mechanical properties of the chromosomes were used to explain sex-linkage, linkage, sex-determination and other observed traits. Interestingly, simple and straightforward correlations were *not* always possible in this later period, though the identification of the chromosome with a linearly arranged string of genes *explained why* they were not. Thus Castle's modest and simpler operationally motivated proposal that cross-over frequency was a linear function of the real distance between genes turned out to be inconsistent when attempts were made to give it a realist (non-instrumentalist) interpretation. The mechanical model of the chromosome of the Morgan school explained why this simple correlation was impossible and the mechanisms of (multiple) crossing over, interference, and differential breakage strength suggested the form of deviations from it.

The picture that emerges from this last case is that it is extremely difficult to specify a fruitful form for correlations in the absence of an identificatory hypothesis. Thus, even the discovery of most correlations follows upon prior proposed identities. But this might be thought to be of little weight: What is really of most interest to the dualist is the circumstances under which identities are eschewed *in favor of* correspondences. This is done in at least two kinds of cases:

One situation in which correspondence is readily asserted is when the theories involved apply to entities which are spatiotemporally distinct. Thus, Rashevsky's observations that the spread of rumors fit very nicely the epidemiological equations for the spread of diseases led none to identify rumors and diseases, except perhaps metaphorically, in spite of a substantial degree of analogy. But this won't help the dualist, since the claim (e.g., of Descartes) that the mental realm is nonspatial is not a claim that it is *spatially* distinct from the physical realm, for this would mean that the mental is *elsewhere* in space. Interestingly, one can view character traits as becoming spatialized through the construction of linkage maps of the chromosome in a way that is suggestive of the form of possibilities for the spatialization of the mental realm. (See Wimsatt, 1974*b*.)

One other situation, perhaps the most common, in which correspondences are asserted rather than identities is also of no use to the dualist, for this is a situation in which the unity of the realm embracing the corresponding entities is already assumed. These are cases where, within a theoretical perspective, one can identify two things as cause and effect, or as mutual effects of a common cause. This is true, as Causey (1972) argues for structural features and the dispositions they produce, for the corresponding variations of thermal and electrical conductivity of the Wiedmann-Franz law, and (to the extent that there are one–one correspondences) between genes and the characters they generate. One might suggest that this allows a totally dualistic interactionism or epiphenomenalism, but I think that the number and variety of identifications likely would make it come much closer to Sperry's "emergent interactionism," which I argue is consistent with reductionism.

If correspondence seems unlikely, what about wholesale elimination of the mental realm? Suppose for example, that dualistic prejudices isolated mental talk sufficiently from progress in neurophysiology (much as religion has become isolated from its earlier task of explaining nature) that in the ultimate confrontation, the mental realm would just "slough off" as neurophysiological results explained more and more.

I also think that this is unlikely—indeed, virtually impossible—because neurophysiology cannot make progess at the level of higher units of functional organization without appealing to the mental realm for guidance . The task would be like asking a molecular biologist to give a molecular reconstruction of elephant physiology from what he knows, together with photographs of elephants taken in the wild at a conservatively safe distance. Constant reference to minute details of the upper-level descriptions of elephant anatomy and physiology are at least necessary (though not yet sufficient) for the task. The rebirth of cognitive psychology and an increasing interest in development, while in part reactions to behaviorism with its emphasis on the contemporaneous external environment are also absolutely necessary for further neurophysiological progress. We must use our current and future intuitions and theories of the mental realm to help to develop our neurophysiological accounts. But our current psychological theories are still in many respects clearly "photographs taken at a safe distance" (and after the fact), and it seems equally obvious that many of the most revealing closeups are neurophysiological and developmental, as Peter Knapp's article (this volume) so clearly suggests.[11a]

The image of the mental realm, or of our theories about it, as an unreactive theoretically isolated skin that could be sloughed off and eliminated (see, e.g., Rorty, 1965), is an image that is only tempting if one ignores the dynamics of reduction and reverts to a statically inspired view of a fragile and fallible upper level which is supported, corrected, and explained by a robust and infallible lower level, to which it offers nothing in return. It is a feature of our conceptual scheme that lower-level phenomena generally explain upper-level phenomena, but it is a mistake to think that upper levels are in special need of one-sided ontological support or that our conception of them is constantly corrected by, but never corrects our conceptions of lower levels.

Furthermore, the mental realm has for us another independent subjective claim to centrality which is related to the distinction between

---

[11a] I believe that Rosenblatt (1962a,b) was the first to point out that a developmental model might be *simpler* to analyze than a "finished" one, as well as to argue that developmental models were required to specify the phenotype with a reasonable amount of genetic information.

first and third-person perspectives. I will say something more about it after I have laid some necessary foundations *via* the analysis of the concept of a level of organization and of how levels can be related.

PART III: LEVELS, AND THEIR SIGNIFICANCE FOR REDUCTION

The Nature and Independence of Levels

"The aim of science is to cut Nature at its joints." This metaphor, in which Nature is compared to some mythical beast which science is to dismember or dissect tells us a great deal about levels of organization. The main point of the metaphor is that, among the many possible ways of cutting up the world, some are easier than others, just as it is easier to cut through the cartilage at the joints than through the bone and muscle in between. So also it implies that Nature *has* joints, or natural units of organization. If so, then explanatory ontological, systematic, and controlling aims of science all coincide at the importance of finding these "joints," and of describing the units in between and how they articulate. Talk of joints also suggests that the units in between can be readily spatially delineated.

Whatever levels are, they are at least major vertebrae among the joints of Nature. It might do very well *for a start* to think of levels as differing primarily in the spatial dimension of the entities which are at the respective levels, so the theories at different levels might be thought of as sieves of different sizes, which sift out entities of the appropriate size and dynamical characteristics. The fact that size and dynamical characteristics *do* so frequently change coordinately suggests size as a major feature in individuating levels. But they *can* vary independently: black holes and bacteria can be the size of a dust mote, though the three will have radically different behaviors in similar circumstances, and this is one of the major complicating factors of a purely scale-based definition of level.[12]

With a joint, if you cut to the left or to the right of it, the going is a lot harder. Similarly, it seems at least roughly true of a level

---

[12] While scale changes alone do not individuate levels, they are an exceedingly important—perhaps the most important—factor at virtually all levels of organization. This can be for a variety of reasons. Different forces can have different ranges either because their force laws vary with different powers of the radius or because in our world some with the same exponent in their force laws are cancelled out at close ranges (electrostatic forces), while others (gravitation) are not. Relationships between forces, often the same relationships, can be exceedingly important in different areas in different ways as Dresden (1974) and Thompson (1961) point out—Dresden for length–volume and area–volume relations in hydrodynamics, and Thompson for surface–volume, cross sectional area–volume, and other relations in a variety of biological adaptions. Weisskopf (1975) does so throughout physics. Dresden's paper is remarkably similar in most of its conclusions to those advanced here. Similar or related views can be found in Simon (1969, pp. 103–104) and Levins (1966, 1970).

that if one, starting with that size "mesh," makes the mesh continuously bigger or smaller and tries to construct theories with the entities that result (many of which we would not consider to be entities at all), the going will be a lot harder—at least until one gets far enough in either direction to be approaching a neighboring level. I assume that this means either that the theories are more complex, or the phenomena are less regular, or usually both, for an imaginary theory constructed at the slightly larger or smaller size scale.

If the entities at a given level are clustered relatively closely together (in terms of size, or some other generalized distance measure in a phase space of their properties) it seems plausible to characterize a level as a *local maximum of predictability and regularity*. Still supposing that levels are to be individuated solely on the basis of size factors, imagine a picture like that of Figure 1a, in which regularity and predictability of interactions is graphed as a function of size of the interacting entity. The levels appear as periodic peaks, though of course they might differ in height or "sharpness," and there is no *a priori* reason why one might not get a picture like that of Figures 1b, 1c, 1d, or even 1e. I suggest below that Figure 1c is probably most like our world, and why.

Suppose that systems, which are relatively changeable in terms of their size and properties over a sufficiently long scale (in some cases, clearly of cosmological or evolutionary magnitudes), are left to do so. One feature that quickly emerges if we take biological organisms as an example is that *under the pressures of selection, organisms are excellent detectors of regularity and predictability*. As Levins (1968) and others have suggested,[12a] organisms tend to act and evolve in something like a cost–benefit manner towards the minimization of uncertainty in their environment.[13] To the extent that this is so, one would expect to find

---

[12a] Discussions of Simon (1957, 1969) and Bronowski (1970) have suggestively similar implications for a broader class of systems.

[13] At higher levels of organization, at least, this is an oversimplification. Thus organisms will tend to evolve in such a way that conditions upon which their survival depends are met in as reliable and simple a manner as is possible, and conditions detrimental to their survival are *avoided* in as reliable and simple a manner as possible. This means, for example that organisms will try to regularize their relations with food (or prey) at the same time as they (or their prey) are trying to *irregularize* their relations with their predators. This leads to obvious conflicts, not only in the behavior of predators and their prey, but between the different desiderata for a given organism.

The formulation given here of levels as maxima of regularity and predictability is thus an oversimplification, though I think it is a good "first approximation" to the problem of characterizing a level, for at least two reasons. (1) The complex behavior described above requires a number of degrees of freedom in the interacting, evolving systems, and thus lower levels of organization are likely to approximate more closely to the ideal "maximal" characterization. (This is a partial explanation for why Figure 2c seems the most likely characterization of the amount of regularity and predictability at different levels in our world.) (2) The higher levels *may* still be describable as a maximization subject to (many) constraints, though it is an interesting question whether as the interactions become more complex an alternative theory of optimization (such as Simon's (1957) "satisficing" theory) should be applied to the individual interactions, and ultimately, to the definition of a level of organization.

the greatest density of organism-types at the places of greatest regularity and predictability—i.e., at or near the various levels of organization.

What natural selection does for organisms, other selection processes do for entities at other levels, both physical and mental. Atomic nuclei and molecules constitute two other levels of organization and foci of regularity. They are so because they are the *most probable* states of matter under certain ranges of conditions. They are not under other conditions. There are no or few molecules in a gas which has been heated sufficiently to become totally ionized, and there are no or few atomic nuclei in a neutron star. The relative probability of different states of matter, even in cases where no further mechanism for this can be found, is itself or represents the effects of a kind of selection mechanism.

Simon's (1969, 1973) hierarchial models of memory, perception, and problem-solving behavior generate levels in a similar manner in the cognitive realm, along criteria which (ignoring disputes over empirical adequacy) should be equally acceptable to dualist and physicalist alike. One of the recurrent features of Sperry's view is an emphasis on hierarchial organization (see especially 1970, pp. 588–9), and his remarks on a hierarchy of control are close in spirit to those of Simon, as well as to those of Pribram (1971a) at this point.

I have so far talked as if the levels were features of an abstract (property) space which did not interact with the systems which move through this space and fill it up in different ways. It is possible, however, and generally preferable (to reduce the dimensionality of the problem) to describe the levels as if they themselves are functions of what kinds of system are in the space and interacting with each other. Thus organisms are an important feature of the environment of many of the other organisms that they interact with. The presence or absence of an organism may have a strong effect on the predictability and regularity of the environment for another organism, and thus, of how close the latter is to a level of organization. (Several relevant examples are discussed by Levins, 1974.) While the complexity of interactions of things at apparently widely different levels is more common (and more severe) for things in the biological realm, the dependence of what constitutes stable states on what else is around is found at all levels of organization. (How stable is any atom of matter when it is next to a corresponding atom of antimatter?)

If organisms and units of other sizes and properties which can be regarded as under selection forces tend to be good detectors of levels of organization, and thus to "congregate" there, and if the location of the stable, regular and predictable regions is itself fruitfully viewed as a

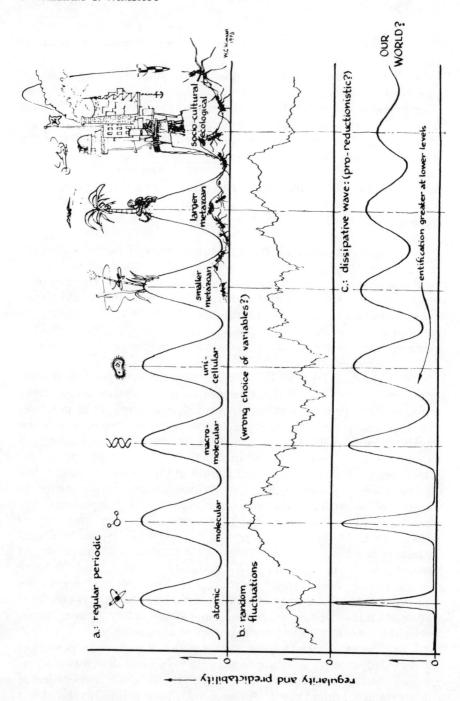

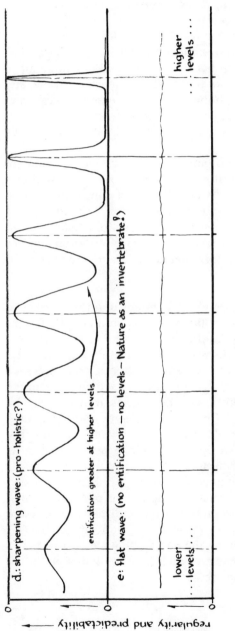

Figure 1. Levels of organization—some conceivable waveforms.

242 □ WILLIAM C. WIMSATT

product of what systems are in the neighborhood, then it seems reasonable to drop the introductory fiction of separate levels and their occupants, and to say that levels of organization just are those places (in a space of properties) where the greatest densities of types of systems are to be found.[14] This is also where one would expect to find the greatest density of types of interaction among these systems.

The identifications made between levels will of course mean that the same system will be found at a *number* of levels, if it has any reasonable degree of complexity, though it will of course be *a* system at only one level. At lower levels, it will be a multiplicity of systems in complex "ecological" interaction and at higher levels, it will appear as a part of a system.

In picking out a level of organization (which we generally do by naming a few characteristic entities and interrelations) we are doing so on the basis of something like a gestalt—a recognition that these entities and these relations hang together more strongly with one another (in terms of frequency and density of connection) than they do with other units and relations. A related dynamical criterion, that of "near-decomposability" has been formulated by Simon. (See his 1969, Chapter 4, or Wimsatt, 1974*a*.)

Donald Campbell (1958) has discussed our tendencies to reify things, and suggests that it is strongly dependent upon the extent to which we find spatially coincident boundaries for a number of different properties and "common fates" or multiple interactions among constituent entities. This definition works well for the entities at a level, and for the levels themselves as entities. Extending this to properties, we might take as real at a given level those properties which are reliably detected by an appreciable proportion of the entities at that level. The situation naturally lends itself to definition of a "degree of reality." One could further specialize this to "real for an entity of type x" as "reliably detected by an entity of type x" or generalize it to real *simplicitur* as "reliably detected by a reliable detector."

On this account then we have a kind of "panphenomenalism" (not to be confused with what is usually thought of as panpsychism) at which entities and things detected by them at different levels are equally real, and none is secondary, in its *reality*, to any other. This is, I think, a necessary move in removing the feeling of austerity that many people appear to fear in reductionism—what, in other words, might be called the "nothing more than" phobia.

---

[14] This claim actually involves a disguised equilibrium assumption, which I will not discuss here.

Ontological and Explanatory Primacy

This characterization of levels and of what it is to be real is neutral with respect to how or whether some levels depend upon or are products of others. The problem now is how to introduce these features in a way that can perhaps satisfy both most reductionists and, I hope, many antireductionists. To do this, it is important to recognize that no subsequent *added* asymmetries compromise the reality and independence of different levels secured above. They merely *add* a way in which higher levels are conceived of as dependent on lower levels.

The feeling of asymmetry arises when one notes that the entities of higher levels are in some sense *composed of* the entities at lower levels. This might be thought to result directly from the asymmetry of the composition relation: If Xs are composed of Ys, then Ys are *not* composed of Xs.   But this asymmetry alone will not explain our feelings of the primacy of lower levels over higher, since the inverse of the composition relation is the partition relation (Ys are parts of X), which is also asymmetric. *Unless there is some reason to choose one relation over the other as more important,* their asymmetries "cancel" and do not explain the particular asymmetry, with the priority of lower levels over higher, characteristic of reductionism. We thus need a reason to single out *compositional* information as presumptively more important than *contextual* information.

One such reason is the presumption of our conceptual scheme that if Xs are composed of Ys, and one wants an *explanation* for the behavior of Xs, one should look at the behaviors and interrelations of Ys, but not (except in special circumstances) conversely. I will refer to this by saying that the direction of *explanatory primacy* is from parts to wholes or in the direction of composition. I suggest that if the general presumptions were in the other direction—that the behavior of parts were generally to be accounted for in terms of the behavior of wholes, the asymmetry would be in the other direction.   This last would be a kind of holism, but more all-embracing than has ever been espoused, since it would have to cover the range from sub-atomic particles to cosmological events.

It is tempting to think that another reason arises in the claim that lower level theories are "more general" than upper level theories, and that upper level theories cover just a restricted special subset of the class of systems that could be made with the entities of lower level theories. Thus, e.g., organisms are held to be "just a special class of physical system." But this is just another way of talking about the importance of what a thing is composed of and is thus another indirect testimony to the direction of explanatory primacy. While it is true that there are many unmade wholes that could have been made with the parts on hand, but never aggregated, so also, there are many parts that could have been fragmented out of the wholes on hand, but never were. There are good physical reasons for the non-occurrence of events of each type. Just as some wholes are radically improbable combinations of parts, so also some parts are radically improbable decompositions of wholes. There is, of course, temptation to think of the unseparated parts as unmade wholes of still smaller parts, and no corresponding temptation to think of the unmade wholes as unseparated parts of still larger wholes. But this is just to repeat anew the importance of composition and the direction of explanatory primacy. If the latter were reversed, we would be thinking of unseparated parts rather than of unmade wholes and higher level theories would be regarded as "more general."

Another suggestive asymmetry is given by considering when we are likely to decide that a term has changed it meaning. Roth (1974) has used meaning change as one of her criteria in ordering "descriptive levels," with a meaning change in a term a *prima facie* ground for saying that the entity or property referred to by the term has been redescribed at a deeper descriptive level. Thus, if we discover that genes are composed of DNA, this is held to involve or lead to a meaning change in the concept of the gene. But if we discover that an atom of iron occurs in the heme group that associates with a hemoglobin molecule, we do not see a meaning change for "iron." We say that we have just learned something more that it can be used for.

This shows how deeply reductionism is embedded in our conceptual scheme, but I suspect that the direction of meaning change is a consequence of explanatory primacy rather than a possible cause of it. If the source of explanations is generally to found at lower levels, then more relevant information about the behavior of an entity will be picked up by discovering a lower level description of it than by looking for descriptions of systems of which it is a part. The most important information about an entity becomes stabilized as part of the meaning of terms that refer to it, so lower-level redescriptions are in most cases more likely to lead to changes of meaning than upper-level redescriptions.

This is further confirmed if we look at a concept for which the relevant explanatory information is found at a higher level. The concept of fitness underwent a meaning change when evolutionary theory lead us to look at the population, the species, or the descendants of an individual as significant units, and away from the individual as the primary recipient of the advantages of fitness. In this case, greater knowledge of the physiology and anatomy of the individual is held to tell us more about the means for achieving fitness, but not about its meaning. The direction of meaning change seems to follow the direction of explanation in the case of individual concepts. It seems reasonable to suppose that the normal direction of meaning change is an effect rather than a cause of the normal direction of explanation.

Where does this presumption of a direction of explanatory primacy come from? One possible source would be the assumption or demonstration that lower-level things are in some sense *more real* than upper levels things. But if the directions of lower and upper can be defined equally well in terms of what is composed of what or of what is a part of what, this would either have to be an arbitrary assumption, or in turn be based on one of the intuitions which lead back to the direction of explanatory primacy. The same applies to the generality of theories, or to the informativeness of descriptions. In other words, I think that any feelings we have about what is more real, general in scope, or specifically described, is based upon feelings about explanatory primacy, rather than conversely.

For present purposes, I will take the notion of explanation in the main as a primitive unexplained notion, and then propose that the direction of explanatory primacy can be defined in terms of the notion of explanation in a way paralleling the definition of the direction of increasing time, in a causal theory of time, in terms of the direction of increasing entropy in a majority of branch systems.[15]

Suppose that it is possible to enumerate[16] all kinds of pairs of things such that one of them explains or is part of the explanation of the other. These will include things from all different levels of organization. I propose that the direction of explanatory primacy is determined by the direction of explanation in the majority of such pairs which differ in level.[17] The direction of explanatory primacy is thus, on this account,

---

[15] See Grunbaum (1963, pp. 253–264) for relevant discussion of this analysis of the anisotropy of time in terms of the statistical form of the second law of thermodynamics. There are, I believe, deeper connections to be found between thermodynamics and the direction of explanation.

[16] This a dubious assumption. It is hard to decide how to enumerate these pairs, or even whether they are enumerable. But since I am only trying to explain a feature of our organization of phenomena, rather than to generate it, I see nothing wrong with accepting our given scientific accounts of the world as a basis for starting, complete with its explanations and levels assignments.

[17] I am inclined to believe that all explanatory pairs which are genuinely at the same level (and not ambiguous, indeterminate, or indistinguishable with respect to level) are cases of temporally successive events related as cause and effect, and thus of a different but not unrelated type than the explanations involving temporally coincident phenomena at different levels. I am ruling out intralevel explanatory relations not because they are of a different type, but because by being intralevel they are "neutral."

simply determined by the fact that in our conceptual account of our world, more things are explained by things which are lower than them in level than by things which are higher that them in level.[18]

Since we are talking about a constituitive feature of our conceptual scheme, a limitation to something like the known (or projected) explanatory pairs would be required, since to assume otherwise would be to assume that our conceptual schemes are based on an omniscience which we do not possess. Various kinds of paradigms play an important role in making such projections. Primary among these are:

(1) The mechanical engineering paradigm of making artifacts by stringing together parts. If the way to *make* a whole is by stringing together parts, then it is natural to think that this is the way to explain a whole as well. Suggesting the origin of this paradigm in engineering techniques of construction also indicates the existence of alternative paradigms: since the dawn of engineering, some craftsmen have lamented that the mysterious holistic construction techniques of organisms were not open to them.

(2) A probable consequence of this paradigm is the evolutionary account of increasing complexity and functional "fit" as an aggregation problem. This was implicit in Darwin's explanation of adaptation as a product of the *accumulation* of small favorable variations, and is explicit in Simon's account of the evolution of complex hierarchially organized systems in terms of the *aggregation* of stable *sub*assemblies (1969, chapter 4).[18a]

What does the direction of explanatory priority have to do with reduction? The primary effect of explanatory priority is to determine in which direction one should look for an explanation of a given phenomenon. This applies first and foremost to phenomena for which one has no explanation at all, but it does not apply only to them. It also applies in cases where one has noncompeting explanations of the phenomenon from both lower *and* higher levels, and leads to a natural tendency to regard the explanation from the direction of priority as somehow more important. It even applies in cases where one has an explanation of the phenomena in question from the unpreferred direction and none in the prior direction; there is a strong tendency to regard

---

[18] Indeed, the change in presupposition concerning the direction of explanatory primacy from Aristotle's day to our own could be viewed as just the product of extending our knowledge of the very small and the very large, both of which generally support reductionistic accounts and thus tip the scale away from the teleology of the middle range. Thus, what was once regarded as primary and real, the dependence of parts on wholes, is now regarded as derivative and apparent.

[18a] The claim to complete generality of these paradigms is contestable, even from within a generally reductionistic tradition. Thus for an alternative or complementary account to that of Simon, see Levins (1973), who argues that many features of organization evolve by differentiation of parts or by their mutual coadaptation in the context of the whole, rather than by aggregation. Levins' description appears to fit developmental phenomena better than Simon's, though the issue is still open. The current dispute over the evolution of eukaryotic cells is a collision of these two views, which is further discussed in Wimsatt (1974a).

the explanation as derivative, heuristic, and just a stopgap measure until one can find the "real" explanation (which is, of course, one from the direction of explanatory priority). In other words, explanatory priority seems to account for an appreciable proportion of the sometimes quite obnoxious behavior of an ardent reductionist. But to see this is also to see that such behavior is really ontologically quite innocuous, though some reductionists mistakenly believe otherwise.

Consider as an example the realm of biological evolution, an area which, because of the cyclic nature of the developmental and selection processes, legitimately permits explanations of the occurrence of a phenomenon from both higher and lower levels. Lower level explanations of a phenomenon—say the particular configuration and composition of the jaw of a soldier termite[19] would proceed in molecular and developmental terms to talk about the genetic and environmental factors relevant to *how* the termite jaw came to have this particular configuration. But it is a tradition in biology that it is also legitimate to ask *why* the termite jaw has this particular configuration, to answer this in terms of its functional design, and to feel that this explains, in some sense, the existence and form of the termite jaw. Since Darwin, this teleological explanation has been given a strictly causal interpretation in terms of selection mechanisms, which has had the effect of turning it into a kind of "how" explanation and thereby making it legitimate.

A selectionist explanation proceeds as follows: The jaws of the soldier termite (which are so outsized that the termite cannot use its jaws to feed itself and must be fed by other worker termites) are specialized for defense and combat with ants, beetles or other potential enemies of the hive.[20] This adaptation and the correlative (colony defending) specialized behavior results in a differential advantage: those colonies that fared better because of it left more "offspring" colonies than those that lacked it and any heritable behaviors responsible for their having fared better were also passed on. The accumulation of such heritable favorable differences leads to the high degree of functional efficiency observed in nature, and in particular to the outsized jaws of soldier termites.

It is true, and not at all antireductionistic, to say that certain functional high-level organizational effects of the division of labor in the colony are the cause not only of the form of the termite jaw, but of the presence of DNA sequences which helped to bring it about. Yet the

---

[19] This particular example is developed at length in a discussion of "downwards causation" by Donald Campbell (1974) and this is based on his account.

[20] In termites and other social insects, the reproductive system is such that the entire colony is a unit of selection. This makes possible degrees of specialization and altruistic behavior that would be impossible if the individual termites were the units of selection and differentially competing among themselves.

suspicion induced by the explanatory priority of lower levels is not dispelled by the substitution of natural selection for special creation as a mechanism consistent with lower level forces and explanations. It has led many to remain suspicious of the importance of functional considerations; they prefer to ignore them entirely in favor of the analysis of straightforward (lower to upper) "how" questions, to treat selection as a disguised tautology rather than admit that there could really be selection *forces* (which would have to be upper-level forces which could have lower-level effects), and to act as if selection of termite colonies is ultimately inexplicable in any other terms than as the solution to a gargantuan Schroedinger wave-equation or whatever the current "lowest" level proposes. These last are clearly illegitimate responses and overreactions to the demands of explanatory priority. (See Garfinkel, 1975, for a more detailed treatment.) Clearly, too, it is responses of the latter sort—not the substitution of natural selection for special creation—which has given reductionism a bad name in many scientific circles. (See Wimsatt, 1972*a*, for more on teleology and selection.)

Once the sources and effects of the presumption of a direction of explanatory primacy are realized, some further things that are often hidden emerge:

(1) Even if explanatory priority is something that helps to confer reality on a level—and thus, in some sense to make lower levels *presumptively* more real than upper levels—it is only one source. The mutual cohesiveness and causal interrelatedness of the entities and properties of a level confer, according to Campbell's (1958) criteria, a reality of its own on each level. This confers a purely level-relative explanatory primacy on *each* level. *This primacy is recognizeable in the fact that no or virtually no explanations are to be found which are not in terms of entities at one level or another,*[21] although there *are* entities which are, for at least some purposes, between levels.

Thus, the Brownian motion of a particle is explained in terms of the kinetic activity of the molecules of the surrounding fluid—not in terms of other things at its "level"—which is in a meaningful sense in between the levels of the fluid and the kinetic gas. It is too small for the law of large numbers to effect the statistical smoothing characteristic of the behavior of a macroscopic gas, but massive enough to reflect light and to move sufficiently slowly to be visible to the macroscopic eye, unlike the invisible particles which move it. (See, e.g., Jeans, 1960, p.

---

[21] This is meant to apply to theoretical explanations for kinds of phenomena, and not to causal narrative explanations for particular occurrences of particular phenomena. The functions and aims of the two are different.

24 ff.) That its behavior is explained in terms of lower level entities is a product of the explanatory primacy of lower levels over higher. That its behavior is *not* explained in terms of other "between level" entities is a product of the explanatory primacy of levels over nonlevels. It is tempting to say that there are no relevant between-level entities to explain its behavior, but there are—namely the appropriate not-too-large, not-too-small collections of molecules impacting with it between distinguishable changes in its motion. If it is argued that those aren't *really* entities, but only artificial constructions of lower-level entities, this is just to make the point anew that Brownian motion particles are between levels, and not at one. The fact that these particles are characterized *primarily* in terms of their behavior (and only secondarily in terms of the properties they must have to produce it) is also indicative that their intrinsic "in-between level" properties have no *further* explanatory interest.

(2) Secondly, the reductionistically inspired feeling that upper-level explanations are always possibly and perhaps even preferably reformulatable in lower level terms (the Schroedinger wave-equation account of the selection forces responsible for soldier termite jaw configurations) are not only heuristically ill-advised. They are simply incorrect, in at least the following sense: *some things have no further explanation at a lower level and for them there is no point in talking about lower levels.*

Thus part of a selectionist explanation of a trait is the path from molecularly characterized gene to the trait in question, but this does *not* mean that as the trait performs its function in a still larger system, the natural explanation one gives of *that* in terms of its own level phenomena derive any more or even as much explanatory force by being redescribed in molecular terms. The trait already has a molecular explanation in areas where that is appropriate (e.g., in the molecular genetic basis for its production) and in other areas there *is* no molecular explanation—it is not a molecular phenomenon. One could "in principle" give a molecular translation of the molar explanation, but that is not an explanation—unless perhaps in some derivative sense entailed by and meaning nothing more than the hypothesized translatability.

This last fact, more than any other, should serve to justify and explain Sperry's "emergent interactionism." His intuitions about a drop of water in a whirlpool (1969, p. 534) are correct and an example of the above point. There *are* no molecular explanations for the gross spiral trajectory it describes (it is not a molecular phenomenon), though there may be for the Brownian motion of a dead bacterium suspended in it.

It also explains how a reductionist could counter Sperry's argument that reductionism leads " . . . to an infinite regress in which eventually everything is held to be explainable in terms of essentially nothing" (p. 167). Such a reductionist, perhaps even Sperry himself, can deny that explanation is, in that sense, transitive, and can thus deny that the explanatory movers of all phenomena must disappear into the microcosm with the progress of a reductionistic research program to lower and lower levels.

Intuitively, explanation is traceable up in level (or forward in time) only as far as the relevant effects, and down in level (or back in time) only as far as the relevant causes. When the phenomena become sufficiently far removed from the causes in question that they are explicable by a wide variety of alternative suppositions, citing the particular cause loses most of its force. If a camel is so heavily loaded that an added straw will break its back, it is perverse to cite the straw in question as the cause. Similarly, if all but 1 in 10^{100} of the initial configurations of a set of gas molecules will result in its obeying the ideal gas law within detectable limits, it is perverse to cite the specific initial configuration as a cause of its being obeyed. As Garfinkel (1975) points out, one of the things such a specific description suggests is that the detail is *relevant*, and this thus hides the fact that not only the specific initial condition in question, but also virtually any perturbation from it, will produce the result in question. The very thing that makes science in general, and reductionistic science in particular, possible—that as one goes up in levels, much of the detail of lower levels can be ignored (Levins, 1966)—guarantees that as one goes down in levels, one will not need *and cannot use* much of the detail one finds for the explanation of upper level phenomena.

This suggests an information-theoretic account of how far we go in looking for an explanation of a phenomenon. If one accepts the "statistical relevance" model of explanation of Salmon, Jeffrey, and Greeno (see Salmon *et al.*, 1971) that we look for factors which give a better partitioning of the phenomena into reference classes, it seems natural that as "dinky computers" we should apply cost–benefit considerations to decide the order of acquisition of explanatorily relevant information and when we should stop looking for more information. By the definition of a level, most regularities, and the most important regularities involving a phenomenon will involve other variables at the same level, so one should look there first for an explanation. Furthermore, if the regularities at that level don't involve too many exceptions, then relatively little is gained for cases which meet them by a further, more exact analysis in terms of microlevel variables. Cost–benefit considerations suggest that explanation will usually stop here in such cases.

But this does *not* apply when the phenomenon is an exception to one of the laws at its level. Then variables at other levels may provide a relevant partition of the *different* reference class (of exceptions to the macrolevel law) to which the phenomenon belongs. In this case, everything is to be gained by a further analysis, since the inapplicability or false applicability of the same level regularity leaves the phenomenon unaccounted for, and any relevant partition of a reference class to which the phenomenon *does* belong is useful.

The normal presumption (from the explanatory primacy of lower levels) in such cases is to look for lower-level variables to explain the deviations as with Brownian motion. Appeals to still higher levels are indicated when disputes over functional considerations arise. (See, e.g. Williams, 1966 on mutation rates; Lewontin, 1970, on predicted frequency of the *t*-allele in *Mus musculus*; and McMahon, 1976, for a general relevant discussion.)

The cost–benefit extension of Salmon's (1971) account is capable of more precise formulation and can explain why we look for explanatory information in the way that we do, why further (lower level) accounts sometimes seem to have no further explanatory force and, more generally, why theories, like phenomena, come in levels.

Complexity and the Incomparability of Levels

It was assumed in the discussions of part II and the preceding sections that phenomena were always comparable with respect to level. Thus, for any two phenomena, one could determine clearly and unambiguously whether they were at the same level, and if they were not, which was higher or lower. I believe that comparability of levels is a necessary condition for reduction, but that comparability may not always be possible for reasons which need not involve an ordinary explanatory failure. (Emergence, like reducibility, requires comparability of levels.) Incomparability of levels presents a serious possible challenge to the psychophysical identity thesis—one which it is important to understand more fully. It is this challenge which permeates the last half of Peter Knapp's paper (this volume) and I think is probably at least partially responsible for the awesome complexity, even as a diagramed abstraction, of the relations among Eccles' (this volume) "three worlds." But how is incomparability of levels even possible?

The most simple-minded reductionistic picture of the world— one that might be had by giving in to all of the prejudices induced by

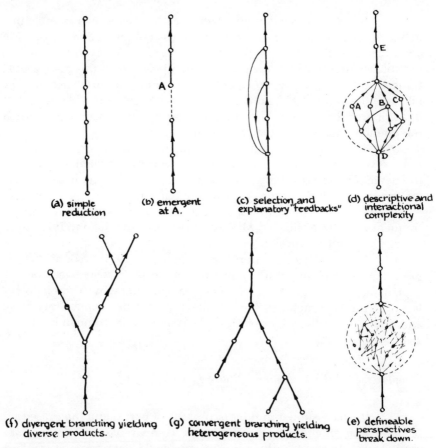

(a) simple reduction

(b) emergent at A.

(c) selection and explanatory "feedbacks"

(d) descriptive and interactional complexity

(f) divergent branching yielding diverse products.

(g) convergent branching yielding heterogeneous products.

(e) defineable perspectives break down.

Figure 2. Complex orderings—of levels and perspectives. Nodes are levels or perspectives—arrows give direction of explanation.

the direction of explanatory priority and unconstrained by the study of any complicated systems of the variety one is likely to encounter in biology, psychology, or the social sciences—is like that of Figure 2a. In this diagram each node represents a distinguishable realm of phenomena (levels, perspectives, or in the more complex cases perhaps only a few closely interrelated types of phenomena). The arrows represent significant causal or explanatory connections. Thus, in Figure 2a, there are distinct levels, but the phenomena of each is explained by and reduced to those of the level below, from which it is clearly distinguished. No phenomena receive explanation from the same or from a higher level. The anathema of this view is that there might be a level, or

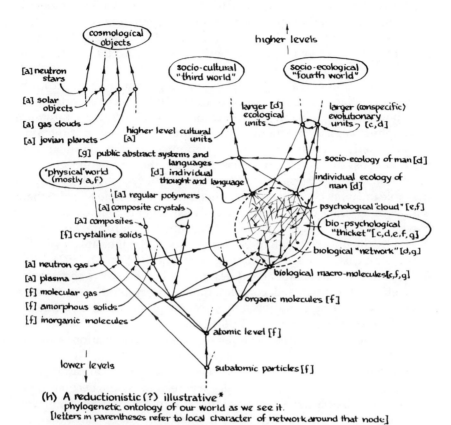

(h) A reductionistic (?) illustrative*
phylogenetic ontology of our world as we see it.
[letters in parentheses refer to local character of network around that node]

* A diagram like this is obviously highly tentative. Although it has been constructed
with many specific relations in mind, I would claim accuracy only of a general qualitative
sort – i.e., for the rough general distribution of network properties, as indicated, e.g.,
by the distribution of letters.   W.C.Wimsatt 1973

even a phenomenon which, as diagrammed in Figure 2b, might not
have an explanation, and thus be emergent.

A more complicated view (Figure 2c) suggested perhaps by a
superficial look at evolutionary theory, has one or two explanatory
feedbacks from higher levels in the hierarchy (e.g., individuals or
populations as units of selection) affecting and explaining phenomena
at lower levels (e.g. the sequences of DNA molecules). At this stage in
spite of the explanatory feedbacks it still seems possible to talk about
distinguishable levels, and even (forgetting the arguments of the preceding section) sometimes to act as if the feedbacks don't really exist,
but are somehow really coded in the upwards arrows in some unob-

vious way. This kind of view is a natural result of a very abstract view of organisms (characteristic of reductionistic interpretations of population genetics—see Williams, 1966, and Wimsatt, 1970) which leaps from genes to populations without tracing the functional or dynamical pathways from one to the other.[22]

In a more realistic view of the organism (Figure 2d), the explanatory relations are more complicated, and it becomes difficult to talk about distinguishable or neatly orderable *levels* for anatomical versus physiological, biochemical versus developmental, or functional versus genetic versus evolutionary mappings of the significance of different subsystems of the organism. Because the interpenetration and interaction of these *perspectives* (they are not levels, but they have a definable unity) is partial and undefined it is not possible to order them as levels at all. If we can't fairly uniformly say what is composed of what or what explains what, then the things in question are not clearly orderable: they not only fail to be clearly at or not at the same level, but there *are* no clear levels. I have argued elsewhere (Wimsatt, 1974*a*) that this situation of interactional and descriptive complexity is characteristic of efficiently organized complex functional systems, and thus an expected product of evolution and selection processes at any but the lowest levels. (See also Levins, 1970.)

One of the notable features of levels of organization is that in terms of any variable or set of variables (such as size), the higher levels seem to become more diffuse—less regular and less localizable (stopping short of the astronomical scale, where they again become more regular)—just like a traveling wave that dissipates in time. The levels thus probably look more like Figure 1c than 1a or 1d. I believe that this is another reflection of the above mentioned explanatory complexity. It is likely that the notion of a level is totally inadequate for this kind of situation, and that a better characterization is derivable from that of the ecological niche. Ecologists have happily (or unhappily) been explicitly wrestling with similar problems for years. (See Whittaker *et al.*, 1973.)

Another complication is a ramification of branches of levels of organization, as is indicated in Figure 2f and 2g. This causes no particular reduction problems (reduction is only to lower nodes on the same branch) unless there is substantial interaction between entities from levels on different branches, which produces situations like those of Figure 2d, 2e, or 2h. Branching occurs when entities at a given level are parts of (for divergent branching, Figure 2f) or made up of (for

---

[22] This view has been widely criticized of late, by Mayr, Waddington, Lewontin and others. See e.g., Waddington, 1970.

convergent branching, Figure 2g) two or more importantly different kinds of systems at higher or lower levels. This process is fundamental to the formation of complex functional organization.

I believe that the "trialism" of Eccles (and Popper) is basically to be handled in this manner, with the abstract sociocultural and the concrete socioecological systems (Figure 2h) on separate branches emerging from the biopsychological "thicket" of connections which is socialized individual man. A branching must occur because the entities or *objects* on the cultural branch (individual mental and group abstract entities) are *complex properties* of socialized man and of the entities on the other branch. This radical ontological split (between properties and objects from the view of the concrete realm) necessitates a branching, and explains many of the differences between abstract and concrete objects.

A further degenerative stage, indicated in Figure 2e, seems possible. This is where the multiplicity of connections and interactions are so multifarous and complex that the perspectives themselves become almost impossible to individuate, or—what may have the same effect, that the perspectives are individuatable but that no agreement can be reached on what available perspectives, if any, truly describe the system. In this sort of situation arguments over definitions of key terminology proliferate—often because, in the absence of useful guidelines as to how they should be defined, there are as many sets of definitions as authors. In this sort of situation too, which seems characteristic of the social sciences, there is a great deal of dispute over "foundational," "methodological," and "philosophical" questions and an uneasy malaise that progress in the disciplines is more cyclic than linear.

Is reduction impossible in such complicated situations? If orderability of levels fails, this means that we can no longer say what is composed of what. On a view of reduction that emphasized ontological simplicity, or regarding upper level things as "logical constructs" or aggregates of lower level things, this would seem to be a crucial failure. The fact that anatomical organs can be viewed as made up of physiological processes and physiological systems as made up of anatomical components suggests that neither view is complete and also that neither kind of entity is really totally made up of the other. I suspect that similar remarks would apply to the relations between the "third world" of Eccles and Popper and the socioecological "fourth world" that they both ignore. There is little temptation to talk about reduction in such a situation.

But when orderability fails (as within the dotted regions of Figures 2d and 2e) it usually only fails "locally." Thus, in Figure 2d, A, B, and C may be unorderable relative to each other, but they are all clearly above D and below E. Anatomical and physiological entities are both clearly composed of molecules, and both clearly parts of ecosystems. Would their local failure of orderability prevent claiming reducibility of ecosystems to molecules? If so, could very messy and hard to define levels, within which there was compositional orderability of things "further apart" but failure for things "closer together" do the same thing?

I believe that this is a more severe version of problems that began in part II, with the argument that *inter*level reduction did not require type-translatability as long as the lower level could explain phenomena at the higher level. We have now seen how far this line can lead. Where ordering fails locally, if the levels in question are sufficiently far apart, I believe that we tend to accept reducibility if we can claim something like explanatory adequacy of one domain for phenomena in another. In practice, I suspect that such a claim would be more often derived from presumptions of explanatory primacy than from demonstrated explanatory adequacy.

If reduction of the mental to the physical is possible, it may be with this residual indeterminacy: It may be unclear exactly what psychology is being reduced to, and unclear exactly what is being reduced to neurophysiology, but the malaise may disappear, leaving only the conviction that the explanatory task is complete, and without ever having invoked forces which were inexplicable at lower levels. Probably that is the most a reductionist can ask, and probably also it is enough. With this, also, we have driven a clear wedge between the ontological and explanatory dimensions of reduction, and it appears that the explanatory dimension is more important.

On the Eliminability of Levels and Generalized First-Person Perspectives

The fact that the psychological realm is representational—and as a result that our psychological *worlds* seem to have at least a dual nature—as subjective as opposed to public cultural (the problem of thought and language), as phenomenal as opposed to real (our sensations and the physical external world), and as subjective and private as opposed to neural or behavioral and public (the first-person–third-person asymmetries that have bedevilled philosophers and scientists alike) is possibly the major problem for neat ordering of levels in psychology. It is possible that at least some of *these* ordering problems are solvable.

One feature of levels as advanced in this paper may cast some further light on first-person–third-person asymmetries in the form of a more generalized analogue. Phenomenalism is an attempt to analyze the world from the first-person perspective of a single person. By analogy, one might suggest that a communal defense of our "ordinary conceptional scheme" (such as Sellars's, 1963, "manifest image") is an attempt to analyze the world from the first-person perspective of a culture or of a species (depending upon how much gets included as "common sense"). This suggests the following "panphenomenalistic" generalization which smacks of Globus' (1972, 1973, this volume) panpsychism without the "bad" connotations of *psychism* or universal consciousness.

A "reliable detector" as defined in the first section of this part is first and foremost a reliable detector of things and properties at its *own* level (though it will not, in general, reliably detect *all* the things at its own level). This is the germ of truth behind a defense of "ordinary common sense" ordinary conceptions and ordinary explanations, though to think that it applies somehow only to us and to our own level is an anthropomorphic conceit.

I suggest further as a general principle that if X is at level L_X, that level L_X is *ineliminable* for X—but ineliminable for cognizing creatures, in 2 distinct senses. The failure to distinguish these has led to mistaken defenses of common sense beliefs as being *conceptually* ineliminable when "common sense" may be better defended in a manner which does not restrict conceptual progress.

(1) To the extent that L_X is *conceptually* ineliminable for X (which I will take as meaning that it is untranslatable into lower level terms) it is so because it involves the predictive regularities of X's own level. This means that theories couched in terms of the phenomena and entities of that level will be the *best* theory (in cost–benefit terms) of any of the theories corresponding to the different levels *for X* to use as a means of increasing X's fitness. The benefits will be high because most of the regularities most important for the survival of X which X can affect with the actions open to it will be regularities of L_X. The cost will be low because the natural information inputs (and resultant categories) will be in terms of L_X interactions, and thus a theory in those terms will demand a minimum of constructions or "theoretical entities." (In this, e.g., the sense-datum theorists erred in ignoring physical objects of roughly ordinary person-detectable size as proper primitives.) This kind of ineliminability obviously presupposes that the system X can be said to have a theory (or internal model) of the environment, and is thus of a certain minimum level of adaptive complexity.

But conceptual ineliminability of L_X for X is only likely if the system in question does not have sufficient computational and manipulatory powers available at sufficiently low cost to make construction of theory at other levels *in addition* worthwhile *for the added predictive benefits to X at L_X*[23].Culture and technology have lowered the cost and raised the benefits sufficiently that we are no longer in all ways *conceptually* tied to our own level, though we have not yet actually achieved—or found it desirable to attempt—the complete sort of translational reduction necessary to talk of conceptual eliminability.[24] Conceptual ineliminability would thus seem to be contingent and dependent upon the costs and benefits of other ways of describing the world in relation to our resources.

(2) For cognitive systems with sensory input a sizeable proportion of the entities and properties of their level L_X will be *sensorily immediate* to X. By claiming that entities and properties in the world are sensorily immediate, I am *not* claiming that they are kinds of sense data, or objects of sense, in the traditional meanings of these terms. (They are, in Globus's, 1973, terms, "distal to the transformation boundary.") Nor am I claiming that we do not interact with the entities of the world *via* sound, light, pressure or heat waves and *via* the normal sensory transducers which these affect. Rather, I am claiming that our interactions with them are sufficiently regular, well-behaved, reliable, and normal that there is *usually* no point in questioning the operations or reliability of these intermediate links. The point of sensory immediacy is not to claim that the entities and properties in the world are *themselves* immediate to the sensing system, but that the *causal interaction* (normally produced by them in an involved but reliable manner) is given immediately to the system acted upon, in a way that makes it ineliminable (though it may be modifiable) by conceptual activity. To say that they are *sensorily* immediate (rather than just causally immediate) is to recognize the role these interactions play in the acquisition of knowledge. Because of this role there is a temptation to treat those things which are sensorily immediate as kinds of facts, and to read their

---

[23] This is chosen as important because it is presumably most closely related to the *biological* functions of consciousness and of conceptual thinking. In this way, at least from an evolutionary perspective, control of or adaptive response to one's environment is the *main* function of science, and explanation, while the main "pure" end of science, is subservient to this.

[24] And if the cost–benefit account of explanation and the account of levels proposed earlier are right, *complete* translation (as opposed to selective partial translation or explication) seems forever unlikely in most areas. See part II above, Dresden (1974), and Boyd (1972).

immediacy as a kind of ineliminability or incorrigibility of these facts to the system which (or person who) has them. This is obviously a mistake, for things in the world cannot be known incorrigibly, and the sensory events which are immediate are not the objects of knowledge.

This mistake has a complementary one, which is especially rampant among those who are suspicious of subjective data of consciousness and advocates of "eliminative materialism." Such writers as Rorty (1965) believe that scientific progress will result in the elimination of the contents of sense experience and their replacement with something else. This error also treats sensory immediates as kinds of facts, which, being facts, are corrigible and replaceable by other facts. I wish to deny that sensory immediates are facts, and thus to deny both that they are incorrigible *and* that they are eliminable, at least by any cognitive act of reconceptualization.

The ineliminability of sensory immediates makes it tempting to describe them as emergent, though this would have to be in a *third* sense (= emergent$_3$) which is distinct from both of the two senses discussed earlier (above in part I), and, most importantly, is independent of the possibility of reduction or conceptual eliminability.

To interact causally with a system X is just to produce an effect on it at its own level, L_X. (Effects produced primarily at lower or higher levels will be interactions with sub or supersystems of X, and only indirectly with X.) Cognitive input is a special case of this causal interaction (*via* its sensory modalities) with a system sufficiently adaptive and complicated in its modes of responding to and interacting with its environment and which receives information pertinent to this interaction efficiently enough (both in terms of energy and coding) that we say that it has an "internal model" of the environment, "acts on the basis of" outputs from the model, and receives information to be "used" in this model through "sensory modalities." All claims to knowledge on the part of the system—putative facts—are outputs of this internal model or representations in it. All sensory immediates are inputs to this model or immediate causes of these inputs.[25] We need and are stuck with our sensory world much as it is because of the physical and biological nature of our sensory receptors. The closest we can come to eliminating objects of sense is by refusing to interact with our environment—not by any cognitive operations on or in our internal

---

[25] The terms in quotes are, roughly, to be regarded as implicitly defined by the context. I am deliberately sliding over a morass of issues here, from what exactly is an "internal model" to what kinds of intrinsic properties a sensory modality must have, to just where, in the interaction between a system and its environment are to be found those causal interactions which are sensorily immediate. I cannot discuss these topics here, though I believe that the approach begun here permits a unified attack on all of them.

model. However far our knowledge of other levels progresses, even complete explanation, reduction, and ability to control things at our own level in terms of this knowledge would affect only the *conceptual* centrality or eliminability of things at our level but not their *sensory* immediacy. I can stop seeing objects around me by closing my eyes, an operation on my sensory channels, but not by any conceptual revolution, which would be an operation on my internal model. *If my knowledge of the world is to be empirically based, the sensory immediacy of at least some things at my level follows, since sensory interaction with the things of this level is the only means open to me of acquiring empirical knowledge.*

A similar relation applies between things as described at our level and the same things described at lower levels as applies between 1st person reports of conscious experience and 3rd person behavioral, psychological and neurophysiological reports of that same experience. To ask about the *conceptual* centrality of our own level is like asking about ourselves "from outside"—in the *third person*, or looking at our brains in Feigl's (1967) "autocerebroscope." It is asking how our level looks through the medium of another level—the lower level which might (in principle) allow its conceptual elimination. To ask about the *sensory* or causal centrality of our level is like asking about ourselves in the *1st person*. Just as I cannot experience except through *my own* sensations, so no system can interact or be interacted with except with something that interacts with it.

I believe that this parallel is no accident. The immediacy of the first person perspective and of our own level is *causal*. When either becomes *conceptualized*, it becomes potentially defeasible, eliminable, or translatable, because it has acquired a basically third person or *representational* character, and it becomes appropriate to ask whether (and to what extent) the representation is correct.

There is a substantial danger of confusion here, because the distinction between first and third person perspectives is probably most usually treated as a distinction between private and public worlds rather than as one of the immediate vs. representational character of sense. The two distinctions are not equivalent: *My* view of the world (or internal model) is both *representational* and *private*, and *public* objects are *sensorily immediate* to anyone who interacts causally with them through sensory channels. Thus, even the normally assumed *coincidence* of sensory immediacy with privacy and of the public with the representational (mistakes encouraged by phenomenalism) is not universal.

I believe that these two distinctions—private vs. public and causal vs. representational—interact in a variety of complex ways to produce virtually all of the paradoxical and involuted intricacies of the

full-blooded human first-person–third-person distinction with its at-
tendant asymmetries. (See Gunderson, 1970.)

The private–public distinction also has broader analogues, in
terms of what it is to be internal or external to a system. If we imagine
the boundaries of systems changing (e.g., as when a set of subsystems
aggregate into a large system—see Simon, 1969, chapter 4), what is
private (internal) to them or public (external) to surrounding systems
changes correlatively. This way of talking suggests spatial inclusion and
boundaries, but Simon's work on near-decomposability of systems
allows generalization to cases where the criteria for defining systems
are relative strengths of interaction (Simon, *ibid.*, Wimsatt, 1974*a*).

But there remains a strong feeling that the inner–outer distinction (or anything like it) as applied to physical systems fails to give our
private–public distinction. Thus, there are physically inner events
(such as the dilation of my capillaries) which are neither public (except
perhaps under the surgeon's knife) nor private (because I am not aware
of changes in my capillaries). Similarly, no amount of cutting will
render my inner-and-private afterimage, intention, or belief outer-and-
public. Being psychologically private, it is clear, is not *simply* being
physically inner, or conversely, and this is the paradox of Feigl's (1967)
autocerebroscope.

The missing fact is that psychologically private events are
representing events in a representational system.[26] All physical systems have a physical inside, but only those capable of behavior which
is, in some sense, representational to itself (whose representational
status is not parasitic upon the actions or intentions of an outside
observer) can have a psychological inside. Similarly, to talk either
about *conceptual* eliminability or about *sensory* immediacy is to presuppose that the system in question has complex representational
capabilities. The capability for representation thus emerges as crucial.
As a physicalist, I believe that this capability is a complex physical
property—but not one which all systems possess. On this view, then,
panpsychism (Globus, this volume) is false.

If construing the concept of representation very loosely helps
Globus to espouse panpsychism, this is a sword that has two edges.
Denying the broad sweep of representation, tethering panpsychism to

---

[26] By this, I mean that they are the kind of events which characteristically represent things. This not
only fails to imply, in many particular cases, that the represented thing exists, but even fails to
imply in some cases (like that of an afterimage) that there *is* something represented, intensionally,
as it were.

I am inclined to add that being a representational system is inextricably connected with having
that function (which is, for organisms, to indicate that selection for that characteristic has played a
role in the evolution of the relevant "hardware"). This condition is clearly not met for Globus'
neutron–pion pair, discussed following.

those systems which have the organizational equivalents, in loosely construed functional terms of embodied interacting nervous systems,[27] means that in the rest of the (physical) world one finds a firm foundation not for the generally accepted (but unrecognized as such) *third* person perspective, but for the paradoxical and elusive *immediacy* of conscious experience.[28] This gives a physical basis for the immediacy of consciousness without postulating an ontological complementarity, and the hope of analyzing the third person perspective as a straightforwardly physical property of complex systems.

Where we have gone wrong is in assuming, anthropomorphically, that the physical world (and not just our view of it) is a third-person world, not a first-person world—a world as represented to us rather than a world of immediate interactions unto itself, as if all of the world, like Berkeley thought, were a representation in the mind of some great perceiver. But in this way, we have to postulate an unobservable *Ding an Sich* which is the cause of our perceptions. The feeling that this unobservability is both inescapable and methodologically intolerable has lead to skepticism with respect to other minds (other first-persons); operationalist, instrumentalist, fictionalist, and other anti-realist interpretations of theories of the real world; and, at the hands of modern behaviorists, even Descartes' last refuge in his own self and more modern versions of introspectionism have been disbarred as empirically useless. The solution must be to put the first-person perspective back into the physcial world of causal interaction from which Descartes and empiricists since have removed it.[29] The world of causal interactions at different levels unifies these two perspectives in an epistemologically complementary way without inducing ontological schizophrenia. Nor can science tolerate this split: We can hardly expect to put our heads together if we leave our worlds apart.

---

[27] I believe that *central* state materialism is false, although physicalism is true. I believe that the psychological involves the functional interactions of a socialized embodied brain with its environment. To locate consciousness solely and simply in the brain, *even though the brain may properly be called the organ of consciousness*, is to commit a kind of functional localization fallacy which is subtler and more seductive, but nonetheless basically akin to calling Broca's area the "speech center," or suggesting that Penfield and Roberts' stimulation experiments located the memories they evoked at the tip of their stimulating electrode.

[28] This insight was inspired by Globus, and by the elegant recursive symmetry of his proposal (1972, p. 294). I believe this point to be a working out of the consequences of his startling assertion that rocks and other inanimate objects could have a first-person perspective. Without that claim, I would have gone on seeing the world as if it (and not my *view* of it) was in the third person. Unlike Globus, however, I think that the first person resides not in an object's private *Ding an Sich*, but at least partially also in the character of its relations with the world. This overall view is also more than passingly Kantian, as Manley Thompson has pointed out to me, and quite Sellarsian, as I come more and more to realize in time.

[29] This subjective aspect of experience is one of the features which Gunderson (1971) has called "program resistant." But if I am right, this type of failure is due not to the limitations of programming *per se*, but to the limitations of our post-Cartesian dichotomy between first and third person.

With this inversion of the problem, we are done: There is no place for the subjective immediacy of consciousness in a third-person world, unless we assume that consciousness is an ineffable something that even neutrons, protons, and electrons have a little of. But in a 1st person world of causally immediate interactions at various levels of organization, there is a hope that we can explain what a representational system is in terms of a sufficiently complex organization of such interactions. With this much, a physicalism (of causally immediate interactions) has won the battle, and without the need for complementarity as more than an epistemological matter.

With this last move, all of the paradox should be gone from Sperry's "emergent interactionism." His statement that "conscious subjective properties . . . have causal potency in regulating the course of brain events . . . " (p. 165) follows naturally in a world in which a third person perspective is a straightforward higher level emergent$_2$ (but explicable) property of a system composed of interacting lower-level physical, chemical, biological, and neuropsychological subsystems, imbedded in evolutionary, ontogenetic, sociocultural, and socioecological environments. The "split" between mental and physical should be no more mysterious than the anatomical split between left and right hemisphere in commissurotomy patients, and no more real than the psychological "split" in normal people. It is no more real because in both cases there is none, and it is no more mysterious, because in all three cases, the explanation is to be found in the nature and structure of lower and higher level interacting systems. If this constitutes a reduction of the mental to the physical, then so be it!

ACKNOWLEDGMENTS

I have learned substantially from my co-conferees, students, and colleagues who have reacted to a series of versions of these remarks. I would like especially to thank David Bantz, Richard Boyd, Donald Campbell, Alan Donagan, Arthur Fine, David Hill, David Hull, David Kolb, Elyse Rasky, Robert Richardson, Nancy Roth, Kenneth Schaffner, Eric Stiffler, Paul Teller, and Manley Thompson. Special thanks are due to Gordon Globus as a frequent source of ideas and as an invaluable critic in helping me to clarify my own ideas. I wish to dedicate this paper to the memory of Frank Rosenblatt, who introduced me to evolutionary and mathematical ways of thinking about the mind. I thank the program on Humanities, Science, and Technology at Cornell University for support as a research fellow, giving time for the revision of this manuscript.

264 □ WILLIAM C. WIMSATT

REFERENCES

Bartlett, F. C., and John, E. R. (1973): Equipotentiality quantified: The anatomical distribution of the engram. *Science* **181**, pp. 764–767.

Blachowitz, J. A. (1971): Systems theory and evolutionary models of the development of Science. *Philos. Sci.* **38**, pp. 178–199.

Boyd, R. (1972): Determinism, laws, and predictability in principle. *Philos. Sci.* **39**, 431–450.

Bronowski, J. (1970): New concepts in the evolution of complexity: Stratified stability and unbounded plans. *Sythese* **21**, pp. 228–246.

Campbell, D. T. (1958): Common fate, similarity, and other indices of the status of aggregates of persons as social entities. *Behav. Sci.* **3**, 14–25.

Campbell, D. T. (1973a): Evolutionary epistemology. In: *The Philosophy of Karl Popper*. Ed. by P. A. Schilpp. LaSalle, Illinois: Open Court, pp. 413–463.

Campbell, D. T. (1974): "Downwards causation" in hierarchically organized biological systems. In: *The Problem of Reduction in Biology*. Ed. by F. Ayala and T. Dobzhansky, Berkeley: University of California Press.

Carlson, E. A. (1966): *The Gene: A Critical History*, Philadelphia: Saunders.

Causey, R. (1972): Attribute-identities in microreductions. *J. Philos.* **69**, pp. 407–422.

Darwin, C. (1872): *The Expression of the Emotions in Man and Animals*. Reprinted, Chicago: University of Chicago Press, 1965.

Darden, L. (1974): *Reasoning in Scientific Change: The Field of Genetics at its Beginnings*. Ph.D. dissertation. Committee on Conceptual Foundations of Science, University of Chicago.

Dennett, D. C. (1969): *Content and Consciousness*. New York: Humanities Press.

Dennett, D. C. (1971): Intentional systems. *J. Philos.* **68**, pp. 87–106.

Dewan, E. M. (1969): Cybernetics and attention. In: *Attention in Neurophysiology*. Ed. by C. R. Evans and T. B. Mulholland. London: Butterworths, pp. 323–347.

Dresden, M. (1974): Reflections on fundamentality and complexity. In: *Physical Reality and Mathematical Description* (Festschrift for Joseph Jauch) Ed. by Charles Enz and Jagdit Mehra. Reidel: Dordrecht. pp. 133–166.

Feigl., H. (1967): *The Mental and the Physical*. Minneapolis: University of Minnesota Press.

Feyerabend, P. K. (1962): Explanation, reduction, and empiricism. In: *Minnesota Studies in the Philosophy of Science*. Ed. by H. Feigl and G. Maxwell. Minneapolis: University of Minnesota Press, pp. 28–97.

Fodor, J. (1968): *Psychological Explanation*. New York: Random House.

Fodor, J. (1974): Special sciences (or: the disunity of science as a working hypothesis). *Synthese* **28**, pp. 97–115.

Garfinkel, A. (1975): *Explanation and Individuals*. Ph.D. dissertation, Department of Philosophy, Harvard University.

Globus, G. G. (1972): Biological foundations of the psychoneural identity hypothesis. *Philos. Sci.* **40**, pp. 291–301.

Globus, G. G. (1973): Unexpected symmetries in the world knot. *Science* **180**, pp. 1129–1137.

Glymour, C. (1973): Testability without meaning: An essay on distributive justice. Department of Philosophy, Princeton University (mimeo).

Gregory, R. L. (1959): Models and the localization of function in the central nervous system. In: *Key Papers: Cybernetics*. Ed. by C. R. Evans and A. D. J. Robertson. London: Butterworths, pp. 91–102.

Grunbaum, A. (1963): *Philosophical Problems of Space and Time*. New York: Knopf.

Gunderson, K. (1970): Asymmetries and mind-body perplexities. In: *Minnesota Studies in the Philosophy of Science* Vol 4. Ed. by M. Radner and S. Winokur. Minneapolis: University of Minnesota Press, pp. 273–309.

Gunderson, K..(1971): *Mentality and Machines*. Garden City: Doubleday (Anchor).

Hanson, N. R. (1961): *Patterns of Discovery*. London: Cambridge University Press.

Hanson, N. R. (1970): A picture theory of theory meaning. In: *The Nature and Function of Scientific Theories*. Ed. by R. G. Colodny, Pittsburgh: University of Pittsburgh Press, pp. 233–274.

Hull, D. L. (1972): Reduction in genetics—Biology or Philosophy? *Philos. Sci.* **39**, pp. 491–499.

Hull, D. L. (1973): *Philosophy of Biology*. Englewood Cliffs, N. J.: Prentice-Hall.

Jeans, J. (1960): *An Introduction to the Kinetic Theory of Gases*. London: Cambridge University Press.

Kim, J. (1964): Inference, explanation and prediction. *J. Philos.* **61**, pp. 360–368.

Kim, J. (1966: On the psycho-physical identity thesis. *American Philosophical Quarterly* **3**, pp. 227–235.

Kim, J. (1971): Materialism and the criteria of the mental. *Synthese* **22**, pp. 323–245.

Kuhn, T. A. (1962): *The Structure of Scientific Revolutions*. Chicago: University of Chicago Press. (2nd ed., 1970).

Levins, R. (1966): The strategy of model building in population biology. *Am. Sci.* **54**, pp. 421–431.

Levins, R. (1968): *Evolution in Changing Environments*. Princeton, N. J.: Princeton University Press.

Levins, R. (1970): Complex systems. In: *Towards a Theoretical Biology*, v. 3. Ed. by C. H. Waddington. Edinburgh: University of Edinburgh Press. pp. 73–88.

Levins, R. (1974): The qualitative analysis of partially specified systems. *Ann. N. Y. Acad. Sci.* **231**, 123–138.

Lewontin, R. C. (1970): Units of selection. *Ann. Rev. Ecol. Syst.* **1**, pp. 1–18.

Longuet-Higgins, H. C., Willshaw, D. J., and Buneman, O. P. (1970): Theories of associative recall. *Quarterly Review of Biophysics*. **3**, pp. 223–244.

McMahon, J. (1976): *The Concept of Fitness in Evolutionary Biology*. Ph.D. Dissertation. Department of Philosophy, University of Chicago (in preparation).

McMullin, E. (1972): The dialectics of reduction. *Idealistic Studies* **2**, pp. 95–115.

Miller, G. A., Galanter, E. H., and Pribram, K. H. (1960): *Plans and the Structure of Behavior*. New York: Holt, Rinehart and Winston.

Nagel, E. (1961): *The Structure of Science*. New York: Harcourt.

Nickles, T. (1973a): Two concepts of intertheoretic reduction. *J. Philos.* **70**, pp. 181–201.

Nickles, T. (1973b): *Reduction and Conceptual Change*. Unpublished manuscript.

Popper, K. (1959): *The Logic of Scientific Discovery*. London: Hutchinson.

Pribram, K. H. (1971a): *Languages of the Brain*. Englewood Cliffs: Prentice-Hall.

Rorty, R. (1965): Mind–body identity, privacy and categories. In: *Modern Materialism: Readings on Mind–Body Identity*. Ed. by J. O'Connor. New York: Harcourt, 1969, pp. 145–174.

Rosenblatt, F. (1962a): Strategic approaches to the study of brain models. In: *Principles of Self-Organization*. Ed. by H. von Foerster and G. W. Zopf, New York: Pergamon Press, pp. 385–402.

Rosenblatt, F. (1962b): *Principles of Neurodynamics: Perceptions and the Theory of Brain Mechanisms*, Spartan Books, Washington, D.C. (Also published by Cornell Aeronautical Laboratory as Report No. VG-1196-G-8, 15 March, 1961).

Roth, N. (1974): *Progress in Modern Biology: An Alternative to Reduction*. Ph.D. dissertation. Committee on Conceptual Foundations of Science, University of Chicago.

Salmon, W., Jeffrey, R., and Greeno, J. (1971): *Statistical Explanation and Statistical Relevance*. Pittsburgh: University of Pittsburgh Press.

Schaffner, K. F. (1967): Approaches to reduction. *Philos. Sci.* **34**, pp. 137–147.

Sellars, W. (1963): Philosophy and the scientific image of man. In: *Science, Perception and Reality*. Ed. by Sellars, London: Routledge, pp. 1–40.

Shapere, D. (1966): Meaning and scientific change. In: *Mind and Cosmos*. Ed. R. G. Colodny, Pittsburgh, University of Pittsburgh Press, pp. 41–85.

Shapere, D. (1969): Notes towards a post-positivistic interpretation of science. In: *The Legacy of Logical Positivism*. Ed. by P. Achinstein and S. F. Barker, Baltimore: Johns Hopkins Press.

Shapere, D. (1974): Scientific theories and their domains. In: *The Nature of Scientific Theories*. Ed. by Frederick Suppe. Urbana: University of Illinois Press.

Simon, H. A. (1957). A behavioral model of rational choice. In: *Models of Man*, Chapter 15. Ed. by Simon, New York: Wiley.

Simon, H. A. (1966*a*): Thinking by computers. In: *Mind and Cosmos*. Ed. by R. G. Colodny, Pittsburgh, University of Pittsburgh Press, pp. 3–21.

Simon, H. A. (1966*b*): Scientific discovery and the psychology of problem solving. In: *Mind and Cosmos*. Ed. by R. G. Colodny, Pittsburgh, The University of Pittsburgh Press, pp. 22–40

Simon, H. A. (1969): *The Sciences of the Artificial*. Cambridge: M.I.T. Press.

Simon, H. A., and Chase, W. G. (1973): Skill in chess. *Am. Sci.* **61**, pp. 394–403.

Sklar, L. (1967): Types of inter-theoretic reduction. *Br. J. Philos. Sci.* **18**, pp. 109–124.

Sperry, R. W. (1966): Brain bisection and mechanisms of consciousness. In: *Brain and Conscious Experience*. Ed. by J. C. Eccles. New York: Springer-Verlag.

Sperry, R. W. (1969): A modified concept of consciousness. *Psychol. Rev.* **76**, pp. 532–536.

Sperry, R. W. (1970): An objective approach to subjective experience: Further explanation of a hypothesis. *Psychol. Rev.* **77**, pp. 585–590.

Sutton, W. S. (1903): The chromosomes in heredity. *Biol. Bull.* **4**, 231–251.

Taylor, C. (1964): *The Explanation of Behavior*. London: Routledge.

Taylor, C. (1967): Mind–body identity, a side issue? *Philos. Rev.* **76**, 201–213.

Thompson, D'Arcy W. (1961): *On Growth and Form*. Abridged edition, edited with commentary by J. T. Bonner. London: Cambridge University Press.

von Bekesy, G. (1967): *Sensory Inhibition*. Princeton: Princeton University Press.

Waddington, C. H. (1970): Paradigm for an evolutionary process. In: *Towards a Theoretical Biology* Vol. 2. Ed. by Waddington. Edinburgh: University of Edinburgh Press, pp. 106–124.

Whittaker, R. H., Levin, S. A. and Root, R. B. (1973): Niche, habitat and ecotope. *Am. Nat.* **107**, pp. 321–338.

Weisskopf, V. F. (1975): Of atoms, mountains and stars: A study in qualitative physics. *Science* **187**, pp. 605–612.

Williams, G. C. (1966): *Adaptation and Natural Selection: A Critique of Some Current Evolutionary Thought*. Princeton: Princeton University Press.

Wimsatt, W. C. (1970): review of G. C. Williams' *Adaptation and Natural Selection*. *Philos. Sci.* **37**, pp. 620–623.

Wimsatt, W. C. (1971*a*): *Modern Science and the New Teleology: I—The Conceptual Foundations of Functional Analysis*. Ph.D. dissertation. Department of Philosophy, University of Pittsburgh.

Wimsatt, W. C. (1971b): Aggregativity and complexity. In: *Proceedings of the 4th International Congress for Logic, Methodology and Philosophy of Science*. Ed. by P. Suppes.

Wimsatt, W. C. (1972a): Teleology and the logical structure of function statements. *Studies in History and Philosophy of Science*. **3,** pp. 1–80.

Wimsatt, W. C. (1972b): The machine in the ghost: The sciences of the Artificial. Invited commentary on the paper, *Chance and Design in Darwin and in Neo-Darwinism,* of Edward Manier at the 1972 Metaphysical Meetings (unpublished manuscript).

Wimsatt, W. C. (1974a): Complexity and organization. In: *Boston Studies in the Philosophy of Science* Vol. 20. Ed. by K. F. Schaffner and R. S. Cohen, Reidel: Dordrecht, pp. 67–86.

Wimsatt, W. C. (1974b): The problem of spatiality in genetics and in the mental realm. In preparation.

9 Introduction

Discussions of the mind–brain puzzle have a way of diffusing to an entire set of broad philosophical issues; perhaps this is why Schopenhauer's phrase, "world knot," seems so felicitous. The following article is such a case, since Globus generates a number of manifestly extravagant claims about the nature of reality and universal consciousness from his "psychoneural *structural* identity thesis," which he distinguishes from the Russell-Feigl-Maxwell "psychoneural identity thesis."

According to Globus, any system can be viewed from "intrinsic" and "extrinsic" perspectives, where the former is coextensive with the system under consideration. He argues that, since the intrinsic perspective must find the "stuff" of the system to be "unbounded," whereas the extrinsic perspective must find the "stuff" of the system to be "bounded," the two perspectives give irreducibly incompatible accounts. At the same time, the *structure* of the system is "one and the same" according to these perspectives, in a rather complicated sense. The structure of input to the locus of the extrinsic perspective conserves the structure of the system under observation and is in turn conserved through successive transformations within the locus of the extrinsic perspective; thus, the structure of the intrinsic perspective is to some extent "conserved" on the extrinsic perspective, and is known "by acquaintance"; ideally, the structure as known "by description" is strictly identical with the structure on the intrinsic perspective.

Since the intrinsic perspective on a certain system is strictly identical with mind, and the extrinsic perspective on that same system finds it to be "brain," according to Globus, the mind–brain puzzle is resolved. Mind and brain are structurally identical, but the "stuffs" so structured have incompatible properties as a function of perspective, which leads to irreducible contradictions. What Weimer (this volume) attributes to ambiguity in the deep structure which generates meaning, and Savodnik (this volume) attributes to the vicissitudes of symbol formation, Globus attributes to intrinsic and extrinsic perspectives finding a configured "stuff" to be unbounded and bounded respectively. Although disparate on this issue, all three appear wary of certain ontological claims and attempt an epistemological unification for the apparent bifurcation of "reality."

Expanding on this solution, Globus proposes a "sophisticated naive realism" in which the structure of reality is known "by direct acquaintance" (*contra* Russell) to the extent that it is conserved within the set of neural transformations, since the structure of mind is in fact that structure conserved. In this radical version of "structural realism," the common-sensical notion that we perceive the world as it is becomes refurbished, since the structure of the world is directly perceived as it is (subject to whatever transformations the brain imposes as a function of inheritance and learning).

Finally, Globus finds no reason to confine mind to human systems; indeed, the logic of his argument compels him to claim that *all* systems have mind, although the kind of mind varies directly as a function of the "richness" of the system. Unlike Pribram (this volume) who finds that "only a difference that makes a difference is worth pursuing," universal consciousness is for Globus an issue of utmost ethical importance, since, if true, it trivializes another one of man's narcissistic beliefs which prevent him from seeing himself clearly as he is. But it will seem to many that Globus' extrapolation of his argument leads here to such improbable conclusions that his structural identity solution is seriously compromised by this alone. For example, what exactly does Globus mean when he talks of a rock's consciousness? Surely the term has been drained completely of its ordinary meaning. How are we to talk of the consciousness of, say, the Pacific Ocean? (At least manifestly, the "spirit" which primitive cultures may attribute to a body of water appears to have little in common with Globus' technical exposition of perspective on systems, although Globus argues that "it is *we* who have misunderstood highly sophisticated mystical thought.")

It is apparent that in addition to science, Globus draws considerable inspiration from what he understands to be the mystical tradition when approaching the mind–brain puzzle, although he presents no reasons which lend credence to this bias; what "feels good in his bones," to borrow Maxwell's (this volume) phrase (or his implicit "themata," following Holton [1973]), is unlikely to enlist sympathetic resonance among philosophers and scientists in general.

REFERENCE

Holton, G. (1973): Thematic Origins of Scientific Thought: Kepler to Einstein. Cambridge: Harvard University Press.

9 Mind, Structure, and Contradiction

GORDON G. GLOBUS

The opposite of a trivial truth is a falsehood. The opposite of a profound truth may well be another profound truth.
—*attributed*[1] *to Niels Bohr*

All around him were what other people called mirrors, which he called leaks. *The entire wall which separated the lobby from the cocktail lounge was a* leak *ten feet high and thirty feet long. There was another* leak *on the cigarette machine and yet another on the candy machine. And when Trout looked through them to see what was going on in the other universe, he saw a red-eyed, filthy old creature who was barefoot, who had his pants rolled up to his knees.*
—*Kurt Vonnegut, Jr. (1973, p. 229)*

In working on the mind–brain problem over the last few years, I have become disheartened on occasion and come to the conclusion that western man is uniquely equipped and situated so as to make that problem unsolvable, even though it may be a rather simple problem indeed. As a scientist, I would like to hold philosophers responsible for this state of affairs! However, the roots appear to lie deeper than mere

---

[1] Personal communication from Alexander Stern.

GORDON G. GLOBUS·University of California, Irvine

271

verbal obfuscation. As Freud pointed out, the Copernican revolution, the Darwinian revolution, and finally the psychoanalytic revolution—the latter being more of a quelled insurrection—all comprised narcissistic injuries to man, who had seen himself variously as the center of the universe, distinct from other forms of life, and consciously determining his own behavior. Perhaps to understand the mind–brain problem, we have to give up further narcissistic notions—that we are the only conscious form of life, that the world *actually*[2] is as we perceive it to be, indeed that we are in *any* nontrivial way distinct from the rest of the natural world. Those of you who have read the brilliant and extraordinary books of Carlos Castaneda (1969, 1971, 1973, 1974) which describe his apprenticeship to a Yaqui Indian sorcerer, don Juan, will appreciate the tenacity with which we, reared in a western philosophical and scientific paradigm, hold onto these narcissistic notions. In this regard, I find that the mystical paradigm has much to offer, when considering the mind–brain puzzle.

In the present paper, I want to offer a solution to the mind–brain problem which trivializes the separation of the human mind from the rest of the natural world. I am hopeful that my argument will prove more compelling than a naive panpsychism; indeed, it may well be that it is *we* who have naively misunderstood highly sophisticated mystical thought, especially as embodied in eastern philosophy and less technologically advanced cultures. It seems to me, for example, that when we separate don Juan's epistemology and ontology from his psychotherapeutic and pedagogic methods, we can discern an indigenous Yaqui philosopher of the first rank behind the therapist and teacher. As another illustration, Capra (1975) has presented superbly the striking similarities between the comprehensive holism of mystical thought and contemporary quantum physical conceptions of a fundamental "interpenetration" of all matter such that "the universe is seen as a dynamic web of interrelated events."

But before enjoining the issue of a universal consciousness, I shall develop what I believe to be a novel solution to the mind–brain puzzle. This "psychoneural *structural* identity thesis" holds that the structure of mind and brain are (in a sense to be explained) *one and the same,* even though incompatible properties *must* be attributed to the mental and neural "stuffs"[3] so structured. This incompatibility is a

---

[2] I am not talking about giving up a *theory* that the world is as we see it; that is simple enough. Instead, I mean *seeing* the world as it is, rather than as we think it is. (cf. J. Krishnamurti's (1972) *Freedom From the Known.*)

[3] I use the term "stuff" throughout in its most general and nondescript sense. I do not mean to attribute any "substantival" properties here. Hence, the phrase "stuff of awareness" does not imply that awareness is a material.

function of "intrinsic" and "extrinsic" perspectives finding the "stuff" to be unbounded and bounded respectively. Irreducible contradiction, it is argued, is inherent to our knowledge of the "stuff" of the world, but this contradiction can be transcended by our knowledge of the fundamental structural unity.

COMPLEMENTARITY RECONSIDERED

I have presented elsewhere (1973a,b,c, 1974) a "complementarity solution" to the mind–brain puzzle which now requires modifications. According to this complementarity argument, any system, Z, can be approached from two perspectives. The *intrinsic perspective* is coextensive with Z itself, whereas an *extrinsic perspective* is not, and thereby entails some other system, Z.* There is only one intrinsic perspective; all other perspectives are extrinsic. Because a system cannot be both coterminous and not coterminous with the same system, intrinsic and extrinsic perspectives are *mutually exclusive.* Since these perspectives must attribute incompatible properties to Z (for reasons to be detailed below), we have a special case of "complementarity."

The sense in which "complementarity" is meant here can be illustrated by reference to the wave–particle duality problem in quantum physics. Complementarity holds that light is not completely accounted for by the experimental arrangements which indicate that light has properties of a wave, nor is light completely accounted for by those experimental arrangements which indicate that light has properties of a particle. Further, these experimental arrangements cannot be applied simultaneously, and light cannot be considered a "wavicle," since the wave and particle properties are patently incompatible. Instead, complementarity holds that light has no reality *independent* of the experimental arrangement by means of which light is observed. "Reality" is relativized by the method of observation.

The connection between this sense of complementarity and the "complementarity solution" is as follows. Since mutually exclusive intrinsic and extrinsic perspectives on Z cannot be simultaneously applied, and since Z has incompatible properties according to these perspectives, we have a unique instance of complementarity, where one experimental arrangement (that is, perspective) is intrinsic to (coextensive with) the system under observation.

There are two considerations which have led me to abandon this formal complementarity approach. First, after a long period of widespread acceptance, the actual status of complementarity in physics itself is now considered problematic (Parks & Margenau, 1968; Margenau, 1963). But more importantly, my assumption that intrinsic and extrinsic perspectives on Z *must* be mutually exclusive, by definition as it were, turns out to be incorrect. *Given a sufficiently rich system*, it is possible for these two perspectives to be united within one perspective, as shown in Gödel's (1931) celebrated proof on formally undecidable propositions. Gödel succeeded in constructing a "self-referential formula," a statement within a (sufficiently rich) calculus which has mirrored within it a metamathematical statement about that statement. (In effect, the formula, F, asserts: "F is not formally demonstrable.") A metamathematical statement assumes an extrinsic perspective on the calculus, while F is intrinsic to the calculus.[4] Since the system Z can be a "sufficiently rich" system—when Z is that system called by observers a "human brain"—an argument from complementarity to a mind–brain solution is seriously compromised.[5]

PHENOMENOLOGICAL ISSUES

It appears that the great majority of contemporary philosophers of the analytic tradition writing on the mind–brain puzzle stubbornly pay no attention whatsoever to their own awareness—the very awareness which is at issue—and indeed, avoid all phenomenological considerations in favor of conceptual and linguistic concerns. This philosophical indulgence, which is a reflection of a characterological style (or better, "grammar") typical of analytic philosophers, makes sensible discussion impossible.[6]

I would like to present my argument in the most simple way that I can, which entails at first some minimal phenomenological considerations,[7] which I present informally and without the cumbersome terminology of Husserl. If the reader is willing to "see" (Castaneda,

---

[4] In a recently completed work, together with Stephen Franklin and Irwin Savodnik, I have considered the relevance of Gödel's proof to the mind–brain puzzle in some detail (1975a, 1975b).

[5] Of course, acceptance of certain self-referential statements leads to grave complications, since that statement is "undecidable" (in some sense, depending on the kind of statement). These "dues" are explored elsewhere (1975a, 1975b).

[6] The phenomenological tradition has a different set of indulgences! Although I shall not focus on this in my discussion, an exclusive reliance on the intrinsic perspective is characteristic of phenomenological philosophers, whereas an exclusive reliance on the extrinsic perspective is characteristic of analytic philosophers. This leads to the peculiar kinds of irreducible incompatibilities between the two traditions.

[7] The crucial moves in this paper are made in the present section, in which the phenomenology of mind and brain are disentangled; the remainder, in effect, massages a tautology.

1971), then tedious and obfuscating discussions can be limited, and entanglement in the world knot elided. With respect to the analytic philosophers, I can only plead—as in any drama—for the "willing suspension of disbelief" on the first reading, so that I might make my case.

The first task is to rid ourselves of ordinary meanings which are imposed on perceptual experience,[8] so that we might be directly acquainted with a perceptual awareness *sans* ordinary meaning. (It is these perceptual meanings that ordinarily entangle us in the world knot.) An array of light reflected from some "real object" to our retinas is just a configuration (an ordering, a structure) of electromagnetic waves of varying frequencies and amplitudes. That I perceive, say, a yellow pad in front of me at this moment, is a function of my (presumably) having learned to *intend* the pad and/or of genetically determined characteristics of my nervous system (for example, retinal contrast mechanisms which help distinguish pad as figure from desk as ground).[9] It is precisely the world-as-intended which gives us so much difficulty in clarifying just what is puzzling in the mind–brain puzzle. This is where the mystical insight becomes so important, since the ultimate goal of meditation can be defined as *direct acquaintance with an unintended awareness,* that is, an awareness to which no "meanings" adhere.

There are myriad meditation techniques for "preventing" meanings. (The cogent phrase used by don Juan is "not doing," implying correctly that "stopping the world" [i.e., the world of meanings socially acquired] entails the cessation of an activity rather than implementing a different activity.) My own "trick" is to fix my head and eyes, direct my attention concentrically to the peripheries of my visual field, and assume a *passive* attitude. To the extent that I am successful in so doing, I lose phenomenal objects, such as the yellow pad in front of me, and experience instead a meaningless *configuration* of "visual stuff" varying in color, brightness and saturation, such that the former yellow pad is resorbed (assimilated) into the whole. This configuration is *continuous,* i.e., it is not "grainy" (Sellars, 1963). Of especial importance, it is *unbounded*—there is no place where my visual world leaves off, no

---

[8] I use visual experience as the paradigmatic case here, since it is easiest to talk about.

[9] Note the unorthodox move here of including biological givens within intending meanings, i.e., a biological intending. The notion here is simply that some constraints imposed upon the configuration of input to the brain are "wired in" and others acquired—in either case, what is given to the brain (the stimulus configuration) is transformed in characteristic ways. According to my formulation, "intending" reflects the operation of a "grammar," i.e., a set of transformation rules embodied in a neural algorithm which also includes specification of the kinds of input accepted into the algorithm.

demarcation between my visual experience and "something else" which is not visual experience;[10] nor can I find this demarcation through any other sensory modality.[11] Thus, my phenomenological claim is only that this kind of visual experience, which I shall term "seeing," is a *continuous and unbounded configuration*.

Now, let us look at the objection that "seeing" is such an atypical case, it is hardly relevant to the general puzzle of mind and brain. If we carefully consider this objection, we shall come to appreciate that most of the usual distinctions made between mind and brain indeed *presuppose* "seeing" in the former case; so our maneuver, rather than being radical, is in fact conventional. (What makes it appear unconventional is its explicitness.)

Suppose I were asked to compare the yellow pad in front of me with a brain; I would have to say that they are equivalently physical. Now suppose I were asked to compare my *experience* of the yellow pad in front of me with brain; but this request would be "naively realistic" nonsense (a position to which Maxwell (1972) has delivered the final *coup de grâce*). The yellow pad in front of me *is* my experience, not some object which I directly perceive as existent in the world-out-there; that is to say, I know the yellow pad by direct acquaintance and it is precisely this yellow pad which I find equivalently "physical" (in

---

[10] Some observers may object to this claim, stating that there is a perceived boundary—a "brownish–blackish nothingness" which surrounds the visual field. It must be remembered that peripheral vision depends on rods rather than cones, and the acuity of peripheral vision is therefore poor. Second, facial shadows from the nose and orbit tend to frame the visual field, depending on the facial structure of the particular observer, and these are vaguely dark-colored. Finally, the eyes have a fine tremor (or "jitter") so that the periphery of vision does extend over a slight range. For these reasons, the periphery of the visual field may be dark and poorly defined, but it is still a function of *input* to the visual system, and is properly considered to be integral to the phenomenal visual field. In any case, the "brownish–blackish nothingness" is *seen* at the periphery of the phenomenal field, and must be considered integral to it. Note that on my usage, "boundary" is not the peripheral rim of the phenomenal field, but the *distinction* between phenomenal field and "something else."

[11] The reader who has difficulty in following this discussion may find this footnote helpful. Suppose I were to claim, "I can *touch* the border of my visual experience with 'something else.' For example, I put a yellow pad against my nose and run my finger laterally along it. Just where my finger leaves my view (and I can still feel the pad) is the demarcation where visual experience leaves off and 'something else' begins." This claim is obviously wrong, since the tactile experience is the same throughout; there is no *tactile* distinction between "something" and "something else," and the tactile experience is the same whether or not I have the visual experience (e.g., if I close my eyes). Let's look at what goes wrong with this claim.

First, we must remember that "the real yellow pad" existing in the world-out-there is known only by description, whether via direct acquaintance with visual or tactile modalities. The input is mechanically deforming forces on the one hand and electromagnetic waves on the other, but both inputs reflect properties of the same entity ("the real yellow pad"). The experience of touching the pad relates to activity in whatever neural centers subserve meaningful tactile perception, and the "quale" of touching is irreducibly (and indescribably) distinct from the "quale" of visual experience which relates to different neural centers; we no more touch our visual experience than we see our tactile experience. (Of course, the same "real object" as transduced at eye and ear is reflected in both experiences.)

everyday sense) to brain[12] (which I, of course, *also* know by direct acquaintance. If it were *my* brain at issue, an "autocerebroscope" would be required).

So there never is any yellow pad with mental characteristics that is incompatible with a brain having physical characteristics, unless I bring that incompatibility along with me as a function of my naively realistic confusions. *"Mental" characteristics are only present during "seeing,"* in which case the yellow pad is resorbed into (assimilated to) the whole configuration. That some philosophers are wont to talk of some manner of yellow pad made up of some kind of "mental stuff" is just another one of those intellectual indulgences rather than something experienced. Because during "seeing," the visual "stuff" has certain "mental" properties, it seems reasonable to conclude that there is some yellow pad which, when disassimilated out of the visual configuration, also has "mental" properties. This conclusion seems especially attractive since the stimulus situation is *constant* whether the yellow pad is assimilated to or disassimilated out of the whole configuration. But as just discussed, the disassimilated yellow pad has *physical* properties. So the yellow pad does not have mental properties; such properties are always a consequence of "seeing" a configuration *qua* whole, rather than disassimilating out a phenomenal object.

THE "MENTAL" AND THE "PHYSICAL"

Let us now consider the classical incompatibilities between the "mental" and the "physical," which provide the puzzle we seek to resolve. Our ultimate strategy is going to be one of accepting certain of these incompatibilities as *irreducible*, and then accounting for their irreducibility in a *unitary* fashion. This strategy is in contrast to the Feigl (1967) and Maxwell (this volume) approach of denying that the "mental" and the "physical" are really incompatible in any of the ways that our commonsensical approaches find so convincing. (I trust that in what follows the reader will not be too quick to conclude that I am totally ignorant of the well-known objections to certain lines of argument, or have overlooked obvious lacunae in my presentation; Prospero-like, I promise to explain all in the end!)

---

[12] Alternatively, the "yellow pad" known by description has "physical" (in a conceptual sense) properties which are equivalent to the "brain" as known by description.

We begin by considering the problem of "grain" (Capek, 1969; Sellars, 1963; Meehl, 1966; Weimer, this volume; Maxwell, this volume) about which so much to-do has been made, probably since Feigl himself has been much troubled by it. (See his "postscript" in 1967.) In "seeing," our awareness is continuous, whereas the brain is "grainy"— composed of discontinuous neurons (discontinuous "somethings," whatever our level of analysis.) If awareness is in some sense "identical" with brain, then how can this manifest disparity in grain be accounted for?

I find this a specious distinction on a number of counts, but primarily as an expression of philosophers' ignorance of biology. (Also see the preface to this volume.) Just because one can discern discrete neural events in space–time does not imply that awareness must also be "grainy" in some way. The *correspondence* between awareness and brain (the "principle of psychoneural correspondence") is not between awareness and the discrete neural entities and events we see in neuro-histology and neurophysiology. These neural events are integral to a *functional whole*, and it is this ("emergent," if you will) functional whole, if anything, which corresponds to awareness (cf. Wimsatt's [this volume] extensive discussion). The neural side of "psychoneural correspondence" is no more grainy than Dewan's (this volume) "virtual governor."

Further, the brain is only "grainy" *when we intend it to be so.* Suppose we are standing up close to a screen on which a microscopic view of the brain is displayed, and fills our visual world. As *we* shift back and forth between "seeing" and "intending neurons," we experience alternating continuity and grain, even though the stimulus input is constant. It is apparent that the grain disparity is a function of a change in what *we* do, rather than reflecting some fundamental distinction about "stuffs" *per se*. Although we find the disparity in "grain" between mind and brain to be reducible, there are also certain *irreducible* incompatibilities, which are next discussed.

Mind is said to be *unextended*, whereas brain is extended, according to the common-sense Cartesian position. Now, to be "extended," an entity must be "here" and not "there"; that is, if there is no location which an entity occupies, then it cannot be said to be "extended." It follows that to be "unextended" can mean that the entity is either *no*where or *every*where, since in either case no distinction can be made between where the entity is and where it is not. To claim, as we have, that perceptual awareness is continuous and unbounded is a *de facto* claim that it is unextended.

Note that to claim the brain is "extended" implies that we

have *intended* the brain. The "phenomenal brain" of our direct acquaintance, which is "here" and not "there," implies the very intending we have eschewed in "seeing." It is only from this extended brain,
known by direct acquaintance, that we infer a "real brain" located out-
there-in-the-world (known "by description"). (If we had not so intended the brain, we could never claim that "brain" is extended—either
by acquaintance or description—since the entity referred to, *qua* entity,
would be assimilated to the whole configuration.)

In addition to the irreducible (but explicable) unextended vs.
extended distinction, mind (in contrast to brain) is either said to be
entirely outside of the causal nexus as explicated by science (or at best
what Feigl [1967] calls a "nomological dangler"), or if connected to the
causal scheme, how this is to be understood remains entirely enigmatic. For example, one of the standard moves against interactionism
(cf. Savage's [this volume] critique of Eccles) is to point out that mind
has no locus at which the "interaction" could transpire.

Now, as physicists usually talk about causality, a finite signal
must connect the causally interacting entities, e.g., a light wave, gravitational wave, etc. For such a signal to either reach mind or emanate
from mind to something else, it would have to cross a boundary. But
mind is unbounded, as we have seen. And again, to say that in contrast
to mind, brain is bounded, and thereby capable of entering into causal
connections, is to create the incompatibility between mental and neural
properties by virtue of our own intending (i.e., by our disassimilating
the brain), rather than the incompatibility being inherent to that considered. Hence, the issue of causal connectivity regresses on the
bounded–unbounded distinction.

At this juncture, we would like to divest ourselves of the
cumbersome issue of intending objects, which makes discourse on
mind–brain incompatibilities so confusing; we do this by bringing to
"seeing" the same intentions used toward objects. Suppose that we
intend the whole configuration we are "seeing" to in fact be an "ob-
ject⁺" just as we might intend any differentiation within that awareness, on dissassimilating the whole configuration, to be an "object*."[13]
Even though the intentional act is constant across these objects, the object⁺

---

[13] This kind of maneuver is discussed extensively in our 1975*b*. In my illustration of "seeing,"
designed for those like myself who are not meditation *adepts*, the perceptual experience was not
completely without intention; indeed, a chromatic configuration was intended (instead of an
object). The present point is that we can "see" the whole configuration and at the same time
intend it to be an object, in the same manner as when we disassimilate a configuration and intend
an object. But even though we intend the same meanings towards our perception in each case, we
have an "object⁺" instead of an "object*." Again, the imposition of meanings by the neural
grammar is imposed on the meaningless stimulus input, but even though we may intend the
"object⁺" to be an object, yet we perceive it to be unbounded unless we "imagine" the boundary.

remains unbounded in contrast to the object* which is bounded. This provides for us the unambiguous and irreducible incompatibility which is at the core of mind–brain (mind–matter) contradictions. *The mental "stuff"* (whatever "stuff" is) *must be unbounded, whereas the physical "stuff"* (whatever "stuff" is) *must be bounded.* We now appreciate that, although the continuity–grain distinction is a function of intending, the extended–unextended distinction (hence the causally connected–unconnected distinction) is not, and therefore is irreducible.[14]

We also note one final irreducible distinction between mind and brain; the former is *private* (uniquely accessible) whereas the latter is *public* (intersubjectively accessible). Sperry's (this volume) elegant work on "split-brains" has complicated this issue somewhat, since there is general agreement[15] that an individual with a severed corpus callosum has *two* minds which are not acquainted with each other.[16]

Now, if utopian neuroscience were to construct a corpus callosum between your brain and mine (thereby eliding the system of sensory receptor–transducers), we would be of one mind, i.e., privy to each other's experience. By virtue of this corpus callosum connecting point-for-point across brains, there is a more comprehensive system with respect to which the intrinsic perspective provides mind. But since this one mind would encompass and transcend both component minds—each of our minds would be assimilated to a larger whole—this does not vitiate the sovereignty of each of our minds *per se*; no one can ever be directly acquainted with my mind as it was *before* the *gedanken* corpus callosum connection was made.

MIND AND THE INTRINSIC PERSPECTIVE

We are now ready to attempt the crucial move in our argument in which we account for why the "mental" and the "physical" have

[14] Other distinctions made between the "mental" and the "physical" are derivative of those already discussed. The qualitative–quantitative and holistic–atomistic distinctions are just the grain issue again. As Feigl (1967) points out, to call mind "purposive" and "mnemic" does not distinguish it from machines, in this cybernetic age. And to hold mind to be "intentional" is only to specify the operation of a grammar, which is also a machine capability, as discussed above.

[15] Eccles' discussion (this volume) of Savage emphasizes that the right brain is likely to be conscious, but only the left brain (with its language area) is conscious of consciousness.

[16] We know that the left brain is conscious because it tells us that it is; at least, when input is arranged so as to reach the left brain only, which contains the language area in most cases, we find no differences from reports from an intact brain. The right brain, which has no speech, cannot *tell* us anything when input is arranged so as to reach it exclusively. However, the complexity of response that can be made by the right brain is consistent with responses that we attribute without hesitation to a conscious brain. (The left brain appears to have no idea as to how these responses are brought about.)

irreducibly incompatible properties. Suppose that Z is what I would term "your brain," as a neurophysiologist, and you would term "my brain," if you had an "autocerebroscope" (a device by means of which you could observe your own brain in the very manner that I do). An extrinsic perspective (E) on Z (whether by me or you) is always able to find a boundary to Z on intending it to be an object, i.e., there is always a demarcation to be found where Z leaves off and "something else" which is *not* Z begins. An intrinsic perspective (I) on Z, on the other hand, is *incapable* of finding a boundary to Z on intending it to be an object, for if Z included a distinction between Z and "something else" which is *not* Z, Z would be more than what it is, which is absurd. *On I, then, Z is unbounded; and since there is only one perspective coextensive with Z, I is irrevocably private.*

It is a curious fact that, as Gazzaniga has emphasized (see Puccetti, 1973), destructive lesions in the retina or optic nerve create a field defect experienced as a black hole, say, in the very center of the phenomenal field, whereas lesions in the corresponding parts of the visual cortex to which the optic nerve projects cause the same field defect but one which is not experienced as a black hole. In the latter case, especially if the connections to the association areas are also destroyed, the patient may be quite unaware of any defect in the center of his phenomenal field. Thus, a lesion in the visual cortex does not create a demarcated rent in the fabric of visual experience; the patient has to figure out that he has a field defect, especially by remembering what the configuration of his phenomenal field once looked like.[17]

But we need not consider esoteric lesions in the nervous system to pursue this issue; we need only consider our own "blind spots." There is a location in the retina called the "optic disc" where there are no receptor cells, since this is the exit point of nerve fibers comprising the optic nerve. Corresponding to this "defect" in the retinal receptive field, there is a "blind spot" in the phenomenal field, when one eye is closed.

Now, there is a rather precise topographic mapping of fibers contributing to the optic nerve onto the lateral geniculate body (a thalamic way station in the visual system) and ultimately onto the visual cortex. It has recently been discovered (Kaas *et al.*, 1973) that there is a small more or less cylindrical zone in a layer of the lateral geniculate which is *cell free*; that is, if there were receptors in the optic disc area, they would project to this zone, but since there are not such

---

[17] Comparably, after certain right brain lesions, the patient may no longer experience the left side of his body as his own. When shown his arm lying on the bed, he may think it is someone else's arm. But he doesn't "miss" the left side of his body, although he may be able to *conclude* it is not experienced, although "his." I thank Jon Sassin for discussing these issues with me.

receptors, the zone is without cells. Presumably, the visual cortex also has a corresponding cell-free zone (although this has apparently not yet been investigated). In effect we have the naturally given equivalent of a central lesion creating a monocular field defect.

It is quite easy to map out and study one's own blind spot, by using a small flag (like the eraser on a pencil) which can be freely moved about. The fact discovered by so doing is that there is *no boundary to the blind spot and no perception of a "hole" in the phenomenal field*. One can easily *conclude* that there is such a hole, but this is not a perceptual acquaintance; no matter how many times one passes the flag through the blind spot so that it first disappears and then reappears, visual experience remains continuous and without boundaries. This small "experiment" provides a compelling demonstration that the phenomenal visual field is unbounded.

This striking clinical condition only serves to emphasize my point that visual experience is unbounded; even with a defect in the center of the phenomenal field, there is no boundary where visual experience leaves off and something else begins. *Pari passu*, the intrinsic perspective on the visual cortex—even a cortex with a lesion punched somewhere within it—can find no boundary to itself.

Now, since the intrinsic perspective on Z finds Z to have properties which are identical with the properties of mind, and since mind is believed by (almost) all to be somehow connected with Z, there seems no compelling reason why we should not *strictly identify "mind" with the intrinsic perspective on Z*. Further, we can readily understand that the "stuff" of Z must always have incompatible properties according to E and I, since on the former, the "stuff" of Z is (or better, can be found to be) bounded, whereas on the latter, it is not (or better, can *never* be found to be) bounded.

But this fundamental disagreement as to the property of boundedness is quite unrelated to the structure of Z; the configuration[18] is identical in each case. (We already know this structural identity to be the case from the principle of psychoneural correspondence, since what corresponds here is obviously the structure of mind and brain, rather than the "stuff" structured.) Hence, the structure of mind and brain is ideally[19] *one and the same*, even though the "stuff" structured is unbounded in the first case and bounded in the second (as a function of I and E respectively). *Contra* complementarity, there *is* a "reality" independent of perspective, and that "reality" is *structure*.

[18] Note that a boundary is not part of the configuration, but delimits the locus of the configuration.
[19] The restrictive term "ideally" will be unpacked in a later section.

THE RELEVANCE OF GÖDEL'S PROOF

In considering the mind–brain puzzle by specifying the results of approaching the same system from I and E perspectives, the question naturally arises, "Is it possible to *combine* I and E perspectives, and if possible, what is the result?" Since this issue can be raised quite formally and rigorously, it would not be surprising to find a mathematical theorem which provides an answer. My colleagues S. Franklin and I. Savodnik and I (Globus *et al.*, 1975*a*, 1975*b*) have shown that Gödel's (1931) celebrated proof[20] provides an abstract and formal model of the mind–brain puzzle. I shall only outline here some of the features of this highly technical discussion.

Consider the unique case of the autocerebroscopic situation in which one is aware of the brain state corresponding to one's preceding awareness. Following Gödel's strategy, and given a sufficiently rich system like Z, it proves possible to construct a self-referential perceptual awareness, A, which is: "B_{des} has the property $\sim P\#$", where B_{des} is the brain state corresponding to A, and $P\#$ is the property of existing in the brain and being causally connected to an input stimulus. It turns out that it is impossible to decide whether or not A is a *veridical* perceptual awareness, for if A is assumed to be veridical, it follows immediately that $\sim A$ is veridical, and vice versa. (This result corresponds to Gödel's, in which it is impossible to determine whether or not formula F ("This formula is not formally demonstrable") is formally demonstrable, i.e., "veridical" within the terms of the axioms and transformation rules of the calculus.

Now, with both F and A, there is another alternative available, other than accepting them as "undecidable" (which places insuperable obstacles to the calculus being "complete" in the one case and empirical knowledge being "complete" in the other). "Biting the bullet," it is possible to *embrace the contradiction as irreducible,* even though such a course is anathema to western "themata" (Holton, 1975) and would appear to completely undermine logic as we know it. But on embracing contradiction, we find it to be not so unpalatable after all, and accordingly are led to reinterpret Gödel's theorem. In the case of A, there is no contradiction as to the structure of mind and its corresponding brain state, and in the case of F, there is no contradiction as to the structure of F and its corresponding "Gödel number." Since there is no contradiction with respect to structure, then *meaning remains inviolate.* The contradiction arises because the "mental stuff" of A (and the "symbolic

---

[20] For a lucid and nontechnical account of Gödel's proof see Nagel and Newman (1958).

stuff" of F) is unbounded, whereas the "physical stuff" of B_{des} (and the "numerical stuff" of a Gödel *number*) is bounded. This contradiction is entirely accounted for by I and E.[21]

The relevance of Gödel's proof to the mind–brain puzzle, then, is that it provides a formal model of the puzzle in an abstract and strictly regulated domain, so that one might look deeply at the issues. On so doing, our conclusion (1975*a*, 1975*b*) is that there is irreconcilable contradiction consequent to the assumption of I and E perspectives on the same system (whatever that system might be) since the stuff of the system appears to be unbounded and bounded respectively, but that this contradiction can be transcended by appreciating the underlying structural unity.[22]

COMPARISON TO OTHER SOLUTIONS

There have been so many solutions offered to the mind–brain puzzle (see Broad [1925] for a discussion of the varieties of moves which have been made), that it is quite difficult to elbow yet another solution into the crowd. The "psychoneural *structural* identity thesis" is very like many, yet (I believe) unique. In order to explicate just how this thesis fits in, the present section compares it to other well known solutions.

First of all, the structural identity thesis is ontologically monistic and epistemologically dualistic, since the fundamental given is structure (relatedness), whereas the manner in which the "stuff" structured becomes known is bifurcated as a function of perspective. Thus, there is no interaction in the classical Cartesian sense; that which interaction is supposed to account for is explained by an unremarked shift in perspective from I to E (or vice versa) which constantly con-

---

[21] I *speculate* that in addition to these two kinds of perspectives, I and E, there may also be a third *imaginary perspective*, which would enrich our conceptual structure. This speculation is derived from a view in which numbers have the property of "passing through themselves" so as to become their own mirror-images turned inside out. (In the complex plane, this is represented as rotation through 180°.) The imaginary part of the complex number gives the extent to which the number is passed through itself. A purely imaginary number is neither outside-out nor inside-out, but a singularity (or "hole") in the complex plane where perspective does not exist because "space" does not exist. That complex numbers are obligatory in the quantum domain suggests that the fundamental event there may be such a movement, with the singularity providing a "wormhole" in a multiply-connected topology. (Spencer-Brown [1972] has considered the logical role of imaginarys in his *Laws of Form*.)

[22] The concordance with ancient Chinese philosophical thought tempts me to call this conclusion the "Tao Principle."

founds the Cartesian argument. *In place of interaction, we have a structure continually subject to transformation*, as exogenous input convolves with endogenous rhythms.

Structural identity covers the same ground as classical noninteractionist parallelism, but where parallelism founders on what keeps mind and brain parallel (or how the two "clocks" were set so that they run in parallel forever after), the thesis proposed here finds but one structure *known in parallel ways*, which ways are epistemologically of equal status. Unlike epiphenomenalism, which is a kind of interactionistic and parallelistic hybrid, mind does not "dangle" impotently (and mysteriously) from brain. Again, what is basic is structure, while the "stuff" structured is either bounded or unbounded depending on locus of observation.

In a formal sense, structural identity substitutes the intrinsic perspective at precisely that place in the argument where emergent theories (see the papers by Sperry and Dewan in this volume) utilize the "emergence" of holistic properties. Further, structural identity elides the difficult problems associated with either intralevel or interlevel reduction (Wimsatt, this volume), since "reduction" is not involved; there is only a shift in perspective, neither of which can be considered more fundamental than the other (Globus, 1973). I find the main defect in emergent theory to be that although emergent properties *qua* mind may well be "different from and more than" the properties of their constituent parts *qua* matter, that the emergent properties are in fact *incompatible* with the material properties does not flow naturally out of the emergentist's arguments.[23] (This criticism may not be applicable to Wimsatt's [this volume] brand of emergentism.) In contrast, the incompatibility of mental and physical properties follows organically from the definitions of perspective, according to the structural identity thesis.

There are a large number of solutions, much beloved by philosophers, which are "counterintuitive," such as (crass) materialism, Ryle's (1949) analytic approach, Skinnerian (1971) behaviorism, and so on. These solutions are counterintuitive, in the sense that they *deny* our ordinary common-sensical understanding and seek to explain away our philosophical perplexities by exposing the arrant irrationality presumed to underlie this common-sensical understanding. Although these approaches have formidable problems in their own right, which

---

[23] I believe that Weimer's (this volume) argument is also weak here. Granting a deep structure which generates mental and physical properties as *ambiguous*, in Chomsky's sense, there remains a conceptual gap from ambiguous to *incompatible*. Many writers tend to gloss over the *contradictions* which arise in relation to mental and physical properties.

I shall not discuss here, I want to make explicit my "methodological theme" (Holton, 1975) that a solution consistent with common sense is preferable to one inconsistent with common sense; the distrust of "ordinary experience" is philosophical chauvinism and "head-tripping" again. (This is "thematic" in the sense that what "feels good in my bones," to borrow Maxwell's [this volume] felicitous phrase, is consistent with ordinary experience, whereas what "feels good in your bones" may be quite the opposite.)

In contrast to Feigl (1967) and Maxwell (this volume), who argue for the "psychoneural identity thesis," structural identity does not hold that mental and neurophysiological terms have the same referent, since mental terms refer to something unbounded, whereas physical terms refer to something bounded. In a sense, this is a return to a fundamental "ontological complementarity" as a function of intrinsic and extrinsic perspectives, although these perspectives connot be considered "mutually exclusive" as in the formal principle of complementarity. At least, the incompatible properties of mind and brain which are irreducible, yet are explicable, by considering the relations of boundedness and "privacy" to perspective.

Although mental and neural terms do not have the same referent, they do refer to the same *structure*. And as already pointed out, rather than explaining away the incompatibilities between mind and brain, the incompatibilities follow organically from the solution. (Whether or not the structural identity thesis will remain immune to the large body of criticism leveled already at the Russell–Feigl–Maxwell kind of solution remains to be seen.)

The present solution also has very different implications for Russell's doctrine of "structural realism" than does the psychoneural identity thesis. According to Weimer (1973),

> Structural realism is structural in the sense that our knowledge of the entire nonmental world, from our bodies to theoretical entities, is of the structural characteristics of that world rather than of the intrinsic properties of those objects comprising it. . . . the formal relationships which characterize the nonmental world are not particular, concrete, always present to the senses, etc. *Structural knowledge is fundamentally abstract knowledge in the sense that it is not what is presented in our experience.* Theoretical entities are specified by reference to their (almost invariably mathematical) structure. "Scientific" knowledge of nonmental entities is limited entirely to this structure, and we cannot attribute to theoretical objects the properties that the nominalist bases his claim upon: that is, the particular and concrete deliverances of our senses. (p. 23–24)

But it seems to me that if the psychoneural identity theorists were seriously to take Russell's "structural realism" in the biological way that Pribram (this volume) emphasizes, then they would come out with something which entails a regression—*horrible dictu!*—to a *sophisticated* form of naive realism. The reasons for this can be briefly put. The stimulus array—say, the electromagnetic waves impinging on the retina—conserves the structure of the "object" from which it has been reflected, since the physicochemical properties of the "object" differentially absorb and reflect certain frequencies, so that their arrangement is reiterated in the reflected array. The structure of the stimulus array is conserved within the retina and as the representation passes centrally into the brain.

Of course, transformations are imposed on that structure by virtue of genetic and acquired "grammars," but *the structure of the "object" must be conserved* to a considerable degree. (Brains which do not conserve sufficiently that structure are at a grave disadvantage in evolutionary selection!) Further, the "stuff" structured varies: from whatever the object "stuff" is, to a light "stuff," and finally to a neural "stuff"—but the structure *per se* is (more or less) maintained.

So it appears that, although the brain transforms this structure enormously, subsequent to passage through the primary reception areas in the visual cortex, we still must assume that the structure—the order, the nonrandomness, the arrangement—of the "object" is in some way conserved. But according to the structural identity thesis, this *same* structure is immediately given within awareness, since awareness is but the intrinsic perspective on that system called "brain" from the extrinsic perspective. Then, *we are directly acquainted with the structure of reality*, where that structure has undergone a set of transformations by virtue of the neural algorithms acting upon the input structure; but since the input structure is *conserved*, we may justifiably proclaim: *"Naive realism lives!"* at least in a sophisticated structural version.

We are now in a position to backtrack in order to unpack a qualifying phrase left over from the preceding section, where it was asserted that the structure of mind and brain is "ideally" one and the same. Since in practice, the brain of the observer on the extrinsic perspective *transforms* the structure of input, the structure of the "brain" known by direct acquaintance is not *strictly* identical with the structure of mind according to the intrinsic perspective. But since the structure of input (assuming that structure faithfully conserves the structure of the system under observation) is in fact conserved to some extent across the various transformations, *to that extent* the structures of mind and brain—both as known by direct acquaintance by subject and observer respectively—can be said to be the same.

But given a utopian neuroscience in which those transformations can be completely specified, the structure of brain *known by
description* by the observer on the extrinsic perspective (the structure
inferred to be "out-there-in-the-world") is unequivocably and strictly
one and the same with the structure of mind on the intrinsic perspective. So we may conclude that the structure of mind (known by acquaintance) and brain (known by description) are strictly one and the
same, whereas the structure of mind (known by acquaintance) and
brain (known by acquaintance) are to some extent the same (which is to
say that they are definitely not *one* and the same, but that the latter
structure to some extent conserves the structure of the former). Since I
see no reason not to state the structural identity solution in ideal form,
my claim is that *mental terms refer directly and neural terms refer indirectly
to one and the same structure*.

It is apparent that the present thesis is a peculiar form of
neutral monism and Spinozan in spirit, but where the neutral "stuff" is
neither a substance nor unknowable, and is explicitly *structure*, which
(as a transformation) we even can come to know by direct acquaintance.
It is also closely akin to double-aspect theory, worked out, as it were,
within a structuralist paradigm, but with clear specifications of what is
meant by "inner" and "outer" aspects of some unknowable *tertium
quid*, and with the contradictions inherent to the mind–brain puzzle
accounted for by virtue of the specification of perspective. The immediate problem of double-aspect theory has always been, "Aspects of
what?" (This "what" is surely not equivalent to a coin seen from two
sides!) Received answers, regressing on neutral monism, have been
aspects of either "something" unknowable or (under the influence of
complementarity) there is no "something" independent of our manner
of knowing it. According to the structural identity thesis, there is a
what—which is structure—and the stuff structured will have incompatible properties according to I and E perspectives.

There is a close but not immediately apparent connection
between the structural identity solution and the position of Cassirer, as
explicated by Savodnik (this volume). What I have called "seeing," a
state to some extent accessible even to those who are not adept in
meditation, is equivalent to the level of the "expressive function,"
whereas the intention which creates "physical objects" is equivalent to
Cassirer's "representative function." In agreement with Savodnik,
there is no mind–body problem at the level of expressive function, for
the simple reason that there is no "body" available to experience at that
level. That at some early primordium in the ontogenesis of an individual there is only "seeing," seems quite reasonable to me; as Knapp (this
volume) points out, the infant follows faces preferentially very early in

life. (I suspect that any primordium which is pure in this regard ought to be placed well prior to birth.)

But this does not dispose of the problem, it seems to me, since it leaves us with mind as a primitive and matter as derivative of our concepts. But the very evolution of these concepts, which, at least to some extent, are built into the genetically given neural grammar (Hayek, 1963; Weimer, 1973), and to some extent are acquired through experience, implies that they in some way promote adaptation to an existent "reality" which the matter-concepts model. So *we* are still left with mind and in some sense "matter," at least when our symbolic consciousness has developed enough to ask philosophical questions, even though the problem disappears when we meditate or regress on Peter Knapp's analytic couch.

Thus, the puzzle does not go away unless we accept a stringent idealism, and it is the ontological status of mind and matter that the structural identity solution seeks to derive, by appealing to the epistemological status of intrinsic and extrinsic perspectives in relation to "the same" system.

UNIVERSAL CONSCIOUSNESS

My defense in these concluding sections of the claim that there is a mind intrinsic to all systems[24] is now but denouement, since it follows trivially from the psychoneural structural identity solution to the mind–brain puzzle. Consider the "prototypical" system z (cf. the "variable" which is a "prototypical" number in an equation). As an abstraction, z can be considered on I and E (in the abstract, as it were). When specialized to any particular system, such as Z, intrinsic and extrinsic perspectives are "actual". Here, z functions as something more than a "mere" Platonic form or *universal*, since as the form of all systems, the "system-template" if you will, it is the Form of All Forms (the "Form of the Good"?!), the *Universal System*.[25] The intrinsic per-

---

[24] I am (provisionally) content with considering systems to be present even in the quantum domain; for example, a proton and a neutron, tossing a pion back and forth at inconceivable rates, is a "system" on my usage. In this, I differ sharply from Wimsatt (this volume).

[25] This claim may be a bit too condensed to be immediately grasped. When we talk about a system, we are talking about a form or arrangement which can be particularized in many different ways according to a particular grammar. The brain *qua* system can potentially be specialized to myriad billions of particular arrangements. So, any "system" is in fact "prototypical." z, as the prototype of systems which are themselves prototypes, thus has a very unique status. If we think of the grammar of any system as insuring that a certain structure or relatedness is conserved across all particularization of the system, then that certain relatedness is a universal, and the universal of all these universals is *relatedness per se*. (I am suggesting that this is [in some sense] a part of Plato's "Form of the Good" and that a structural solution to the problem of particulars and universals might be developed along these lines.)

spective on z is in fact "mind," where the "kind" of "mind" varies as a function of the particularization.

To take a gross example, a brain and a rock are systems differing enormously in "richness" of structure, and the respective "minds" accordingly differ enormously. (The change in a rock's organization when you hit it with a hammer and in your brain's organization when you hit your finger with a hammer are considerably different in degree!) The difference between the minds intrinsic to rock and brain is such that the mind intrinsic to brain is myriad billions of times more aware than that of rock, but still, the difference is *only quantitative*. Although I appreciate that most will consider it to be ridiculous to attribute awareness to a rock, for my purposes, I choose to emphasize the awareness intrinsic to rock; *we have had more than enough emphasis on the awareness intrinsic to brain already*!

At heart, the issue is just that there is no place to unarbitrarily draw a line (or even a range) in a hierarchy of systems increasing in complexity, above which we can say that mind occurs and below which it does not. The notion that awareness somehow emerges at only the highest orders of complexity is human chauvinism at its worst. This is *not* to say that awareness of awareness does not emerge with increasing complexity; it obviously takes a system of extraordinary richness to model itself.[26] Nor is it to say that the capacity for representation does not emerge with increasing complexity. What I am arguing is that awareness—sheer awareness—which does not represent anything, just *is*, as the intrinsic perspective on any level of complexity that we might consider.

Naive panpsychism attributes an essentially human consciousness to other animate and even inanimate forms. In contrast, my (hopefully) sophisticated panpsychism holds that the kind of consciousness is a function of the system-as-particularized under consideration. If pushed to the wall—as Professor Sperry would artfully contrive!—I would argue that the measure of degree of consciousness is the richness of structure of that system per unit volume and time.

CODA: IN DEFENSE OF "PANPSYCHISM"

Even though it has not rained in 6 months, it is possible to hike through the Southern California "desert." On rounding a sharp

---

[26] Gödel's proof requires a calculus of a certain "richness" of axioms and transformation rules in order to construct self-referential formulae; not every calculus will do.

turn in the foothills, I come upon a line of yellow flowers silhouetted against the distant mountains, thrust up on dusty foot-high stalks, sturdily askew. I feel delighted, and exclaim, "The flowers experience joy!"

But this is the kind of "native panpsychism" that I do not wish to espouse. Clearly, I attribute *my* "joy" to the flowers! What exactly is it, then, that flowers experience in what I purport to be a "sophisticated panpsychism?" It is certainly fair of the "hard-nosed" materialist to object, "I have not the vaguest idea of what you are talking about." But it is also fair of me to complain that I cannot convey a flower's experience in terms of *his* language; my materialistic friends need to "listen" in the same way that they need to "see"!

The awareness of the flower is the faintest whisper of awareness, a primordial hum hardly distinguished from background noise during its brief season; yet it is immeasurably more conscious than the rigidly ordered rock enduring nearby; further, the evanescent system of flower changes richly over time, whereas change in the tedious rock follows a geological time constant measured in aeons.

Given any system—"brain," "flower," "rock"—there must always be two perspectives on it, intrinsic and extrinsic to the system, which provide contradictory accounts of the stuff of the system, but attribute one and the same structure to it. What is respectively brain, flower, and rock on the extrinsic perspective is self-referencing consciousness, dim protoawareness, and imperturable ur-awareness on the intrinsic perspective.

Our science-conditioned minds find this almost impossible to fathom. Yet camping within the protective confines of an ancient thick-limbed California oak rooted in the nidus of a valley, and appreciating the richness of its symmetry and convoluted strength against the night sky, it does not seem preposterous to reflect on this great oak-entity from the intrinsic perspective, which the Indians would have called the "spirit of the place." The spirit indwelling to the powerful oak, which has pervaded this place for generations of men, is recognized not to be a romantic fancying of primitive animistic minds, I have argued, but an irreducible feature of the world, as understood by nonwestern men. In the present paper, I have tried to present this understanding within the western paradigm.

But I suspect that in order to be convinced that everything is "conscious" in this sense, and that we are therefore only trivially distinguishable from the rest of the natural world, something more than the kind of philosophical and empirical arguments presented above is required, even in the unlikely event that the arguments were to prove quite correct. This is precisely where, I believe, mystical insight contributes to the resolution of the mind–brain puzzle.

ACKNOWLEDGMENTS

I thank Stephen Franklin and Irwin Savodnik for many amiable and not-so-amiable discussions which have deeply influenced my thinking. I thank (not unambivalently!) William Wimsatt for critical comments which served to entirely demolish my "conference paper," and forced me to write the present one, which he also has reviewed and contributed to.

REFERENCES

Broad, C. D. (1925): *The Mind and Its Place in Nature*. London: Routledge and Kegan Paul.
Capek, M. (1969): The main difficulties of the identity theory. *Scientia* **CIV**, 1–17.
Capra, F. (1975): *The Tao of Physics*. Berkeley: Shambhala.
Castaneda, C. (1969): *The Teachings of Don Juan*. New York: Balantine.
Castaneda, C. (1971): *Separate Reality*. New York: Simon & Schuster.
Castaneda, C. (1973): *Journey to Ixtlan*. New York: Simon & Schuster.
Castaneda, C. (1974): *Tales of Power*. New York: Simon & Schuster.
Feigl, H. (1967): *The "Mental" and the "Physical."* Minneapolis: University of Minnesota Press.
Globus, G. (1973a): Unexpected symmetries in the 'World Knot,' *Science* **180**, 1129–1136.
Globus, G. (1973b): Consciousness and brain: I. The identity thesis. *Arch. Gen. Psychiatr.* **29**, 153–160.
Globus, G. (1973c): Consciousness and brain. II. Introspection, the qualia of experience, and the unconsciousness. *Arch. Gen. Psychiatr.* **29**, 167–176.
Globus, G. (1974): The problem of consciousness. In: *Psychoanalysis and Contemporary Science, Vol. III*. New York: International Universities Press.
Globus, G., Franklin, S., and Savodnik, I. (1975a): Gödel's Theorem and the mind–brain problem. I. An undecidable awareness. (Unpublished manuscript)
Globus, G., Franklin, S., and Savodnik, I. (1975b): Gödel's Theorem and the mind–brain problem. II. A psychoneural structural identity solution. (Unpublished manuscript)
Gödel, K. (1931): *On Formally Undecidable Propositions of Principia Mathematica and Related Systems*. London: Oliver and Boyd.
Hayek, F. A. (1963): *The Sensory Order*. London: Routledge, 1952. Reprinted by University of Chicago Press.
Holton, G. (1975): On the role of themata in scientific thought. *Science* **188**, 328–334.
Krishnamurti, J. (1972): *Freedom From the Known*. London: Victor Gollancz, Ltd.
Kaas, J. H., Guillery, R. W., and Allman, J. M. (1973): Discontinuities in the dorsal lateral lateral geniculate nucleus corresponding to the optic disc: A comparative study. *J. Comp. Neurol.* **147**, 163–180.
Margenau, H. (1963): *Philos. of Sci.* **30**, 1 and 138.

Maxwell, G. (1972): Russell on perception: a study in philosophical method. In: *Bertrand Russell: A Collection of Critical Essays*. Ed. by D. Pears, New York: Doubleday.

Meehl, P. (1966): The compleat autocerebroscopist: a thought experiment on Professor Feigl's mind/body identity thesis. In: *Mind, Matter and Method*. Ed. by P. K. Feyerabend and G. Maxwell, Minneapolis: University of Minnesota Press.

Nagel, E., and Newman, J. F. (1958): *Gödel's Proof*. New York: New York University Press.

Parks, J. L., and Margenau, H. (1968): *Int. J. Theor. Phys.* **I,** 211–283.

Puccetti, R. (1973): Brain bisection and personal identity. *Br. J. Philos. Sci.* **24,** 339–355.

Ryle, G. (1949): *The Concept of Mind*. London: Hutchinson.

Sellars, W. (1963): *Science, Perception and Reality*. London: Routledge and Kegan Paul.

Skinner, B. F. (1971): *Beyond Freedom and Dignity*. New York: Knopf.

Spencer-Brown, G. (1972): *Laws of Form*. New York: The Julian Press.

Vonnegut, K. (1973): *Breakfast of Champions*. New York: Delta.

Weimer, W. (1973): Psycholinguistics and Plato's paradoxes of the *Meno*. *Amer. Psychol.* **28,** 15–33.

10 Introduction

In considering the structure of consciousness, Pribram seeks to provide a practical answer to a practical problem, in the tradition of scientific pragmatism and clinical medicine. What constitutes the answer here is far different than if one asked a theoretical question; philosophers differ from many scientists in this regard. Thus, Pribram suggests a "cuddleness criterion" for consciousness which includes (especially furry) animals and excludes plants and Scrivenish computers, since the consciousness of plants and computers makes little difference and "only a difference that makes a difference is worth pursuing." Practically speaking, consciousness is tied to protoplasm. From this perspective, the issue of computer consciousness may appear to be a tedious Talmudic controversy. An opposing view holds that it is precisely these limiting cases where the issue becomes enjoined that our clearest notions can be developed. Thus, our conception of the physical universe becomes altered extraordinarily when we approach the special case of velocities near the speed of light.

For Pribram, consciousness is "a property by which organisms achieve a special relationship with their environment." A variety of characteristics of this property can be discriminated and are accessible to empirical inquiry. For example, why do some perceptions seem to be located in the environment and others inside of us? Mathematical equations have been developed in some instances which describe the sensory processing that accounts for the attribution of a perception to the world out there, and thereby directly bear upon the relationship of an organism to its environment. Further, the "smooth control of input–output relationships in the central nervous system" refers to a relationship of organism to environment which we refer to as "habit." When this smooth transition of input to output does not occur, the relationship is referred to as conscious, that is, *consciousness and habit are reciprocal*. Pribram's deceptively simple conceptualization can encompass an enormous amount of empirical data, and he emphasizes in his illustrations that the brain is complex enough to account for the extraordinary richness of our consciousness. In the context of his philosophical predilection for "constructional realism," Pribram consistently focuses on the importance of *structure* when considering brain functioning.

It appears to be Pribram's contention that an "ultimately understandable biological process" can be multiply realized as neural activity, consciousness, and in other forms. He proposes that integral to this is a holonomic process, little dealt with by biologists, comparable to an optical information processing technique (holography) by means of which two sets of light waves, one of which may derive from an object while the other serves as reference, can be "frozen" into a photographic plate (hologram) and "revived" when the hologram is reilluminated by the reference. (The hologram contains only the interference pattern of the intersecting light waves so that the object is in no way apparent in it.)

Although Pribram's analogy to optical information processing systems which produce three-dimensional images is intriguing, it is difficult to encompass consciousness within this conception, for it is unclear how the properties of holonomic functions relate to the properties of consciousness. Consciousness is surely not like the hologram, a seemingly random configuration of dots. Nor is it like a holographic image, which is just an array of light, nor is it like a convolution of electrochemical waves. That the brain functions to some extent holonomically is certainly a bold and cogent hypothesis, but precisely how consciousness fits into this holonomic functioning remains obscure. And if consciousness is *in correspondence* with these holonomic functions, this is but a restatement of the principle of psychoneural correspondence, with an "update" on the neural side. It is perhaps this kind of inconclusive outcome which underlies the belief that the problem is basically philosophic rather than scientific.

10 Problems Concerning the Structure of Consciousness

KARL H. PRIBRAM

While still in the practice of neurosurgery, I was called one day to consult on a case some 200 miles distant. A 14-year-old girl had fallen from a rapidly moving automobile when its rear door inadvertently opened. She had lacerated her scalp badly, and, when the emergency procedures to stop the bleeding were accomplished, I was called, because the family physician was afraid that the patient's head injury would become exacerbated by the additional trauma of a long trip by ambulance. I was informed that the girl's condition was critical and that everyone feared she was moribund.

When I arrived on the scene some 3 to 4 hours later, the situation had deteriorated further. The girl had not even been moved to a nearby hospital and was lying in a bed at a farmhouse near the scene of the accident. She was not expected to live.

I entered the bedroom. Blinds were drawn. Blood-soaked bandages were wrapped around the girl's head. Only a small part of her face showed, and it had a sickly coloration. She was hardly breathing.

The distressed family made room for me at the bedside. As was my custom, I said, "Hello, Cathy" (the girl's name) as I took her

KARL H. PRIBRAM·Stanford University

hand to feel her pulse. Much to my amazement, Cathy opened her eyes and said, "Hello, Doctor"! Cathy was conscious!

My whole approach to the consultation changed. I quickly looked at the girl's eyes to see if her pupils were of equal diameter, which they were, did the essentials of a neurological examination, such as lifting her head to rule out stiffness due to bleeding inside the head, and then went on to ascertain that all limbs were movable, etc. But my attention became focused, not on the neurological, but on the remainder of a thorough physical examination. I noticed that, in moving her right arm, the patient expressed considerable discomfort. And very quickly I ascertained that some ribs had been broken and had punctured the girl's right lung. She was indeed in critical condition, and I ordered an oxygen tent to be brought immediately from the hospital since our patient's trouble was not in her head but in her chest. Recovery ensued rapidly once the locus of the problem had been identified.

This case history points up the set of problems concerning the concept "consciousness" that I want to take up. (1) The concept consciousness is not just some esoteric theoretical football to be tossed to see whether interception by man-made computers can take place: my attribution of consciousness is of practical concern to those who are so graced; (2) consciousness is related primarily to brain function; and (3) consciousness sometimes involves the identification of self: Cathy responded only when I addressed her by name.

ACHIEVING CONSCIOUSNESS

My story, I believe, indicates the usefulness of the concept consciousness. I inferred that Cathy was conscious from occurrences that, in this particular circumstance, were, in fact, surprising. What then are the categories of episodes from which I infer consciousness?

The first category is that of life, based on the occurrence of growth and replication in some asymmetrical mass showing varied parts. The second category is that of movement in space. In short, I tend to view animals, especially furry animals, as conscious—not plants, not inanimate crystals, not computers. This might be termed the "cuddleness criterion" for consciousness. My reasons are practical; it makes little difference at present whether computers are conscious or not, and, in the Jamesian tradition, I hold that only a difference that makes a difference is worth pursuing.

How does consciousness make a difference? Ryle (1949, p. 136) suggests that the concept of mind in general and such concepts as perception, attention, interest, and consciousness in particular take their origin in occurrences that indicate that the conscious, interested, or attending organism minds, i.e., heeds his surroundings. Also in this view, consciousness derives from the interaction of an organism with his environment—it is therefore meaningless to ask whether consciousness "intervenes" or interacts with either the organism, his brain, or his environment. In this sense, consciousness describes a property by which organisms achieve a special relationship with their environment. We have easy access to this relationship when it becomes manifest in the behavior of the organism. Here the term "behavior" should be understood in a larger sense than its usual English connotation. The German "Verhaltung" and the French "comportment" come closer since they connote English "bearing" as well as more active behavior. Thus a question we need to address is whether we can also access these manifestations of consciousness by looking at the behavior of restricted parts of the organism such as his brain.

A useful analogy comes from mechanics: although we speak of gravity as a property of a mass, this property becomes manifest only when interactions among masses occur. So we may loosely talk of locating gravity at the center of a mass or of consciousness in the center of the head, but only in the case of consciousness do some still seriously entertain the proposition that if we go dig deeply enough, we will assuredly find "it." But neither the sophisticated earth scientist nor the brain scientist would argue against coming up with some samples that might explain specific characteristics of the "gravitational" or "conscious" process.

What are some of these specific characteristics of consciousness? We look to see, we listen to hear, we remember what we see and hear, and sometimes the looking and the listening. And sometimes also we remember that which we have forgotten. In addition, of course, we can let others know we have seen and heard and we can even talk about it. So we have a variety of characteristics to be explained. They range from asking practical questions about "seeing" (for some of us are blind), through those that deal with "looking" (since so often we see *only* what we look for), and remembering (because much of our behavior is based on *antecedent* rather than on concurrent episodes), to the more difficult problems about forgetting (it's so damned *selective*), and talking (the *sine qua non* of academic and other *human* endeavor). Finally we must face the issue of who is "we" or who am the I that manifests such conscious characteristics (the clinic is full of people in search of *their* identities). Analyzed into such components the problem of consciousness becomes somewhat less awesome and certainly amenable to scientific investigation.

BRAIN AND CONSCIOUSNESS

A second main topic was brought into focus by Cathy's case history: consciousness and brain are somehow intimately interwoven. Some would have us believe that consciousness is a brain state, but such statements are a mixture of mind talk and brain talk (Mackay, 1956) that irritate the purist. Another possibility would be that certain brain states result in consciousness, and this is what I implied in the previous section. But such statements also run into difficulties: if brain states can result in conscious experience, we should be able to replicate the brain state and thus produce a computerized robot who is conscious. My friends in computer and other physical sciences seem to welcome this as an ultimate achievement—I should like to point out to them only one among many difficulties: the emergence of an SPCC which would attempt to legislate the scientists' activities in order to prevent cruelty to computers.

Somewhat more seriously, the question entertains the possibility of consciousness and self-consciousness as emergent properties of certain kinds or amounts of neural (and therefore, perhaps of other) organizations and addresses the issue of the primacy and privacy of subjective experience. Critical philosophy has given a lead in exploring these problems in a logical fashion that allows scientific inquiry to proceed. Most of these analyses have come out on the side of a monistic and against a dualistic interpretation of the mind–brain issue, although multiple aspects of an identity are ordinarily allowed. I have elsewhere (Pribram, 1971a, 1971b, 1972) made the case that, in fact, these are not multiple aspects but multiple realizations of an ultimately understandable biological process. However, many biologists, including Sir Charles Sherrington, Wilder Penfield, Sir John Eccles, and Roger Sperry, are dissatisfied with this sort of explanation because they cannot as yet visualize a brain mechanism that readily transforms nerve impulses into subjective experience. They then come to wrestle with the converse problem that experience alters brain structure and function.

The issue can perhaps be stated somewhat more clearly by asking what sort of transformations allow spectral energies to become transformed into neural, and back again. We have little difficulty in grasping the principles of a camera which stores spectral qualities and quantities on film, which, when illuminated by other spectral energies, produces an image corresponding to the original qualities and quantities. It is but a step to store the spatial phase of the relationship between these qualities and quantities rather than the qualities and quantities themselves. And, as we know, such films (known as "holograms") are in some respects (see below) even more versatile in reproducing images corresponding to the original.

My proposal here is that there are a set of properties manifest in organized (i.e., spectral) energy that we have been slow to comprehend fully when engaged in trying to understand biological organization. Only during the past quarter century have we come to appreciate the power of the concept "information" in describing communications of any sort. Information is not the property of any single event, but the property of the relation between them, their sequence, their hierarchal structure, their arrangements. Information becomes encoded in such organizations and decoded from them. Codes are languages (Pribram, 1971b) and languages are the key to the structure of consciousness (Cassirer, 1966; Langer, 1951), not only in the sense ordinarily used by critical philosophers, but in a deeper sense that "the limits of my language *are* the limits of my world" (Wittgenstein, 1922, italics mine).

I believe that the particular code, the particular transformation, that makes subjective experience, conscious awareness, such a difficult topic is that biologists have yet dealt only minimally with the implications of holonomic processes. As we have seen, holographic encoding presents for study just the kind of problem that has troubled neuroscientists, biologists, psychologists, and philosophers for centuries. How are images reconstructed? Where are these images located? What is the physical property that makes superposition of the functions of neighboring elements mandatory? How can a pattern, the encoded information, be transmitted without transmission of the substance or medium in which the communication occurs?

CONSTRUCTIONAL REALISM

My proposal is therefore that the basic function of brain is to generate the codes by which information becomes communicated. Some of these codes are like those used in optical information processing—they are holographic. Thus image construction and projection occurs, and, when the system becomes sufficiently complex, it no longer functions only as a self-contained unit, but begins to act more like an open parallel processing mechanism. Characteristic of such open systems is that when they are endowed with memory they generate feed-forward processes that select, become voluntary (see below), rather than just respond to input. It is therefore readily conceivable that an open parallel processing system would generate images against which input determined images are compared. The question remains whether such images are simply epiphenomena since the encoded representations are in fact doing the work of comparison—a question couched as a dualism that may sound as strange to us some years hence as asking whether it is the gravity of one mass that is responsible for the gravity of another—when it is the interaction between the masses that allows the inference of gravity in the first place.

Thus, in philosophy I have become a constructional realist. This approach to the mind–brain problem allows me to view sympathetically the problems that have given rise to the "emergent property" theory of consciousness espoused by Sperry and the "trialist" modification of dualism used by Eccles to deal with the problem of free will— though my fundamental philosophy differs substantially from theirs. I want now, therefore, to show how this constructionalism transcends earlier formulations without denying the vitality of the issues.

For me, the problem of emergent theory revolves around the interaction between the emergent and its supposedly "material" substrate. Emergence theory, as I have heard it variously exposed, is invoked to handle those properties of a material universe that seem somehow somewhat immaterial. Thus the wetness of water, and its floatation on cooling to ice, seem less "material" than the molecules of H_2O and their constituents. But physicists have come to suspect the ultimate materiality of their observations of the universe—yet we are all agreed that a recourse to a complete subjectivism, whether cloaked in the terminology of instrumentalism or phenomenalism, leads only to a rather sterile solipsism. My response to this dilemma has been to turn the problem on its head and to suggest that we actualize a variety of experienced realities by con-struction: by composing, realizing, embodying the structures inherent in those experiences. Some of these realities may be most practically viewed as constituting a "material" level or universe; others, in practice, gain more credence when their reality is construed as subjective: that is, shown to depend more directly on individual observation and interindividual variation.

When realities are thus viewed as constructions, what does it mean to ask "do emergents interact with their substrates?" Do we worry the issue of just how "wetness" affects molecular structure or how "icing" influences the binding properties of hydrogen and oxygen? We do and we don't. We don't ask the question as it is asked of consciousness and brain by some philosophers and physiologists and thus make the mistake of crossing categories warned against by Kant (see Barrett, 1968) and by Whitehead and Russell (1927). Rather, we ask what structural combinations are involved when H_2O acts as a wetting agent and what are the differences between these structures and those that produce ice. We can then pose questions about interaction in structural terms—what is the difference in interaction among the components of the structures in the wetting and the icing realizations of the basic substructure of H_2O.

Translating this approach to the problem of brain and consciousness, we ask not how brain and consciousness interact, but how the organization of interaction of basic brain elements differs in the states characterized by automatisms and those characterized by consciousness. As noted already, this form of reduction is not a pernicious reductionism that denies reality to consciousness or "explains" all the manifestations of consciousness in brain terms. Conscious awareness is a realization as real as is brain. In understanding the origins of the organization of consciousness we employ reductive procedures leading to the structure of brain, but in understanding the organization of brain we employ procedures that are equally reductive and which lead to the structure of awareness. And who is to say that one of these reductions is more fundamental than the others? Or who would claim that these reductions provide the total panorama of the realities we call "consciousness" and "brain"?

THE DISPOSITION TOWARD SELF-CONSCIOUSNESS

The third main question raised by Cathy's case history concerns her awareness of self, identified by her name. How does self-consciousness come about?

A student enters my office, sits down in a chair opposite me and asks me to explain holography. I demonstrate how images can be reconstructed from a piece of film that itself does not look like an isomorphic representation of the object to be imaged. I point to the image, but when I try to apprehend it, touch it, the image disappears. The image is not located in the film, yet a representation of the object is located there, and from this representation the ghostlike image can be conjured by the appropriate incantations of the input. Where then is the "image" stored? Certainly not on the film, here only the representation occurs. Where is the image "located" when it does occur? Certainly not in the film itself. The image is projected beyond the film (in a transmission hologram) or inside the apparatus (in a reflection hologram).

I ask the student where she sees the book I am holding. She points to it and says, "Why there!" She is puzzled by my question.

I now say to her, "My, you look pretty today, Eva." Whereupon she changes her bearing slightly, blushes a bright crimson, smiles and acknowledges my compliment. I now ask her where she feels beautiful. The blush, which had just begun to subside, returns full-blown and she says, "All over, it's just a feeling I have inside."

Why does Eva perceive the book as out there and feel the glow of beauty as inside herself? After all, the stimulation that initiated her perception occurred at the retinal surface and the stimulation that initiated her feeling occurred in the flushing of her body surface—both in surfaces between "Eva" and her "environment."

A series of experiments by Bekesy (1967) gives at least a partial answer to this age-old philosophical puzzle. Bekesy had modeled the cochlea of the ear by making a device that placed five vibrators on the surface of the skin. The frequency and phase relationships of the vibrators could be varied. When placed on the inside of the forearm or thigh, the sensation produced was that of a point source which could be made to move along the surface by changing the relative rates of the vibrators. Then Bekesy placed two of these devices on his subjects—one on each limb. He would now play with the phase relationship between the two devices. At first the subject would feel the point source to jump from one limb to the other, but after some exposure—usually several hours—he would begin to localize the source of stimulation to a point between the limbs. In short, he now projected the somatosensory source into space much as stereophonic sound becomes projected into the space between two loudspeakers.

Bekesy's original findings of ascribing a movable point source to a set of phase related vibratory stimuli was described in terms of inhibitory interactions imposed by the receptive surface and the central processing of sensory input. Such inhibitory interactions are present in the visual as well as the auditory and somatosensory systems, and Bekesy produced some preliminary evidence which suggests that the taste mechanism may also be organized in this fashion. A great number of facts, such as the occurrence of Mach bands (Ratliff, 1965), of metacontrast (Bridgeman, 1971), and apparent motion (Cornsweet, 1970) can be explained readily by these inhibitory processes.

The mathematical equations used by Bekesy (see Ratliff, 1965) and others to quantitatively describe the inhibitory mechanisms are sets of reversible transforms that superpose the effects of neighboring stimuli. These mathematical descriptions, often called holonomic transformations (McFarland, 1971), are of the same genre as those used by Gabor (1948) when he invented holography to enhance the resolution of electronmicroscopy. In short, there is a resemblance between the equations that describe sensory processing and physical holography.

This resemblance led me to propose that we take seriously the analogy between neural processing and physical holography (1966, 1971b, 1974, Pribram, Nuwer, and Barron 1974). Work on the visual system has supported this proposal: the system as a whole and cortical cells in particular have been found (Campbell, 1974; Campbell *et al.*, 1968, 1969; Pollen, 1971, 1974) sensitive to spatial frequency (e.g., the distance between neighboring edges of a grating.

In view of these similarities between sensory processing and physical holography, the projection of images away from the receptor surface becomes somewhat less of a mystery. When the appropriate phase relationship between neighboring excitations occurs, the source of those stimulations becomes attributed to space between the surfaces. The mystery is not completely solved, for it was Eva and I who saw the images in my hologram demonstration. Who sees the images produced by the neural holograms occurring in the sensory systems?

INTENTIONALITY

So we turn to the enigma that is central to any discussion on consciousness: the problem of self-consciousness, the question of who am I?

There is a good deal of evidence that self-awareness is achieved gradually and that it is relatively fragile. Spitz has described the development of the smiling response (1946) and the emergence of "yes" and "no" (1957) as infants begin to differentiate themselves from their caretakers. Piaget (1960) has suggested that full awareness of a self is not attained until the age of 7 or 8. Experiments show that only the great apes and man can recognize marks placed on his body or face as identifying his image in a mirror (Gallup, 1970). Lesser apes (gibbons) and monkeys (F.P. Patterson and K. Pribram, unpublished observation) fail to have such reactions which demand a simultaneous recognition of body image and an external projection of such an image. All of this evidence, added to my simple demonstration with Eva, suggests that the disposition toward self-consciousness needs to be constructed and is not universal among organisms.

What then might be the critical aspects of the mechanism that allows the simultaneous perception of a body image and its external representation? In subtler form, this is the problem of intentionality discussed so extensively by Brentano (1960) and the postcritical realists. Intentionality is the capacity to identify the difference between agent (self) and percept (externally projected image) and to perceive both simultaneously. The concept thus involves intention or volition (see below) as well as self-consciousness.

Elsewhere (Pribram, 1971b) I have argued that subjective awareness is the reciprocal of smooth control of input–output relationships in the central nervous system, that only when performances become habitual and experiences become habituated does processing become automatic. Dishabituation to novelty engages the junctional and dendritic mechanisms of the brain where the slow potential microstructure, the holographic representation of input, is produced. Only with repetition do patterns of these slow potentials intercorrelate sufficiently to generate the nerve impulses necessary to action. Each slow potential pattern is assumed to leave its residue at these synaptic junctions and dendritic locations and so participate in generating the correlations. In short, to the extent that our experiences fail to correlate, to the extent that our actions are uncontrolled by habit, to that extent they are voluntary and we are conscious.

Ordinary consciousness is thus achieved by a mechanism (somewhat like a hologram) that disposes the organism to locate fresh experiences and performances at some distance from the receptive and expressive interfaces that join organism and environment. In this respect the body image is that which cannot be projected, and self-consciousness develops from the remainder of consciousness when external attributions fail to "materialize." When sufficient complexity develops in the system controlling these receptive and expressive interfaces, the distinction between those interfaces that project their image into the environment and those that do not can be processed simultaneously, i.e., they become disjoined to operate as separate channels. Ross Ashby (1960) has given a precise account of how a multiply interconnected mechanism can become disjoined when parts of it come under the control of separate environmental inputs. And I have, on the basis of experimental evidence, made a case for the specific neurological mechanisms involved in preserving and dissolving this common control apparatus (Pribram, 1969). But before we discuss this neurological mechanism, let us dispose of some of the problems that concern the "intention" part of intentionality.

VOLITION

Let me therefore apply the constructional approach to the problem of brain and free will. As Sir John Eccles (this volume) has so elegantly demonstrated, our knowledge of the functions of the motor cortex of the brain has increased tremendously over the past few decades. I want to add to his exposition some data of my own, because their import has not as yet been fully appreciated and bears directly on the problem of volition.

Man discovered about one hundred years ago (during the Franco-Prussian war) that he could electrically excite the exposed cortex of his fellows and so produce in them a variety of muscular contractions. Since that discovery, brain scientists have argued as to the nature of this relationship between brain cortex and muscular contraction. Some have shown a highly specific topological correspondence between brain and muscle locus. Others have emphasized the variability of movement that is produced by stimulation of the same cortical locus when the conditions of stimulation and of the position of the body parts are varied. This argument became encoded in the question as to whether muscles or movements were represented in the cortex. I repeated many of the earlier experiments and found the facts to be pretty much as described. In addition, however, I found (Malis, Pribram, and Kruger, 1953; Wall and Pribram, 1950) that the primate motor cortex receives a rather direct input from peripheral structures (exteroceptive, proproceptive, and interoceptive) and that it could therefore appropriately be conceived to be a sensory cortex for motor function much as the occipital cortex is the sensory cortex for optic function. The question remained as to the nature of this "motor" function.

An answer to this question came from cortical removals made in man (Bucy and Pribram, 1943) and monkey (Pribram, Kruger, Robinson, and Berman, 1955–56). Even extensive removals failed to paralyze any particular muscle or muscle groups. Nor did cinematographic analyses show any specific movement (sequence of muscular contractions) or sequence of movements to be disrupted by the ablations. Yet skill in certain tasks was impaired (latencies for completion of latch box puzzles became prolonged). I interpreted these results to mean that neither muscles nor movements were represented as such in the cortex—that instead, actions, the specific environmental outcomes of movements were represented.

It was to be many years before I would understand how an act such as writing a word or building a nest could be encoded in such a

308 KARL H. PRIBRAM

way in the brain that the resultant representations could control movements to produce a desired environmental consequence. The answer
came from experiments by Bernstein (1967) and confirmation came
quickly from the laboratory of Evarts (1967).

Bernstein performed a very simple experiment. He dressed
subjects in black leotards, had them perform skilled actions, such as
hammering a nail or running rough terrain, and took cinematographic
pictures against a black background. Before taking the pictures, however, he had pinned white swatches of cloth to the leotards at the
locations of major joints. The photographs therefore were running
spatial displays of the perturbations in time of these white swatches.
Bernstein then performed a Fourier analysis on the wave form of the
photographic displays and found he could predict within a few milli-
meters where each next blow of the hammer would be directed or
where each next step in running would land.

What Bernstein could do, his brain could do and what Bernstein's brain can do, ours can also accomplish. Again, a mathematical
tool similar to that used by von Bekesy and others in the analysis of the
brain's inhibitory mechanisms, and by optical-information scientists in
the construction of holograms, was shown to have tremendous explanatory power. Direct evidence of this comes from experiments by Evarts,
who showed that neurons in the motor cortex of monkeys do not fire
proportionately to the amount of lengthening or shortening of a muscle
involved in depressing a lever. Instead firing is proportional to the
weight attached to the lever, i.e., the force necessary to move the lever.
It is not the muscle or its contraction, it is the act, the use to which the
muscle is put, the predicted end that needs to be achieved, that is
reflected in the activity of the cortical cells.

The fact that actions, not just movements or muscles, are
represented in the motor cortex has far reaching consequences. It means
that I can with my left hand write Constantinople with muscles that
have never been engaged in such a performance or anything like it. It
means that chimpanzees can build nests with materials such as news-
papers out of which no previous chimpanzee nests have ever been
built. It means, therefore, freedom in the composition of an action—a
freedom usually discussed by psychologists as response equivalence,
but which is more, since pen, pencil, or typewriter can be chosen to
achieve the same act.

Thus we have at hand an explanation of the origins of the
brain organization that leads to acts such as moving the eyes and head
about, the writing of plays and essays and the apparently self-generated
variety of directions that the activities of men deploy. We even know a

good deal about the machinery of accomplishing this sort of freedom. As already noted, Ashby detailed a mechanism whereby the operation of a system could come to be determined by inputs processed in parallel. Since his classic studies, it has become clear that this sort of parallel processing is constructed of a feedforward, open loop, rather than a feedback, closed loop, mechanism. Further, such parallel processing, open loop, feedforward systems display all the characteristics of voluntariness in that they run themselves off to completion in a preprogrammed fashion. Therefore, some of the mystery of volition is rapidly yielding to the precision of scientific analysis performed in the spirit of constructional realism.

TRANSCENDENTALISM AND THE LOGICAL PARADOX

But perhaps the most striking impact of a constructional approach to the problem of consciousness comes from observations of transcendental experiences. As already noted, certain brain structures have been found to control the join among the various feedback and feedforward mechanisms of the brain (Pribram, 1969). These structures (circuits centering on the amygdala) also become the site of pathological disturbance in man. Epileptogenic lesions of the medial part of the pole of the temporal lobe of the brain near the amygdala episodically disrupt self-awareness. Patients with such lesions experience inappropriate *deja vue* and *jamais vue* feelings of familiarity and unfamiliarity and fail to incorporate into memory experiences occurring during an episode of electrical seizure activity of their brains. In a sense, therefore, these clinical episodes point to a transcendence of content, a phenomenon of consciousness without content, a phenomenon also experienced in mystical states, and as a result of Yoga and Zen procedures—a transcendence of the dichotomy between "self" and "other" awareness.

As illustrated by Globus's (this volume) defense of panpsychism and Eccles's (this volume) defense of the soul, many scientists desire not to eschew the mystical and feel that certain transcendent properties of consciousness cannot be ignored: perhaps we must lapse into dualism after all, if we are to be happy ever after. The constructional realist needs no recourse to such counsels of despair. At a recent and most eventful gathering, called by Alan Watts and John Lilly at Esalen Institute, I learned of the work of G. Spencer Brown (1972), a student of Wittgenstein's and Russell's. As an engineer, Brown (and his brother) devised for British Railways a gadget that could automatically monitor the number of wheels entering and exiting their tunnels irrespective of the recursions a particular wheel of a partially halted train might perform. As a mathematician, Brown quickly realized that in devising the gadget he had performed some unorthodox arithmetical twist which, upon scrutiny, turned out to be the invention of an imaginary number in the Boolian algebra. Pursuing the problem further, he found that this invention became necessary because his system had to deal with oscillation. Oscillations occur when negative feedbacks are imperfectly timed. And oscillations may never stop—thus, when the system had to deal with an infinite calculus, the invention became necessary. As a pupil of Russell and Wittgenstein, Brown was seized by the idea that he had encountered the Whitehead–Russell dilemma of the logical paradox ("this statement is a lie") in the form of an oscillation and that his solution had transcended the paradox. Spencer Brown told us of some of the implications for philosophy of his mathematical discovery (see also Keys [alias G. Spencer Brown], 1972) and we developed others for ourselves.

In this spirit, von Foerster pointed out that the problem of the existence of a reality external to us, so persuasively discussed by Hume (1888) and Berkeley (1904), had a solution akin to that proposed by Spencer Brown. To paraphrase the ensuing discussion: If I had to choose to regard my subjective reality as purely private and you regard yours in like manner, we have a choice. We can either retreat to our own corners and deny the world, or, like oscillating wheels, shuttle our private experience between us through communication. In order to keep such communication open—infinite—we "invent," construct, a real world which includes the distinction between the "other" and the "self." In short, here again is evidence that self-consciousness is a construction, a construction as real as any other admitted by the constructional realist.

So you see, the constructional realist has a ball. His reality is not bounded by the material universe though he sees no virtue in denying its reality. Russell (1959) suggests that the structural properties of the physical world are the job of science to discover. He defines intrinsic properties as those that are undiscoverable. I prefer to think of intrinsic properties as those in which structural properties are embedded. They have a special relationship to the structural properties: they actualize, make possible the realization of the structural properties. Thus, we know a Beethoven symphony by its structure, but this structure must become realized in the notations on sheet music, the recorded inprint on a plastic disc, the arrangement of magnetized minerals on a tape, or the orchestrations at a concert. The intrinsic properties of paper making, printing, laboriously constructing 33⅓ rpm records and playback phonographs, the invention of wire recording and its gradual development into present-day tapes and cassettes, seem to have little to do with the structure of a symphony—yet they are essential to its realization. In biology, realization of genetic structures is dependent on the morphogenetic field in which the genetic material is embedded, and interestingly, early formulations of holographic-like processes were addressed to problems of morphogenesis (Pribram *et al.*, 1974). In short, I want to suggest that Russell's intrinsic properties are those in which structural properties must become embedded in order to be realized, become embodied. Further, I might point out that these intrinsic properties are the concern of and take up a considerable portion of effort expended by experimentalists, engineers, artisans, and artists who are engaged in realizing scientific and artistic structures. Yet, as Russell emphasized, these intrinsic properties are unknowable, in the sense of scientific theory, since they are subject to vagaries of the moment, are apparently unrelated to each other in any systematic fashion and can be appreciated, in the final analysis, only individually and subjectively, as in the case of the symphony, by listening. I repeat, however, constructional realism is not a reductive materialism. Though historically derived from the multiple-aspects theories of the critical philosophers, it differs sharply from them in giving primacy to realizations as embodiments of structure, not to those undefined somethings whose aspects are to be viewed. It is an understanding of structure, and of the intrinsic organizations in which structures become embedded, that is elusive and that has to be worked toward by observation and analysis. In this sense, constructional realism is more akin to William James's neutral monism and Russell's ideas on structural and intrinsic (embodied) properties and on the morphogenetic field.

Thus, the constructional realist is not afraid of spelling out the laws of transcendence—nor the brain organizations that make such laws possible. There is for him no more mystery to the mystic than to the induction process that allows selective derepression of DNA to form now this organ, now that one. The organizations that produce voluntary behavior and those that give rise to transcendence are yielding to our analyses. What we must face squarely is that such analyses do not dispel the "mystery" engendered by the operation of these processes in synthesis—that we need not polarize as opposites the hard-headed analysis and the search for structures and the wonder and awe when we view the embodiment of those structures. We have seen at the conference which gave rise to this volume that those most productive of scientific fact have maintained throughout a lifetime of contribution just these spiritual qualities—and that as scientists, they are as ready (and capable) to defend spirit as data. This is science as it was originally conceived: the pursuit of understanding. The days of the cold-hearted, hard-headed technocrat appear to be numbered—the constructional realist delights in the vistas that are opened by this renewed view of science.

REFERENCES

Ashby, W. R. (1960): *Design for a Brain: The Origin of Adaptive Behaviour*. New York: John Wiley & Sons, (2nd ed.)

Barrett, T. W. (1968): The relation between mind and brain. *Confin. Psychiatr.* **11**, 133–153.

Bekesy, G. (1967): *Sensory Inhibition*. Princeton, New Jersey: Princeton University Press.

Berkeley, G. (1904): *Three Dialogues Between Hylas and Philonous*. Chicago: Open Court.

Bernstein, N. (1967): *The Co-ordination and Regulation of Movements*. New York: Pergamon Press.

Brentano, F. (1960): The Distinction between mental and physical phenomena. In: *Realism and the Background of Phenomenology*. Ed. by R. M. Chisholm. New York: The Free Press, pp. 39–61.

Bridgeman, B. (1971): Metacontrast and lateral inhibition. *Psychol. Rev.* **78**, 528–539.

Brown, G. S. (1972): *Laws of Form*. New York: The Julian Press, Inc.

Bucy, P. C. and Pribram, K. H. (1943): Localized sweating as part of a localized convulsive seizure. *Arch. Neurol. Psychiat.* **50**, 456–461.

Campbell, F. F. (1974): Transmission of spatial information through visual systems. In: *The Neurosciences: Third Study Program*. Ed. by F. O. Schmitt and F. G. Worden, Cambridge: MIT Press.

Campbell, F. W., Cooper, G. F. and Enroth-Cugell, C. (1969): The spatial selectivity of the visual cells of the cat *J. Physiol.* **203**, 223–235.

Campbell, F. W., and Robson, J. G. (1968): Application of Fourier analysis to the visibility of gratings. *J. Physiol.* **197**, 551–566.

Cassirer, E. (1966): *The Philosophy of Symbolic Forms. Vol. 3: The Phenomenology of Knowledge*. New Haven: Yale University Press.

Cornsweet, T. N. (1970): *Visual Perception*. New York: Academic Press, Inc.

Evarts, E. V. (1967): Representation of Movements and Muscles by Pyramidal Tract Neurons of the Precentral Motor Cortex. In: *Neurophysiological Basis of Normal and Abnormal Motor Activities*. Ed. by M. D. Yahr and D. R. Purpura, Hewlett, New York: Raven Press.

Gabor, D. (1948): A new microscopic principle. *Nature* **161**, 777–778.

Gallup, Jr., G. G. (1970): Chimpanzees: self-recognition. *Science* **167**, 86–87.

Hume, D. (1888): *A Treatise of Human Nature*. Oxford: Clarendon Press.

Keys, J. (1972): *Only Two Can Play This Game*. New York: The Julian Press, Inc.

Langer, S. K. (1951): *Philosophy in a New Key: A Study in the Symbolism of Reason, Rite, and Art*. New York: Mentor Books.

McFarland, D. (1971): *Feedback Mechanisms in Animal Behaviour*. New York: Academic Press, Inc.

Mackay, D. M. (1956): The epistemological problem for automata. In: *Automata Studies.* Ed. by C. E. Shannon and J. McCarthy. Princeton, New Jersey: Princeton University Press, pp. 235–252.

Malis, L. I., Pribram, K. H., and Kruger, L. (1953): Action potentials in "motor" cortex evoked by peripheral nerve stimulation. *J. Neurophysiol.* **16**, 161–167.

Piaget, J. (1960): *The Child's Conception of the World.* Paterson, New Jersey: Littlefield Adams and Company.

Pollen, D. A. (1971): How does the striate cortex begin the reconstruction of the visual world? *Science* **173**, 74–77.

Pollen, D. A. (1974): The striate cortex and the spatial analysis of visual space. In: *The Neurosciences: Third Study Program.* Ed. by F. O. Schmitt and F. G. Worden, Cambridge: MIT Press.

Pribram, K. H. (1966): Some Dimensions of Remembering: Steps toward a neuropsychological model of memory. In: *Macromolecules and Behavior.* Ed. by J. Gaito. New York: Academic Press, Inc., pp. 165–187.

Pribram, K. H. (1969): The neurobehavioral analysis of limbic forebrain mechanisms: revision and progress report. In: *Advances in the Study of Behavior.* Ed. by D. S. Lehrman, R. A. Hinde and E. Shaw, New York: Academic Press, Inc., pp. 297–332.

Pribram, K. H. (1971a): The realization of mind. *Synthese* **22**, 313–322.

Pribram, K. H. (1971b): *Languages of the Brain: Experimental Paradoxes and Principles in Neuropsychology.* Englewood Cliffs, New Jersey: Prentice-Hall, Inc.

Pribram, K. H. (1972): Neurological notes on knowing. In: *The Second Banff Conference on Theoretical Psychology.* Ed. by J. Royce, New York: Gordon and Breach, pp. 449–480.

Pribram, K. H. (1974): How is it that sensing so much we can do so little? *The Neurosciences.* Cambridge: MIT Press, 249–261.

Pribram, K. H., Baron, R. and Nuwer, M. (1974): The holographic hypothesis of memory structure in brain function and perception. In: *Contemporary Developments in Mathematical Psychology.* Ed. by R. C. Atkinson, D. H. Krantz, R. C. Luce and P. Suppes. San Francisco: W. H. Freeman

Pribram, K. H., Kruger, L., Robinson, F. and Berman, A. J. (1955–56): The effects of precentral lesions on the behavior or monkeys. *Yale J. Biol. & Med.,* **28**, 428–443.

Ratliff, F. (1965): *Mach Bands.* San Francisco: Holden Day.

Russell, B. (1959): *My Philosophical Development.* New York: Simon and Schuster.

Ryle, G. (1949): *The Concept of Mind.* New York: Barnes and Noble.

Spitz, R. A. (1946): The smiling response: a contribution to the ontogenesis of social relations. *Genet. Psychol. Monogr.* **34**, 57–125.

Spitz, R. A. (1957): *No and Yes: On the Genesis of Human Communication.* New York: International Universities Press, Inc.

Wall, P. D. and Pribram, K. H. (1950): Trigeminal neurotomy and blood pressure responses from stimulation of lateral cerebral cortex of Macaca mulatta. *J. Neurophysiol.* **13**, 409–412.

Whitehead, A. N. and Russell, B. (1927): *Principia Mathematica.* Vol. 1, 2nd ed., Cambridge: Cambridge University Press.

Wittgenstein, L. (1922): *Tractatus Logico-Philosophicus.* London: Routledge & Kegan Paul, Ltd.

11 Introduction

Prefaces to articles, like social introductions, are usually formal, and have a certain covert tendency to become articles in their own right. Rather than providing such a preface to Maxwell's provocative "afterthoughts" on the relevance of scientific results for the mind–brain problem, we present the "natural" preface, that is, the particular discussion between philosophers and scientists which provided him with a stimulus for his paper. But since this discussion of science and the mind–brain puzzle in fact reflects the major emergent focus of the conference—as scientists tried to "shoot the gap" in that formidable Minnesota line!—the discussion also stands on its own as an independent contribution. The "discussion," which was constructed from a verbatim transcript, has been severely edited in the service of coherence, readability, and entertainment value.

11 The Role of Scientific Results in Theories of Mind and Brain: A Conversation among Philosophers and Scientists

E. M. DEWAN, JOHN C. ECCLES, GORDON G. GLOBUS, KEITH GUNDERSON, PETER H. KNAPP, GROVER MAXWELL, KARL H. PRIBRAM, C. WADE SAVAGE, IRWIN SAVODNIK, MICHAEL SCRIVEN, R. W. SPERRY, WALTER B. WEIMER, WILLIAM C. WIMSATT

Maxwell: Pribram has emphasized that consciousness is important, practically important, even. It is very heartening to hear this coming from a tough-minded scientist. He comes to grips with Ryle's "ghost in the machine" and comes to the conclusion that ghosts (of the kind that rile Ryle) really exist, and that they too are important. He talks about the world within, the reality of the subjective feelings as we live through them—through pains, joys, sorrows, red patches in the visual field, and so forth. But does this imply dualism? Pribram's answer is a resounding

"No!" His main reason appears to be that we have at least the beginnings of a neural and psychophysiological science that will account for, that is, give us the *mechanism* for, the production of these feelings.

Does this falsify dualism? I think the answer here is again a resounding "No!" and for extremely important reasons which are relevant to all of the problems relating to mind and brain. Dualism is not falsifiable in that, no matter what data we have or what data we are going to get, the dualist can always accommodate them within his system quite easily. I believe that dualism is consistent with and indeed can account for both our subjective feelings as we live through them and report them and any neurophysiological findings that we may come up with. However, this holds not only for dualism in its various forms (interactionism, parallelism, epiphenomenalism) but also for psychoneural identity theory and other kinds of monism.

As C. Wade Savage has noted earlier in this conference, many philosophers consider the empirical findings of science to be not very relevant to the "philosophical mind–body problem" because theories about mind–brain relations do not seem to be falsifiable and, in general, the data are only very tenuously connected with the theories. Such philosophers find that scientific data turn out to be very unimportant and unexciting. But the same thing can be said for *any* scientific theory of much depth, scope, or generality. Any such scientific theory can not only be made consistent *with* but can be made to account *for* and to *explain* whatever data we may ever obtain.

Eccles: May I register my disapproval now!

Maxwell: Pribram makes the interesting comparison between consciousness and brain, on the one hand, and massive bodies and gravity on the other. He says that we recognize that gravity is a kind of interaction of masses. Nobody believes that, if you dig deep enough into a ball, you will discover (observe) gravity, but, in the case of consciousness, there are still some who entertain the belief that, if we just dig deep enough into the brain, surely we will find (observe?) consciousness. Although this belief is absurd, it is not too clear just why it is absurd to suppose that, no matter what means (what instruments, etc.) we acquire for observing the brain, no matter what we do, we will never be able to observe consciousness by, say, ripping open Pribram's skull and examining his brain. Even if I had Herbert Feigl's imaginary "cerebroscope," by means of which I could see the neurons firing or even the electrons whirling around in his brain, I would never see his feelings of pain, love, hate, etc.

This is probably the biggest stumbling block of the mind–brain issue, especially for those who want to maintain an identity theory of mind and brain; and I think that, *considered in one way*, any identity theory is obviously absurd. We *know* (we tell ourselves) what the brain is; if we break open the skull, we find a bloody mess—grey matter, white matter, and so forth. If we look at it under a microscope or use other instrumental techniques, we see still other things, but we do not come any closer to seeing feelings of pain, joys, sorrows, and so on—nor could we ever come any closer, as has been clearly emphasized by Leibniz and others.

Now, for those who want to maintain some sort of identity theory, I think that one way out of this seeming absurdity has been clearly put forth by Bertrand Russell (in, e.g., *Human Knowledge: Its Scope and Limits*, New York: Simon and Schuster, 1948). The main point is that we don't ever really *see* anybody else's brain. If I break open a skull and do what we call in ordinary language looking at somebody else's brain, what I see is *not* somebody else's brain; what is in my visual experience is a portion of my own brain. The word "see" here no longer does the work that is needed to be done. Why is this? Neural activity in my own brain is both necessary and sufficient for my visual experience in all its richness. In brief, what this means is that *we do not see matter*. We do not have direct visual experiences of tables and chairs, and thus we do not have direct visual experiences of anything that is not an ingredient of our own (private) experience. Things are not what we think we perceive them to be; naive realism is false. Our concepts, or better, our *beliefs* about what matter is, have to be changed drastically.

What we come up with, as Russell has clearly explained but has been ignored generally, is that our knowledge of the material, external world, our knowledge of "the physical," is knowledge only of *structure*. (Here, Pribram and I appear to be in agreement.) In the light of results from physics, neurophysiology, and psychophysiology, we must realize that our knowledge is of certain structural and/or formal features of the external world, but we do not know what comprises its intrinsic or *first order* properties.

Once we see this, it seems to me that we remove the difficulties involved in identifying a certain portion of the physical world with our subjective experience. If we recognize that we don't know what the real nature of the brain is because we don't know the real intrinsic nature of anything physical, the possibility is left open that the brain is at least partially composed of thoughts, feelings and the rest of our subjective experience. I mean this quite literally, although to tell the whole story I would have to make clear that we must get rid of substance metaphysics altogether and reject *matter* or *substance* in favor of an *event ontology*. To say that the brain is partially composed of mental events, is to say that some of the events in the causal network that correspond to (are the constituents of) what we commonsensically call "the brain" are our directly known thoughts, feelings, jealousies, and sorrows. They are just as physical as any other events in the brain, in that they are in the causal network; and if they are in the causal network, they are in the space–time network, if we accept Russell's attempt to construct space–time out of the relations among events. As Russell has noted, there is no more difficulty about saying that some events are both mental and physical than there is about saying that some men are both bakers and fathers.

I should make it clear, however, that this is not a materialistic identity theory or a materialistic monism. The *mental* does not become any *less* mental by being identified with (a portion of) the *physical*. I hesitate to call the view *physicalism*. In fact, as Feigl used to say, "If you give me a couple of martinis, a good dinner, and a couple of after-dinner drinks, I would admit that I am strongly tempted toward (a rather watered-down, innocuous) panpsychism."

Gunderson: Only a certain kind of after-dinner drink, isn't it?

Maxwell: Yes, green chartreuse! The cause of this temptation is very simple. It seems reasonable to suppose that, since all events are presumably in the causal network and thus in the space–time network, then there is only a *difference in degree* between those events that go to make up my conscious awareness and other events in the world. Otherwise, we would be left with a *kind* of mental–physical dualism, although it would not be a mind–brain dualism. This difference in degree *is*, no doubt, tremendous, so that I don't find any absurdity in supposing that it is the *only* difference.

Eccles: Maxwell states that any scientific theory of sufficient generality can be accommodated to any scientific observations that can be made. This must be untrue, because falsification is the very essence of the scientific method. I am speaking as a scientist for the scientific method that is used by scientists. The effort is always to put up a series of ideas going beyond our present experimental understanding and factual material, and then do experiments which might or might not conform with the prediction, which then has to be modified. We are all the time changing theories on the basis of the experimental data. This is what I do as a practicing scientist.

Maxwell: On the basis of the history of science, and examination of case histories, we find that, although of course theories have changed as new data come in, nevertheless, if you are stubborn enough and you want to cling to a particular theory, then you can always do it just by modifying some of the auxiliary theories, some of the assumptions about initial conditions, some of the so-called *background knowledge* (if you want to use Popperian language) and so forth. And this not only holds for evidence counting against theories; it can also hold for evidence counting in favor of theories.

Eccles: As Max Planck says, quite often this is the case. Scientists are not convinced by counterexperiments, but their mistakes die with them. And that is how false theories are eradicated from science.

Dewan: I'd like to agree with Eccles. When I would like to make a theory, I go to great pains to make it testable in the sense of being refuted. If two or three experiments all go against what I predicted, I say to myself, "Too bad! That theory is not so good!" and I throw it away.

Scriven: But that is being a good boy. You are telling us tales from the kindergarten book. Everybody knows that this is the model of how science is *supposed* to proceed. When Maxwell says that this is not in fact what really is possible, he is after something more subtle, namely that science doesn't always proceed the way that it is supposed to proceed.

Pribram: We all agree to that. What we are saying is that some of us actually practice what is being preached, and Eccles is a very good example!

Maxwell: This matter is at the heart of the issue. We are trying to decide here whether or not scientific findings are relevant to the mind–brain problem. My contention is that they are very relevant indeed, but I am trying to explain why many philosophers have *thought, erroneously*, that they were not relevant. These philosophers have thought that no matter what your position, no matter whether it is dualism of one or another kind, or a version of monism, or something else—that all of these positions seem to be consistent with any sort of data that we have or that is conceivable. I want to say that this slippery relationship between theories and data may indeed hold, but this does not prove that scientific findings are irrelevant for the mind–brain theories. If it did, it would be easy to go on and prove that the observational evidence is irrelevant for any very important scientific theory. It is a matter of degree. Most theories that are commonly considered to be scientific ones are a little closer to the data than are most so-called "philosophical" theories.

Now, you can ask yourself several things about a theory. Does it explain the data? As I said, all the theories of mind and brain explain the data. Do they account for the data in an elegant and simple manner? Moreover, are they *plausible?* This can mean several things. How well do they fit in with the rest of our world picture, whatever it happens to be? *How good do they feel in our bones?* How do they strike us? Do we like them? Would we estimate what I call their *prior probability* to be relatively high? I think that we ask and answer (implicitly, at least) such questions in scientific inquiry, and I think that as in the case of science, we do so in the case of the mind–body problem. Again, the difference between theories of mind and brain and less exalted theories is a difference of degree and not a difference of kind.

Gunderson: As Maxwell presents the Russellian twist, we don't really see the physical object, the brain, at all; what we think we see is a portion of our own brain. Now, I think that move is crucial. Do you want to generalize that across sensory modalities, so that when you hear things, you only hear portions of your brain? I am not sure how well that works. Do we smell a portion of our own brains?

Pribram: As the Bèkèsy-type experiments have shown, we project an external world based on characteristics of the stimuli, such as their phase relationship. It is possible to perceive a tactile vibration applied to the two thighs as being in the empty space between.

Maxwell: If you are hung up on ordinary language, of course "seeing" a portion of our own brain is problematic. You have to recognize that words like "see" and "hear" are *naive–realist* terms that presuppose certain commonsense beliefs about perception. But these beliefs turn out to be false, so the word "see" with its ordinary meaning is no longer applicable. When I say I *see* part of my own brain, of course this is no longer accurate, since in reality I don't *see anything* in the *ordinary* sense of the word. But the visual experience involved *is* an event that is a constituent of my brain, and *nothing* that is not a part of my brain is an ingredient of my visual experience, although other things or events including the physical object that we mistakenly *think* that we see *are* causal ancestors of the visual experience. It is in such a new but related sense of "see" that we *see* (parts of) our own brain. The same applies, full-force, to *hearing* and *smelling*.

Eccles: I take issue with Maxwell's statement that neuronal events are both necessary and sufficient for visual or auditory experience. I do not believe they are sufficient, since these neuronal events may occur while I am unconscious. The other thing I have to be is *attentive*. Visual stimuli have been pouring into my eyes constantly throughout this day, but only a few of them have been in my visual experience. I choose to ignore, and can ignore by intention, these visual experiences and concentrate on others. So I think the necessary *and* sufficient is not correct.

Maxwell: These are contingent matters. It might turn out (I am convinced that it *would* turn out), for example, that when you are conscious the pattern of your neuronal activity is different from what it was when you were unconscious, and it might turn out that when you were not attentive the pattern of your neuronal activity was different from when you were attentive.

Eccles: But when I am conscious, there are still extreme ranges of visual experience. All the other information that is coming in, for example, sounds, also determines whether or not we have visual experience. Neural activity relating to visual stimuli is not sufficient. By shifting my attention, I can become aware of my left big toe which I haven't been aware of all day.

Maxwell: Being a (an interactionist) dualist, you naturally would hypothesize that neural activity is only necessary but not sufficient; being a monist, my hypothesis would be that it is both necessary and sufficient. Some of the neural events that go to make up the complex of events that constitute the brain's activity just *are* our acts of awareness, our acts of seeing red patches, and so forth. As far as *logic* is concerned, this may be false and it may be true. The identity theory as well as all dualist theories are contingent hypotheses.

Scriven: What we really have is a set of theories which are all too flexible, so that people can wave whatever flag they like the color of, fairly confident that nobody can make them take it down. Now let me put a challenge to the scientists. Is there something in your field of expertise that strikes you at the moment as a phenomenon which really rules out some theory? If not, is there some phenomenon in your field of expertise with respect to which you feel in particular need of some kind of solution for the mind–body problem? Finally, is there any way in which we philosophers can be helpful to you scientists?

Sperry: Since stimulation of the cerebellum in a conscious subject yields no conscious effect, this suggests that panpsychism is a lost cause, since panpsychism says that everything is consciousness.

Globus: All it suggests is that the cerebellum isn't hooked up to the language system. In your own split-brain studies, you argue that the minor hemisphere is conscious even though it can't talk about it.

Sperry: I was hoping you wouldn't think of that!

Eccles: I think that we could help this discussion if we distinguish between consciousness and self-consciousness. In the latter, we know of ourselves as self-conscious beings, in knowing we are able to examine our own mental processes. It is quite clear that this is not the case with animals, but I wouldn't deny them consciousness. I think they have a different kind of experience, as would be the case for the human minor hemisphere, which doesn't know that it knows, or at least can't tell us about it, whereas the dominant hemisphere can. This is one of the really challenging empirical findings by Sperry which is quite relevant to theories of mind and brain.

   Many years ago, following Sherrington, I suggested that there was a brain–mind liaison somewhere in the brain, but we did not know where it was. And now at least we've got the scientific evidence from split-brain subjects that it is in the dominant hemisphere—not in the minor hemisphere, not in the brain stem, and not in the cerebellum! Even though there are perhaps 200 million fibers which can conduct some 20 times per second between the two hemispheres, it is only the dominant hemisphere that has self-conscious awareness.

Pribram: To respond to Scriven, I believe that biological data are most relevant. The contribution of the biologist's approach is in the working out of mechanisms taken one step at a time. For example, now we have some idea of what DNA looks like and then immediately we get into the repressor story, and a derepressor story, and all of that, and as we try to work it out, gradually the problems seem to dissolve, rather than anything else. Consider the problem of vision. We know the physical instigators of sensory processors, we know enough of what goes on in the retina, and what goes on at the geniculate nucleus, visual cortex, and temporal cortex, and so on, so that we begin to have all the intermediary steps. Then, the problem of vision no longer bothers us as an overly mystical sort of thing. We have enough steps worked out so that we understand vision, but, when you look at the problem *overall*, it still has the same mystery it always did! But you have a feeling of being reasonably comfortable with the mystery. My feeling is that the problem of consciousness will dissolve in similar fashion with the stepwise progress of biology. This is what I mean by "the biologist's approach."

Savodnik: Pribram's comment brings to mind an image of a Gothic cathedral which rises and rises so high, and gets smaller and smaller, until it fades away into the sky, so that the experience you have is that you practically can walk your way into heaven! I am wondering whether we actually are trying to walk our way into the soul in the same way. Perhaps all this neuroscientific data actually obscures the issues. The problem is still just as hard as it was before all the data were introduced. That is why I think the data are, in a sense, irrelevant at times.

Knapp: When you talk about no theory ever being confirmed by data, you probably could make a good case for it, but one place where a theory has proved remarkably inelegant is Descartes' theory that the mind and the body interact in the pineal gland. That notion has not appeared in many journals lately!

Sperry: There also was a centrencephalic story about 20 years ago, in which evidence supported the idea that the consciousness is centered in the brain stem, but when you divide just the forebrain and find the split in consciousness between the two sides, the centrencephalic idea is eliminated.

Scriven: But really what you are pointing out to us is that the soul has been shuffled around from pillar to post; that is progress, but it doesn't look as if philosophy has helped you much.

Pribram: We are talking about consciousness again as if it were a single thing. Now, the reason for talking about the centrencephalic system being related to consciousness was with regard to the sleep–wakefulness states in contrast to the state of unconsciousness, that is, the state of stupor. When you have tumors around the third ventricle, or if you disturb the third or fourth ventricle, you do in fact make the patient go into stuporous states. Further, there is considerable biochemical evidence that mood states are controlled by biochemical processes located around what used to be called the centrencephalic system, but which I would call "core systems of brain." But this is not the kind of consciousness we have been talking about here. We've gone a step further in talking about perception, detailed kinds of awareness, and self-consciousness. The core systems have something to do with the problem of consciousness and we know very specifically what they have to do with particular aspects of the problem. Again, this is all part of a stepwise biological solution.

Scriven: So you are telling us about the machinery, but I am inclined to think that no amount of telling about the machinery will handle the conceptual problem. For example, once you understand how a computer is going to do certain jobs, you must look from the inside of the computer to the computer, in the way things look from the inside of us to us. Then somebody says to you, "Is there interaction or not?" Then, you don't know what to say, because it doesn't seem to be important what you say.

Gunderson: The scientists have been talking about things like *where* consciousness is. You can shift from the ear lobe to the pineal gland and so on. But the relationship between wherever-you-put-it and mental states as you experience them still remains quite perplexing.

Eccles: Mental states have to be related with or correlated with the operations or processes in the brain that are specifically concerned in generating these mental states. Would you agree with that?

Gunderson: Of course, but just saying that does not explain the mind–body relationship.

Eccles: At least it is defining the problem much better than it has been in the past. We are getting on. Don't expect a problem like that to be solved in the next generation or two. But we can make it a much better problem.

Gunderson: But consider the relevance of neurophysiological data to the explanation of the relationship. The question is, supposing that you have a lot of data which suggests that the mental is located here, or there, or wherever. How does that explain the relationship?

Eccles: For the past 20 years progress has been fantastic! The questions that we now ask, the ways we can answer them, and so on, is quite different from what it was 20 years ago. Don't be too impatient! The hardest problem a man can ever have is the relationship of his own brain processes to his mental states! But don't be defeated because we haven't got there yet.

Gunderson: I just don't see any progress in understanding the mind–body relationship, from the pineal gland to wherever you have gotten now. All I see is a lot of *neurophysiological* progress.

Pribram: But the difference between how this was conceived of by Ralph Gerard when he taught me my first course in biology and the way we can look at it now is like the difference between night and day.

Maxwell: The reason Gunderson and Scriven can't see any progress is because they stubbornly and persistently cling to a naive direct perceptual view of the world. If they give that up, they could see the way open to progress. You can talk to scientists about this, but you can't talk to philosophers! They are too . . . stubborn!

Sperry: Suppose you could work out the brain mechanisms involved in the perception of red in great detail, and then suppose you could show that if you change those mechanisms a little bit in particular features, you'll get green. Or with another change, you'll get a sense of taste. When you reach that point, I would think you would be in position to understand these mental properties.

Globus: Granting you a "utopian neuropsychology," would you then say that your data supports epiphenominalism, interactionism, double-aspect theory? A demonstration of a *correlation* between phenomenal experience and neural events is not the problem. The problem is how might we go from that empirically supported correlation to a theory which will account for it. This discussion keeps going around and around in a circle.

Wimsatt: The discussion of location versus the relationship between mind and body abstracts from the scientific process in a dangerous way, because it suggests that you can decide *where* consciousness is, and then learn *what* the relationship is. If you look at the dynamics of an identification, you will find something quite different; there is feedback from localization to a certain extent, to learning something more about the relationship and then using the relationship to further localization and so forth. I think there is only one very good case study of this in any system approaching the complexity of the mind–body relationship. It is quite illuminating to consider the history of the localization of the genome. For Mendel, the genes were "factors" that did not have to be located anywhere. But this led to discoveries of localizable DNA molecules. There is a very complicated interaction between the spatial hypothesis and what the genome does. Suppose I say to you, " 'Yellow body' is three times as far away from 'red eyes' as is 'curly wings.' " It is not clear what it means to attribute a spatial location to these character traits, and yet we in fact can say that it has a meaning. I think in part what we have to be very careful about here is that we are not suffering from a lack of scientific imagination.

Weimer: The philosophers line up and say that data are irrelevant to the problem, whereas the scientist's position is that only the data are *really* relevant. But I do not think that there is any real conflict here. What the philosophers are saying is that the data which are relevant to the mind–body problem are irrelevant with regard to the potential confirmation or refutation of one or another theory. And what the scientists, granting that this is so, are saying is, what we've learned when we learn more about the mind–body problem are, precisely, these data. For instance, consider the formulations of dualism that were available to Plato and contrast them with the ones available to Eccles. If you take a look at the history of monism, you'll find that there are enormous changes, and that data are enormously relevant, since, in effect, they structure the whole way that we construe every problem involved. Yet, we do not know the role of data, if you will, in the confirmation or falsification of scientific theories.

Unidentified: It just seems so obvious that I wonder why we really wondered about it! Let's go to lunch . . .

11 Scientific Results and the Mind–Brain Issue: Some Afterthoughts

GROVER MAXWELL

Rereading the transcript of the preceding "Conversation among Philosophers and Scientists" left me feeling unsatisfied or, rather, unfulfilled. It was not so much the old familiar feeling that, I suppose, most of us in the academic game have had more than once—the feeling that, "When he said *so and so*, I should have said *such and such*. That would have been a good lick!" On the contrary, it left me with the impression that all of us, including even me, did pretty well—pretty well, that is, given the material that we had and had had before us at the conference. My regret was that, in view of the interest in the matter and its crucial importance, we had not had more formal presentations on the relevance of scientific knowledge for the mind–brain issue.

This is one excuse for inserting *this* paper on the subject here. Another is that the "Conversation . . . " was triggered by some discussion remarks of mine in response to a paper by Karl Pribram (this volume). The present essay *is* intended as a general one, and I have made every effort not to reply either directly or by implication to any of the points "made against" me, indeed, not to "make points" against

GROVER MAXWELL·Minnesota Center for Philosophy of Science, University of Minnesota *any* of the remarks contained in the "Conversation . . . " Whether or not I have succeeded in this resolve is, no doubt, difficult to decide, for the "Conversation . . . " certainly has been stimulating and suggestive and has played a large role in generating the material for this paper.

Since there are some readers who are not (professional) philosophers, I have tried to keep jargon at a minimum and have explained at some length matters which the philosophers will find unnecessarily elementary. I beg the indulgence of the latter group for these two breaches of professional mores.

The concern of this essay *is* the mind–body problem, and, if it were possible, I would stick to *it* and pass over general issues about the relationship between science and philosophy. But the view that scientific results can have little or no relevance for philosophical problems is currently so popular and so firmly held that it must be dealt with if one wishes to argue that science is not only relevant but indeed that it provides the means for untying the world knot (the mind–body puzzle). I *have* dealt with it in detail elsewhere (Maxwell 1970*a*, 1972, and, esp., 1975, 1976), so I shall be brief and thus, I fear, somewhat dogmatic here.

Before making any critical remarks, I should like to give a short statement of what I take the nature, the task, and the method of philosophy to be. The concern of philosophy is with basic, fundamental, foundational principles (assumptions, beliefs, etc.). Such principles may sometimes be explicit, but often they are implicit, tacit, and, perhaps, unconsciously held. (Some of them may be missing altogether. This might be the case in an area about which we would say that its "foundations" are incomplete or unsatisfactory—for example, confirmation theory today [or, as some would call it, "inductive logic"], or, in physics, quantum theory.) The belief in the existence of the "external" (mind-independent) world—the belief that, say, my desk continues to exist when no one is aware of it—may be said, not too inaccurately, to be an example of an assumption or a belief that is *tacit* and, perhaps, *unconscious* (until, or course, one becomes initiated into philosophical circles). (Some would have it that such philosophical musings are misguided, oversophisticated [or sophistical], contrived, unnatural, pathological, and otherwise naughty. I disagree. I have encountered more than one happy, healthy, well-adjusted four- or five-year-old who invented, quite independently, and struggled with puzzles very similar to Kant's antinomies on the finitude of space and time. This, of course, doesn't *prove* my point, but, *prima facie*, it seems to favor it.)

How do such foundational principles (and/or beliefs, etc.)

differ from less exalted ones, ones for which we might try to collect (observational) evidence, perhaps designing and performing experiments, so that they might be *confirmed or disconfirmed*? The answer, I am firmly convinced, is that they differ only in degree and not in kind. And sometimes the difference in degree is quite small: there is a continuum (with no singularities) from the most basic foundational principle to the most lowly "empirical" generalization. In other words, *philosophy* and *science* differ from each other only in degree and not in kind. (By "philosophy" here, I am referring to epistemology and metaphysics, in general, and philosophy of science, in particular. I wish to leave entirely aside the question as to whether very similar or very different considerations apply to the realm of *values*.)

Before giving arguments for this contention, it should be useful to consider some of the reasons that it sounds so outrageous to many contemporary ears. (For more details than can be included here, see Maxwell, *ops. cit.*) The central objection to my position might run as follows: "*Scientific* statements, even the most highly theoretical ones, must be such that they can, in principle, be confirmed or disconfirmed by experimental, observational evidence. It must at least be the case for a *scientific* proposition that there *could* exist evidence that would count either in favor of it or against it. *Scientific* disagreements can, in principle, always be settled by a proper assessment of an appropriate kind and amount of evidence. (What holds for scientific knowledge also holds for virtually all of our [legitimate] common sense knowledge.) Philosophical propositions," the objection continues, "are radically different. They can not only be 'saved' *from* and made consistent *with* any conceivable evidence; many of them are such that their proponents, by means of ingenious and convoluted machinations, can make them *explain* or *account for* any conceivable evidence. This should generate healthy suspicion and distrust of (traditional) philosophical propositions and should, as it indeed does, lead us to an agonizing reappraisal of the entire philosophical enterprise. As a result, we see that the only function of a *legitimate* philosophical statement is to convey[1] information about the *language, the concepts,* and the *logic* that we use to express our knowledge, beliefs, etc., about the world and ourselves. (Legitimate) philosophical activity can consist only of the analysis of language, conceptual analysis, or logical analysis. For, in what other area could philosophy stake a defensible claim? We have

[1] According to some, philosophical statements can only *show* or otherwise "express" information; they cannot (explicitly) *assert* it. It is now recognized by most, however, that statements made in an appropriate metalanguage can explicitly *assert* the (linguistic, conceptual, or logical) information that is "conveyed."

seen above," the argument proceeds, "that statements and issues of a factual—a contingent, an *empirical*—nature are in the realm of science (or, sometimes, of good old everyday common sense) and are to be settled by collecting and weighing evidence and that philosophical issues are not amenable to this kind of settlement. Therefore, philosophical statements, views, positions, theories, etc., must be void of any factual, contingent, 'empirical' content and, at best, can only be about linguistic, conceptual, or logical matters. Q. E. D. "

As congenial as this view about the nature of philosophy (and of science) may be to contemporary philosophers (and, no doubt, to many scientists) and as much as I used to extol it myself, I believe that it is grossly mistaken and that the argument, sketched above, in its favor is drastically unsound. However, I do agree emphatically with one of its apparently damning premises; it is true that almost any philosophical theory can be "saved" in the face of any conceivable evidence and can, indeed, be made to explain or account for any evidence whatever. But, unfortunately for the argument in question, *the same is true for any scientific theory* that is of any appreciable degree of interest and importance and which goes beyond the lowest "empirical generalization." So that, if the premise in question is the ground for the intermediate conclusion that philosophical propositions are devoid of factual, contingent, or "empirical" content, it follows that every scientific proposition that is of much interest or importance is possessed of the same kind of distressing vacuity. What is wrong here? The obvious but not very helpful answer is that neither (intermediate) conclusion follows from the premise and that some propositions that are such that they can be "saved" in the face of all conceivable evidence, etc., etc., can nevertheless have factual, contingent content. (Omission of the word "empirical" from the preceding sentence, which, in a way, is the key to the whole matter, as well as my using it in "shudder quotes" in this essay, will be discussed presently.)

The discomforting facts about the rather extreme tenuousness and deviousness of any connections that lead from evidence to scientific theories have been revealed clearly and forcefully by recent studies in confirmation theory—by uniformly unsuccessful attempts to "justify induction" and/or to develop an "inductive logic," by attempts such as Popper's, again unsuccessful, to "save empiricism" by utilizing *falsifications* (actual *or* possible) of theories by observational data in order to circumvent the "problem of induction," by Russell's devastating negative results and, at best, indifferently successful constructive efforts to deal with problems of confirmation, and by many others. The reasons for such failures were first elaborated, as far as I have been able to tell, partly by Russell and partly by Duhem, although Hume had long before provided the central theme with impeccable clarity and force. Russell emphasized the (deductively demonstrable!) fact that commonly employed "inductive inferences" or "inductive arguments" yield, in principle, false conclusions from true premises infinitely more often than they yield true ones. (Included under "commonly employed 'inductive inferences' " are induction by simple enumeration, Mill's Canons, and most kinds of statistical inferences that are presented in textbooks.) For, it is easy to demonstrate that, for every such inductive argument with true premises and a true conclusion, there exists an infinite number of arguments, each of which has the *same form* as the first, has premises that are all true, and has a *false* conclusion. (The conclusions of these arguments are also mutually incompatible in addition to being incompatible with the true conclusion.) As Russell [1948] remarks, this shows that induction leads infinitely more often to incorrect, unacceptable results than it does to correct ones *unless* it is bolstered by (extremely strong) contingent but unconfirmed[2] assumptions. As we shall soon see, an entirely analogous result can be demonstrated for the only other kind of procedure that seems to be available for confirmation, or for nondeductive inference, or for relating evidence to theories (the *hypothetico-deductive* or, better, *hypothetico-inferential* method). These considerations show, quite conclusively, I think, that all attempts to justify or vindicate induction, any kind of nondeductive inference, or any kind of confirmation methods in a manner acceptable to empiricism—and, thus, to the vast majority of contemporary philosophers—that all such attempts are bound to fail (for reasons, ironically enough, that can be established by "logical analysis" alone). It follows that, except for statements that report direct observations of the moment, *there are no empirical statements* in the sense of "empirical" that is used in contemporary circles. There are no statements of much scope, interest, or importance that are decidable or, even, confirmable or disconfirmable on the basis of only the data plus logic (including "inductive logic," if there were such a thing).

Popper's valiant attempts to "save empiricism"[3] in the face of all of this, most of which he would grant and, indeed, enthusiastically endorse, must now be considered briefly. His views are so well known that I shall omit any exposition of them and proceed directly to criticism. Unfortunately for Popper, statements that go any way at all

---

[2] Not confirmed by any means acceptable to empiricists (or to rationalists, for that matter) and, thus, not confirmed by means acceptable to most contemporary philosophers. For discussion of the nature of such assumptions, see Maxwell (1975, and in press).

[3] He puts the matter in this manner in Popper (1962).

beyond the lowest level empirical generalization—statements that are of any appreciable scope, interest, or importance—are no more falsifiable by observational evidence than they are verifiable (or confirmable).[4] The reasons are, mostly, the familiar Duhemian ones: such a theory alone will not, as a rule, yield any evidence statement (any observation statement or its denial) as a *deductive consequence* and, thus, in isolation, it cannot be falsified by any conceivable observational evidence. In practice, that which *does* deductively imply observation statements is a conjunction of the theory of interest with other, *"auxiliary" theories* ("background knowledge") together with (singular) statements of initial conditions *a large portion of which are usually about unobservables.* Thus, if such a conjuction entails a certain observation statement and, after we have done our best to see that all of the initial conditions are fulfilled, the entailed observation statement turns out to be false (the predicted result does not occur), what has been *falsified,* of course, is the conjunction; the culprit may be one or more of the auxiliary theories and/or one or more of the assumptions about unobservable initial conditions, and the theory being tested (the "theory of interest") may, for all we know, be true.[5]

[4] Popper (1959) recognized this, but goes on to say that it's all right, because scientists ought to use certain "methodological rules" which *do* "make" theories falsifiable. Crudely, but not, I think, unfairly, Popper's "rules" may be summarized: Assume that all of the operative auxiliary theories and other "background knowledge" are true so that if the predicted observation does not occur, it must be the theory of interest that is false. I have given detailed arguments elsewhere (Maxwell, 1974, 1975) that use of such rules, unless it is completely arbitrary and *ad hoc*, rests on strong presuppositions that are unconfirmed (and "uncorroborated") and that, therefore, stand just as much in need of justification or vindication—if they are to "save empiricism"—as do induction or other confirmation procedures. Moreover, I have argued that some of the presuppositions are false and that the rules *neither are nor ought to be* taken too seriously by practicing scientists. To cite just one argument, quite often the auxiliary theories that are used to relate the theory of interest to the evidence are less well confirmed (or "corroborated") than the theory being tested. A striking example from recent history of science is the "detection" of the neutrino (see Maxwell, 1974); so that if the results *had* been negative, no one would have thought that the "neutrino hypothesis" had been falsified.

[5] Popper (1974) contends that such conjunctions do not need to contain statements about initial conditions in order to be inconsistent with (and, thus, falsifiable by) the special kind of observation statements that he calls "basic statements." Presumably, this is because his basic statements contain assertions to the effect that the initial conditions do hold *and* that the predicted outcome does not transpire. But his contention can stand only if all the initial conditions, in a given case, are observable. Consider a case where the initial conditions required, say, that a certain system be at thermodynamic equilibrium or that a given planet was not being acted upon by any unobserved bodies or by other undetected forces. The potential falsifiers would be (something like), "When a system [such as this] is at thermodynamic equilibrium and when [the other initial conditions] are fulfilled, then, [nevertheless], such-and-such a result does not transpire" (and an analogous one for the astronomical case). But these potential falsifiers are *not*, of course, observation statements, and Popper (1959) clearly specifies that his *basic statements are* observation statements. It is true that he was not very happy about this, even at the time, and said that he could have just as well said that they were statements about macrophysical objects. But, of course, the latter condition does not hold, in general, for unobservables. He may want to change his mind about the observability–macro requirement and allow some basic statements to be (partially) about unobservables. But this surely would wreck his program to "save empiricism," in particular, and his efforts to provide any kind of deductive link (indeed, any viable link at all) between observable evidence and scientific theories. And, it would, I should think, transform his conventionalism about the acceptance of observation

I have answered Popper's replies to these kinds of objections in the footnote just designated, in the one preceding it, and, at more length, in Maxwell (1974, 1975). I have used footnotes for this, not because of any underestimation of its importance—on the contrary—but in an effort to preserve unity and simplicity of presentation. For its purpose, I shall assume that the Duhemian position, as I have outlined it here, is correct and urge the reader to study the footnotes at a convenient time. I have discussed the elementary and rather well

---

statements (already too bitter a pill for most empiricists to swallow) into a full-fledged conventionalist view of science.

I grant that these *particular* unwelcome results can always be circumvented by patching up theories by adding to them postulates of a certain kind. (They are a kind of "correspondence postulates," in Carnap's (1963) terminology.) Such postulates could quite conveniently be considered to be among the auxiliary theories and, thus, subject to the kind of "methodological rules" discussed in the preceding footnote. For example, in the thermodynamics case, we could add a postulate to the effect that all systems that have been isolated as carefully as possible for such-and-such period of time and in which measurements of temperature, pressure, etc., at various places in the system and at various times agree with each other and remain constant, and etc., etc.—that all such systems are at equilibrium. *This* particular postulate is not too bad, although we do know from contemporary thermodynamic theory that, at best, it only holds statistically. (I shall let pass, here, Popper's provisions for "making" statistical theories "falsifiable," although I think that they are as ad hoc and unsatisfactory as his other *methodological rules*.) For the astronomical example, the postulate added would be something to the effect that, whenever we have pointed our telescopes, etc. in all directions and have made all other plausible efforts to detect extraneous bodies and forces, no such bodies or forces are present. This would be a very questionable postulate or auxiliary theory (quite apart from the fact that it is, at best, a statistical one—for, almost certainly, we would sometimes fail to detect extraneous forces that are nevertheless present, no matter how assiduously we looked for them), and a methodological rule that abjures us to accept it as true for the purpose of "making" the theory of interest falsifiable would be a bad rule. For example, its adoption, at a certain stage of inquiry, would have resulted in the "falsification" of celestial mechanics and have prevented, at least for a time, the discovery of the planet Uranus. Popper could quite correctly reply that, on the contrary, it was careful attention to this "postulate" or "auxiliary theory" that *resulted*, eventually, in the discovery of Uranus. However, this shows, it seems to me, that there is only a verbal—or rather a formal—nonsubstantive difference between dealing with, e.g., extraneous forces as unobservable (perhaps in some cases, as in this one, merely unobserved-at-the-time) initial conditions, on the one hand, and incorporating them into postulates or auxiliary theories, on the other. The substantive point is that, either way, such factors amount to one more obstacle in the way of falsifying theories of interest and provide one more reason for rejecting Popper's methodological rules. Recall that the "rules" direct us to turn our fury towards the theory of interest so that it "becomes" falsifiable and, thus, to be gentle with the auxiliary theories rather than subjecting them to the same kind of severe scrutiny. Such a policy *might well* have overlooked Uranus and "falsified" celestial mechanics. (Or, if unobservables *are* accepted into initial conditions and, thus, into *basic statements*, why not accept, *by convention*, the basic statement to the effect that [the other] initial conditions obtain *and* there are no extraneous bodies or forces present, and the orbit of Neptune does not coincide with the one predicted by our theory of celestial mechanics? In which case, the same unhappy chapter in the history of science would have had to be written.)

At this point, some defenders of Popper might be tempted to abandon his "methodological rules" but to claim that, even so, the conjunction consisting of the theory of interest and the auxiliary theories, etc. (including those that incorporate what I prefer to consider unobservable initial conditions)—that this (rather enormous) conjunction *is* falsifiable by observational evidence. This is true, *provided that* neither the theory of interest nor any of the auxiliary theories are statistical ones, a condition which, I believe, will almost never hold, since those "auxiliary theories" that incorporate initial conditions will almost always be statistical ones; but let this pass, for the moment, and assume that such conjunctions *are* falsifiable. Such a "defense," however, unless something else is said (I don't know what), renders the Popperian position indistinguishable from that of the Duhemians and brings us back to exactly the same point in the text at which we had arrived when we took time out for this footnote.

known details of the logical structure of the relations among theories of interest, auxiliary theories, initial conditions, and (observational) evidence at some length here because they, together with a point to be emphasized soon, not only undermine Popper's program but also take us to the heart of the confirmation predicament.

We have already noted not only the Duhemian point, that a theory of interest can be saved in the face of any data—any evidence—whatever by means of making appropriate changes and exchanges among the auxiliary theories (and the other necessary conjuncts), but also that by using similar manipulations, the theory can actually be made to *account for* (to *explain*, to yield [together with the other conjuncts] as a deductive [or, sometimes, as a statistical] consequence) any such evidence. This is always possible, moreover, when it is required, as of course it *should* be, that the theory of interest function nonvacuously in accounting for (explaining, entailing or implying statistically) the evidence. It is also easy to show (again, indeed, to demonstrate [deductively]) that, *given any conceivable evidence in any amount whatever, there will always be an infinite number of mutually incompatible theories each of which will account for (explain, [deductively] entail* or, if statistical theories are appropriate, *statistically imply) the evidence*. And this result holds not only for "theories of interest" but also when we designate as *theories* the entire, enormous conjuncts that are required to account for (entail, etc.) the evidence. This delivers, I believe, the *coup de grace* to Popper's program, already mortally wounded by the Duhemians. For, even if falsification *were* possible, it would get us nowhere. No matter how many theories we falsified, there would always, in principle, remain an infinite number of theories that entail (would account for, etc.) the evidence at hand, only one of which is true.

However, Popper's program is no worse off (and no better off) than any of the other confirmationist (or "corroborationist") procedures that most philosophers (and, I suppose, most scientists who are at all self-conscious about their methodology) accept as articles of faith today. What we must accept is the abject impotence—total, chronic, and permanent—of evidence so long as it is paired exclusively with logic (even with Inductive Logic—whoever she may be). And since Empiricism refuses to recognize as legitimate anything other than knowledge that issues from the union of these two, she must join Hume, perhaps the first and the last consistent empiricist, and embrace total skepticism. The so-called "paradoxes of confirmation" and other popularly discussed difficulties fade into insignificance beside—indeed, they are just special cases of—these general and elementary logical considerations that, we have seen, seal the doom of empiricism.

If anyone has remained with me this far, he may very well be losing what patience he has left. For example, I can just imagine someone (in particular, I imagine Sir John Eccles!) bristling and coming up with a rejoinder such as, "Come, come now, Maxwell! I am neither intimidated by nor very much impressed with your logico-philosophical bag of tricks. As a practicing scientist I am not interested in your infinitude of logically possible, mutually incompatible competing theories. Surely most of them are so silly, contrived, implausible, and convoluted that they aren't worth considering. Anyway, in any *one* real scientific context, no one is going to think up or, at any rate, propose seriously more than one or two of them. And let us suppose, even, that someone does. We could always use our good old scientific horse sense to decide which of them are too silly to be considered. Moreover, we can use the same kind of horse sense to see when the evidence counts heavily enough against a theory for us to consider it falsified, even though it could be 'saved' by substituting complicated, far-fetched, silly, or *ad hoc* auxiliary theories, etc." Bravo! Something sort of like this *is* what happens in scientific *and* in common sense contexts. But before proceeding, let us pause to note that using "good scientific horse sense" is using something in addition to evidence plus logic and that *silliness* (or the absence thereof), *plausibility*, far-fetchedness, etc.,[6] are not logical properties. This calls attention to the central principle of epistemology, which is that if knowledge (or, even, a significant amount of true belief) is possible and if any reliable assessment or confirmation of our knowledge claims is possible, humans must possess two remarkable (extralogical) kinds of abilities.[7] They must be able to make guesses, have hunches, in other words, to *propose theories* that have a much greater chance of being true (or close to true)

---

[6] It might be thought that *ad hocness* and perhaps *simplicity* (low degree of complication or convolution) can be characterized by purely logical terms and, thus, can be used as a basis for eliminating all but one member of a family of competing theories, providing a way out of the confirmation muddle, rescuing empiricism, etc. But it is easy to show that, given any of the usual meanings of *ad hoc*, no theory (or singular hypothesis, even) is *ad hoc* unless it is *logically equivalent* to all or a portion of the evidence (see Maxwell, 1974). And I believe that I have shown (Maxwell, 1975) that *simplicity* offers no hope as far as accomplishing the hoped-for miracle is concerned.

[7] It may well be true that we have no good *reasons* to believe that knowledge, confirmation, true belief, etc., are possible, but surely it is also true that we have no good reasons for believing in their impossibility (provided we are willing to abandon *un*reasonably stringent requirements for certification of knowledge, confirmation, etc.). It is perhaps, then, moot whether it is "rational" to hope, or *believe*, or have faith that knowledge, etc., is possible. However, it seems obvious that it is not *irrational* to so hope and believe, although I have no desire to begin any debate about the words "rational" and "irrational." It even seems to me that we would be well advised to act as if knowledge, etc., *were* possible. I am not quite sure what this means, but I think that it might be explicated by means of decision-theoretic considerations. Whether or not this, if true, amounts to a "vindication" of such beliefs or modes of action, I do not know. Ironically, it is somewhat similar to one part of Reichenbach's attempted justification of induction. I say "ironically" because he had set himself what I have tried to show is the impossible task of justifying an evidence-plus-logic-alone method.

than would be the case for random selection among the possible theories, each of which is equally well supported by the evidence-plus-logic, and they must be able to make not-too-hopeless (subjective) estimates of the *prior probabilities* of those theories that *are* proposed and considered. This restates the imaginary contention of Eccles in a less elegant, less colorful but somewhat more precise manner. Since the data-plus-logic are always neutral toward a .bewildering multitude of competitors, we must use our horse sense to discover ("think up") and propose a small subset of these theories and to choose among those proposed, selecting those kinds that, we believe, turn out most often to be true.

For the purposes of this essay, the point to be emphasized that has emerged from these considerations is that scientific theories (of appreciable importance, interest, etc.) and many "philosphical" theories, *including theories about mind and brain*, are all in pretty much the same boat. Why has this not been noted, indeed, why has the contrary been so strongly maintained? Well, scientists, blissfully unaware of the finer points of logic chopping, have gone right along using their horse sense to propose theories and to (subjectively) estimate their *prior* probablities (at least they have done so tacitly or implicitly) in order to eliminate some of those proposed and to calculate (again, perhaps tacitly and implicitly) *posterior* probabilities or degrees of confirmation of those not eliminated. Philosophers and "inductive logicians," not entirely aware that scientists were doing this (or believing that they ought *not* be doing it even if they were), maintained the comfortable faith that, although Hume's problem ("of induction") remained unsolved, somewhere (maybe in Plato's Heaven) a solution existed, and that evidence-plus-logic-alone could decide among—confirm or falsify—*scientific* theories. Being more familiar, or course, with "philosophical" theories, they were aware that this did not hold for them and, thus, went on to infer that philsophy and science must be forever disjoint. Only Russell, Duhem, and a few others have noted that scientific theories (of appreciable important, etc.) are little, if any, better off.[8] Before continuing, let me admit and insist that there are extenuating circumstances. *Some* philosophical problems *are* mostly logical, conceptual, or linguistic in character,[9] and *most* philosophical problems have important, sometimes crucial, logical, and conceptual

---

[8] Quine has noted it but has drawn therefrom, I believe, some mistaken conclusions. Unlike Quine's, my refusal to draw a sharp line between science and philosophy depends in no way upon a rejection of a sharp analytic–synthetic distinction. Nor does the confirmation predicament, at least part of which Quine correctly recognizes and insists on, give any viable support to rejection of the latter distinction. For a detailed discussion, see Maxwell (1976).

[9] As are *some* chemical, psychological, physical, etc., problems. Recall, for example, what Einstein accomplished by a logico–conceptual analysis of the notion of *simultaneity*.

components (as do many scientific problems). For example, most of the negative results vis-a-vis confirmation theory upon which I have drawn so heavily herein have been obtained almost entirely by logical and mathematical means; and I believe that the "free-will" problem is mostly a linguistic and conceptual one (although I am not entirely comfortable with any of the solutions that have been proposed for it). Moreover, problems that are popularly called "philosophical" problems are, generally speaking, perhaps even a tiny bit more loosely connected with evidence than are those that are considered to be *scientific*. (What this means will be discussed presently. For a more detailed discussion, see Maxwell [1976]).

As a case study, let us now take some of the principles that we have been considering and use them to dispose of *one* mind–body theory, the kind of mentalistic monism that has been called "subjective idealism." The "case study" will be a long one, but much of the material that is developed in it will be used later when we are more substantively concerned with the mind–brain problem. For the benefit of nonphilosophers (if such persons exist), subjective idealism is the contention that nothing exists except minds and their contents, or, at any rate, that we can have knowledge of nothing else and, therefore, have no right to assume that anything else exists. For those offended by the phrase, "minds and their contents," there are many alternative ways of stating the position. We could, for example, speak of *sense experience, sense contents, items of direct (private) experience*, etc. No way of expressing the view will please everyone, and some contend that it cannot be meaningfully stated at all. We must brave their wrath and proceed. The position, in my opinion, is very similar to most varieties of phenomenalism. At any rate, most of what I shall have to say about it will also apply to phenomenalism.

The battles against this view, I believe, have been all too frequently "won" too easily. Many of the defects, for example, in Berkeley's already very clever and rather compelling exposition of it are quite easily removed. In particular, there are no insurmountable logical, linguistic, or conceptual obstacles in the way of its acceptance. (I know how heretical this sounds but hope that the reader will bear with me, for arguments' sake if for nothing else.) It is true that the view presupposes that we can meaningully talk about mental events (or their "ingredients"—items of private experience, "sense contents," feelings of joy and sorrow, etc.) This rather modest assumption is challenged today by many philosophers, who subscribe to the Wittgensteinian "argument against private languages," or to something similar to it. There is neither the space nor the patience, here, to deal with such hangovers from narrow positivist verificationism—with the epistemologistic fallacy of conflating the meaning of a statement with its "method of verification" (or confirmation). I have treated the matter (with the help of an apostate positivist—he was never a very devout one) in Feigl and Maxwell (1961) and in more detail in Maxwell (1970a). I shall only say now that the objection is completely demolished, I believe, by applications of the considerations about confirmation theory and their implications for science and philosophy that are given above. However, the argument that I shall give *against* subjective idealism is general in character and can be applied, *mutatis mutandis,* against a number of other philosophical views. For example, I should hope that anyone who still balks at "private languages," etc. and who holds that our talk is mainly (though not necessarily exclusively) about medium-sized material objects will see how the argument, whatever its defects may be, would be used against an instrumentalist view of scientific theories. (Instrumentalism is the view, crudely put, that "ordinary" material objects [or some other kind of observables] exist but *not* the unobservables [electrons, fields of force, etc.] that some [misguided noninstrumentalists] contend many scientific theories are about. What *are* they about? "Nothing," says the instrumentalist, "they are *mere* instruments, calculating devices, cognitively meaningless sounds or marks on paper or blackboards").[10] It is, at the least, meaningful I have been arguing, to claim as does the subjective idealist, that we are directly aware of (are *acquainted with,* have direct knowledge of, etc.) items in our direct (private) experience, whether they are (or are called) sensations, sense contents, feelings, thoughts, emotions, etc., that we are directly aware of (are acquainted with, directly observe, etc.) nothing else and, finally, that these items are the only *direct referents* of the descriptive (nonlogical) terms of our language. I want to claim not only that this is *meaningful,* but I should like to grant that it is *true*—for the time being and for the sake of argument, if for no more and nothing else.[11]

The subjective idealist now plays one of his two aces. "If we can only observe sense contents, items in our own minds (call then what you will), if the only properties, objects, etc. with which we are acquainted or (directly) know anything about are mental in nature, how, then, can we even form any idea or concept of other properties or

[10] For arguments against contentions such as those of Nagel (1961) and Carnap (1963) to the effect that the differences between instrumentalism and realism (or between phenomenalism and realism—*or* between subjective idealism and realism) are mere linguistic differences see, e.g., Maxwell (1970a), to say nothing of the material that has preceded and that is to follow here.

[11] It is easy enough for *me* to grant these preliminary contentions of subjective idealism because, as a matter of fact, I am firmly convinced that they are not only true but that they are extremely important, especially for the mind–body problem and that they are virtually forced upon us by contemporary physics, physiology, psychophysiology, etc. But more of this later.

entities of any sort? Obviously we cannot," he continues, "and if we cannot form any concept of nonmental items, certainly we cannot talk about them, we cannot refer to them directly *or* indirectly and, *a fortiori*, we cannot have any knowledge (direct *or* indirect) of them or any right to suppose that they exist." A great many contemporary philosophers, including myself, have considerable respect for this argument, but few of us accept its conclusion. Most of these philosophers, apparently, feel that the inference is valid or, rather, could easily be made so by supplying relatively unproblematic missing premises. Believing that the conclusion is absurd, they take the argument to provide a kind of *reductio* proof of the falsity of the premises. I contend that the argument is invalid and remains so after addition of any reasonable missing premises, so that it is perfectly consistent to reject the conclusion and maintain the premises. In so doing, however, I agree that I am obliged to explain how we can have a right to believe in the existence of unobservable properties and other entities and how we can "talk about them" or refer to them (indirectly). But it will be convenient to wait until the subjective idealist has played his other ace. "Suppose that, *per impossibile*, we *could* form meaningful concepts of mind-independent entities, talk about them—refer to them indirectly, whatever this may mean. Even so, " continues the attack, "there would not be the slightest reason to believe that they existed. There would not be—could not be— any evidence from which we could reasonably infer any thing about the nature of such entities or, again, even that they exist." Many seem to be even more impressed by this argument than by the former one. However, it is grossly defective and is plausible only when an extremely naive view of confirmation is held, the view that the only legitimate modes of nondeductive inference are simple inductive ones. Hypothetico–deductive (or, better, hypothetico–inferential) explanations of events of which we are directly aware by assumptions (theories) about mind-independent entities provide excellent confirmation of such assumptions provided the prior probabilities of the assumptions and of the (directly experienced) evidence fall within certain (very wide) intervals. Let us return, then, to the first argument.

Long ago, Bertrand Russell (see, e.g., Russell, 1905 and 1912) explicated the important distinction between *knowledge by acquaintance* and *knowledge by description* and explained, with his theory of description (definite *and* indefinite), how it is that we are able to refer, *indirectly* to (or to *denote*) entities with which we are not acquainted. When we say, "The author of *Waverly* was knowledgeable" ("$(\exists x)(Wxw.(y)(Wyw \equiv x = y). Kx)$"), then, provided one and only one person did write *Waverly*, we have managed to denote that person or to refer (indirectly) to him (or her), in one perfectly good sense of "refer" and, moreover, to say something about the author, even though we have not observed him, are not acquainted with him, and may not have any idea as to *who* he was (or is). This indirect reference is accomplished by using an existentially quantified (individual) variable[12] and words whose *direct* referents *are* items (things, properties, etc.) with which we are aquainted.

In what amounts to a development of Russell's theory[13] Frank Ramsey (1931) provided the formal apparatus for clarifying our indirect reference to unobserved and unobservable *properties, sets,* etc. The details need not concern us here. They are similar to those of Russell's method for referring indirectly to individuals; in the "Ramsey sentence," existenially quantified *predicate* variables (or other variables of higher logical type) are used to refer indirectly to properties, sets, sets of sets, etc. (The resulting descriptions are always indefinite ones.)

Applying these results to the subjective idealist's first argument, we see that we have the means for talking about, referring (indirectly) to, expressing (possible) knowledge about, etc., items with which we are not acquainted, which are unobserved and, even, unobservable, whatever one may take such unobservables to be. For the subjective idealist, everything is unobservable except sense contents and other mental entities. However, Russell's theory of descriptions, in general, and Ramsey sentences, in particular, make it clear that there is no difficulty at all in talking about, hypothesizing, and theorizing about entities, which, for the subjective idealist as well as for others, are unobservables. Whether or not this enables us to form *concepts* of mind-independent entities is, perhaps, moot. What *is a concept*? It is true that, in our new language that we have *reformed* to accommodate the subjective idealist and the rest of us who hold that only sense contents, emotions, etc. are observable, there are no descriptive terms that refer directly to mind-independent objects. This however, is no obstacle to our saying all that we need to say about them (using indirect reference) nor to our *knowing* a great deal about them—by confirming and disconfirming hypothetico-inferentially our theories and hypotheses about them, as explained above.

What I have done so far is to defend the subjective idealist's claim that there are no logical, linguistic, or conceptual barriers that prevent his position from being meaningfully asserted. Then, I count-

[12] In English, words like "some," "something," and other "logical" words perform the function of such variables.

[13] That Ramsey's device is an extension of Russell's theory of descriptions does not seem to have been generally recognized.

ered his claim that *only* his position can be asserted, showing how, even when one grants (as I *do*) that the only observables are mental entities, there are no logical, conceptual, or linguistic barriers to talking about and having knowledge about mind-independent entities. So far, our work on this issue *has* been purely logical, linguistic, and conceptual. The subjective idealist has failed to *establish* his position by logical, linguistic, and conceptual means, but, we have seen, his position cannot be *refuted* by such means either.

This, in my opinion, is entirely as it should be. Subjective idealism is a *contingent* theory, true in some possible worlds and false in others (which include the actual world, I believe). To evaluate it and its alternatives we must go beyond the realm of the logical, the conceptual, and the linguistic and consider the evidence and other factors necessary for confirmation or disconfirmation. The evidence, of course, is the whole of our experience—our sense experience, our experienced emotions, thoughts, etc., etc., including any regularities, irregularites, anomalies, etc. in it that we remember or have recorded (or that we *think* we remember or *think* that we have recorded).

Let us suppose, first, that the worst possible situation exists— the situation in which confirmation or disconfirmation would be the most difficult. Let us suppose that subjective idealism and whatever alternative to it we are considering—some kind of realism—account for the evidence (*explain* our experience) equally well. Even in such a case, I claim that, given the evidence, *realism would be much better confirmed than subjective idealism.* For, we have seen above that one indispensable factor in the calculation of degree of confirmation is our estimate[14] of the prior probability of the theory of interest. I would estimate the prior probability of realism to be *much* higher than that of subjective idealism. Are the readers appalled that, in such a case, I would stake my defense of realism and my rejection of subjective idealism on a pure guess, a (subjective) hunch about prior probabilities? Dear friends, as I have asked elsewhere (Maxwell, 1976), what is the alternative? We have to do pretty much the same thing,[15] as was already so clear to Hume, when we "bet" that our next mouthful of bread will nourish rather than poison us.

The actual situation is not quite as bad, although it will,

---

[14] Although we must depend on our *subjective* estimates of prior probabilities, the prior probabilities themselves (as well as the posterior ones) are objectively existing relative frequencies. (Roughly, they are the relative frequency with which theories that *resemble* the theory of interest in certain relevant respects are true or close to the truth. For details see Maxwell [1975, 1976]).

[15] Not exactly, it is true. Remember, however, that both hypotheses *can* be "made" to account for all of the evidence and, crucially, that we have to make a guess about the prior probabilities before we can say that the "nourish" hypothesis is the better confirmed.

doubtless, leave many just as unhappy. The auxiliary theories that are needed in order for subjective idealism to account for all of the evidence (our experience) are different from those that are required in order for realism to do so. In computing the degree of confirmation or the posterior probability of a theory on the basis of the evidence at hand, there are a number of equivalent ways to handle the prior probabilities (prior to the evidence in question) of the auxiliary theories. For our purposes, it will be convenient to consider, first, the posterior *and* the prior probabilities of the entire conjunction (of the theory of interest, the auxiliary theories and other "background knowledge"). Now I maintain that the auxiliary theories, etc., that must be conjoined with subjective idealism in order that the evidence be accounted for are much more convoluted, complicated, contrived, etc. and, therefore, are much more *implausible* than those that are required in order that realism do so. We should, then, estimate their prior probability to be much lower and, thus, that the prior probability of the entire conjunction in the case of subjective idealism to be much lower than for the case for realism. Since the evidence is the same for both cases, the degree of confirmation or the posterior probability of the conjunction containing subjective idealism will be much less than that for the one containing realism. It is true that it does not follow, deductively, from this that the degree of confirmation for subjective idealism is less than that for realism. What does follow is that in order for subjective idealism to account for the evidence, that is, *in order for the evidence to be relevant, to give any support at all to subjective idealism, we must assume that theories with extremely low probabilities are true, while this is not the case for realism.* We are, thus, entitled to conclude that the evidence gives very little support to subjective idealism but, given our estimates of the relevant prior probabilities, that it gives strong support to realism.[16] We should, therefore, conclude that, on the basis of the evidence, subjective idealism is, in all probability, (contingently!) false and that (some variety of) realism is (contingently) true.

Fortunately, now that these lengthy, general considerations are completed, we can make short shrift of the mind–body problem. It

[16] I cannot take the space, in an article already becoming too long, to go into details about what these various auxiliary hypotheses might be or why I consider the ones necessary for subjective idealism so much less plausible than those for realism. To mention only one, subjective idealism must either account for our ability to communicate with "other minds" or go on to embrace what many claim is its "logical conclusion," solipsism. I would certainly estimate the prior probability of the latter position to be very low, and any auxiliary (nonrealist) hypothesis that I can imagine that would account for the communication with other minds seems fantastic and unlikely indeed.

is not the purpose of *this* essay to *solve* it but, rather, to argue for the crucial relevance for it of experimental and theoretical scientific results. It is true that in doing I shall indicate what I think its "solution" to be, but I shall reserve for another occasion detailed arguments in its favor.

There are a number of obvious but often forgotten ways in which scientific or, even, common-sense knowledge (actual and/or conceivable) can have important implications for the mind–body problem. For example, Aristotle, with his usual scientific acumen[17] announced, so I am told, that the function of the brain was to cool the blood, the seat of the soul being, I suppose, in the heart. If this were true, we would have a mind–heart or soul–heart problem but no mind–brain one.

More seriously, there can be no doubt that contemporary developments in neurophysiology and psychophysiology, rudimentary as they may be, count heavily against a radical interactionist dualism. (By "radical interactionist dualism," I refer to the contention that *some* mental processes are radically autonomous, being neither [directly] caused by nor regularly correlated with [or "paralleled by"] brain processess.) On the other hand, if the evidence were very different from what it is, if, for example, there were evidence of the existence of disembodied minds, evidence that people really can "leave their bodies" as some do claim to do, or evidence of survival after the destruction of the body, etc.—if there were evidence of this kind, it would be reasonable to conclude that radical interactionism is true. Of course, it would *not* thereby be proved, nor would alternatives such as, even, materialistic monism be falsified. However, the auxiliary theories that would be necessary to "save" materialism in the face of such evidence would be so bizarre as to be given a prior probability near zero. The evidence being what it actually is, the prior probabilities of the auxiliary theories that would have to be assumed to save radical interactionism should be estimated to be very low.

Recalling that we have already, on a scientific or, at any rate, a contingent basis, disposed of radical mentalistic monism (subjective idealism[18]), we see that the viable alternatives that seem to remain are (nonidealist) mind–body (mind–brain) monism, psychophysical paral-

---

[17] Other examples: Women have fewer teeth than men, and elephants can be cured of insommia by rubbing salt into their hides (see Russell, 1946). He also revived the naive realist view of perception and knowledge of the world, a view that had already been demolished by the pre-Socratics, especially by Democritus and the other early atomists (see, e.g., Anderson, 1974).

[18] I am not competent to deal with *absolute* or *objective* idealism. However, from what I am told, I would guess that its prior probability is low.

lelism, epiphenomenalism, and a view, let us call it, "*mild* interaction-ism."[19]

Many philosophers contend that there is no "difference that makes a difference" among the last three (dualist) positions. I have a considerable amount of sympathy with their contention, especially in view of the unsatisfactory state of our knowledge about the nature of causation. Nevertheless, I believe that the contention is wrong. It is true that the three positions (as well as mind–body monism) can all be made to account for all actual and possible evidence, assuming that they are logically, linguistically, and conceptually acceptable. But as we know, *ad nauseum*, by now, this is very unexciting and by no means entails the no-difference-that-makes-a-difference contention.

Both parallelism and epiphenomenalism are extremely im-plausible intuitively. This, of course, does not *entail* that their prior probability is low, but, often, even in science *and* in everyday life we have to base our (sometimes vital and crucial) estimates of prior proba-bilities and, thus, our eventual selection or rejection of theories or hypotheses on nothing more than intuitive plausibility. In cases where there is more to go on, well and good! But all that we can do, in a given case, is the best that we can. These two positions are implausible, apart from the feeling of mystery engendered by dualism, in general, and the *preestablished harmony* required by parallelism, in particular, because of the strange network of causal relations that they involve. Whatever the meaning of "cause" may be, it seems as certain as anything is certain that, if there *is* any such thing as causation, then my getting pricked by the pin *caused* an intense feeling of pain, which, in turn, caused a quick flash of anger. My guess is that the prior probability of this is so high that I must assign to parallelism, which it contradicts, a very low one. And it seems equally certain that the pain and the anger *caused* me to slap away at the arm of the person who pricked me. This, in turn, causes me to estimate a very low prior probability for epiphenomenal-ism. (Also, as Smart [1963] and others have noted, there does not seem to be anywhere else in the universe the kind of total causal impotence that epiphenomenalism requires mental events to be possessed of. It

---

[19] *Mind–body monism* is the denial that "the mental" and "the physical" are drastically different from each other. The following three positions deny this denial. According to *parallelism* each kind of mental event (or mental state, etc.) is invariably accompanied by its own peculiar kind of physical correlate, but there is no causal interaction in either direction between the mental entity and its parallel physical event (or state, etc.). *Epiphenomenalism* (not to be confused with the unrelated (perceptual–epistemological) theory called "phenomenalism") assumes that the same kind of corre-lation exists but that the physical events *cause* the mental ones *and* that the mental events, however, have no causal efficacy at all. *Mild* interactionism, assuming the same kind of correlation, holds that there is causation in both direction. These crude characterizations are sufficient for our purposes here. They may be ignored by professional philosophers.

seems unlikely [contingently unlikely, *I* would add] that such "nomological danglers" exist.[20])

Mild interactionism, although *prima facie* more plausible, is also beset with causal anomalies. There are danglers of a sort here, too. For many mental events would have *two* causes, and not in the usual innocuous senses of there being a (large) number of serial events in the same causal chain *or* of there being two or more necessary events in the *set* of events that is sufficient to produce the effect. It is rather a queer kind of "overdetermination." Each cause, the mental one and physical one, it appears intuitively, is *sufficient*, quite independently of the "other" cause, to produce the effect. For example, the feeling of pain alone seems sufficient to produce the brain state or event that initiated the efferent neural impulse that was responsible for my slapping the hand, as does *also* the brain state or event that neurophysiology assures us preceded *it* and, indeed, caused it (also?). Our reflections lend, for example, considerable plausibility to the contention of parallelism that the physical realm is *causally closed*. All of this produces the inclination to estimate a quite low prior probability for mild interactionism.

The only possibility that remains seems to be some kind of mind–brain monism, and, since we have rejected radical mentalism, we seem to be left with some variety of mind–brain identity. But, as we shall see in a moment, this seems, *prima facie,* not only implausible and improbable but downright absurd; indeed, when a few facts that seem trivially obvious are taken into account, it seems logically or, at best, conceptually absurd. If mental events really are just brain events—just physical events—then *all* events are physical events. Is this not just plain old materialism[21]—nothing more? Materialism denies the existence of *bona fide* mental events (states, etc.) altogether or, at best, tries somehow to sweep them under the rug (by holding, for example, that mental entities are not at all like what we think they are—indeed not even like what we *think* that we directly experience them to be—that when we *do* come to understand what they *really* are like, we shall see that indeed they are *nothing but* neurons firing, electrons jumping from one energy level to another, etc.).

It is difficult to know how to give *arguments* against material-

---

[20] Unlikely that nomological danglers exist, *not* unlikely that mental events exist, even though Smart and other materialists *do* seem to want to infer *something* like the nonexistence of the latter from the nonexistence of the former. Nonmaterialists, such as Feigl (1960), infer, correctly I believe, simply that mental events are not nomological danglers.

[21] Sometimes nonphilosophers take materialism to be simply either parallelism or epiphenomenalism. (See, e.g., Gunderson [1970].) This is reasonable because these positions make mental entities second class citizens, or lower. However, they do acknowledge the (full-fledged) existence of the mental, and they are not usually classified as materialisms by professional philosophers.

ism, just as it would be difficult to give arguments against someone who maintains that I am feeling no pain and that my flesh is not being seared while my bare foot is being held firmly against red hot coals. I can only protest that I am more certain of the existence of my sense experience and emotions, and I am more certain about their nature, as I live through all of their qualitative richness than I am of anything else, including the most "firmly established" scientific principles, to say nothing of any philosophical view. I, therefore, estimate the prior probability of materialism to be very near zero. Again, admittedly, this is not much of an argument and is, perhaps, not a very exemplary attitude. But let us recall once more that in science and in everyday life, we often have to make crucial decisions on the basis of prior probabilities that have been estimated on just such bases. Moreover, I do not believe that there are any viable arguments for abandoning *these particular* beliefs about our experience so intuitively congenial and so strongly held. However, somewhat ironically, I shall argue presently that some of our beliefs that are almost as intuitively certain as these must be abandoned in the face of contemporary scientific findings. However, these will, in fact, turn out to be the beliefs that start the materialist on the wrong track. The rejection of them will make clear why I contended above that there is no scientific sanction for abandoning the beliefs that the materialist wants us to give up.

We have rejected both (radical) mentalism and materialism. Does this leave hope for *any* kind of monism and for a mind–brain identity theory, in particular? It might seem that we are worse off than ever. We have seen that we know intimately and quite fully what our experience and the items in it are like. And, we common-sensically believe, we also know almost as intimately and in considerable detail what physical objects, events, etc. are like, whether they be tables, chairs or brains that we can see (that we *believe* that we can see) or whether they be neuron firings, electrons that go from one energy level to another, etc. We know, then, what *the mental* is like and what *the physical* is like, and is it not obvious that they cannot be identical? As I once heard Benson Mates remark, it makes about as much sense to identify a mental state with a brain state as it does to identify a billy goat with a quadratic equation. And, indeed, given these obvious "facts" that we know about the mental and the physical, it isn't just that we estimate the probability of their identity to be near zero, but there seem to be genuine conceptual obstacles to identifying them with each other. Here is another point at which scientific results come to our rescue. They imply that we must surrender some of the beliefs so dear to materialists and, evidently, to just about everybody else. (These beliefs *are* so deeply embedded in common sense that they usually operate only at the tacit, implicit, or, perhaps, unconscious level.) It turns out, however, that, when we do accept the necessity of abandoning them, the materialist has the matter entirely reversed. It is not our concepts or, better put, our *beliefs* about the nature of the *mental* that must be radically altered but, rather, our notions about the nature of the *physical* that must be drastically revised.

Before proceeding, let us recall that we defended the conceptual legitimacy (the "meaningfulness") of the subjective idealist's contention that everything of which one is directly aware is an ingredient of (or occurs in, or is a content of, etc.) his own private experience. Although we expressed sympathy, we left open the question as to whether or not the claim is true. I now want to argue briefly that it *is* true. However, I do not believe that its truth can be established by purely logical, linguistic, or conceptual means, nor by appeals to "epistemological primacy," and certainly not by the (alleged) certainty, incorrigibility, etc., of judgments about one's own experience. The crucial argument is, again, from science. Physics, physiology, and psychophysiology virtually force us to conclude that, for example, a blue patch of color of which we are visually aware is exemplified in and only in our minds (or in our brains—to leave *this* issue open for the time being). (Considerations from these sciences also corroborate what should be pretty obvious already—that each one's experience is indeed private unto oneself.) It is, of course, very fashionable today to maintain the philosophical irrelevance of "the causal theory of perception." But this is just one more instance of the general prejudice that scientific results are irrelevant for philosophical issues. (For a detailed discussion of the relevance of the "causal theory of perception," see Russell [1948] and Maxwell [e.g., 1972].)

The conclusion reached above about the blue patch of color holds for all of the sensory qualities. Admittedly scientific theory does not *prove* (deductively) that these properties are exemplified only in our experience and that, for example, the table top that we think we perceive to be brown is not brown because it is not colored—color exists only in our private experience. What it does show is that we have no good reason for supposing that it is brown. For, a complete physical, neurophysiological, and psychophysiological account of everything that happens when I do what we commonsensically (and, strictly speaking, somewhat mistakenly) call "looking at a brown tabletop"— such an account would not mention anything brown[22] until the psycho-

---

[22] In the usual, primary sense of "brown"—*brownness* as we are directly aware of it in visual experience.

physiologist mentioned the visual *experience* of brownness. Again, this does not *prove* that table tops, in particular, and, indeed, "mind-independent, external" objects, in general, are *not* brown, but it does make the assumption that they *are* brown as gratuitous and unwarranted as the assumption that there are now exactly 5481 imperceptible demons dancing on this page.

If, then, naive realism is to be rejected—if physical objects are not at all like we have believed them to be—believed, indeed, that we *perceived* them to be, what *are* they like? How do we know that they exist? How can we formulate and confirm or disconfirm knowledge claims about them? Here, the material developed in our "case study" above again stands us in good stead. Insofar as we know anything about physical objects (and we have reason to believe that we know a great deal), they are like what our well-confirmed theories (reformulated so that all of their "observational terms" refer to items of our [private] experience) say that they are. If we want to be strictly correct—for most purposes we do not need to be—the theories are formulated as Ramsey sentences. This kind of indirect reference to the entities, the properties, individuals, sets, sets of sets, etc. of the mind-independent, "external," or *physical* (in *one* sense of the term) realm makes explicit our ignorance about *what* these properties, etc. *are*. What is expressed is our knowledge *that* they are (they exist) and our knowledge about their higher type (higher *logical* type) properties, relations, etc.—in other words about what Russell terms their *structural* properties. (The lower type properties of the physical realm are what he calls *intrinsic* properties, and our ignorance as to *what* these *are* is indicated by our referring to them only by description—by indirect reference, as described in our "case study.")

I have discussed all of this in detail elsewhere (e.g., Maxwell, 1970*a*, 1970*b*, 1972), giving arguments where appropriate, etc. Here, I am concerned mainly to reemphasize that *it is mainly science* rather than the traditional philosophical arguments *that makes the rejection of naive realism*[23] *mandatory* and to go on to use this result in our "solution" of the mind–brain problem (with which we have almost finished).

Since physical objects, states, and events are not at all like we common-sensically believe them to be, or, at any rate, we have no good reasons for believing that they are, since our best scientific results—up to *this* point—provide knowledge only about their structural properties and leave entirely open the question as to what are their *type-one*, or *intrinsic* properties, then, *the possibility is entirely open that some of these*

---

[23] The realism that we accept is similar to though not identical with so-called *representative realism*. Our "case study" above showed that the usual arguments against representative realism are grossly unsound.

properties just are the ones that are exemplified in the events that constitute our own private experience. If this is true, then *mental events are* indeed *one kind*—perhaps a rather special kind—*of physical events.*

Let us pause to reflect on the important step that we have just taken. Science urged upon us the rejection of naive realism (as well as the acceptance of an alternative kind of realism). We see, then, that we are not directly aware of mind-independent ("physical") entities; we do not really observe them. They provide (crucially important) links in the causal chains that produce our perceptive experiences, and something (structurally) similar to our common sense perceptual "knowledge" can be *rescued* (and confirmed) by reformulating it as (theoretical and/or hypothetical) *knowledge by description* (using Ramsey sentences or other, equivalent devices). "Biting the bullet" and admitting that we do not observe ("external") physical objects and, thus, do not have observational knowledge of what their intrinsic properties are and, moreover, that those intrinsic properties that we mistakenly attributed to them are, in all probability, exemplified only in our ("internal") private experience—all of this removes completely, in the manner explained above, the enormous intuitive and conceptual obstacles to identifying *the mental* with (a portion of) *the physical*. It emerges from this that scientific results not only often have crucial implications for those (numerous) philosophical propositions that are *contingent* in nature but, also, they can rescue us from seemingly hopeless *conceptual* quagmires such as the one that detained us after we have rejected, above, subjective idealism, parallelism, etc. Therefore, even those who (mistakenly!) hold that all philosophical problems are conceptual, linguistic, or logical in nature, cannot validly infer from this that scientific (or other contingent) knowledge is irrelevant for philosophical issues. (For a general [non-Quinian] discussion of how contingent knowledge can have a [usually indirect] bearing on "purely" conceptual or linguistic matters, see Maxwell [1961].)

It is true that giving up our common sense beliefs about perception, the nature of physical objects, etc., is a pill that goes down hard and certainly not a step to be taken lightly or hastily. It might seem, using the jargon that we have developed, that the prior probability of these beliefs is so high that they should stand in the face of any evidence whatever. However, as Russell (1959) noted, we are faced with a painful choice, a choice, moreover, that cannot be avoided by pleading the "philosophical" irrelevance of "the causal theory of perception." We are faced with the choice no matter what the nature of philosophy may be; whether one chooses to call it a "philosophical choice" or not, it will not go away. Russell's choice concerns the kind of considerations given above about the situation that we commonly call, "looking at a brown tabletop." We must choose between admitting (1) We do not see a tabletop, (2) We do not see anything brown (i.e., we do not have brownness exemplified in our visual experience[24]), or (3) physics, neurophysiology, and pychophysiology are grossly false. We have chosen (1), but, as Russell points out (in different words), choosing either (2) or (3) would have resulted in even more violence to the evidence and to our intuitions and would have involved rejecting beliefs for which we should estimate even higher prior probabilities than we do for those that we must abandon as a result of choosing (1). It could be pointed out that we did not consider a fourth alternative. We could have chosen to interpret physics, neurophysiology, etc., instrumentalistically—in which case the theories of these sciences would be neither true nor false and therefore not true. I am not sure, however, that this would free us from choosing among the first three alternatives. For these theories, although they had become mere calculating devices, would still yield

---

[24] Quite a few philosophers assure me, in all apparent seriousness, that they do not know what this means (meaning, of course, that they deny that it *has* any meaning). Philosophy, being the study of basic, often implicit and unconscious, beliefs, *should* be full of surprises including *prima facie* absurd avowals. We should, therefore, in general, learn to be tolerant and at least go through the motions of having an open mind (as Herbert Feigl says) in the face of such strange denials. I must admit, however, that I am tempted to reply to this particular instance of know-nothingism with: "You know perfectly well what I mean." Such a denial may (or may not) be based partially on something like Ryle's (1954) ruminations about "success words," according to which the word "see" is used appropriately only when we have successfully *seen* an external, mind-independent object. (Rylians will, no doubt, also object to the use of the last three or four words in the preceding sentence. However, I cannot remember exactly how he put it, and it is impossible for me to obtain a copy of his work at present.) If Ryle were correct, this would seem to make my use of the phrase, "brownness exemplified in . . . visual experience" as an alternative to "see anything brown" even more admissible instead of rendering it naughty. But, I am told, the meaninglessness of my expression is also partly due to inappropriate (nonordinary) use of the word "experience" (or, perhaps, also of "visual," "exemplified," "brownness," etc.). This illustrates, in my opinion, a very common fault of ordinary-language philosophy. It refuses to recognize (and at times seems to be *based* on such a refusal) the myriad of (very useful and desirable) ambiguities and vaguenesses that make "ordinary language" such a flexible and expressive instrument. *Contra* this school of philosophy and other old-time positivists, we can use it to say almost anything we want to say, including things philosophical.

Let us suppose that words like "see" *are* most commonly used in "success" situations of the kind *required* by Ryle. But they can also be used in different (though related) ways even, I should say, while retaining virtually the same meaning (*intension*)—or, if the meaning does change, a large amount of "core meaning" remains common to the different uses. For example, we talk of "seeing in our mind's eye," or when remembering a *vivid visual* experience (!) (forgive me! How else should I put it?), we say, "I can just see it (him, her) now!" And surely we, quite properly, speak of *seeing* things in dreams (or should we speak rather, of *visual experiences*?) There is just no good reason that we cannot see something (or have a visual experience of something) that is not an ordinary material object. In a still more different though still closely related use of "see," we can, with perfect propriety, speak, as Russell (1948) does, of *seeing our own brains* (every time we have a visual experience).

Finally, we must recall that we actually never succeed in seeing a mind-independent, physical object, although we usually mistakenly think that we do. If this allegedly basic use of "see" were the only legitimate one, then we would never *see* anything. (This is consistent with the (attempted) "success" use being the basic or, even, the first-learned use [or attempted use]. We can learn from false beliefs [and unsuccessful though *apparently* successful attempts] provided that they are not too hopelessly off the mark. How this might be done, I have discussed in Maxwell [1970a].)

the same observation statements one of which, we have argued, is something like, "If mind-independent objects *are* observable, then they are *not* observable," which entails, of course, that mind-independent objects are not observable. (See Maxwell [1960] for the details of a similar argument as well as for general arguments against instrumentalism.) This argument depends, however, on whether or not statements like, "So-and-so's are observable" are, themselves, observation statements, so I shall not press it here. The main thing is that instrumentalism seems completely unacceptable. We saw in the "case study" above that there are no viable logical, linguistic, or conceptual obstacles to realism, and it seems undeniable that the preponderance of the evidence, when reasonable estimates of the requisite prior probabilities are used, is overwhelmingly in favor of realism (vis-a-vis scientific theories as well as elsewhere).

Let us return to the point at which we had rejected naive realism in favor of an ontology and epistemology that acknowledge our ignorance of the intrinsic properties of physical entities but recognize and avow their existence, as well as the legitimacy of our knowledge claims about their structural properties. To best utilize this result for the mind–brain problem we need to replace (common sense) *substance* metaphysics with an *event ontology* (in the manner of Russell [1927, 1948] and Whitehead, e.g. [1925]). *An event* is, roughly speaking, the instancing or the exemplification of a property, for example the occurrence of a blue expanse in the visual field or a twinge of pain (not to be taken to imply that all events are necessarily experiential). Substance ontology is objectionable on conceptual—perhaps logical—grounds (e.g., the absurdity of "bare" [propertyless] particulars). On the scientific side, contemporary physics is best formulated, in my opinion (again following Russell [1927, 1948]), using an event ontology. In such an ontology, *things* or *objects*, etc., are replaced by families of events, families of families of events, etc., causally related to each other in certain intimate ways.

The brain (perhaps it would be better, strictly speaking, to abandon the word "brain" with its naive–realist and substance–metaphysics connotations and say something like, "the entity that takes the place of the brain"), according to our event ontology, is a huge family of families of families, etc., of events. We now rephrase our earlier statement of mind–brain identity by saying that, in view of the considerations cited above, the possibility is entirely open that some of the events that *are among the constituents of the brain are mental events,* our sense experiences, our feelings of joy, our thoughts about Nirvana (as we live through them and know them in all of their qualitative richness).

At this stage, there are no reasons for not giving free range to our strong intuitions that mental events are both causally efficacious (vis-a-vis other mental events and [other!] physical events) and susceptible to (causal) production by (other!) physical events. Now if we follow Russell (1927, 1948), as I believe that physics and, perhaps, neurophysiology and psychophysiology will eventually indicate we should, and regard (physical) space–time as a construction out of the causal relations among events, we can say that mental events are just as much in time *and in space* as are other (!) physical events—since they are, we hold, just as much in the causal network. We see, then, that replacing our old notions about *the physical*, including (physical) space, with scientifically more adequate ones removes any conceptual obstacles to saying that mental events are in space. In fact, I am confident that it removes virtually all of the stock objections to a genuine mind–brain identity theory. All mental events are physical and some physical events are mental. As Russell (1959) notes, there is no more difficulty about saying that a given event can be both mental and physical[25] than there is in saying that a given man can be both a baker and a father.

The last point makes it evident that this identity theory is *not* a variety of materialism. Mental entities remain entirely mental and none the less so for being physical as well. It can be called, quite fairly, a kind of "physicalism." All events are physical and none the less so just because some of them are mental. Therefore any laws expressing regularities among them can be called, quite fairly, physical laws; whether some of the laws involving brain events are quite similar to or quite different from other physical laws is, of course, an open question. Certainly it is a kind of "identity theory;" mental events are identified with (though not replaced by) physical events. Whether or not it is a monistic theory is, perhaps, moot; Russell says that we should remain agnostic as to whether the events in the rest of the world are (intrinsically) similar to or very different from that subset of brain events that constitute the mental. If they are radically different, then a *kind* of dualism, but *not* a mind–brain dualism, remains; while if they differ only in degree (assuming this means much of anything) a kind of monism—a much watered-down panpsychism—would seem to be true. Fortunately, this is not an issue that has to be settled in this paper.

We must note here that Russell's construction of (physical) space–time out of the causal relations among events was sketchy and programatic and left important problems unsolved. Once someone

---

[25] This is *not*, however, *neutral monism*. Although Russell never explicitly disavowed the term, it definitely does not appropriately signify, in any of its usual (phenomenalistic) senses, his later views on mind and body.

completes it or a similar program, a number of difficulties, among them the "grain" problem (see, e.g., Sellars [1965] and Meehl [1966]) will, I believe, disappear. The "grain" objection, put very crudely, asks, "How can a 'mental' event such as the exemplification of a color patch in the visual field, which is smooth, continuous, and nongappy, be identical with a physical state or event, which, according to physics, has a gappy, discontinuous structure (an array of elementary particles, or of quantum transitions, or of singularities in a field, etc.)?" Well, in Russell's construction, a point in physical space–time is a family of events, and, while of course a point, by definition, is not extended, the events that are its members can be extended (*and* continuous) in space–time in two respects. An event, or rather its "ingredients" such as a color patch can be extended in *visual* space(–time), and an event can also be extended in physical space–time in that it can be a *member* of more than one point. It might be thought that this can't help much; for would it not be implausible to *over*extend an event, *a member of a point*, to cover a large region of the brain; and is it not likely that in, e.g., seeing a colored expanse, a large region of the brain is involved? I believe that part of this difficulty results from picturing "a large region of the brain," etc., in terms of common-sense space, which is a mixture of "phenomenal" space and physical space and which we have *replaced* with a network of causal relations among events. Whether this is true or not, I do not believe that this objection can be evaluated properly without proposing and analyzing in detail a number of possible brain models for perceiving, sensing, etc. In a holographic model, for example (see, e.g., Pribram, 1971), a relatively large region of the brain could be involved and yet each of a large number of very small regions within it would provide for (contain events that would be identical with—how *should* one express it?) sensing a patch of color. This is crude, merely suggestive, and, no doubt, would have to rejected or drastically modified if it were developed in detail. However, I do not believe that we should be discouraged by the "grain" argument until we have proposed and examined a large number of psychophysiological theories.

In this paper I have tried to show that scientific results have great relevance for the mind–body problem and, indeed, that a scientific approach to the problem seems to offer the most promising results. This is mainly because, as I have argued at length, there is at most a difference in degree and not a difference in kind between scientific problems and philosophical ones. The mind–body problem is very near the middle of the continuum; in fact I believe that it is nearer the scientific end (if we want to insist on retaining such a distinction even though there isn't too much point to doing so—save for academico-administrative convenience—but as Quine astutely reminds us: The universe is not the University).

We have seen that the "scientific" procedure of weighing the (observational) evidence—with proper use of the requisite prior probabilities—is appropriate and vital for a considerable portion of philosophical problems, in general, and for the mind–body problem, in particular. Another often unnoticed but crucially important way in which science has implications for philosophy is from the *theoretical* direction. Theory (admirably well confirmed) leads us to abandon naive realism. This in turn, we saw, enables us to formulate a viable mind–body identity theory. Theory also indicates, I claimed, that we should adopt an event ontology and then proceed to base our theory of (physical) space–time on the network of causal relations among events. This also greatly facilitates the development of and lends added credence to our mind–body view. We also indicated how neurological and psychophysiological theories coupled with this space–time theory might point the way to a solution of the "grain" problem. Finally, we saw how scientific developments can even point towards ways of solving "purely conceptual" components of a problem. Theory, in refuting naive realism, removed conceptual obstacles to an identity theory as does also the space–time theory just mentioned.

BIBLIOGRAPHICAL ADDENDUM

In presenting the mind–body theory sketched and defended here, I have referred most often to the work of (the later) Bertrand Russell. I have studied his work on the subject more recently and have it more at my fingertips than material from other sources. Moreover, I believe that his is the most nearly complete theory (although, admittedly, one must piece it together from various parts of his writings). Especially vital to the mind–brain issue is his event ontology and his views about space and time. However, several important thinkers have arrived, each more or less independently of the others, at positions very similar to Russell's. First of all, there is the justly renowned work of Herbert Feigl (e.g., 1960, 1971, 1975), to whom I am indebted in this and a number of other areas even more than to Russell. Unfortunately, many who are superficially acquainted with his mind–body views classify him as a more or less old-fashioned materialist. This is entirely mistaken. In fact, I can bring this addendum to a speedy completion by referring to his recent account of the independent development of the mind–body positions of Russell and of Moritz Schlick (Feigl, 1975). Not only does Feigl include a fascinating comparison of the views of these two philosophers, but he mentions a number of others who developed and defended similar views. Among them are Kant, Durant Drake, Roy Wood Sellars and other American "Critical Realists," and the late Stephen Pepper.[26]

ACKNOWLEDGMENTS

Support of research by the National Science Foundation is gratefully acknowledged.

REFERENCES

Anderson, R. M., Jr. (1974): *Externality and the Frontal Lobes: An Experienced Interplay between Philosophy and Science.* Unpublished manuscript.

Carnap, R. (1963): Replies. In: *The Philosophy of Rudolf Carnap.* Ed. by P. A. Schilpp LaSalle (Ill.): Open Court, p. 868.

Feigl, H. (1960): The Mental and the physical. In: *Minnesota Studies in the Philosophy of Science Vol. II.* Ed. by H. Feigl. M. Scriven, and G. Maxwell, Minneapolis: University of Minnesota Press. (This long essay was reprinted with a "Postscript," in paperback by the University of Minnesota Press in 1967.)

Feigl, H. (1971): Crucial issues of mind-body monism. *Synthese* **22**, pp. 295–312,

Feigl, H. (1975): Russell and Schlick: A remarkable agreement on a monistic solution of the mind–body problem. Erkenntnis **9**, 11–34.

Feigl, H. and Maxwell, G. (1961): Why ordinary language needs reforming. *J. Philos.* **58**, pp. 488–98.

Gunderson, K. (1970): Asymmetries and mind-body perplexities. In: *Minnesota Studies in the Philosophy of Science Vol. IV.* Ed. by M. Radner and S. Winokur, Minneapolis: University of Minnesota Press.

Maxwell, G. (1960): The ontological status of theoretical entities. In: *Minnesota Studies in the Philosophy of Science Vol. III.* Ed. by H. Feigl and G. Maxwell, Minneapolis: University of Minnesota Press.

Maxwell, G. (1961): Meaning postulates in scientific theories. In: *Current Issues in Philosophy of Science.* Ed. by H. Feigl and G. Maxwell, New York: Holt, Rinehart and Winston.

Maxwell, G. (1970a): Theories, perception, and structural realism. In: *Pittsburgh Studies in Philosophy of Science Vol. IV.* Ed. by R. Colodny, Pittsburgh: University of Pittsburgh Press.

Maxwell, G. (1970b): Structural realism and the meaning of theoretical terms. In: *Minne-*

---

[26] Schlick's views on the matter were published in 1918 in his *Allgemeine Erkenntnislehre* (2nd. ed. 1925, Berlin: Springer), which is now available in an English translation by Albert E. Blumberg (Schlick, 1974). References to works by the others mentioned above as well as many other important ones are in Feigl (1975).

sota Studies in the Philosophy of Science Vol. IV. Ed. by M. Radner and S. Winokur, Minneapolis: University of Minnesota Press.

Maxwell, G. (1972): Russell on perception: A study in philosophical method. In: *Bertrand Russell: A Collection of Critical Essays*. Ed. by D. Pears, New York: Doubleday.

Maxwell, G. (1974): Corroboration without demarcation. In: *The Philosophy of Karl Popper*. Ed. by P. A. Schilpp, LaSalle (Ill.): Open Court.

Maxwell, G. (1975): Induction and empiricism: A Baysian-frequentist alternative. In: *Minnesota Studies in the Philosophy of Science Vol. VI*. Ed. by G. Maxwell and R. Anderson, Minneapolis: University of Minnesota Press.

Maxwell, G. (1976): Some current trends in philosophy of science. In: *Boston Studies in the Philosophy of Science Vol. XXXII*. Ed. by R. Cohen, Clifford Hooker, and Alex Michalos, Boston and Dordrecht: Riedel Publishing Co.

Meehl, Paul E. (1966): The compleat autocerebroscopist: A thought-experiment on Professor Feigl's mind–body identity thesis. In: *Mind, Matter, and Method: Essays in Philosophy and Science in Honor of Herbert Feigl*. Edited by Paul K. Feyerabend and Grover Maxwell, Minneapolis: University of Minnesota Press.

Nagel, E. (1961): *The Structure of Science*. New York: Harcourt, Brace, and World, pp. 141–52.

Popper, K. R. (1959): *The Logic of Scientific Discovery*. New York: Basic Books.

Popper, K. R. (1962): *Conjectures and Refutations*, New York: Basic Books.

Popper, K. R. (1974): Replies. In: *The Philosophy of Karl Popper*. Ed. by P. A. Schilpp, LaSalle (Ill.): Open Court.

Pribram, K. (1971): *Languages of the Brain*, Englewood Cliffs (N.J.): Prentice-Hall.

Ramsey, F. (1931): *The Foundations of Mathematics and Other Essays*, New York: Humanities Press.

Russell, B. (1905): On denoting. *Mind. 14*, and In: *Readings in Philosophical Analysis*, Ed. by H. Feigl and W. Sellars, New York: Appleton-Century-Crofts, 1949.

Russell, B. (1912): *The Problems of Philosophy*. New York: Oxford University Press.

Russell, B. (1927): *The Analysis of Matter*. New York: Harcourt, Brace.

Russell, B. (1948): *Human Knowledge: Its Scope and Limits*. New York: Simon and Schuster.

Russell, B. (1946): *A History of Western Philosophy*. New York: Simon and Schuster.

Russell, B. (1959): *My Philosophical Development*. New York: Simon and Schuster.

Russell, B. (1956): *Portraits from Memory*. New York: Simon and Schuster.

Ryle, G. (1954): *Dilemmas*. Cambridge: at the University Press.

Schlick, M. (1974): *General Theory of Knowledge* (Trans. Albert E. Blumberg), Vienna and New York: Springer-Verlag.

Sellars, W. S. (1965): The identity approach to the mind–body problem: *Rev. of Metaphysics*, **18**, 430–451.

Smart, J. J. C. (1963): Materialism, *J. Philos*. **60**, 651–62.

Smart, J. (1972): Further thoughts on the identity theory, *The Monist* **56**, 149–62.

Whitehead, A. N. (1925): *Science and the Modern World*, New York: The Macmillan Co.

Contributor Index

Subject Index*

---

* This index was compiled in the spirit of creative endeavor by Kathleen Costa.

Ryle   The Concept of Mind

London: Hutchinson & Co.

Chomsky, Syntactic Structures

Popper Objective Knowlige: An
Evolutionary Approach

Oxford Univ Press

Levi

Engard

8008 Iltis DC

243-1027